The Essex Coastline
– then and now

by Matthew Fautley & James Garon

First published in 2004 by
Potton Publishing
65 The Dingle
Winterbourne Down
South Gloucestershire

ISBN 0 9548010 0 8

Designed and produced by
The Short Run Book Company Limited
Unit 1, Orpheus House
Calleva Park
Aldermaston
Berkshire
RG7 4QW

Contents

Chapter one – the Essex coastline

Whether you like long rambles along remote stretches of marshland, or whether you just prefer an occasional short stroll along the beach, it is hoped that this book can spur you on to explore new areas of the Essex coastline. It is difficult to define the attraction that the Essex coastline has to offer. Indeed, some people don't realise that they have a hidden gem on their doorstep. This beautiful landscape has so many different aspects that it would be wrong to single out any one particular feature. In any event, every person would probably have their own answer. Most people enjoy the tranquil marshland scenery; many are also intrigued by the wildlife, particularly the wildfowl that flock across the mudflats. Town-dwellers often appreciate the peace and relaxation of just sitting on a remote sea-wall, watching a stress-free world go by, and some people are interested to discover the history of the salt-marshes, of lost islands, attempts to reclaim the marshes, and the constant battle against the tide.

This book is not just about walks around the coastline, but also describes its colourful and varied history. It concentrates on the countryside *between* the towns, and is especially aimed at people who enjoy relaxing strolls along quiet footpaths, as an antidote to the bustle of modern life. Anyone who has obtained this book with the intention of finding out more about their particular coastal town will be disappointed. Specialised books already cover almost every Essex town and village, and local councils and tourist offices are always able to provide further information.

This book covers all the Essex coastline, following each river upstream to its tidal limit. Once you include all the creeks and inlets, this comes to a total of over 370 miles of coastline – roughly the distance from London to Edinburgh!

The boundaries of Essex have been re-drawn several times over the centuries, but the county has always been broadly defined by the River Stour to the north, and the River Thames to the south. In between, the coastline is deeply indented by three major river systems: the Colne, Blackwater and Crouch. These five rivers all have a different and distinctive character, and each has therefore been given its own chapter in this book:

- **The River Stour** – This area has a wonderfully wide variety of landscapes, from the woodlands of the Stour, through the hidden and forgotten islets of the Walton Backwaters, to the developed seaside towns of Frinton and Clacton.

- **The River Colne** – This area offers an intriguing contrast between wide rivers and narrow creeks, with several unique nature reserves dotted around the estuary. The peninsula near Old Hall contains some of the wildest and most remote landscape to be found in the county.

- **The River Blackwater** – Downstream of Maldon, the river opens out into an enormous estuary, several miles across. The sea-wall can be followed almost uninterrupted around its entire perimeter, with wide views across an ever-changing landscape. Most of the walks here are very remote and rural, almost guaranteeing peace and tranquillity.

- **The Rivers Crouch and Roach** – Just off the main rivers, this flat landscape is carved up by a maze of narrow creeks. These confusing backwaters offer probably the most enjoyable walks in the county. Special treatment has been given to the six islands of the Essex Archipelago (Wallasea, Potton, Rushley, Havengore, New England and Foulness). This archipelago is perhaps the epitome of Essex marshland – remote, forgotten and inaccessible – with the bleakest and most extreme scenery in the county. Access is not as easy as other parts of the coastline, but it is certainly possible to arrange a visit. Intrepid walkers who make the effort to organise a special visit are rewarded by an amazing landscape of isolated marshes, within a few miles of the suburbs of Southend-on-Sea and yet virtually undisturbed from one year to the next.

- **The River Thames** – In between the commuter towns and industrial developments, a surprising number of marshes have remained undisturbed along this river-front. Pockets of wildlife such as Vange Creek are virtually ignored by the nearby town-dwellers, and these are well worth exploring.

Each chapter ends with a short bibliography of recommended books. Many of these books may go out of print, but it is usually easy to find copies at public libraries and small local bookshops. An enormous amount of information can also be gleaned from the Internet, but web-sites are often only transitory, remaining on-line for just a year or two, and are therefore generally not included here.

Each season of the year brings a different flavour to the coastline. The scenery is prettier in the summer and this is obviously a popular time for many casual walkers, but the warm weather can make the footpaths quite overgrown, with long and tussocky grass. Furthermore, the sunshine sometimes brings out too many people for you to relax and truly enjoy the peace of the remote marshes. The winter, on the other hand, may bring cold and bracing winds, but if you wrap up against the weather, you get the extra reward of watching the winter wildfowl flocking around the mudflats, and crisp days can be amongst the best to take in tje austere beauty of the landscape.

Many visitors to the Essex coastline are keen to learn about the wildlife that thrives here. You rarely need to walk for long before you spot a tern or an oyster-catcher. The quieter marshes are a Mecca for bird-watchers, with many rare birds making an occasional appearance. Foxes and even seals are not unheard of, and do not forget that the saline environment provides many habitats for unusual plants. A short chapter at the end of the book offers just a quick taste of a few of the birds and plants that are special to the marshes. However, this is an enormous topic and there is no hope of doing justice to the wildlife in such a short space. Instead, you are recommended to seek out more information in one of the many excellent specialist books on sale.

Until the 20th century, roads were very poor around the remote marshlands of Essex, and a lot of goods were transported by boat instead. These isolated communities often tended to be quite lawless, with crimes such as smuggling being particularly rife. The low-lying marshes were also damp and unhealthy places to live, a problem not helped by the lack of fresh water, which often had to be brought in from outside. In this unwholesome climate, diseases took their toll on the unfortunate inhabitants. One of the most frequent ailments was "the ague", a type of malaria. Numerous remedies for the ague were used, such as the drinking of gin laced with coal-dust.

One fact that surprises many people as they learn more about the Essex coastline is that the landscape has changed considerably over the centuries. New sea-walls have enabled land to be reclaimed from the sea, creeks have been dammed and then drained, and entire islands have been abandoned and even disappeared completely. Everywhere you walk around Essex, you can see where land has been lost and gained. In this way, the map of the coastline has been re-drawn many times over the centuries, reflecting man's endless battle against the sea.

But why do we need sea-walls at all? In some cases, they enabled landowners to increase the size of their farms. Furthermore, any land reclaimed in this way tends to be extremely fertile and valuable. The island of Foulness, for example, was extended piece by piece over the centuries by constructing a series of earth embankments over the tidal mudflats. (Note that the word "dyke" is sometimes used to refer to the sea-wall itself and sometimes to the ditch or "borrow-dyke" behind – to avoid possible confusion, we try to avoid using the word in this book.) Other sea-walls were built to protect existing land from the encroaching sea. It was often possible to reduce the length of the sea-defences by damming the smaller creeks. In this way, you can find the remains of many creeks around the Essex marshes that are now totally cut off from the open sea. These are given the local name of "fleets" and are usually obvious on the map. Some farmers also built embankments inland, around the edge of their property. Known as "counterwalls", these were designed to protect them in case their neighbour's land became flooded.

Since the end of the last Ice Age, the whole of the British landmass has been slowly shifting. The western edge has lifted upwards, resulting in raised beaches and other unusual formations, whilst Essex and the eastern coastline has been slowly sinking back down again. Since Roman times, this has averaged a foot per century, although the rate has not been regular. In recent times, this has accelerated because global warming is melting the polar ice-caps. In 1972, for example, the government passed an Act to prepare sea-defences for a 1 in 1000 chance of a sea-wall breach by the year"2030. Already this estimate has been"revised ten-fold, to just 1 in 100. Some studies have even suggested that tides are now rising at the rate of 5 feet within 30 years.

Today, almost all of the coastal land around Essex lies below the level of high tide. Furthermore, as the tides rise inexorably each year, it also becomes more expensive to keep improving the dams and barriers to hold back the sea. It"is clear that these methods are all doomed to fail eventually, and that this interventionist approach cannot continue indefinitely. As a result, this form of "hard" engineering is gradually being replaced by "softer" solutions. In some places, barriers are being built (or removed) to adjust silting and erosion patterns. Intensive agriculture has also reduced the need for farmland, and a few areas of land are being deliberately breached and allowed to flood in order to provide a natural buffer against the tide and waves. Every now and then, the old-fashioned style of hard engineering briefly rears its head once more, such as the idea of more hugely expensive barriers across the River Thames.

The government's role in flood protection is only given a brief mention in this book, largely because the departments are re-organised so frequently. Responsibility for deciding general policy (in England, at least) was transferred in 2001 from MAFF (Ministry of Agriculture, Fisheries and Food) to DEFRA (Department of Environment, Food and Rural Affairs). However, the actual work has been carried out over the years by a collection of different "operating authorities". These have included water boards, local councils, Internal Drainage Boards, and the National Rivers Authority. On 1st April 1996, it became the responsibility of the Environment Agency to "supervise all matters relating to flood defence in England and Wales".

Walking along the coastline

Anyone who intends to visit the Essex coastline regularly is recommended to buy a tide-timetable (annual booklets are on sale at most boating shops). Some sea-walls are best walked at low tide, perhaps because of the wildfowl or special features such as tidal fords. Indeed in a few special places the walks are only possible at low tide. In some places, there may also be a risk of getting cut off by the tide – these are very clearly mentioned in the text and must be treated very seriously. **Do not under-estimate the danger**! Many people have drowned because they failed to understand the importance of the tide. The height (and time) of the tide can also be affected by the wind and weather, so make sure that you consider these walks carefully in advance.

Many people are surprised to find that they enjoy the marshes more during the middle of winter, when the bleakness of the landscape takes on a special quality. You need to be prepared for bitterly cold winds as well, but at the other extreme, make sure that you also dress sensibly for a summer walk as well – a sun-hat (and cream) will obviously be useful during hot weather, but many people forget to take a good supply of water on the longer, more remote footpaths. However, by their nature, walks along sea-walls are flat and easy, without any hills to tire you out.

There is a lot of nonsense written about the laws of trespass. Fortunately for walkers, access to the Essex coastline is generally much better than in most other parts of the country. In 1949, the government introduced the National Parks and Access to the Countryside Act. This new law required every county council in Britain to prepare a definitive map of all public roads and footpaths in their area. The definitive map drawn up by Essex county council included a public right of way along almost all of the sea-walls. On the whole, the local councils have protected these rights of access carefully over the years.

However, it is inevitable that, from time to time, you may come across an illegal obstruction blocking the public footpath. You are strongly urged to report these incidents to the Highways Department of the county council (the number is in the telephone directory) in order that future visitors do not have to be inconvenienced too. In the meantime, note that you do not usually have to turn around at a blockage and go home: the law entitles you to follow the nearest reasonable alternative route, *even* if this involves crossing private land. Do not be intimidated by signs imploring you to "keep out" – the law is on your side if the public right of way is impassable for *any* reason.

That said, we scarcely need to say that every responsible visitor to the coastline should respect landowners and other users of the countryside, and stick to the correct footpaths. It would be an unusual person who manages to follow the "wrong" sea-wall, but there are few signposts to indicate the correct place to join and leave the coastline. For these, good maps are highly recommended. In Britain, the only maps worth buying are those produced by the Ordnance Survey. There are two series of interest to the casual walker:

- Landranger 1:50,000 (pink covers, approximately an inch to a mile). These are the minimum necessary – every walker should ensure that they own a copy of the local map.
- Explorer 1:25,000 (orange covers, approximately two inches to a mile). These have recently superseded the older green Pathfinder maps.

The "Explorer" maps contain much more detail and are therefore much more helpful (e.g. they mark the ditches and fences around fields). However, they are also sometimes inaccurate, particularly with respect to the existence (or not!) of sea-walls, and also often out of date. In a few cases, this is not their fault, particularly in military areas where surveyors have not been allowed access for many years. However, other examples are more difficult to explain, such as the eastern ford onto Two-Tree Island which is still marked, though it actually disappeared over 100 years ago.

Every writer eventually comes up against the problem of metric vs imperial. Whilst the metric system will inevitably dominate in Britain, we believe that the traditional units of feet, yards and miles are more widely understood amongst ordinary walkers, and are therefore used in this book. However, it is possible that we have let some metric units creep in occasionally where appropriate – we apologise if this causes confusion!

Indeed, just like the Ordnance Survey maps above, it is almost certain that this book contains other mistakes and inaccuracies. With the speed of change and development around our coastlines, some of the descriptions contained in this book will probably be out of date even before it is published. The authors would therefore be extremely grateful for any information or further knowledge that might help to improve later editions. On the whole however, the small details of the Essex coastline may change, but its character remains timeless and unchangeable – explore it all and enjoy it.

Chapter two – the River Stour – to Clacton

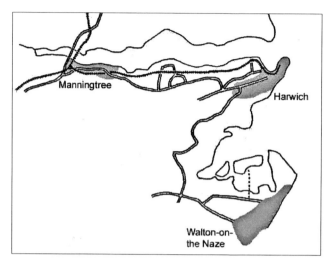

Each chapter in this book describes one section of the Essex coastline, starting from the north-eastern corner of the county and gradually heading southwards. This first chapter covers most of the land east of Colchester. In this part of the county, the rivers Stour and Colne cut deeply into the coastline, forming a large peninsula.

Once known as the Tendring Hundred, this peninsula is bounded on its northern side by the River Stour, the northernmost river in Essex. The Stour runs in an west-east direction, separating the counties of Suffolk and Essex. In these lower tidal reaches, the river is very wide, often over a mile across, with expansive views more akin to the open sea. The River Stour has a different atmosphere to the other Essex rivers, with rolling countryside sloping gently down to the river-banks.

Along the end of the Tendring peninsula, a series of towns have built up along the coastline. Harwich is a popular stepping-stone for holidays on the continent of Europe, with large vehicle ferries leaving from the quayside at Parkeston. Further to the south, the seaside resorts of Walton-on-the-Naze and Frinton-on-Sea sprawl along the coastline for several miles, almost joining up with the nearby town of Clacton-on-Sea.

However, in the midst of all this bustling activity, a large but beautiful inlet stands almost unnoticed. This bay effectively divides the Tendring peninsula into two parts, and yet very few people know that it even exists. These are the quiet backwaters of Hamford Water, with a collection of small islands interwoven by a network of creeks. Hamford Water is a delight to explore, and, despite their inaccessibility, the islands also have a fascinating history. The area contains a wealth of wildlife, and the peace and solitude is a perfect antidote to the hectic pace of the nearby towns.

❋ ❋ ❋

Cattawade Marshes

The county of Essex is, broadly speaking, separated from its neighbour Suffolk by the River Stour. Although it is only the lower reaches of the river which constitute the true coastline of Essex, this meandering river passes through some delightful countryside, and is well worth exploring. This area has strong connections with the famous landscape artist John Constable, who was born in the nearby village of East Bergholt in 1776. Whilst many of his contemporaries travelled around Europe for their scenes, Constable got most of his inspiration from the countryside around Suffolk and Essex, and yet his works were more popular at the time in France than they were in England. Today, the National Gallery in London displays some of his more famous paintings. such as Flatford Mill and The Hay Wain.

The River Stour was used as a means of transport, but soon after flowing past Dedham Mill and Flatford Mill, the banks begin to widen out and the water becomes shallower. To allow boats to reach the open sea at all states of the tide, a short canal had to be dug just below Flatford Mill, linking the river to a deep water channel further downstream. This canal, running to the north of the old river, is barely two miles in length. It is now disused and today forms the boundary between Essex and Suffolk, though maps dating from 1805 show that the original boundary followed the natural river all the way to the sea. The land between this tidal river and the canal is low-lying marshland, an area sometimes referred to as the Cattawade Marshes.

Unfortunately, there are no public rights of way across the rough grasslands of Cattawade Marshes, but from the southern end of the sluice, there is a very pleasant footpath along the south bank of the River Stour. After about half a mile the river narrows, and sticking out of the river at this point are a series of upright wooden posts. These are the remains of a small bridge that used to cross the river, and if you look across the water at the marshy terrain opposite, you can still see the straight lines of the drainage ditches that ran alongside the track. This was the main route of access onto this section of the Cattawade Marshes, and was probably used to graze sheep.

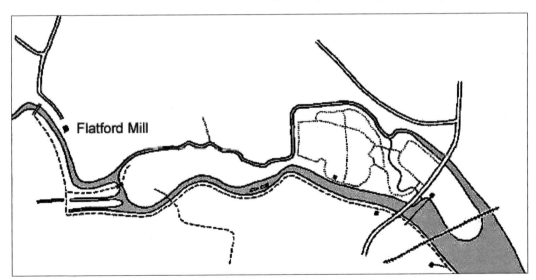

With the river-banks now starting to rise noticeably above the surrounding fields, the river meanders gently for the next mile, passing a few small grassy islands in the river, the first of which has been named Reed Island. As you walk further downstream, you may notice that Cattawade Marshes are neatly split into two regions. The western half is still rough and undrained, whereas the eastern half has been enclosed in a series of earth embankments, although the area inside these embankments is often underwater.

Aerial photographs of the area show that there are a large number of these walls, often weaving in and out and intertwined with each other, presumably the remains of failed efforts over the years to keep the area drained. Just inside these embankments can be seen a couple of derelict farm buildings, which now stand in almost a foot of water.

As you approach the busy road bridge over the Stour, a raised track can be seen across the river, leading from the main road into the marshes. It is said that this was part of a recent attempt to use the area as a tip for industrial waste, but thankfully nothing came of the idea, and the land around Cattawade Marshes is now a quiet spot for people and wildlife alike. Indeed, a small picnic site was recently built on the northern bank here. Some old maps show a ford crossing the river around this spot, but there is no sign of this ford today.

The road bridge up ahead is known as Cattawade Bridge or White Bridge, and it carries the A137 from Colchester to Ipswich. As well as being a useful access point for motorists, it is also convenient for public transport. Several buses travel along this route, and Manningtree railway station is just half a mile to the south. Alongside this bridge can be seen the first of many tidal defences that line the Essex coast. About twenty years ago, a flood barrier was built across the River Stour at this point, enabling the Water Authorities to protect the low-lying, and highly productive, arable land further upstream from floods. Similar barriers can be seen all round the coastline of south-eastern England.

Only a few hundred yards separate Cattawade Bridge from the next bridge, the last over the River Stour. This is a railway bridge, carrying the main line from London to Ipswich, and then to Norwich. This spot is rarely quiet for long, and it is better to push on quickly. Across the river lies a small area of saltings known as Hogmarsh. This lies at the junction of the River Stour with Cattawade Creek, where the canal finally enters the main river. With some of the best birdlife in the area, this tidal marsh was donated to the Essex Wildlife Trust by Lt. Col. C. A. Brooks in 1973. It has been designated by the Nature Conservancy Council to be a Site of Special Scientific Interest (usually abbreviated to SSSI). These sites, which have special legal protection against development, comprise most of the wild coastline of Essex, and many of them are owned or managed by the Essex Wildlife Trust, who have a particular interest in maintaining and protecting the wildlife.

Just around the next corner, a view of the River Stour estuary opens up. Here the character of the river changes enormously. At high tide, the river is a wide expanse of water, almost a mile across, but at low tide vast mudbanks are exposed, leaving just a small channel. Large boats still travel as far upriver as the twin villages of Manningtree and Mistley, which lie ahead.

The coastline between the railway bridge and Manningtree has long suffered from erosion, and the embankment that used to protect this land from flooding has recently been strengthened. Vast amounts of earth and stone were amassed to produce a large and wide sea-wall, capable of withstanding the fiercest of storms. In order to protect the wall from erosion, rocks and stones were piled up along its foot to undermine encroaching waves.

Manningtree

The footpath enters the village of Manningtree through a small car park in Riverside Avenue. The village has a long history, largely relating to the river. One of Manningtree's most famous inhabitants was Matthew Hopkins, otherwise known as the

Witchfinder General. During the unrest that followed the English Civil War, many people hired witch-hunters to discover women who were practising witchcraft, and hundreds of women were executed on the proclamation of witch-hunters such as Matthew Hopkins, including several women from Manningtree in 1645. He was said to be in such demand that he could earn up to £1000 for each witch he brought to trial, a much greater salary than in his previous job as a lawyer.

Manningtree contains a mixture of modern buildings and old Georgian frontages, including a few Dutch weavers' cottages dating back to before the Huguenot settlers. The name of the village was traditionally thought to mean "Manna's tree," the word "tree" often referring to a cross, as in the names Braintree or Coventry. Indeed, on John Norden's 1594 map of Essex, the village is marked as "Mannatre". However, there is growing belief that it could simply mean "a place of many trees", from the Old English word "manig" meaning "many", in the same way that Aintree means "one tree". Support for this theory comes from a document of 1274 which refers to the village as "Manitre".

Mistley

From Manningtree, a busy road heads eastwards through Mistley Place Park. This 'B' road is known as "The Walls", and leads straight towards the neighbouring village of Mistley, just one mile away. As you enter the village, two towers stand beside the road. These, the Mistley Towers, are all that now remains of a church designed by the famous architect Robert Adam in 1776. When the church was demolished in 1870, the towers, which stood at its eastern and western ends, were retained. A local landowner named Richard Rigby also engaged Robert Adam to design a large spa town at Mistley, but this ambitious scheme was later abandoned.

The Mistley Towers

The name Mistley means 'mistletoe wood', but there is little mistletoe to be seen today. Mistley is a busy village, largely taken up by the EDME malt works which line the road. The ancient process of malting involves laying out barley to germinate. Known as "green malt", this can then be used to produce brewing sugar. The offices are on the south side of the road, and the factories are on the north.

The deep water channel of the River Stour veers off its central course to pass very close to the south bank here. At the foot of Furze Hill, large docks have been built to take advantage of this. The quay was extended in 1849, and when the main Harwich railway was built, a short siding was added to take freight trains to the malthouses. Today large stacks of timber can sometimes be seen on the quayside, and flocks of swans often feed off the waste from the maltings.

Musical instruments and stained glass are made in the Mistley Quay Workshops, and it is possible to visit their showrooms. In recent years, Mistley has also tried to attract tourists by opening up the Essex Secret Bunker, an old nuclear shelter from the days of the Cold War. Otherwise, the village has little to interest the walker, and unfortunately there is no way back to the riverside for another mile and a half.

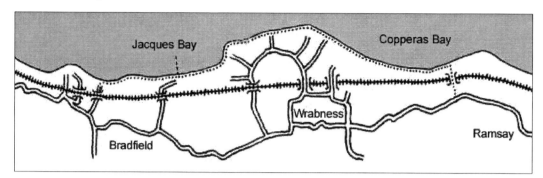

Walking eastwards along the narrow B1352, the road eventually passes quite close to a railway line and then several lanes lead off to the left. The first is not a right of way, but the second leads back to the river-bank within a quarter of a mile. Known as Ship Lane, it can be extremely muddy after heavy rain. It leads to Jacques Bay, the name given to a slight inlet in the banks of the River Stour, which is more than a mile wide by this point. At low tide however, the water recedes over half a mile, revealing a wide expanse of soft mud, which in places is covered with plants which have adapted to withstand the salty conditions. A channel leaves the main river and veers to within a few hundred yards of the shore here. Known as Jacques Fleet, it was used in bygone days by local farmers to transport their goods. In order to reach the creek even at low tide, stone tracks were laid across the mudflats. There used to be three of these "hards" in this area alone, but two of these have since been covered by thick layers of mud, and are impossible to locate, even from aerial photographs. The third hard can still be found, close to the buildings of Ragmarsh Farm. Although rapidly silting up, it is still possible to walk out a hundred yards across the mudflats to Jacques Fleet at low tide.

As you walk eastwards along the muddy shoreline, you pass the site of an old depot, and arrive at a small dam. This is one of the few points along the River Stour with road access – a narrow track called Wall Lane leads down to the dam from the outskirts of Wrabness. Until the dam was built, a narrow creek flowed half a mile inland here. Today, the creek has largely disappeared but the land inside the dam is still low and marshy.

Beyond the dam, the land rises gently, and green fields lead up to the promontory known as Wrabness Point. This is really a tautology, since the suffix 'ness' means a peninsula or a point of land. This higher vantage point gives a wide view of the Stour, and across the river lie the prominent towers of the Royal Hospital School. This school was originally founded in Greenwich *"for the sons and grandsons of seafarers,"* but it was moved to the present site in 1933. In years gone by, this stretch of the river was quite dangerous for ships because of a shallow shoal of mud near the centre of the channel, known as a "horse" to the mariners. It eventually disappeared, however, after extensive dredging.

A narrow sandy beach around Wrabness is backed by cliffs up to fifty feet high, some appearing rather unstable. A few stone paths provide a safe way down between the beach huts and chalets to the beach. Local people often use this beach to launch small boats, or simply to walk their dogs in the evening, and the area is usually full of life.

One 18th-century map shows that there was once a simple jetty here called "Cunningford Loading". It is said that a few of the wooden posts survived until the early 1900s, and were used by barges bound for London.

At Stone Point a mile or so further on, the chalets and beach die out, and the river shore returns to salt-marsh, with a narrow sea-wall providing a dry path around a promontory that was once known as Taylor's Point. You are now entering a bay called Copperas Bay. The name suggests that locals once collected fossils which were rich in copperas. Technically known as iron sulphide, this is often produced when London clay is exposed at the surface to the action of waves. The copperas was collected and allowed to decompose naturally to iron sulphate (sometimes known as green copperas or green vitriol), which was used in the manufacture of sulphuric acid and other chemicals. For example, it was once once mixed with verdigris to produce a cure for sheep scab, or used as a black dye for Essex cloth.

The bay consists of three separate offshoots from the main River Stour. These were called Wood Fleet, Long Twill, and Carrington Creek. At high tide, however, the rising waters cover the mudflats, and the bay becomes one large area of shallow water.

After passing Shore Farm, you pass the small copses of West Grove and East Grove. This stretch of the river is probably best visited at low tide, when the vast mudbanks are exposed by the tide and teeming with birdlife, including numerous oyster-catchers and other waders. Indeed, the wildlife is so varied around this stretch of the coastline that a large portion of the bay has been bought or leased by the RSPB as a bird reserve, and the neighbouring Copperas Woods are owned by the Essex Wildlife Trust. The trees of Copperas Wood and Stour Wood are remnants of the original forests that used to cover enormous areas of Britain, although in the last few hundred years some of the native trees have been replaced by sweet chestnut, with the aim of making poles for local hop plantations.

The footpath follows the edge of fields around Copperas Bay for about a mile, and eventually reaches a large wooden bird hide, set amongst the trees. Although the town of Harwich is still a few miles away to the east, there is no footpath to it along the banks of the River Stour. Instead, the right of way turns inland, and crosses the railway. A very muddy track leads through Copperas Woods, an extensive area of chestnut trees sprinkled with bluebells in spring, to the main road a few hundred yards away. Our route now heads east along this road into the picturesque village of Ramsey. (Do not confuse this with the village of Ramsey Island, further south in Essex on the shores of the River Blackwater.)

Ramsey

The village has been much quieter ever since a bypass was built. The main attraction of Ramsey is the windmill at the far end of the village. This style of windmill is known as a "post mill" because the entire structure rotates about a post, as opposed to a conventional "cap mill" where only the top part rotates. This is in fact only the latest of a succession of mills which have stood in Ramsey over the centuries. A water mill used to stand just upstream of the bridge, using the tidal power of the river to work its machinery. More detail on this type of mill can be found later near St. Osyth. However, the river gradually silted up, and this tidal mill, dating from at least the 14th century, was finally replaced by the current windmill in 1845. Today, the tidal limit of the river is three miles downstream of the bridge. The name of the village probably derives from the two Old English words "hramsa", meaning wild garlic, which presumably grew here, and "ey", meaning island. (The word island was often used to describe a plot of dry land in a marshy area.)

Returning to the northern edge of the village, the walk continues from the farm at East Newhall eastwards along a straight track called Ray Lane, and a fast pace can easily be made past Marsh Farm towards Parkeston. Although the track lies close to the shores of the River Stour, the ground actually slopes away from the coast, and hence the only views are those looking inland. However, the railway here runs right along the banks of the river, and train passengers get a very good view of a secluded bay, and when the tide drops, a marvellously intricate area of creeks and mudflats is revealed. Amongst the myriad of retreating channels, with names such as Ray Creek, Deep Fleet and Bramble Creek, lies a region known as Sunken Island. Although its name suggests that the area was once dry and habitable, it was probably never much more than a marsh used for grazing sheep. Today it remains a quiet backwater providing undisturbed habitats to marshland birds such as shelduck, wigeon, pintail and grey plover.

About fifteen minutes' walk from East Newhall, a prominent footpath leaves the track to the right. This is the original line of the railway, which was diverted in 1972 to allow trains to reach Parkeston Quay. Its two-mile length can still be walked today, part of it through a golf course, and it is a popular footpath with local inhabitants from Harwich. Although this route is slightly shorter, and perhaps more pleasant, the original track is a more faithful path, sticking more closely to the coast, and is the actual right of way.

Soon after the junction, the track begins to enter the industrial area surrounding Parkeston, passing alongside an oil storage depot. A few centuries ago, the character of this land was entirely different, for the ground on which you are now walking was once a small island, known as Ramsey Ray Island. Gradually over the years, silt blocked the creek which separated the island from the mainland, but even on a map drawn as recently as the mid 1800s, this track is shown as being the only route onto this land. It led to the buildings of Rayisland Farm, the predecessor of the modern-day Ray Farm. During the 1870s, several hundred acres of land were reclaimed during the construction of the new quay. This effectively joined Ramsey Ray Island to the mainland, and today it is hard to trace the original coastline.

Parkeston Quay

Just after skirting a large building, the path leads onto tarmac roads. The first road you meet is called Refinery Road, the main entrance to the refinery complex being on your left. A few hundred yards further on past a warehouse, you enter the side-street of West Dock Road. Following this street to the right, you soon come to a mini-roundabout where you meet the main 'A' road leading into Parkeston.

If you were to turn left at the mini-roundabout, you would enter the grounds of Parkeston Quay. This enormous port takes its name from the first chairman of the Great Eastern Railway, Charles H. Parkes, who in 1883 opened *"Parkeston Quay as a terminal for the packet-boat service to Holland."* It was an expensive undertaking, costing £500,000 to build, and a large extension was opened at its eastern end in 1911. It now also handles cross-Channel ferries to Germany, Denmark and Norway, as well as large quantities of container freight.

The quay was largely constructed on land reclaimed from the River Stour, and the building of the railway embankment created a couple of large brackish lagoons, though these were recently filled in and drained to provide more space. The area is now served by one railway station, but originally a small side-line led over a bridge to a second station, called Parkeston Quay West. This was mostly used for freight, and was closed in 1972. The quay has little to offer the walker, and so it is best to push on into Harwich.

From the south of Parkeston Quay, a new relief road leads into the centre of Harwich. These are the last few miles of the River Stour before joining the North Sea, and this stretch is quite different from the rest of the river further upstream. It used to be very peaceful, but the arrival of the new road has changed all that. New earth embankments are being built across the mudflats, reclaiming sections of the bay for developers. At the time of writing, the latest construction project, Phoenix Europark, is gradually taking shape on the western half of the bay.

For the time being however, there is still enough open space to make it worthwhile turning off the road and walking along the foreshore instead. At low tide the water recedes half a mile from the shore, revealing a wide expanse of undulating sand-dunes covered with thin green vegetation. This is the plant glasswort (*Salicornia europaea*) which is capable of withstanding the salty conditions.

Harwich

The end of the beach walk is marked by a collection of large buildings beside the river, built on another redeveloped area of land called Bath Side. Just before reaching the first of these, a path leads back to the road, quite close to the railway station. The coastal route now follows this road to the left, past the entrance to the Harwich and Dovercourt Sailing Club.

Harwich has always had a strong naval tradition. Samuel Pepys was once the local member of parliament, and although he is often remembered for his diaries around the time of the Great Fire of London and the Plague, it is not widely known that he was also the Secretary of the Admiralty. The town was referred to in a document in the year 1274 as 'Herwyz', and the borough was created soon after by Edward II in 1318. The name originally came from the two Old English words "here", meaning an army, and "wic", which means a settlement. The town therefore derived its name from its status as a military base, perhaps referring to the Danish military camp which was set up here in the 9th century.

Just beyond a quiet level-crossing, you come to George Street. The main bus and railway stations are a short way to the right, but our route is to the left alongside a shipyard containing large numbers of discarded buoys, many of which still have the names of their original ports painted on the outside. Indeed, Harwich still services all the buoys that mark the shoals around the Thames Estuary.

Behind this shipyard is the jetty for the train ferry to Zeebrugge, and this is also the main shipbuilding area. Very soon the side street joins up with the main road, known simply as The Quay. Just around the corner you come to Ha'penny Pier, built in 1851, and named after the price of the original toll. You can still take one of the regular passenger ferries across the river to Shotley Point, where numerous boats are moored inside a small marina. Ferries also run from here to the busy port of Felixstowe, where a thriving new port has been constructed on reclaimed land. Do not get confuse the name of this ferry, however, with the small seaside village of Felixstowe Ferry, a few miles further to the north.

Ha'penny Pier stands at the very tip of a long peninsula where the River Orwell flows into the River Stour, and the resulting estuary provides an excellent shelter for shipping. Known originally as Orwell Haven, it is protected from fierce storms by the spit of Landguard Point. During the Napoleonic wars, a large fort was constructed on this long promontary because of its strategic location at the mouth of two major rivers. The fort was converted for active use during the Second World War, and parts of it are open to visitors.

Whilst discussing the possibility of siting a third London airport on the Maplin Sands in south-east Essex, it was seriously suggested that a barrage could be built between Harwich and Landguard Point. This would have reduced the cost of maintaining many miles of sea-defences along the River Stour and the River Orwell, and provided a permanent safe dock for thousands of vessels upstream of the barrage.

Shipbuilding in Harwich goes back a long way. The large shipyard of Navyard Wharf dates back to at least the 17th century, and was used by the Navy from 1660 until 1827. In 1943, it was taken over again by the Navy for the war effort, and finally passed back into private ownership in 1962. This industry blocks public access to the coastline, but the roads which run alongside soon rejoin the coast on the eastern side of the promontary.

Kings Quay Street and Outpart Eastward soon lead back to the coast on the far side of Navyard Wharf, and the buildings of the port of Felixstowe are directly across the river. This port was built relatively recently, and contrasts strongly with the old buildings of Harwich. Indeed, if you follow the beach southwards past Harwich Green, you come across an old Wheel Crane standing in the middle of a small green beside the coast. It was built in 1667 to load and offload ships from the Navyard shipyard, which used to stand on this site, and was operated in a treadmill fashion by local labourers who walked inside the large wheel. It was moved to its present position in 1930.

Just beyond the crane stand a couple of disused lighthouses. The Low Lighthouse stands beside the shore, and the taller High Lighthouse can be seen a little way inland. They were built in 1818, taking the place of earlier wooden structures, and were used to guide ships past the shallows of Landguard Point until 1863, by which time the main course of the River Stour had changed. The channel of the river is now marked by buoys instead. In 1896, Trinity House gave the lighthouses to Harwich Corporation for a nominal sum, and the Low Lighthouse is now home to a Maritime Museum. The High Lighthouse also contains a museum, containing vintage televisions and wirelesses.

The next stretch of the coast is along a short promenade called Harbour Crescent. A circular fort stands inland just behind a row of houses. This is the Redoubt, built between 1808 and 1810, during the Napoleonic wars. (Similar structures can be found at Dungeness, Hythe and Eastbourne.) Today the Redoubt contains a small museum which is open daily during the summer, and on Sundays during the winter. The promenade ends at a long stone breakwater that sticks out five hundred yards into the sea. The far end of this breakwater is the easternmost point in Essex, albeit man-made. (For the purists, the easternmost *natural* land is further round the coastline at Walton-on-the-Naze.) The surface of the breakwater is very uneven and slippery, and walking along it is certainly not recommended in strong winds.

It is hard to imagine that this was once the site of busy industry, but in the early 19th century, Harwich had a lot of cement works. The nearby cliffs contained a lot of septaria, a hard-setting clay sometimes also known as Roman cement stone. Before long, the extraction of the clay caused serious erosion of the coastline, and the town's harbour was at risk. Eventually, in 1845, the Commission on Harbours of Refuge recommended that a breakwater be built, and that no more clay should be removed. The local companies had to turn instead to dredging for the manufacture of their cement, and the industries continued to thrive until outside competition caused their decline in the 1870s. The last kiln closed in Dovercourt in 1890.

Dovercourt

Near the head of the breakwater, on Beacon Hill, are a large number of old buildings constructed during the Second World War to protect this part of the shore from German attack. These ugly ruins are soon left behind however, and the walk for the next mile or so is along the seaside promenades of Dovercourt. This suburb dates back to before the Norman invasion. It was referred to around the year 1000 as "Douorcortae". Like the town in Kent, the word "Dover" is derived from the Celtic word "dwfr" which simply means water. The word "court" is not so certain, however, but may come from the Old English word "cort", which was used to describe a short piece of land. (To this day, the French word "court" means short.) Dovercourt therefore may have originally meant "short piece of land by the water".

During the week, the stroll along Marine Parade is usually very peaceful, for this is largely a residential suburb of Harwich. The coastline walker will probably be glad to learn that the town is gradually being left behind, because these walks along stone and tarmac paths can get very tiring on the feet after a few miles. Towards the end of the promenade, two more lighthouses can be seen. Standing on tall stilts, these black and white iron beacons replaced the older Harwich lighthouses back in 1863. Although both are now disused, there are plans to preserve and restore them.

A few hundred yards south of the lighthouses, the last roads and hence the last buses and public transport leave the coast, and although the breakwaters continue for another half mile or so, this is the last real civilisation for at least four miles. A good path continues along the outside of Dovercourt Holiday Camp. This is where the BBC filmed the television series 'Hi-De-Hi', and it is closely followed by a caravan park. The ground can be a little uneven around here, because this land has been reclaimed from the sea.

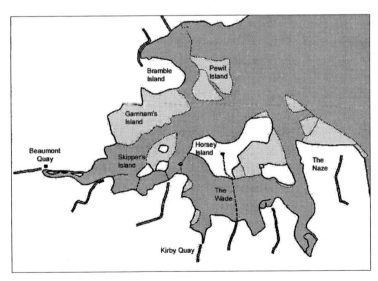

From Dovercourt, the coastal footpath heads southwards into open countryside. Indeed, it is now entering the first real marshland to be encountered around the coast of Essex. The footpath follows the top of an embankment that was built relatively recently to prevent high tides from flooding the rich agricultural land behind it. In common with much of eastern England, this part of Britain is slowly sinking, and the waters are lapping ever higher up the embankments. Indeed, until the 20th century, there was no need for an embankment at all, and the land which is now on the seaward side of the sea-wall used to be farmed for crops. This state of affairs is demonstrated by the wartime pill-box that now stands alone by the water's edge, a good four hundred yards outside the present sea-wall. You may notice that most of the small tidal channels which drain the marshland are quite straight. This does not occur naturally – it is a man-made phenomenon, because many of these creeks are the remnants of ditches dug by farmers to drain their fields. There are many similar examples of this around the coast of Essex.

As you walk around the small inlet of South Hall Creek, you will notice that large rectangular hollows lie just outside the sea-wall. These are oyster-beds, dug out in the last few centuries to store oysters and fish. However, the oyster and fishery industries were never very important around this stretch of the coast, and although the remains of oyster-beds can be seen almost anywhere in the salt-marshes of Essex, their main industrial centre today is further south around the River Colne.

The path around the bay is a little over a mile in length. At the far side, there is a whole series of pill-boxes. One of these wartime structures is built into the sea-wall itself, and here it is possible to leave the embankment and follow the edge of the salt-marsh northwards to reach a second pill-box stranded in the middle of the bay. Such a detour is not recommended, however, because the going is rough and often muddy, and there is a chance of getting cut off by the incoming tide.

The first pill-boxes were built around the east coast of England in 1916. They got their name because the original structures were round with an overhanging roof. During the Second World War, it was decided that hexagonal pill-boxes were easier to construct, using walls of reinforced concrete sixteen inches thick. Doors were added to a few of them, but most had only a simple anti-blast wall just inside the entrance, sometimes with an extra anti-ricochet wall at the centre. In 1941, military experts changed their defence strategy, preferring to use more centrally defended military bases instead, and the pill-box system was abandoned.

A third pill-box can be seen a few yards out to sea, in the centre of some fence-like structures that have been built out across the mudflats. Made of hundreds of twigs and branches woven between upright posts, these are often known as faggots and are used to trap particles of mud, sand and vegetation as the tide ebbs. The aim is to slow down the erosion that is slowly eating away the coastline, and to give plants such as eel-grass and sea purslane a chance to recolonise the mudflats. Similar techniques are increasingly being used in various forms to protect and re-establish Britain's coastlines, especially in low-lying areas such as East Anglia.

The sea-wall continues southwards, giving a clear view of the shipping out at sea. Just a few hundred yards further on from the bay, a low embankment is visible inland, snaking through the fields away from the sea-wall. This was once the original coastline, the site of a creek which used to drain into the sea at this point. In mediaeval times, sea-walls followed most creeks and their tributaries upriver to their tidal limits. Over the centuries, however, the growing threat of flooding by the sea has meant that these embankments have had to be built progressively higher and stronger. In order to save money, it has been a common policy to dam small creeks, hence reducing the length of embankments that need to be maintained. This practice is still going on today, and many examples can be seen around the Essex coastline.

This small creek was dammed some time before the turn of the last century, and the building which lay half a mile inland near the head of the creek, called Lower Barn, was demolished soon afterwards. Small farms and farm buildings were often built in locations where they had access to the sea, because, in the days before good road communications, boats provided one of the most convenient methods of transporting large bulky items from place to place. It would be interesting to postulate that the demise of Lower Barn may have been caused by the damming of the creek, hence cutting off a vital supply route, but this is just speculation – there is no evidence to suggest that the creek was navigable.

This short stretch of sea-wall is therefore technically a dam, but it is difficult today to establish where it joins up again with the original sea-wall. The creek today is mainly dry, and the second embankment has largely disappeared. A pill-box now stands near the point where it rejoined the coastline.

The sea-wall soon begins to veer westwards, and here a long sandy spit, marked on the more detailed Ordnance Survey maps as Irlam's Beach, heads out into the sea. This is prominent even at high tide, and is often quite popular with children who play in the pools nearby. However, this is not recommended because the tide washes up large amounts of litter, including fragments of glass, and the spit is largely surrounded by soft mud.

Hamford Water

Past Irlam's Beach, the character of the coastline changes quite radically. The sea-wall, rather than looking out onto the open sea, now follows around the edge of Hamford Water, a delightful inlet a few miles across. This marshy bay is off the beaten track and quite secluded, and remains in a wild natural state. Even common seals have been spotted here from time to time. It is possible to explore some of its small low-lying islands, most of which have now been abandoned to the elements. Washed over by the tides and visited only by migrant birds, each has its own individual character and history. At first site, Hamford Water may appear to be just one large uniform salt-marsh, carved up into hundreds of small patches of land by the thousands of tiny muddy channels which criss-cross its surface. To those who know where to look, however, there is plenty of interest, and its varied wildlife also appeals to naturalists and bird-watchers.

A hill-top tower in the distance marks the far side of the bay. This is the Naze Tower, built originally as a shipping beacon. It is only about three miles away as the crow flies, but in order to reach it, you have to walk nearly 14 miles. Although the path is occasionally quite rough underfoot, the scenery is outstandingly beautiful, a peaceful antidote to the bustle of town life, and most people are quite sad to leave Hamford Water behind.

One avid admirer of the tranquillity of the area was the author Arthur Ransome (1888-1967). His popular children's series, *Swallows and Amazons*, was mostly set in his homeland of the Lake District, but in 1939 he based one story around Hamford Water. In this book, *"Secret Water"*, he tells of the adventures of the children who call themselves the Swallows and the Amazons, along with their new friends, the Eels, as they attempt to draw a map of Hamford Water. Although he uses false place-names throughout, his descriptions of the terrain are mostly accurate. A more detailed insight into the basis of all the Swallows and Amazons stories can be found in Christina Hardyment's excellent book *"Arthur Ransome and Capt. Flint's Trunk"*.

The path heads westwards, with a wide expanse of salt-marsh to the left and large arable fields to the right. By standing on the top of the sea-wall and comparing the height of the land on either side of the embankment, it is clear that the agricultural ground inland is many feet below the level of water at high tide. According to detailed

Ordnance Survey maps, a typical spot height is about one metre, but it is often forgotten that this is above *mean* sea-level, and that the tide around these coasts will vary about 3 metres either side of this average. In other words, without the sea-wall, these fields would be under 2 metres of water at every high tide.

The extensive mudflats of Hamford Water have been declared a Site of Special Scientific Interest (SSSI) in order to protect the delicate balance of its wildlife, and, although it is occasionally possible for walkers wearing stout boots to probe a short distance into the marshes by leaping from one raised area to the next, the muddy reaches of Bridgedock Creek effectively prevent people from straying too far from the sea-wall. The best method of exploring the marshes outside the sea-wall is by following one of the man-made paths which snake through the swarths of sea purslane (*Halimione portulacoides*). One such path can be found about a mile from Irlam's Beach, where the sea-wall turns sharply to the right. A track leads from here to a rickety wooden bridge and then wanders apparently aimlessly for a few hundred yards before dying out on the banks of Boat Creek. This is one of the few marshland tracks in Essex which has been maintained and is still in use today. At the end of the path, a couple of low punts may be found moored in the saltings. It is important that these boats should not be touched because they are the private property of local wildfowlers, whose shots can sometimes be heard echoing across the water after the first of October, the start of the wildfowling season.

Pewit Island

This path once had a much more important purpose than wildfowling, however. Throughout the 19th century, this track provided the only access to a isolated community known as Pewit Island. Sheep and cattle were kept on this remote island, which was surrounded by a low embankment to keep the grazing land free of salt-water. A network of ditches across the island provided an elaborate drainage system, using simple pottery pipes. Some remains of these can still be seen today.

The precise history of the island is very sketchy – its first appearance on a map is in 1771 (spelt 'Pewet'), though it had probably been grazed for many years before then. A map of 1840 showing the land without sea-walls was probably just inaccurate, but the Ordnance Survey map of 1881 shows the most detail of all. The land was in two sections – the larger northern half was Pewit Island, and the southern smaller half was named New Island. A terrace of four small red-brick cottages stood near the boundary between the two sections, with a freshwater well nearby.

Pewit Island was permanently occupied, though the farmers who lived in the small building must have fought a perpetual battle against the sea. On the 29th of November 1897, Essex was hit by one of the highest tides ever experienced around these coasts. On a day that was later dubbed "Black Monday", waves lashed the sea-wall and water poured over the top of almost every sea-wall in the area, and over 30,000 acres of rich agricultural land were inundated. Fortunately no lives were lost in the disaster, but the livelihood of numerous farmers was destroyed. Salt takes a long time to leach out of the soil, and therefore no useful crops could be grown on the flooded land for nearly ten years. In addition, hundreds of miles of sea-wall had to be replaced. Some landowners didn't have the money to repair the damage, and many farms were simply abandoned to the sea. Pewit Island was one such place – no attempt was made to restore the devastated embankments, and the farm was evacuated. Around 1904, a further series of high tides ensured that the island would never be used again, and the area has slowly reverted back to its natural state.

The island took its name from the peewits who used to nest in the short grass on the island, but since 1897 the grass, no longer grazed, has grown tall and unchecked, and the peewits have left. Gradually, the island fell into ruin. Swirling waters covered the island at every tide, and in 1923 the farm buildings collapsed. Locals say that the raised path leading across the marshes to the island was dynamited by wildfowlers so that they could get their punts down Boat Creek without obstruction and hence circumnavigate the island. The erosive forces of water have now enlarged the gap to a width of some thirty feet.

It is virtually impossible to see any sign of Pewit Island today from the sea-wall, but there are a few remains to be found if you visit the site. The only means of access today is from the end of Irlam's Beach. About half a mile along the sandy spit, it is necessary to wade across Dugmore Creek. Although at low tide this is firm and only a few inches deep, it cannot be stressed strongly enough that at high tide this becomes a deep river some fifty feet across with very powerful currents. The length of time for which this creek remains safe to cross will vary according to the time of month, the wind, and numerous other factors. Sometimes it will be open for three hours either side of high tide, sometimes for just half an hour, and at some tides, particularly when there is a strong north-westerly wind, it may not uncover at all. *Please beware! We recommend that slow walkers or those inexperienced with the tides in this area do not attempt to visit Pewit Island.*

Having taken heed of this warning, walkers who do cross Dugmore Creek and climb up the mudflat opposite will at first find themselves in a desolate landscape of mud and salt-water vegetation with little sign that humans have even passed this way before. The sea-wall that used to surround this section of Pewit Island was washed away by the tide many years ago, and it is necessary to follow the coast southwards for another half a mile before any remains of embankment can be found. The ground is rough and tiring on the legs; the easiest walking is down on the empty mudflats, but if you venture up to the land's edge occasionally, you may notice that some of the tiny channels which intersect the saltings are perfectly straight. These are the remains of the ditches which used to drain excess water off the grazing land.

After a time, the coastline turns sharply westwards. This is the wide channel which separated the two sections of the island, and is still walled on both sides by the original embankments. Protected from the main force of the tides, these sea-walls still retain much of their original height, and local wildfowlers often refer to them as the "High Walls," as opposed to the "Low Walls" which surround the rest of the island.

About a third of a mile up this creek, the "High Walls" suddenly stop. This is the point where the embankment crossed the creek and the two sections of the island were joined. Clearly, the sea-walls have been so severely breached that there is little chance of getting across the creek to explore New Island, except by boat. Just a hundred yards to the north lies the site of the farm, although this involves the awkward crossing of several very muddy channels. A large pile of red bricks and roofing slates is all that remains of the structure today, and standing in this lonely spot it is easy to imagine the isolation that the farmers must have felt. It is possible to explore the interior of the island and perhaps find remains of the pipes which were used in the drainage system, but numerous small channels cross the island, and it is safer to retrace your steps around the edge of the island before Dugmore Creek is covered over once again.

In such a remote and wild region, suggestions to build a railway across this island appear absurd, and yet such a proposal was seriously considered at the height of the railway era in 1882. The aim was to link the towns of Harwich and Walton-on-the-Naze, and would have included constructing a massive bridge across Hamford Water, with a fifty-foot opening section for shipping. No precise plans were drawn up for this venture, and the idea was soon shelved, but it was not the first time that such a link had been turned down. In 1869, a mainland link via the villages of Wix and Tendring was abandoned, even though seven years' work and £26,000 had already been sunk into the project.

Whether you choose to visit Pewit Island or decide simply to enjoy the scenery from the mainland, make the most of it because in a few hundred yards a fence crosses the sea-wall and a large notice leaves you in no doubt that the next stretch of coastline is private. Walkers are forced to make a long detour inland, because an explosives works has been built near the shore on an area of land known as Bramble Island. Although it is unlikely that this ground was ever completely surrounded by water, writers often used the word 'island' to describe any coastal land which was difficult to reach except by boat.

The sea-walls of Bramble Island, like most around Hamford Water, were destroyed in the floods of 1897, but an explosives company bought the land and repaired the embankments with the intention of building a new factory. However, the company went backrupt and the island flooded again in 1905. It was sold soon after to a French-owned company called Explosives and Chemical Products Limited (later abbreviated to Exchem) who constructed a large works on the site. They too experienced serious flooding, first in 1928, then again in 1949. The buildings were also badly damaged during the severe floods of 1953, during which the nightwatchman drowned. Soldiers were required to help drain the site and repair the sea-walls. The water-logging also made the explosives unstable and large quantities were carried eight miles out to sea on a wartime Mulberry barge, which was then deliberately sunk. The site of this barge, still potentially dangerous, is marked by buoys.

No explosives have been made here since 1985. Now known as Exchem Organics, the company manufactures instead a wide variety of industrial chemicals. However, security still has a high profile, and all that can be seen behind their high sea-walls is a row of trees, an old disused look-out tower and the occasional corrugated iron hut. Aerial photographs show a complete network of tracks and low buildings, each protected by a large mound of earth originally built to limit the damage should an accidental explosion occur.

When you reach the fence, turn inland and follow the path to a track which leads up the hill. On the left are large fields where you can often pick your own strawberries during the summer months. At the top of the hill, you reach Clacton Road, the B1414 which links the towns of Harwich and Clacton. Buses occasionally run along this quiet winding country road, and there is a small shop and a 13th-century pub (Ye Olde Cherry Tree) in the village of Little Oakley, half a mile to the right. The coastal route continues to the left.

After half a mile, you pass the main entrance to the Bramble Island works. At the foot of their private side-road, appropriately named Dock Road on Ordnance Survey maps, is Great Oakley Dock. During the 19th century, this was one of the busiest docks in Hamford Water, and Exchem still use it today to carry goods to and from the works. At one time, there was a second landing-stage, known as Joy's Dock, on the south-east side of Bramble Island, but this has not been used for many years. There are also records of a tidal mill somewhere in this area way back in the 12th and 13th centuries, and although it is mentioned again around 1560, there are now no traces of it.

If you were to continue along the B1414, you would pass Great Oakley Hall and enter the village of Great Oakley. Our route, however, leaves the road well before this. Just around the corner from the works entrance, follow a quiet leafy lane for about half a mile, after which a finger-post points out where the public footpath leaves the lane. Do not be unduly worried if you miss this signpost – the two routes lead eventually to the same place. Your view down the hill is blocked by trees, but at the foot of this hill an Ordnance Survey map of 1905 clearly shows a few houses named the 'Decoy Cottages', and another building nearby called 'Decoy House'. These names refer to the now-disappeared Old Moze Hall decoy pond, a special pool which was used in previous centuries for catching wildfowl. There was intense rivalry between this pond and another nearby decoy in the grounds of Great Oakley Hall, which brought in over 10,000 fowl in one year. They closed in 1840 and 1841 respectively. (Detailed information about decoy ponds can be found later in this book, during the description of the Dengie peninsula.)

Eventually the footpath emerges onto the B1414, near a sharp bend (note that the right of way was changed recently, and older maps will now be out of date). Unfortunately here you have to join the road and follow it for a few miles in a south-westerly direction. It is possible to cut off a few of the corners. For details on the rights of way, consult an Ordnance Survey map. Just after Lower Barn Farm, the road passes near Quay Farm, where you can rejoin the shores of Hamford Water.

The stretch of coastline that you have missed by taking this inland route is named Garnham's Island, another of those areas which is called an island despite never being surrounded by water. You can get a wonderful panoramic view of Garnham's Island from the B1414 (where the footpath rejoins the road). Whilst there is normally no public access to this stretch of the coastline, it may be possible to get permission from the local landowners to visit this area. A description is only included here for completeness.

Along the shoreline, clumps of short grass struggle to grow out of a bed of soft mud, interwoven with deep channels which fill with sea-water at every tide. This area has the unusual name 'Cunnyfur Ooze', which may be related to the 'Cunningford Loading' at Wrabness on the River Stour. It is hard to envisage that this wild region of tidal marshland was once dry land used for grazing animals. It never had drainage ditches like those on Pewit Island, nor did it ever have its own farm buildings, since it was usually managed by the owners of Old Moze Hall. (The word 'moze' is the old English word for marsh.) Like much of the low-lying ground around these coasts, it did, however, require embankments to protect it from flooding, and these held back the tide for hundreds of years.

During the high tide of 1897, however, storms destroyed much of the sea-wall, and a large part of the land was inundated. The swirling waters eroded deep channels into the island, and although attempts were made to repair the damage by damming these channels, this proved ineffective against further storms in the early 1900s. Garnham's Island, like Pewit Island, was eventually abandoned to the sea, and a new embankment was built further inland.

Today, aerial photographs still clearly show the line of the original sea-wall around Garnham's Island. Half a mile south of Old Moze Hall, it is possible to walk out along the remains of one section of this wall. It is gradually eroding away with each tide, but it is an eerie experience to safely walk out into the middle of the bay, surrounded by oyster-catchers and terns, with tidal marshland on either side of you. The ruined sea-wall comes to an end after just half a mile, where a wide channel has eroded a hole through the embankment. On the far side of the water, two lines of wooden posts stick out of the mud. These are the remains of a final attempt to repair the sea-wall after the devastation of 1897.

The next public access to the shores of Hamford Water is from the main B1414 road, roughly half-way between the villages of Beaumont and Thorpe-le-Soken. Walk down a side track called Quay Lane towards the buildings of Quay Farm. Just as you approach the buildings, a finger-post points out where the public footpath turns right. After a few yards, you emerge from the undergrowth at the head of a narrow creek. This is the site of Beaumont Quay, which still contains the rotting timbers of an old barge called The Rose. If you look downriver, you will notice that one of the waterways leading to this site is almost perfectly straight. This is the man-made Beaumont Cut, an artificial canal that was dug in order to provide better access to the wharf, and this gives an indication of the importance of this quay in centuries past.

It is known that Beaumont Quay was used in Roman times, and some historians have claimed that the road leading down to Quay Farm is just one part of a long Roman road which used to lead inland to the village of Tendring and hence to the important Roman military centre of Colchester. The quay's more recent claim to fame occurred in 1831 when the wharf was rebuilt using stone from the original London Bridge. However, with the improvement of local roads, sea traffic gradually declined and the waterway silted up. Beaumont Quay is too far upstream for the leisure industry, only being in water for a few hours at each tide, although more convenient docks have survived by catering for the recent upsurge in pleasure craft. The wharf was last used between the wars, and today the site is quiet, with very little sign of its past industry.

The route eastwards from Beaumont Quay is a peaceful stroll along the top of a low sea-wall, following the winding creek downstream on its southern bank. The landscape is truly rural, and the tranquil surroundings give the impression that you are about as far away from it all as you can get. Moreover, the entire character of this corner of Hamford Water changes according to the state of the tide. At high tide, the colours of the sky are reflected in the water as it gently flows around the saltings, filling up nooks and crannies, whereas at low tide waders wander unperturbed around the mudflats.

However, civilisation has not been completely left behind yet, for after two thirds of a mile the sea-wall rounds a corner and approaches a group of waterside cottages. A few small sailing craft are usually moored nearby, and boating enthusiasts are usually so evident at weekends that car parking space is severely restricted. This is Landermere Wharf, a small dock which, as well as being used for hundreds of years to bring in heavy goods, was also once a commercial concern. First used in Elizabethan times, it was sold in 1760 to Richard Rigby who also owned the port at Mistley. The main cargoes were coal, corn and Scandinavian timber, though quiet backwaters such as these also thrived in the past on the profits from smuggling. Perhaps the most common illicit commodity was alcohol, which would have been shipped in quietly at night, probably with the full knowledge of locals.

Remote coastlines have always been a problem for customs men, particularly around inland bays such as Hamford Water where boats carrying contraband could be moored, waiting for a suitable opportunity to approach the wharf and offload. The King's Head pub used to be situated near Landermere Wharf, and reputedly lost its licence in 1913 after a smuggling incident. Whether this is true or not is difficult to ascertain, but it is a fact that smuggling and poaching have been practised along these coasts for centuries. Records show, for example, that a group of men were caught poaching oysters in 1676 and were fined £40.

Landermere Wharf had its own tidal mill in 1292, which was rebuilt in 1493, although there is no clue to its precise location. Detailed information on this type of mill can be found later near St. Osyth. Walkers are required to leave the sea-wall and follow a path along the edge of a field to a row of houses called Gull Cottages. A track leads back to the road, half a mile to your right, but because of the lack of parking space, car owners are requested to leave their cars near the main road. This is the last access to the sea-wall for a good few miles.

If you turn left down the track, you soon rejoin the shores of Hamford Water, and pass a short sandy beach where rows of wooden posts indicate the ruins of old piers and small jetties. After the last building, the appropriately named 'White House', there are wide views of the bay. Where the path turns sharply southwards, a tiny rickety wooden bridge gives access to a low earth embankment which leads out into the middle of the bay. The purpose of this embankment is not clear; the fact that it is straight tends to imply that it is not a natural feature. Possibly it was built by wildfowlers, or is a remnant of the original coastline. Certainly it is known that large quantities of land have been abandoned in this area in the past.

The next stretch of sea-wall can become rather overgrown during the summer months, and it may be preferable to walk along the foot of the embankment instead. An inlet just around the corner was the site of a small quay around 1900, but, like many other small jetties around the coast of Essex, today it is deserted and overgrown. The scenery is truly wild, with extensive mudflats dotted with clumps of vegetation capable of withstanding the salty conditions.

The path continues in an almost straight line through beautiful surroundings for nearly half a mile before passing close to the ruins of a small red-brick building. This was part of the Batt's Hall estate, whose lands also included the island across the creek. This small island is one of a group of three, each of which had its own separate sea-wall. First mentioned in 1696, they were referred to collectively as Holme's Islands, but records show that in 1758 a local man named John Skipper took them over from the previous tennant, John Hibbs, for an annual rent of £22. In an army survey conducted in 1805, they were marked with the new name of Skipper's Island, and this is the name by which they are now more generally known.

Between 1805 and 1840, John Skipper joined the three sea-walls together to make one single island. Although his embankments suffered badly in the floods of 1897, the damage was repaired without too much trouble. However, a storm in 1948 caused a large breach on the western side of the island, and although it was roughly patched up, the storms of 1953 reopened the breach and also washed away a section of embankment on the north side of the island. As a result, the main outside sea-wall was abandoned, and Skipper's Island once again became three separate raised areas of woodland, connected by saltings.

Just across the creek is the western portion of Skipper's Island, sometimes known as The Heronry because of the birds which used to settle here. The herons have now left the island, but the small copse of elm trees is still surrounded by its original protective sea-wall, although one short stretch on the far side is fighting a losing battle against the elements. The tide punched a hole through this sea-wall around 1975, and attempts to stop the gap with wooden posts and long planks did not have much success.

Around 1990 therefore, heavy engineering machinery was brought across onto the island in order to replace the sea-wall with a new stronger embankment. However, the heavy plant required could not be brought in by boat because, even at high tide, the water in the creek is only a few feet deep. Instead, the owners made use of an old tidal ford which used to lead across onto the island. This track has been disused for so long that the stones have become covered with several inches of mud and silt, and although it is still strong enough to take heavy vehicles across, it is now difficult to see. Starting just west of the Batt's Hall ruin, the best clue to its exact site is given by the break in the vegetation where it leaves the sea-wall. A muddy track about six feet wide leads out into the creek with a slight curve to the left, passing just to the right of a couple of tall posts.

It is known that a lot of land has been lost around these coasts through the centuries, and that on numerous occasions the sea-wall, breached by violent storms, has had to be abandoned and new embankments built further inland. There is some evidence that the inlet between here and White House was once farmland inside the sea-wall. Could it be that the path leading out across the saltings (from the wooden bridge near White House) follows the remains of the original coastline?

Walkers wearing wellington boots may be able to follow the ford right out into the middle of the creek. The track is only uncovered for about four hours at each tide, though the exact length of time depends largely on the time of month, the strength of the wind, and various other factors. It is probably best to walk along the ford about an hour after the water has receded, because the mud needs time to drain. It is very difficult to see any sign of the stone surface of the track – it is almost all hidden under the mud – but occasionally the vegetation cover is slightly different and may indicate its position. It may be necessary to search around to find the firmest ground. The mud is rarely more than four inches deep, although this may vary after strong storms or powerful tides, and, in any event, is a little deeper where the old track crosses the main channel. A couple of upright posts have been set into the bed of the creek to indicate the correct route. In this inhospitable muddy terrain, a stout branch or walking stick is useful for prodding the mud ahead in order to find the firmest ground. If you inadvertently stray from the route of the original ford, the mud very quickly becomes deep and dangerous.

If you do venture out across the ford, please do not walk around the island at the far end. Skipper's Island is private property and the wildlife is very easily disturbed. Because of modern farming methods, marshland wildlife is becoming increasingly rare, and everyone should help in the effort to preserve the few natural habitats that remain. The island has even been designated a Site of Special Scientific Interest (SSSI), and careless wanderers can easily undermine hours of work by the warden.

Back on the mainland, the sea-wall continues in a generally eastward direction, although there are many zigzags in the route. The embankment along this stretch is tall and wide, and the easy walking coincides with some of the wildest views of the intertidal saltings to be found around Hamford Water. It is possible that some of these saltings were once dry land inside the sea-wall, and that they have now been lost to the sea. The original coastline would have left the present sea-wall after what is now a small inlet, and rejoined the present coastline a few hundred yards further on. The scenery also changes from day to day according to the weather and the tide. At high tide, the clumps of sea purslane and eel-grass appear like tiny islands in the gently flowing water, and at low tide the exposed mudflats are frequented by numerous oyster-catchers and other waders whose loud calls echo across the windswept marshes.

Skipper's Island

After about two-thirds of a mile, a path leaves the sea-wall and heads out across the saltings towards the water's edge. It crosses the muddy channels using narrow plank bridges, built in 1947. Unlike the marshland path further north near Pewit Island, however, many of these bridges are quite fragile and have no hand-rail, and it is probably safer to stay near the sea-wall. The track leads to the edge of the vegetation where a stone causeway is uncovered for two hours at each low tide. This is the easternmost access onto Skipper's Island. (The causeway can also be seen from the sea-wall a hundred yards further on.) It was constructed using some quite substantial stone blocks and wooden piling and is much more evident than the mud-covered ford further upstream.

Skipper's Island was out of bounds during the Second World War because of a nearby anti-aircraft camp on the mainland, and so the causeway was allowed to slowly erode and silt up for six years. By 1945, its surface was in a poor condition, and the high cost of repairs after the war meant that the owners could only afford to patch it up temporarily. The causeway has deteriorated ever since and great care must be taken when crossing it today, since the covering of mud and moss makes it extremely slippery. *In any event, the causeway is privately owned and you are only allowed across if you have obtained written permission in advance.*

This tidal causeway leads to the central portion of Skipper's Island, which is still joined to the western section by John Skipper's original sea-wall. The Heronry was part of the Batt's Hall estate, whereas the rest of the island was owned by Birch Hall. In most marshland communities, the landowners usually made an arrangement to maintain a common causeway or bridge, so the existence of two separate crossings indicates that there was probably some rivalry between the two neighbouring farms.

The third small island that completes Skipper's Island is hidden from view. Known as the Round Field, it lies to the north in the centre of the saltings, and is now virtually inaccessible. The track which led to it across the saltings has now completely eroded away, and it is now surrounded by tidal marshes with channels barring any access on foot. Surrendered to nature, its small copse of trees supports many species of birdlife, and is particularly reknowned for its colonies of grey and ringed

The (eastern) tidal causeway onto Skipper's Island

plover. Another unique feature of this area is the abundance of the rare plant hog's fennel (*Peucedanum officinale*), which in the British Isles is only otherwise found in Kent.

This northern section lies entirely within John Skipper's original sea-wall, which, although wildly overgrown, can still be followed up the eastern side of the island until a break in the embankment bars further progress. This was the 1953 breach which led to the island being abandoned. The sea has gouged a deep hole here in the sea-wall, and the strong current created by the water flowing in and out of this new tidal channel at each tide is today gradually eroding away the last remains of John Skipper's work. This breach illustrates the precarious position of much of the low-lying farmland around the coast of Essex. No matter how much land we reclaim from the sea in developments such as Parkeston Quay, the sea will always win it back in the end.

Skipper's Island was owned for many years by E. Fred Williams who, along with his brother Rowley, spent much of his time maintaining the island and protecting its unique wildlife. He arranged that, upon his death in 1972, the island would be leased in perpetuity to the Essex Wildlife Trust as a bird reserve. Under their auspices, the island has been managed ever since by a resident warden, who spends most of his time looking after the land or working from the buildings on the central portion of Skipper's Island.

When the original farm building burned down in 1947, the owner decided to live in a houseboat moored nearby. By the time Fred Williams acquired the island in 1955 however, the houseboat was in a poor state of repair. He therefore arranged for three simple bungalows to be constructed on the island. The main building visible on the island is named 'Fred' after him, and a little distance inland there stands a second bungalow called 'Rowley' after his brother. Several boats are usually to be seen standing alongside the island. Although some of these are no longer in working order, others are frequently used as the main means of access to the island, since the causeway is covered for such a large proportion of the time.

There are numerous paths leading across and around the outside of the island, but the best views are obtained from the top of the observation tower which can be seen sticking out above the tree-tops. Constructed in 1960, its rickety structure does not make it amenable to those who suffer from vertigo, but it does give excellent views not just of Skipper's Island, but also of the whole of the Walton Backwaters.

Visitors are not permitted onto Skipper's Island unless a prior arrangement has been made with the warden.

Back on the mainland, the sea-wall passes a private track that heads inland to the farm of Birch Hall. Where the embankment turns a sharp corner, the entrance to a wartime building can be seen just inland in a large square mound, now largely covered with grass. The path then follows around the curved edge of a thin peninsula with good views down Kirby Creek. Two hundred yards from the ruin, it is just possible to spot a low grassy embankment jutting out from the sea-wall. Directly opposite this embankment, across the water, is a tiny clump of raised saltings called Honey Island (marked on some nautical maps as Honywood Island). There is another low grassy embankment crossing Honey Island, and a third embankment leading to Horsey Island beyond, though it is hard to see from the mainland. These were all once joined together, blocking the waters of Kirby Creek.

Horsey Island was recorded in the year 1212 as "Horse hey", and has been inhabited for many hundreds of years. In the middle of the 19th century, an ambitious plan was devised to join it permanently to the mainland. A dam was built from Horsey Island across Honey Island and on to this peninsula on the mainland. However, this is as far as the project went, and the second dam, at the other end of the island, was never constructed. Locals say that the planners probably ran out of money, since the work involved in blocking the powerful tidal currents of these wide creeks was probably greater than they had expected. The scheme was abandoned, and because the dam that they had already built was being eroded by the daily tidal waters from both sides, it was soon washed away. By 1881, the section between the mainland and Honey Island had been breached, and the second section collapsed soon afterwards. Today, the only remaining traces of this grand venture are on the saltings, above normal high tides.

A good example of land being abandoned to the sea occurs just around the corner. Where the present sea-wall bends sharply to the right, traces of an older embankment can be seen continuing almost in a straight line out into the intertidal mudflats. It is difficult to ascertain precisely when the course of the sea-wall was changed, but it was certainly before 1810 because the earliest Ordnance Survey maps show the coastline in its present position.

The path continues in a southerly direction for half a mile, and, just after the route of the original embankment rejoins the sea-wall, the coastline makes an abrupt turn at the head of a small creek, winding around a low hill on which the farm of Marsh House has been built. As the path detours around this low mound, another old embankment may be seen a hundred yards out to sea. This original shoreline rejoins our path on the far side of the hill, where unfortunately a refuse tip rather spoils the scenery inland.

The sea-wall is now approaching the head of Kirby Creek, and just around the next corner you will find the remains of an old quay. Just before the quay, walkers have to climb over a short stretch of rough ground that was once another small refuse tip, and use a short wooden plank to clamber over a narrow ditch. You will then find yourself in Quay Lane, a small side-track that leads from the village of Kirby-le-Soken down to the site of Kirby Quay. No commercial traffic has used this wharf for about seventy years, but in its heyday this was a thriving concern. In 1824, this was described as:

"an area abounding with hares and partridge. The Quay or Wharfe connecting Mercantile business with a family concern ... capable of containing two vessels... on the Wharfe is a corn granary, dwelling house, counting house, lime kiln and lime house, store house, stable and enclosed coal yard."

The main exports from this quay were wheat and barley, but it also carried hay and straw to London for the horses there, and in return manure was imported for use as a fertiliser. Lime was also produced at the small nearby lime-kiln, and a brickworks was built to the west of Quay Lane in 1893. Coastal marshlands frequently had their own small-scale brickworks, using silt from the mudflats to produce bricks for local buildings.

Kirby Quay, Hamford Water

Of the buildings that originally made up the quay, only the corn granary and the storehouse now remain. The corn granary, which dates from the 16th century, was partially converted into living accommodation in 1913, and in 1922 it was fully changed into a private house. Now called Quay House, it affords beautiful views out across the creeks from its isolated location on the water's edge. However, there was a danger that, at high tide, sea-water might get into the foundations, undermining the structure of the building. To prevent this, the whole house was recently jacked up five feet and strengthened.

Quay Lane provides the first access to the sea-wall for miles, and many walkers use this route to reach the coastline, walking down from the village of Kirby-le-Soken. The unusual name derives from around the year 900, when a 'Peculiar Jurisdiction' created the 'soke' of Kirby. This meant that land was put under the jurisdiction of a central manor for the payment of taxes and judicial purposes. Sokes were also created at the neighbouring villages of Thorpe and Walton, which became known as Thorpe-le-Soken and Walton-le-Soken, although the latter is now known as Walton-on-the-Naze. The jurisdictions were finally withdrawn by Henry VIII.

The name Kirby comes from the two Old Norse words "kirkja", meaning church, and "by", meaning a village. Hence Kirby originally meant "village near the church", and although this is a common place-name in Britain, it is significant that Kirby-le-Soken and Thorpe-le-Soken are the only places on the coastline of Essex whose name does not appear to derive from the Anglo-Saxon. It is possible that, like Harwich and Canewdon, there was once a small Danish settlement here.

In the same way as Landermere Wharf further to the west, smuggling was rife here in the 19th century. Illicit imports probably provided most of the supplies to the two local pubs, the 17th-century Ship, and the 14th-century Red Lion, which has its own priest-hole. There are stories that the Red Lion (originally just The Lion) was connected to a secret location out in the saltings by an underground tunnel, and that this enabled contraband to be smuggled in under the very noses of the customs officers. It is also said to have been used by Huguenot refugees, and although it was rumoured to have been bricked up only as recently as 1946, the likelihood is that the "tunnel" was probably nothing more than a quiet footpath, perhaps the track leading to the sea-wall which is now known as Malting Lane.

The coastal footpath continues between Quay House and the old storehouse. This leads to a concrete sluice at the very head of Kirby Creek. Behind this sluice is Pilot's Pool. When the quay was working, this sluice was operated so that the pool would fill up with sea-water as the tide rose, but would hold back the water as the tide receded. At the lowest point of the tide, the sluice would be suddenly opened to allow the water to rush down the creek in a sudden burst, thereby preventing the creek from silting up.

At the far end of the pool, a tiny old thatched building can be seen, protected from flooding by its own small embankment. A stone causeway leads across Kirby Creek to this black weather-boarded cottage. It was once the old pilot's cottage, but it is not hard to see how it got the name "Witch's Cottage". The path climbs to the top of the sea-wall, and follows it to the left. It is sometimes a little overgrown in summer, but the scenery is rural and beautifully wild. In the fields just inside the sea-wall, archaeologists have found what is known as a red hill. This is a site where Romans are believed to have evaporated sea-water in order to obtain salt. (More information on these red hills can be found later in this book, during the description of Mersea Island.) Unfortunately, there is little to be seen today without close inspection.

About a third of a mile out from Kirby Quay, the sea-wall turns sharply to the east. This is known as Peter's Point, and provides one of the best views of the mudflats, which extend for almost a mile in every direction. At high tide, the waters cover the flats to a depth of just a few feet, producing a vast inland sea, but at low tide a wide plain of extensive mud is exposed. The mudflats support numerous waders, such as oyster-catchers, which are instantly recognisable by their distinctive "piping" call.

Just around Peter's Point, a line of small paving stones and a few upright wooden posts are all that remains of an old track leading out across the saltings, probably once used by wildfowlers. The coastal path then continues in an easterly direction for just a third of a mile before it reaches a large concrete ruin from the Second World War, probably an anti-aircraft gun site. Here a rough gravel track heads inland back to the village of Kirby-le-Soken. This is called Island Lane, and although officially the public have no right to drive cars along it, it seems that vehicles are tolerated *provided that they don't cause an obstruction.*

Horsey Island

However, Island Lane does not stop when it reaches the sea-wall. It continues over the top of the embankment, down a concrete slipway on the other side, and out across an area of tidal mudflats known as The Wade. It follows a rough track nearly a mile long before reaching dry land on the shores of Horsey Island. Tidal fords are an increasingly rare phenomenon in these days of good roads and bridges, and a track that seems to stretch almost endlessly across such inhospitable terrain is a remarkable sight indeed.

Most tidal routes are built above the level of the surrounding mud in order to prevent the surface from silting up, but the gravel surface of Island Road was laid down so long ago that the stones have now sunk down into the mud, and the track

The Wade onto Horsey Island

actually forms a cutting, sometimes as much as a foot below the level of the mudflats. Nevertheless, the track is today in a reasonably good condition, although it needs regular maintenance, and the local inhabitants are still able to drive their farm vehicles across to the island.

Today, the mud is occasionally up to a foot deep, particularly after strong storms and very high tides, and the track, marked by wooden posts at intervals, is still sinking slowly. It must be remembered that this track is completely covered at high tide, and that although it only takes twenty minutes to walk from one end to the other, the tide can come in extremely quickly. Before venturing out a long way across The Wade, it is not only essential to know the time of the next high tide, which is usually printed in local newspapers, but it is also important to understand how the wind can affect the tide. For example, a strong north-westerly breeze can actually prevent the tide from leaving Hamford Water in the first place. In any event, walkers should not wander around Horsey Island at the far end. It is private land, and the description of the island that follows is purely for completeness.

It is not known when people first settled on Horsey Island. There are unsubstantiated claims that buildings existed on the island as far back as 1536, but the first definite evidence appears in 1594 on a map by John Norden, who described the area:

> *"Ther is within the Nase nere Waltham a proper ilande, Horsey Ilande, verie good for feede. It is inuironed with creeks, which leade to certayne ladinges, as to Landymer lading and other suche places, wher they take in wood, which carrie it to London, or els where."*

The island has some excellent grazing land and is farmed organically, but it has always been susceptible to flooding. One of the earliest recorded floods was in 1691, after which Sir Harry Carpenter of Birch Hall paid local labourers £30 to repair the damaged sea-walls. The storms of 1897 washed over the island, and the land was severely flooded in both 1949 and 1953, but, unlike most of the other islands around Hamford Water, the embankments were repaired, and Horsey Island remains occupied to this day. In fact, it holds the distinction of being the easternmost inhabited island in Britain.

The track from the mainland enters Horsey Island at its southern tip, beside a simple wooden jetty where small boats are often moored. Old maps indicate that a track used to lead across the island to a second landing stage about 400 yards to the west of here, near a tiny creek called Boathouse Creek. A raised track still leads out towards the water's edge from this site, and a few wooden posts indicate where boats were once tied up. Interestingly, a map from 1881 shows that this creek had been shortened by cutting out the meanders, perhaps to avoid grounding boats on the mud when the water was shallow. Further west, along an inlet called Furze Bay, the shores of Horsey Island become high enough that no embankment is required. The saltings here are known as Stock's Marsh.

At the western end of the island, just beyond another small landing stage, are the remains of the dam which, as described earlier, was built across Honey Island in order to connect Horsey Island to the mainland. In the early 1900s, this area was reportedly the regular haunt of a local wildfowler called Ambrose. When Ordnance Survey engineers visited the island to survey the area, the islanders informed them, tongue-in-cheek, that this promontary was called 'Ambrose Point'. The surveyors faithfully copied the name onto their maps, and the man's name was immortalised and is still marked on "Explorer" maps to this day.

This western section of Horsey Island contains a large freshwater pool, surrounded by large bushes and trees. There was once a small jetty here also, but today boats are asked not to anchor along this stretch of Kirby Creek because the muddy bottom of the creek is used to cultivate oysters. More oyster-beds are located to the north of the island, to the east of a large marshy bay. Among the myriad of tiny channels in this bay is Barge Creek, which winds its way amongst the saltings to the sea-wall close to the farm buildings. As the name suggests, Barge Creek meets the sea-wall at what was once a small wharf. A line of vertical posts embedded in the mud is all that remains here today. A few isolated trees along the shore provide shelter for the nearby farm buildings, which overlook a wide expanse of tidal marshland. A couple of tracks weave their way through the maze of saltings, crossing the narrow channels by means of a series of flimsy bridges made of short wooden planks, many of which have rotted through.

Horsey Island is mostly made up of good quality soil which has been well drained, but the eastern end, comprising nearly a third of the total land area, has been left largely unimproved. It is used only as rough grazing for sheep and horses, often found congregating around the tall windpump which stands isolated in the middle of the fields. This thin peninsula is separated from the central portion of the island by a high earth embankment. This appears to be what is known as a 'counterwall', an inland embankment designed to limit the damage caused by flooding if one of the nearby sea-walls should fail. Many such counterwalls are to be found around the coasts of Essex, particularly in the southern half of the county.

A map of 1838 shows that there used to be extensive saltings off the island here, but because it lies at the entrance to Hamford Water (also known to some mariners as West Water) this corner of the island takes the full brunt of storms that come in off the sea. As a result, the saltings, which protect the island against the powerful erosive force of the waves, have been gradually eaten away, and finally the sea broke through the sea-wall, perhaps during the storms of 1897. A small triangular plot of land was abandoned and a new embankment was built a hundred yards further inland. It is still possible to find traces of the original embankment outside the present sea-wall. Nevertheless, the land is still eroding away. Groynes have been built across the mudflats, and a series of old barges are now permanently moored off the island. These efforts will help to slow down the erosion, but it seems that it is only a matter of time before this land is inundated again.

When this happens, it will not be the first time that the occupants of Horsey Island will have lost part of their island to the ravages of the sea. This eastern peninsula is all that remains of an enormous area of land that was reclaimed from the sea in the early 19th century. At some stage between 1805 and 1838, the owner doubled the size of Horsey Island by building new embankments around Kirby Salt Marshes and draining the enclosed land.

However, the venture was only a partial success because, within a few years, the sea quickly broke through one of the new sea-walls to the east of the island. Only a small part of this new land was restored, and this remains today as the eastern promontary of Horsey Island. Some sections of these embankments still exist to the east of the marshes, and can best be seen from The Naze further round the coast. However, a firm track still led across the waters of Stand Creek and onto the lush vegetation of Standcreek Salts, and the farmer still managed to graze his animals on this abandoned marshy land for some years to come. Eventually this practice was discontinued, probably because the crossing was becoming too soft and muddy, although the site of the track is still clear today.

Around the mid 1800s, a second attempt was made to reclaim a small portion of Kirby Salt Marshes. This time, rather than joining it onto Horsey Island, it was made into a self-contained island called Hedge-end Island. In order to reach this new area of grazing land, the farmer had to cross Stand Creek onto the tidal Standcreek Salts and then walk along the crest of his old failed embankment (possibly the "hedge" in the island's name?) Covering an area of about one hundred acres, the island was drained by a couple of long ditches, and a curious tiny rectangular embankment was built in its north-western corner. Maps dating from the 19th century mark a small oblong object in this corner, probably a barn for storing winter feed for the animals.

Hedge-end Island did not survive for long, however. A map of 1881 shows that the embankment leading to the island was eroding badly, and had to be shored up by a breakwater. By 1889, the sea had finally broken through, cutting all access to the island except by boat. A few years later, perhaps in the 1897 floods, the sea-wall on the eastern side of the island was washed away, and the island was abandoned and reverted to salt-marsh once again. This was not the first time, however, that Hedge-end Island had been flooded. Detailed aerial photographs show that outside the southern sea-wall, and running roughly parallel to it for half a mile, there used to be a second embankment, though this may date from the earlier half of the century when Hedge-end Island was part of the much larger Horsey Island.

Today the south-eastern flank of Horsey Island is wild and full of birdlife. Paul Gallico chose this island as one of the locations for his film "The Snow Goose", though the gull colonies have suffered in recent years from predators such as foxes and rats. A low grassy sea-wall winds its way past a wooden barn through an area abounding with typical marshland birds such as redshank, godwit and curlew, all undisturbed by human activity. Just inside the island can be seen a small square pool. On older Ordnance Survey maps, this was marked as New Decoy Pond. (A decoy pond was an old method of catching wildfowl.) It was used until around 1840, when it had to be abandoned because of problems with the supply of fresh water. In its heyday, the pond had six narrow offshoots leading into a dense plantation of trees, and bore little resemblance to what you can see today.

Heading south from the decoy pond, you come to the promontary where you meet up again with Island Road, having done a complete circumnavigation of Horsey Island. To the east of this point is Hedge-end Salts. This is the site of the old sea-wall leading out to Hedge-end Island when all this marshland was part of one large island, over 150 years ago. Today there is no sign of the old embankment to be seen, which is perhaps a little unusual since the tidal forces are not very strong on this sheltered side of the island. Some people explain this by claiming that Hedge-end Island never was fully joined to Horsey Island, and that the planners ran out of money before the project was finished. A map of 1881, however, shows the island to have been completed, and the idea that Hedge-end Island was indeed once just a part of a much larger Horsey Island is clear when the marshes are viewed from the air, from where the original route of the connecting sea-wall can be seen. Aerial photographs, in fact, show quite a confusing number of lines across these saltings and there is obviously a lot more to learn about the history of these islands. Some of the lines may represent different stages in the development of the shape of Horsey and Hedge-end Islands, although others were undoubtedly just man-made footpaths enabling the farmer to reach Hedge-end Island after it had become separated from Horsey Island. The remains of one such path can be seen crossing a narrow muddy channel via a wooden plank bridge.

Back on the mainland again, the sea-wall continues eastwards from Island Road. Passing an area of saltings known as Dennis's Sand, it curves gently to the right to pass around the head of Coles Creek. Although the scenery from this stretch of sea-wall is pretty and the walking is easy underfoot, it is not a right of way, and members of the public are unfortunately forced to walk along the road to reach the town of Walton-on-the-Naze, now just two miles to the east.

Soon after you enter the suburban sprawl of the town, a quiet narrow farmtrack called Rigdon's Lane may be seen on the left. Detailed Ordnance Survey maps indicate that this passes some farm buildings and joins up again with the sea-wall. In practice, however, this track dies out long before the coastline and provides no access to the sea-wall. In any event, it is not a right of way, and walkers will have to continue along the main road into town.

A couple of hundred yards further east, another road leaves the B1034 on the left. This track, named Coles Lane, does stretch as far as the sea-wall, but unfortunately it is a private road leading to Titchmarsh Marina, a large and exclusive marina offering a safe berth for over 400 yachts and pleasure cruisers. It was constructed in 1973 by Titchmarsh & Son. There had been plans to build a marina on this site for many years. Indeed when the railway to Walton-on-the-Naze was being built around 1864, there were plans to add a small siding to provide rail access to a proposed dock, although this idea was soon dropped.

The ground around Titchmarsh Marina was recently used as a refuse tip. This can be an effective means of disposing of hundreds of tons of domestic refuse. Provided that prospective sites are chosen carefully and with sensitivity, and are initially surrounded by tall wire fences to prevent rubbish from being strewn around by strong winds, this is a useful means of disposing of household refuse. Once the site has been covered with soil, the ground takes only a few years to recover, and, apart from the height of the ground above sea-level, is virtually unrecognisable within ten years. Unfortunately, some of the refuse tips around Essex are not looked after as responsibly as this site, and examples of this will inevitably be found later around the coastline.

Coming into the town of Walton-on-the-Naze along the B1034, you eventually arrive at a busy road junction. Turn left towards the town centre. The second lane on the left is called Mill Lane, and this leads back to the water's edge. As you walk down this lane, a large round tower can be seen to your left beyond a caravan site. This is one of a number of fortresses built during the height of the Napoleonic wars.

Martello towers

Around the turn of the 19th century, the growing strength of Napoleon's army began to worry many British military leaders, who believed that he would soon attempt to invade England. In 1801, several new gun batteries were built around Walton to protect this part of the coastline. As the threat of invasion grew, more and more precautions were taken. In Kent, a new canal was dug to allow materials to be easily transported to the coast. This was named the Royal Military Canal after the reigning monarch, King George III.

In 1808, the decision was taken to constuct hundreds of strong fortresses around the coasts of south-east England. Between 1809 and 1812, a total of 105 towers were built, stretching from Suffolk to Sussex. These became known as Martello towers. There appears to be several opinions over the origin of the name Martello. Around that time many towers on the west coast of Italy, and on some neighbouring islands, were called "torri di martello". The word 'martello' here was the Italian word for the hammer which was used to strike a large bell to warn the local people of approaching danger.

There is, however, a second theory for the origin of the word. In 1793, after a request from the Corsican General Paoli to help repel the occupying French troops, British soldiers began attacking French installations on the island. Despite heavy

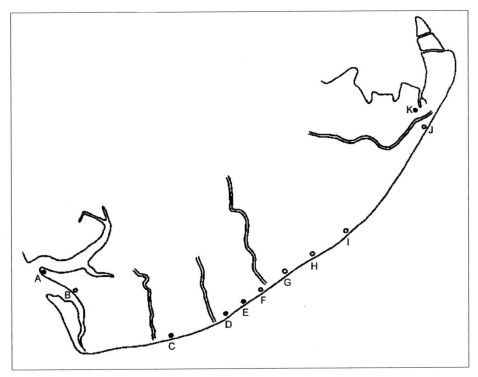

Location of the Martello towers in Essex

shelling, the siege lasted for months because of the impregnability of the French fortresses. One particularly strong tower was on Cape Mortella in north Corsica, on the Gulf of San Fiorenzo. When the British finally succeeded in ousting the French, they remembered the difficulty that they had encountered in taking this tower and used a similar design when constructing the new forts in England. The idea is that the name 'Mortella' was copied incorrectly, and hence the new English forts were called 'Martello' towers.

The best known Martello tower is at Aldeburgh in Suffolk. Of the 56 towers planned for Essex, only 11 were ever built. Protecting the coastline between St. Osyth and Walton, the Essex towers were built to a much simpler design. The outside was elliptical in shape, but they had a circular interior. As a result, the walls varied in thickness from 6 to 13 feet.

Since they were sited either on marshes or beside the sea, the Martello towers were always damp, and diseases such as malaria were rife. Because of the soldiers' continued bad health, the towers were abandoned by 1818. Three of them were demolished soon after, and today only five Martello towers remain standing in Essex. Most of these are in a poor state, including the one seen here in Mill Lane. The town of Walton originally had a second tower, but this was badly eroded. It was sold in 1835 for the high price of £1255, and was then promptly demolished. The best preserved tower is at Point Clear, which we will meet further round the coast near St. Osyth.

Mill Lane leads to a series of boat-yards at the head of Walton Channel. The first one on your right is Hall's Boat-yard, one of the oldest family boatbuilders in the area. At the end of the lane are the private premises of the Walton and Frinton Yacht Club, but there is also a public slipway here at Old Mill Quay, whose name suggests that there used to be a mill in the vicinity. In fact there used to be two. A large wooden windmill used to operate a few hundred yards downstream on the west bank of the creek, but of more interest are the remains of the tidal mill which used to be situated here at the head of the channel.

Some Essex mills had to use the power of the tide to drive their machinery, since the flat landscape produced very few streams with a current strong enough to turn a mill wheel. Each tidal mill had its own man-made pond with sluices that let in sea-water at high tide. As the tide dropped, however, the sluices were closed, and the trapped water was fed through a short mill-stream, turning the wheel as it flowed out of the pond. This meant that the machinery could only be worked when the tide was falling. The miller therefore had to arrange his few hours of work each day to coincide with the tide, even if this was in the middle of the night.

The Domesday Book recorded over 5000 water mills in Britain, of which 151 were in Essex, although perhaps only a tenth of these relied on tidal power. Today the remains of only a handful of tidal mills can be found around the Essex coastline, and there is only one still in working order. This is in the village of Thorrington, near Brightlingsea, and is well worth a visit.

Walton tidal mill was operated continuously for sixty years by John Archer from 1832 until his death in 1892. The extensive mill buildings then lay idle and disused until their demolition in 1921. By a curious quirk of fate, the nearby windmill fell down of its own accord later that same year. It is still possible to follow the outline of the old mill-pond, which is now known as Walton Mere. This is surrounded by a low stone wall which meanders around the inlet, and was used for a time as a boating pool.

This area was once a bustling harbour, busy with fishing boats and barges carrying coal from the north-eastern coalfields. Large amounts of stone were imported from Kent for use in local buildings, and there was a good trade in sand and gravel from the nearby villages of Frinton and Great Holland. Today there is no commercial traffic – only pleasure boats now sail up Walton Channel, and the slipways and boat-yards are only busy at weekends. At the far side of the mill-pond, a footpath follows along the crest of the sea-wall around a caravan park. This is technically not a right of way, although it seems to be regularly used by locals from the town. It leads along the banks of Sole Creek and heads out of town along the western side of The Naze.

The Naze is an unusual phenomenon for a flat county such as Essex. The word "naze" means a promontary and has the same derivation in Old English as the word "ness" which can be found in place-names all around Britain. The Naze was originally called Eadwulf's Ness ("Eadulfes naesse") according to a document dating back to 1052. It is nearly an island, more than a mile square, with a low flat western front surrounded by tidal marshes and creeks, but rising on its eastern side to a high cliff which drops sharply down onto a sandy beach on the shores of the North Sea. It is connected to the mainland by a narrow isthmus barely a few hundred yards across, and here the town of Walton-on-the-Naze grew up. Today the town makes an excellent base for an enjoyable stroll around the Naze.

After about half a mile along the sea-wall, where a slipway leads into the creek, a deep depression can be seen just inside the embankment, now untidily filling with refuse. This was once a short inlet called Foundry Creek, where a small dock allowed barges to offload. This dock had the unusual name of Port Said. The iron works of Warner's Foundry stood at the head of this inlet during the 19th century, and the upper reaches of the main Walton Channel are still sometimes referred to as Foundry Reach. After the dock stopped working, Foundry Creek was no longer used by shipping, and a dam was therefore built across its mouth to prevent a recurrence of serious floods, such as those of 1953. Old maps show that the salt-marshes along this stretch of coastline used to be covered with many small tidal streams and creeks. When the early farmers decided to reclaim this land by enclosing it permanently in an earth embankment, they had to dam all these small creeks at their narrowest convenient point, and this explains the meandering nature of the sea-wall today.

At this slipway, a footpath heads back inland towards a sharp corner in the main road. This is the last access point to the sea-wall before you set off around the head of the Naze, and here you really leave the last vestiges of the town behind you. The scenery gradually returns to one of wild isolation as you head northwards along the flat grassy top of the embankment, following the creek of Walton Channel towards the sea. After a few hundred yards, the stretch of water known as The Twizzle branches off this creek towards Titchmarsh Marina. A "twizzle" was a colloquial word for a fork in a stream or river, and it seems particularly appropriate here. Continuing northwards along the sea-wall, the remains of the embankments around Hedge-end Island are visible. (The island is described earlier in this book.)

The Naze was originally used as a large golf-course, but the club-house burned down during the Second World War, and the land was sold after the war to a Chinese gentleman. He in turn sold The Naze to a a large consortium with plans to build an enormous leisure complex here, complete with a hotel. Local residents expressed some concern about the proposals, and a public inquiry was set up. After a series of long wrangles, it was eventually decided that a large leisure complex was not appropriate, and planning permission was refused. The land was instead sold to the council, who set up a nature reserve here. The first warden was John Weston, and upon his death it was renamed the 'John Weston Reserve' in recognition of his work.

Despite the presence of the nearby nature reserve, large amounts of the Walton Hall Marshes were drained in the 1960s to make way for intensive crop farming, and the only beautiful terrain is outside the grassy sea-wall, where the combination of tidal creeks, saltings and mysterious remnants of lost and forgotten islands provide a subtle contrast to the occasional yachts which sail up the channel towards the moorings around Walton-on-the-Naze.

Some years ago, low concrete slabs were added to the top of these embankments to effectively heighten the sea-wall and act as further protection against tidal flooding. Soon afterwards, however, the warden of the local nature reserve began to discover large numbers of dead shelduck chicks just inside these sea-walls, and it soon became apparent that the young birds were unable to cross these new barriers and reach the waters of the creek, and were therefore unable to go scavenging for food. The problem was quickly solved by the construction of concrete ramps to enable the weak chicks to get across the sea-wall. An example of this unusual feature can be found about a mile out of town.

Not long afterwards, the sea-wall turns sharply to the right, but the very tip of The Naze still lies about half a mile further north across the tidal saltings. A large area of this rough vegetation was also originally enclosed, but the sea had broken through this embankment by the start of the 19th century and eroded a wide ditch across the land. This ditch became known as Cormorant Creek, and formed a barrier across The Naze. A new sea-wall was built around the land south of the creek, and this is the next part of the walk. The area north of Cormorant Creek, however, was abandoned to the tides, though there are some low embankments visible in the saltings from the air which appear to indicate that half-hearted attempts were made at some point to reclaim this land. Today the northern section of The Naze forms an excellent nesting ground for migrant birds, and the area is protected as a bird reserve.

The sea-wall follows Cormorant Creek, sometimes also known as Watch Vessel Creek, for almost a mile and emerges on the eastern side of The Naze near a sewage works. The only access to the bird reserve is northwards from here across an area of rough ground which used to get covered by high tides. Today, however, Cormorant Creek is slowly silting up again, and the reserve only becomes inaccessible at exceptionally high tides. If you enter the bird reserve, you are asked to follow the sand spit which has formed along the eastern shore of the marshes, and not to wander into the area of muddy saltings to the west, where hundreds of birds have made their nests.

Walking over the sand is quite tiring to the feet, and you are warned that some sections of the reserve may get cut off at high tide by deep channels of water. About two thirds of a mile from the sea-wall, a wide creek can be seen just to your left. This is Stone Creek, and at high tide the waters here often flow over the top of the spit, and the area of marshes beyond, called Stone Marsh, becomes a stranded island. In Arthur Ransome's book "Secret Water", the children name this Flint Island, and it is likely that the author was aware that Stone Age flints have occasionally been found on the beaches here. Stone Marsh is surrounded by gentle slopes of soft sand and mud, and small boats often use this as a temporary mooring. At the end of the beach is Stone Point, the extreme tip of The Naze, and here a wide view can be obtained of the mouth of Hamford Water, known as Pennyhole Bay.

❈ ❈ ❈

Back on the mainland, the path along the top of the sea-wall starts to head down the eastern side of The Naze. On older Ordnance Survey maps, a public right of way is marked as running parallel to this embankment, a hundred yards out to sea. Like South Hall Creek near Dovercourt, this is because the public right of way was originally designated to follow the sea-wall which existed at that time, a stretch of coastline named the Tamarisk Wall after the relatively rare flowering shrub (*Tamarix anglica*) which grew there. As the tides gradually eroded this sea-wall away, the authorities made no attempt to maintain it, and eventually the sea broke through during the storms of 1953. Before the wall was completely washed away, samples of tamarisk from the wall were replanted near the hides in the bird reserve. Stone from the old Tamarisk Wall was used in sea-defences further south along the coast at Jaywick, and in 1954 a new embankment was built a hundred yards further inland.

In the 19th century, this area was also used as a rifle-range, but the region is now peaceful and quiet again. Remains of an ancient Neolithic settlement have been found on the beach here. As you walk southwards, the land gradually rises, and soon there is no longer any need for an embankment to prevent flooding. This is the easternmost natural ground in Essex, although the end of the man-made breakwater at Harwich extends a fraction further.

The shoreline on this eastern side of The Naze gets higher and higher, and tidal marshland gives way to the tall East Cliffs. These are up to seventy feet high in places, and parents should be careful to keep young children away from the edge. Most of Essex is based upon alluvial soils or London Clay, which is around fifty million years old, and hence cliffs are a rare site around the Essex coastline. The unusual situation here is caused by a weak top layer of Red Crag silt and sandstone which is being rapidly eroded away by the sea. In geological terms, this sandstone was formed relatively recently, just two million years ago. It was laid down in a shallow coastal basin, and is therefore rich in fossils. Locals were keen to collect fossilised wood because it was rich in iron sulphate, known as copperas. Like at Copperas Bay near Harwich, this was used in the manufacture of sulphuric acid and other chemicals.

A good footpath heads southwards along the edge of the slope, and at the highest point there stands the Naze Tower. About 80 feet high, this structure is a prominent landmark for miles around, and was built by Trinity House in 1720 to act as a navigational aid to sailors far out to sea, though it is possible that earlier towers may have stood on this site for hundreds of years. In more recent years, the tower contained *"wireless apparatus for communicating with passing vessels"*. The local district council is named after the nearby village of Tendring, which also gives its name to the peninsula on which Walton and Clacton stand. This village was mentioned in the Domesday Book in 1086 as Tendringa, which in the Old English language may mean "dwellers by the beacon".

Nearby public conveniences indicate that we are now returning to the outskirts of Walton-on-the-Naze, and a short lane called Sunny Point leads to a car-park popular with walkers at weekends. A small cliff-side path takes you down to a promenade with pleasant views of the Jubilee Beach. The town centre is now just one mile away along the coastal road of Cliff Parade, which soon joins up with the main B1034 road. The town was called Waletuna in the 12th century, and comes from the two Old English words "walh" and "tun", which together meant "village of the foreigners". To the Anglo-Saxons, "foreigners" were usually Celts – the principality of Wales got its name from the same root.

Large amounts of this coastline have been eroded by the tides over the years, and much of the town of Walton, including the original church, have been swept out to sea. The last service was held in the old church in 1798 before being engulfed by the advancing waters, and it is today several hundred feet out to sea. It is said that ruins have been found on a shoal called the West Rocks, nine miles offshore, and legends tell of people hearing the church bells still ringing out across the waters! A large part of the cliffs collapsed into the sea in 1996, and the cliffs are still said to be eroding at the rate of about six feet per year. Evidence of this can be seen in the two wartime pill-boxes on the beach – these were originally built on the top of the cliff.

The main road splits into two near the town's bus station. This may prove to be useful to people wanting to walk around the coastline of the Tendring peninsula. This is also the narrowest part of the isthmus leading onto The Naze. The tidal mill-pond is just a hundred yards away. There is a story that a whale was beached on these shores in 1326, and although much of its meat was taken by local people for their own use, it is said that the tongue was saved and taken by horse to the Bishop of London as a mark of respect.

A coastguard station lies at the end of the pleasure pier just ahead. A 300 foot long pier was first built on this site in 1830, but was dwarfed by a second structure of 1875, nearly 800 feet long. It was soon destroyed in a storm, but in the 1880s an even longer pier was built to replace it. Nearly half a mile in length, it is said to be the second longest pleasure pier in England. (The famous Southend Pier is the longest.) As well as the usual amusement arcades and snack bars, the pier also offers ten-pin bowling, and is popular with fishermen. The railway station stands very close to the coast here, and this line, built in 1867, provides a quick route to the town of Colchester, twenty miles to the west. The local museum is open during the months of August and September. The Old Lifeboat House in East Terrace contains a detailed history of the nearby towns and their development.

Frinton-on-Sea

Numerous groynes and breakwaters protect these shores and the beaches are often busy during the summer. A wide promenade follows the coast southwards, and there is very little break between the towns of Walton-on-the-Naze and Frinton-on-Sea. The town of Frinton-on-Sea grew up around the outskirts of an old village, whose name comes from a Saxon warrier called 'Fritha'. One hundred years ago, Frinton was still just a small village with only 55 houses, but in 1903 the Midlands landowner Sir Richard Cooper began to develop the area as a seaside resort. He landscaped the sea-front, creating gardens along the foot of the cliff, and opened a large golf course nearby in 1905. Today the town is quiet and mainly residential, and has been aptly described as "the haunt of gentlefolk". Although there are plenty of hotels, pubs are very scarce and the town has no nightclubs, nor any of the more lively amenities of some modern seaside resorts.

Sea-front at Frinton-on-Sea

The coastal road, known simply as The Esplanade, runs along the top of a high embankment. This stretch of coastline is called The Greensward. Sir Richard Cooper donated it to the people of Frinton on the condition that there would be no pier, roundabouts, ice-cream vendors or similar trappings of a conventional seaside resort. When new sea-defences were built between 1902 and 1908 at a cost of £32,000, a wide promenade was constructed, and the cliffs alongside were sloped, drained and turfed.

The Esplanade eventually dies out and the coastal route follows the crest of a large sea-wall out of town. Although this is one of the highest sea-walls in Essex, the only views are those of the open sea and a neighbouring golf course, built in 1905. The ruins of a couple of Second World War buildings provide the only items of interest, and this walk is only useful for providing a breath of fresh sea air, since the hard concrete surface will soon tire the limbs.

Early in the morning is perhaps the best time to walk this type of coastline. The bracing wind builds up a good appetite for breakfast, and a dense sea-mist frequently hangs low over the fields and ditches. Known as the "haar", this is characteristic of the east coast of Britain, and it forms a mysterious landscape as you stroll high above the still mist along the top of the embankment. It is easy to see how the nearby village of Great Holland got its name – this flat fertile ground is very reminiscent of the reclaimed lands of the Netherlands. In fact, the name "Holland" is derived from "hoh land", meaning simply "low land".

Before long, a wide meandering ditch called Holland Brook can be seen making its way to a sluice in the sea-wall. In Saxon times, it was owned by a gentleman called

Gunner, whose name was given to the Gunfleet Sands which can sometimes be seen far out to sea when the tide is low. This long sand-bank runs parallel to the coast about six miles offshore, and over the years has caused many problems to sailors. A buoy was placed on these sands in 1628, the first marine marker of any kind off the Essex coast.

Clacton-on-Sea

A small car-park near Holland Haven is the first sign that you are entering Holland-on-Sea. This is now just a suburb of Clacton-on-Sea, but the famous Clacton pier is three miles further along the uninspiring conrete promenade. The original wooden pier was built between 1871 and 1873, and has been extended many times. Its entertainment centre provided the starting ground for such personalities as Tony Hancock and Roy Hudd, although the sea-front today seems to have been taken over by the usual ice-cream kiosks and amusement arcades.

Recommended bibliography:

The River Stour – Russell Edwards
Stour from source to sea – Vernon Clarke
A walk around old Harwich – Harwich Society
Secret Water – Arthur Ransome
Arthur Ransome and Capt. Flint's trunk – Christina Hardyment
The story of Kirby-le-Soken – Irene Johnson
The first 124,999,061 years of Walton – Peter Boyden
Walton 1880-1967 – Peter Boyden
Walton-on-the-Naze in old picture postcards – European Library
Martello towers – Sheila Sutcliffe
English Martello Towers – R. M. Telling
12 family rambles around Frinton and Walton – Hilary Russell
Frinton before the Stuarts – Peter Boyden
Tendring – land of milk and hunnye – Peter Ford

Chapter three – the River Colne – Clacton to Tollesbury

The Essex coastline is deeply indented by five main rivers, all aligned in an west-east direction. All apart from one, that is, because the River Colne flows southwards into the North Sea. The Colne also has the shortest tidal stretch of the five rivers: its tidal limit is in the centre of Colchester, only seven miles from the open sea.

During these seven miles, the river changes dramatically. Near the town of Colchester, the low hills gently slope down almost to the river-banks. Before long however, the valley widens out into classic Essex scenery – vast areas of coastal marshland, now reclaimed and protected by a strong sea-wall. Near the mouth of the River Colne, the floodplain has grown to a width of several miles.

In this way, the River Colne offers a wide variety of scenery, and there are plenty of excellent short walks to choose from, particularly along some of the smaller creeks and tributaries. The area is also full of unusual items of interest, such as an old tidal mill, currently being restored, or an impressive new flood barrier.

Standing near the mouth of the River Colne, Mersea Island is one of the largest islands in Essex, with a length of almost five miles. Mersea is relatively well known and is a popular destination for daytrippers. In contrast, very few people visit the region just to the west, around Wigborough and Salcott. With all the tributaries and creeks, the Colne estuary includes around eighty miles of coastline. This quiet countryside contains some of the wildest creeks and marshes anywhere in Essex. It is possible to walk many miles along the sea-wall without meeting another soul. The Tollesbury Wick Marshes probably contain the most isolated landscape in the area. This is ideal territory for people who prefer long walks through remote marshland scenery, many miles from civilisation.

Clacton-on-Sea

The village of Great Clacton was first recorded around the year 1000 as Claccington, an Old English word meaning 'village of Clacc', a person whose name in turn means 'hill dweller'. It later consisted of two parishes: St. Paul's, formed in 1878, and St. James's, formed in 1907. The area was connected to the rail network in 1882 to help the neighbouring village of Clacton-on-Sea to develop as a tourist resort. Today the villages have grown and merged to form one single large town, one of the most popular seaside resorts in Essex. From Clacton pier, a coastal promenade runs parallel to Marine Parade, and reaches the outskirts of the town within half a mile. On the edge of the town is a large holiday camp built around a large round tower, once used as a meteorological station. This type of fortress, with its immensely thick walls, is known as a Martello tower. Eleven of these strong towers were originally built around the coastline of the Tendring peninsula during the Napoleonic wars, and are described in the previous chapter.

Jaywick

From the town of Clacton, the coastal route heads southwards along the sea-front promenade. It follows the top of a large sea-wall, built in 1880 to protect the low-lying ground inside from high tides. A second Martello tower stands beside the sea-wall in the middle of a small golf course. This is an area known as Eastness, and from here it is only half a mile to the small town of Jaywick, built on the site of a 19th-century rifle-range. In 1928, the land was bought by a man called Mr. Steadman. He built a road to the sea, and developed the area as a seaside resort. Within three years, two hundred chalets had been built on this site, and this had increased to two thousand by 1933.

Jaywick suffered badly in the great floods of 1953. On the night of 31st January, an exceptionally high tide broke through the protective sea-walls and flooded the town, making many people homeless. Thirty-seven people drowned that night, one of the highest casualty rates on the east coast. Although the embankments were quickly rebuilt and strengthened, the town never fully recovered, and the seaside chalets today show none of the prosperity enjoyed by neighbouring Clacton.

From Jaywick, a stone footpath continues along the top of the tall sea-wall past the rows of small chalets, and after half a mile it makes a gentle curve to the right. This was once the tip of a long promontary called Lion Point, but during the 19th century a large area of land was reclaimed from the sea, and further developments took place in the early 1900s in the shallow bay to the west. Consequently, the original promontary is barely noticeable today, although the name Lion Point is still occasionally used. A low embankment winding its way inland marks the line of the old coastline, and the shallow curve of the original bay is still followed by the buildings, and can clearly be seen on maps of Jaywick.

In the 19th century, a decoy pond was constructed a short distance inland near Cockett Wick Farm in an attempt to catch some of the highly prized wildfowl that frequented this peninsula. Known as either Lion Point Decoy or Wick Decoy, it was described as being *"two miles south-south-east from St. Osyth"*. This decoy pond was never a successful venture, and although a pool of water still exists on the same site, it cannot be seen from the sea-wall. On the other hand, it is impossible to miss the Bel Air Caravan Park which lies just ahead. In the middle of hundreds of caravans and mobile homes there stands a lonely Martello Tower, a solitary relic of the area's history which appears to be forgotten by the locals and similarly ignored by visitors. Although it is one of the best preserved Martello towers around this coastline, it is currently used as a store by the site owners, and is usually kept firmly locked.

Seawick

The caravan park stands on the edge of the village of Seawick, the last of the developed tourist sites along this stretch of the coast before you head out into open countryside. The road leading into Seawick lies a few hundred yards further west, and from here it is possible to catch a bus back to Clacton or St. Osyth. The main road, appropriately called Beach Road, also crosses the sea-wall, leading along the shoreline. It continues as a rough track for another mile or so. This section, known as St. Osyth Beach, is very popular with locals, and one stretch has been set aside as a naturist beach.

The footpath continues westwards along the top of the embankment, soon leaving the buildings behind and heading into the quiet and undisturbed landscape of St. Osyth Marsh. With open fields inland and unspoilt tidal marshland to the left, this is a much more peaceful and natural environment than the golf courses and caravan parks around

Clacton, and walkers who have tramped the long miles along the coast from Clacton and Jaywick will find this refreshing. Usually the only sounds to be heard above the raw gusts of the wind are the cries of gulls or the piping of oyster-catchers as they swoop over the saltings. It is a pleasure to be in open countryside once again, undisturbed by the ravages of developers.

A wide grassy footpath heads westwards along the top of the earth embankment for about a mile before turning suddenly to the left, revealing a collection of small buildings. This land was purchased in 1934 by the Lee-over-Sands Estate Company, who built a few bungalows here and started to construct a golf course. The outbreak of the Second World War halted any further development, and Lee-over-Sands remains largely unchanged to this day. A rough track cuts through the sea-wall and leads onto the tidal marshland, splitting into two. The left fork leads down to a large bird hide, but a more prominent feature is the line of giant concrete blocks on the shoreline here. Amongst them is a hexagonal concrete shelter, which gives a clue to their wartime origin. During the Second World War, this remote peninsula was considered to be vulnerable to German invasion and the blocks were placed here to hinder enemy landings.

The right fork, called Beach Road, leads down an uneven track past a row of wooden bungalows. This land is so low that it is often covered at high tide, and many of the structures are raised up on wooden stilts. A footpath continues westwards to a narrow wooden bridge which leads onto the extensive tidal spit of Colne Point. This was originally called Westness, probably related to the area near Jaywick known as Eastness, and has had a long and busy history.

Colne Point contains a rich mixture of landscapes, from saltings to sand spits, and provides a wide variety of habitats for both animals and plants. From about the year 1600 onwards, sea holly (*Eryngium maritimum*) was collected and used for confectionery in such candied sweetmeats as eryngo. It was also used as a cure for tuberculosis and *"obstructions of the urine, liver and gallbladder"*. Although its popularity died out in the middle of the 19th century, the saltings were still scoured for sea kale, a plant commonly found on shingle ridges. This was used as a vegetable, and became so popular that it nearly became extinct in Essex.

During the First World War, a billet of forty men was stationed at the nearby buildings of Lee Wick Farm, and after the war gravel works were set up on Colne Point. A short tramway was built to carry shingle from the sand spit to a nearby jetty, where it was transferred onto barges waiting below. For centuries, local farmers had removed sand from Colne Point to use as ballast for their ships, but gravel removal on this large scale helped to trigger immense erosion of the soil. The works were closed in the mid 1960s and in 1968 the land was bought by the Essex Wildlife Trust, along with the neighbouring farmland of Wigborough Wick. The area is now managed as a nature reserve, and is usually open only to members of the Trust, although walkers who write in advance to the Trust's headquarters at Fingringhoe may be given special permission to visit the reserve.

A footpath runs from the wooden bridge across the marshes to a couple of bird hides over a mile away at Sandy Point, but, as with any coastal area, once you leave the sea-wall you must pay great attention to the tide. At high water, a large portion of Colne Point is cut off from the mainland, effectively becoming an inaccessible island, and many inexperienced people have had to be rescued by boat after becoming marooned in the marshes. It is still possible to follow the raised line of the old gravel works' tramway to the edge of Ray Creek, where a gaunt wooden skeleton is all that remains of the long jetty. Today it is difficult to envisage that such industry existed here just thirty years ago, for Colne Point now has a remote atmosphere, providing a quiet and welcome refuge for many endangered birds and animals. A few relatively rare plants can also be found along the spit, including sea holly, sea bindweed and yellow-horned poppy.

Footbridge onto the sand spit at Colne Point

From the buildings at Lee-over-Sands, the sea-wall heads westwards for a short distance before making a gentle sweeping curve to the north, and a concrete pill-box dating from the last war marks the beginning of the River Colne estuary. Looking out across the nature reserve, you can clearly see the long wooden jetty used by the gravel companies, and, closer to the sea-wall, the remains of oyster-beds form muddy rectangular pits in the vegetation. Although these have been disused for many years, similar beds are still in use around Mersea Island where the oyster industry is still thriving.

After a few hundred yards the sea-wall passes close to a sewage works, and here the public right of way turns inland, leading either across the fields to Wigborough Wick Farm or back up the lane past Lee Wick Farm. However the grassy embankment continues for nearly a mile in a northerly direction. From its crest, a track can be seen heading out into the marshes. Several such tracks were once used by local farmers to gather plants from the saltings and graze their animals, and in the 19th century there was a footbridge across the creek here.

Point Clear

A little further up the coast, the embankment dies away and a couple of wooden jetties jut out into the water. Although boats are rarely moored here, the local landowners have erected a tall wire fence across the marshes, and prominent notices warn potential trespassers that guard dogs are kept on the premises, though it is not clear what they are supposed to be guarding. From the south side of these landing stages, a private path heads inland up a slope called Beacon Hill. It leads along the side of a field to a row of houses at the top, the outskirts of the village of Point Clear. These buildings look out over the mudflats of Ray Creek, and have a marvellous view of the marshes of the Colne Point Nature Reserve, where a couple of bird hides can be seen on the saltings at the end of a long promontary called Sandy Point. One old map refers to this promontary as Horsewash Spit, and it is known that oysters have occasionally been cultivated around these marshes.

A Martello Tower used to stand near the top of Beacon Hill, but in 1967 it was inexcusably demolished to make way for a characterless housing estate called Beacon Heights. A few hundred yards east of the estate, a small side-road named Beacon Way leads northwards past a post office to the main road. The coastal footpath, however, heads west through Point Clear. Half a mile down this road, a short footpath on the left leads back to the sea-shore. A good track follows around the coast, leading out to the end of a thin peninsula. This promontary used to be called Blockhouse Wick, but today it is generally known as St. Osyth Stone Point.

An extensive beach has always protected this land from the worst of the storms, but rapid erosion of the sand and shingle eventually led to the need in the early 19th century for a sea-wall to be built around its edge. Around 1860, the peninsula was used a rifle-range, and large-scale development only really began around 1900. Today, the majority of the land is covered by an enormous caravan site, but the continuing threat of erosion by the sea is demonstrated by the recent decision of Anglian Water to construct a large stone breakwater along its eastern shoreline.

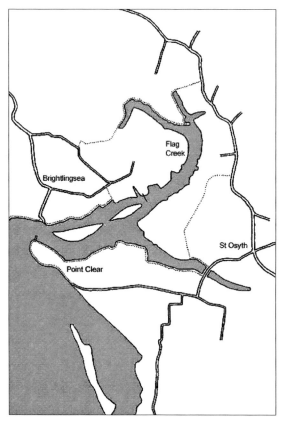

Amongst the caravans and chalets there stands a large round tower. This squat and rather unimposing structure is another Martello Tower, the last that we will encounter around the Essex coastline. Like the other towers to the east, it was built during the Napoleonic Wars to protect against the invasion of England, and is constructed of immensely thick walls capable of withstanding a long siege, as described earlier. Of the eleven towers which were originally built in Essex, this is the best preserved and the most strategically positioned, standing as it does at the entrance to the River Colne and looking across to Mersea Island. It also saw a brief active service during the Second World War, when a small battery was constructed on its flat roof. Today it houses the East Essex Aviation Museum – opening times are sporadic, so it is best to phone in advance on Colchester (01206) 428028.

At the very tip of St. Osyth Stone Point, where a few small permanent houses have been built, a short sand spit juts out from the land. Nearby, a stone slipway leads down the shingle beach to the waters of Brightlingsea Creek, named after the small shipping town on the opposite bank. A ferry used to run across the creek at this point, carrying people from Point Clear to their daily work at the shipyards of Brightlingsea, but unfortunately this stopped recently. Around 1900, a scheme was proposed to bridge the creek, providing a direct road link between the expanding towns of Brightlingsea and Clacton, although the closest that this idea ever came to fruition was during the First World War, when Australian engineers used the creek to practise building pontoons and suspension bridges.

It has been rumoured that a long time ago a stone ford used to lead at low tide directly across Brightlingsea Creek, perhaps before the sea eroded the deep central water channel. Most local historians claim that such a ford never really existed, and believe that the rumours may have derived from confusion with an existing ford just north of Brightlingsea, or perhaps even from a local legend that a tunnel used to lead underneath the creek from Brightlingsea to St. Osyth. All the same, maps dating from 1840 and 1895 clearly show a track heading across the tidal creek, though it is possible that the cartographers were simply inaccurate when drawing up the map, mistaking it for the ferry route which crossed the water at this point.

The mouth of Brightlingsea Creek is clearly popular with boating folk, but it is not so obvious that the area has long been associated with oysters, which have been cultivated in these muddy creeks since the 13th century. Indeed, as you walk eastwards along the top of the earth embankment, which was raised a couple of years ago to give better protection for the local inhabitants, it is possible to spot rectangular shapes in the saltings. These "oyster-beds" were enclosed with low earth walls to create pools of sea-water in which young oysters were allowed to grow before being sent to local markets, as well as to London and further afield.

After half a mile, the path turns a little corner and the oyster-beds become much more pronounced, forming a long row of shallow pits at the foot of the sea-wall. From the air, it can be seen that the saltings are liberally sprinkled with smaller oyster-beds right down to the high water mark. In their heyday, oysters were a valuable commodity for these remote marshland communities and suitable land was at a premium. A high price was paid for the rights to a plot of saltings, and none of it was wasted. Today it seems very short-sighted of many people to view these marshes as waste ground, fit for nothing except drainage and consequent development.

As you continue eastwards past the ubiquitous caravan sites, the creek splits into two, and the two channels of Brightlingsea Creek pass either side of a long thin marshy island. This used to be known as Cindery Island. The name 'Cindery' is believed to derive from the Old English language, meaning "a low lying piece of land". There is a story that a local man, who had to cross the creek every day to get to Brightlingsea, grew tired of rowing his boat all the way around the long island. Eventually he decided to dig a channel through the island at its narrowest point to make a much more direct route to his place of work. Ever since that time, the tides have gradually eroded away the saltings, and the two parts of the island are now separated by a muddy gap over a hundred yards wide, marked on Ordnance Survey maps as 'The Folly'.

The oyster-beds eventually come to an end, and the sea-wall begins to change course, heading in a south-easterly direction along the banks of a small tributary of the main Brightlingsea Creek. This short stretch is called St. Osyth Creek, a narrow winding channel of water which almost completely dries out at low tide. After a sharp bend to the left, the sea-wall passes alongside the back doors of a row of secluded cottages and the surroundings begin to take on a much more traditional rural atmosphere. The scenery is most pleasant at low tide when the countryside appears to come to life as waders cover the exposed mudflats on either side of the water channel.

Boats have used this creek as a waterway for hundreds of years, and the remains of a small wooden jetty can still be seen just ahead on the south bank. As you approach the head of the creek, there are a number of confusing earth embankments amongst the saltings, and their original purpose is unclear. The head of navigation lies a short distance upstream, where a wide dam has been built across the creek. The dam carries a relatively busy road, and parents with young children should take care here since some drivers travel quite fast along this stretch.

Until recently, this dam was used to create a pound for a nearby tidal mill. Covering an area of around forty acres, it worked in a similar manner to the tidal mill back at Walton-on-the-Naze, with water being allowed to enter the large pound as the tide slowly rose. At low tide, the water escaped by running along a narrow mill-stream, turning the machinery by means of a couple of large undershot wheels, in this case for up to eight hours per tide. A mill has stood on this site since at least 1285, but the last mill building was constructed in 1720. It ceased working some time around the last war, during which it was badly damaged, and it gradually fell into decay. During a violent storm in 1962, its roof was blown off, and the owners could not afford the necessary repairs. Although the white weather-boarded building was demolished soon afterwards, there are many surviving photographs of the mill and its internal machinery. Today, there is a sluice gate in the dam and the mill-pond is partially tidal.

St. Osyth

The village of St. Osyth lies a short distance up the hill to the left. An ancient priory stands at the top of the slope, with its magnificent crenellated gatehouse standing beside the road. It is known that the priory was founded in the 7th century AD, but, like most events during the Dark Ages, its history is at best sketchy, and it must be remembered that some of the snippets of information that have been passed down over the years may have been embellishments added by later ill-informed historians.

At that time, England was roughly split into three kingdoms – Northumbria to the north, Wessex to the south and west, and Mercia in the centre. However, these divisions were not clearly delineated, because poor communications meant that the rulers were unable to maintain a strong influence over their subjects. As a result, there were frequent clashes between the Angles and the Saxons along the regions bordering Mercia and Wessex. The Saxon inhabitants of Essex were likewise frequently involved in violent battles against their neighbours, the East Angles, and modern-day writers who believe that the county of Essex should be treated as part of East Anglia appear to have forgotten that Essex and East Anglia were at war with each other for hundreds of years.

In the early part of the 7th century, Christianity was rapidly spreading throughout the country, and this gradually helped to unite the warring factions. The first Christian king of the East Angles, Frithewald, arranged for his daughter Osytha to marry a Saxon whose name was variously spelt Sigebehrt or Sighere, presumably with the aim of securing peace between the two kingdoms. A story tells how a banquet on their wedding night was interrupted when a stag was sighted in the vicinity of the building. Most of the men immediately leapt on their horses and took chase after the stag, and so the concept of the 'stag night' was born!

It is said that Osytha was unhappy with the arranged marriage because she had previously taken vows of chastity, and so she fled to set up a abbey here near the coast. The village, which had previously been called Chich, was renamed St. Osyth in her honour. Unfortunately, she later came to a sticky end. When Danish pirates raided this part of the coast in the year 653, she was beheaded for refusing to abandon her Christian religion and worship their pagan gods instead. Her estranged husband Sigebehrt later inherited the throne of East Anglia from Osytha's father, and went on to play a significant part in English history.

Today the buildings are owned by the de Chair family, and the main house is used as a convalescent home. Even the ornate gateway is now a private residence, although the chapel and art gallery are open to the public between May and September. The priory also has extensive grounds, and peacocks are often to be seen strutting around the gardens.

Back at the mill dam however, the coastal footpath continues back down St. Osyth Creek on its north bank, passing at first through a small boat-yard. This was built on the site of the docks for the old tidal mill, and a century ago most of the traffic here was large commercial barges. Today the area comes to life at weekends when a few enthusiasts arrive to maintain their pleasure craft.

It is not long, however, before the path rejoins the sea-wall and begins to follow the meandering creek downstream towards an area known as Howland's Marsh. Unfortunately the right of way leaves St. Osyth Creek within a few hundred yards and heads inland across the fields towards a copse of trees known as Nun's Wood. It is a great pity that there is no public footpath around the coast here, because the embankment continues downstream amongst some beautiful scenery, and its wide and relatively flat top would make for an excellent countryside path. Although the landing stage which is marked as "Fred's Hard" on more detailed Ordnance Survey maps is no longer visible, the views are of true undisturbed countryside, with sheep and cattle quietly grazing in open fields.

In the summer of 1989, the owners of St. Osyth Priory sold 186 acres of land to the Essex Wildlife Trust, who have started to set up a nature reserve here. In order to secure the purchase of Howland's Marsh, the Trust obtained grants from the Nature Conservancy Council, the Royal Society for Nature Conservation, and the World Wide Fund for Nature, but a large part of the money came as a donation from an anonymous lady (now deceased), who incidentally also helped the Trust to buy part of Fobbing Marsh in south Essex. The warden allows visitors to follow a permissive path to a hide overlooking Flag Creek, but otherwise the sea-wall is still out of bounds.

Howland's Marsh stands right next door to a large gravel works which has dominated the next stretch of Brightlingsea Creek since 1962. As you walk up the hill back towards the main road, you will notice, through the trees on your left, that a small conveyor belt runs parallel to the track. Although now disused, this used to carry gravel which had been extracted from the nearby pit. Open fields on the other side of the path are part of the grounds of St. Osyth Priory. These cover an area of 560 acres and, amongst other forms of wildlife, are home to a herd of fallow deer.

At the top of the hill, you meet up with Colchester Road, the main B1027 road which leads from Colchester to Clacton. This is even busier than the road across St. Osyth Creek, and you should watch out for cars which frequently drive along it at breakneck speeds. Directly across the road, it is possible to get a glimpse through a gap in the hedge of more of the extensive gravel workings. In 1988, the company which owns this land made an application to extend their workings by seventy acres.

Unfortunately there is no more access to Brightlingsea Creek for quite a distance, and pedestrians are forced to walk along the main road for about a mile. As you follow it northwards, you will notice that some of the disused gravel pits to your left have been usefully turned into refuse tips. This was also once the site of St. Martins Farm and a small dock called Wellwick Wharf, whose name is still reflected in the nearby Wellwick Farm. A hundred yards past the Flag Inn, there is a pronounced dip after which the road climbs up a gentle slope known as Hollybush Hill.

Before long, a small public footpath leaves the road to the left, leading down to a confusing maze of tracks through a wood. When it finally emerges from the trees, you will find yourself at the head of Thorrington Creek. This is a short tributary of the main creek and is usually a quiet and undisturbed spot. Looking inland, an old earth embankment can be seen snaking through the fields into the distance. If a section of sea-wall should happen to collapse during a violent storm, a large area of the low-lying farmland nearby would become inundated with sea-water. In order to limit such damage, landowners have frequently built simple embankments around their fields to contain the flood. These "counterwalls", as they are known, can be seen in many places around the coast, although modern farmers tend to rely more heavily on the main primary sea-wall.

At high tide, small waves gently lap against the sea-wall, and as the waters recede, they reveal a large area of silt and mud on which a couple of large boats are beached. The only signs of activity come from the nearby caravan site, built on the site of a brickworks. Like Kirby Quay in Hamford Water, many marshland communities had to have their own facilities for making bricks, since the nearest natural stone outcrops are as far away as Kent.

The public right of way continues down the western side of Thorrington Creek, following the rather overgrown sea-wall opposite the caravan site. Just ahead is a rather interesting feature which is quite common in the marshlands of Essex. The sea-wall suddenly makes a sharp turn to the right and follows around the outside of a small inlet before returning to the edge of the creek and re-establishing its original line. This is a classic sign that, at some point in the past, the sea-wall in this area was breached and that, by the time the landowners could repair the damage, the powerful erosive force of the tide had scoured a deep channel through the earth embankment. In such cases, it is often simpler to construct a new embankment just inland, rather than to attempt the difficult task of stopping up the hole.

The sea-wall soon reaches the tip of a thin peninsula. This is the head of Thorrington Creek. From here you can look back down the main creek and see the jetties and some of the machinery belonging to the gravel works which necessitated the long diversion inland. Closer to hand, a small inlet lies to the east directly across Thorrington Creek. Old maps show that there was once a small dock here called Flag Wharf, and indeed this whole stretch of the river is usually known as Flag Creek. A malt-house once stood beside the wharf, and may have had some connection with the Flag Inn up on the main road.

From this peninsula, it is only about a mile to the head of Flag Creek, although it can be an exhausting walk in summer when the sea-wall becomes rather overgrown. Nevertheless the scenery is delightfully rural with wide open countryside in all directions, and at dusk foxes can often be seen in the fields nearby. When the sea-wall begins to veer to the left, a small path leaves the embankment and runs along the edge of a field, joining a track heading towards the nearby buildings of Marsh Farm (previously called Greatmarsh Farm). It is believed that this was the site of a small tidal mill, referred to in 1594 as Borfleet Mill. Some historians have suggested that it was instead located at the head of Thorrington Creek, but the site here is more likely since Bore Fleet was an old name for Flag Creek. The tidal mill, which should not be confused with another Borfleet Mill closer to the town of Harwich, dates back at least to the time of the Domesday Book, and finally stopped working in the mid-1700s. Today, there are no signs of the tidal mill, and the area retains a remote atmosphere.

The creek ends just around the corner, and although the sea-wall heads downstream again, following the opposite bank of the river around the promontary of Eastmarsh Point, the far side of Flag Creek is private land and you have to make another long detour inland. If you take a small path up the hill to Marsh Farm House, you can follow Stoney Lane inland past an old wartime pill-box. To the left, a flooded gravel pit has been recolonised by all sorts of wildlife, and today makes quite an attractive scene.

When the track veers to the right after a few hundred yards, a small path forks off to the left. Although this path can occasionally become a little overgrown with brambles, it soon comes out at Robinson Road on the outskirts of the town of Brightlingsea. Follow this lane to the left for half a mile, watching out for heavy lorries which occasionally thunder down this road on their way to the gravel extraction works. It is possible to rejoin the coastline by turning right at the East End Green road junction and looking out for a small footpath amongst the buildings which soon appear beside the road.

This small path soon emerges on the shores of Brightlingsea Creek, overlooking a wide expanse of green saltings. The two Cindery Islands are directly in front of you and looking across the channel of water, you can see the opening into St. Osyth Creek, which was described earlier. During the 19th century, locals used the tidal marshlands which border this reach of Brightlingsea Creek for cultivating oysters, and remains of their rectangular pits can clearly be seen amongst the saltings.

This is not the only industry to have made use of the marshes. During the late 17th century, the incidence of scurvy amongst sailors was reduced by scouring the saltings for the plant '*Cochlearia officinalis*'. Sailors took dried bundles of this plant, better known as scurvy grass, and added it to their food, "*its bitter taste being disguised with spices.*" It was not until the early 1800s that more palatable citrus fruits were introduced instead. The marshlands also provided the locals with a good supply of seaweed, called "dacksun" or "ducksun". When large quantities of this seaweed were washed up on the shoreline after storms, it was collected and sold to local farmers for use as fertiliser.

Away to the east, a long thin iron jetty reaches out from the sea-wall towards the deep water channel. This is used by a local gravel extraction company, and there are signs in the saltings around it that some of these marshlands were once enclosed by an old embankment, now long abandoned. Unfortunately, it is difficult to explore this area thoroughly because the sea-wall to the east is not a right of way.

Brightlingsea

The coastal sea-wall heads westwards past a couple of disused slipways towards the mouth of Brightlingsea Creek. After about half a mile, the footpath detours inland around a private wharf which was built recently on the site of an old boat yard. These are the outskirts of the town of Brightlingsea, which gives its name to the creek nearby. The name was first recorded in the Domesday Book in 1086 as Brictriceseia, which means "Beorhtric's Island". This peninsula regularly used to become an island during the Saxon era at times of flood, and was marked as an island even on a 16th-century map. The name Beorhtric is Anglo-Saxon for "bright ruler", although nothing is known about this person. As with many Old English place-names throughout the country, the suffix "ling" was added to the personal name. By the year 1212, the town had became known as Brihtlenggesseya, and this was gradually corrupted over the years to the modern name Brightlingsea.

The right of way leads to a large public slipway beside the creek. The shipbuilding industry here goes back many centuries, and the town is often claimed to be one of the famous Cinque Ports. In fact the original five were Dover, Hythe, Romney, Hastings and Sandwich. Brightlingsea was only added to this list later, along with nearby Wivenhoe and the Sussex towns of Winchelsea and Rye. These towns collaborated during the 12th century to provide a combined defence of the English Channel, and received *"special privileges in return for providing men and ships for the navy,"* which were only withdrawn in the 17th century.

Henry VIII founded a naval station at Brightlingsea, although more recently, in Victorian times, the shipyards here have become famous for their racing yachts. The town is now suffering from a significant downturn in trade, forcing the closure of three of the local shipyards, including the large James and Stone boat-yard, but the area still retains a strong nautical atmosphere. It is a popular berth for small craft, and is home to organisations such as the Colne Yacht Club and the Brightlingsea Sailing Club. The town appears to contain hundreds of marine engineers, chandlers, sail manufacturers and boat repair workshops, and the riverside is a thriving spot at weekends during the summer. From the main slipway, small ferries used to run to Mersea Island as well as to Point Clear just across the creek, although both of these have now stopped.

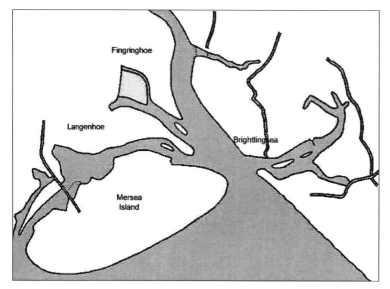

The coastal footpath heads out of Brightlingsea past a long row of beach huts and a caravan park. Across the creek, the low Martello Tower sticks out above the chalets on St. Osyth Stone Point, and looking westwards there is a distant view of East Mersea on the far side of the Colne Estuary. Right at the very mouth of Brightlingsea Creek, on a small promontary called Westmarsh Point, there stands a curious leaning tower. This octagonal structure, known as Bateman's Tower, marks the end of Brightlingsea Creek with its gravel pits and private sea-walls, and the start of an open stroll up the shores of the River Colne. The character of the coastline also changes completely, from a narrow backwater full of quiet hidden recesses to a wide river with an easy footpath along its banks.

The footpath alongside the River Colne heads north-west along the top of a wide sea-wall. You may notice that this large embankment follows an unusually straight line. This is because this was once a railway-line, built towards the end of the 19th century as a convenient method of transporting goods to and from Brightlingsea. The track was completed in 1866, and proved to be an immediate success. However, the low-lying Brightlingsea line was very susceptible to flooding, and the sea frequently cascaded over the top of the embankment during severe storms and high spring tides. It is possible to see, along some stretches of this coastline, that rows of upright wooden stakes have been driven into the mud a few feet from the foot of the embankment. These were designed to prevent waves from eroding away the main embankment.

The opening of the railway was a considerable engineering achievement, since a new embankment had to be constructed to carry the track throughout its entire length.

Sometimes this new embankment was inside the existing sea-wall and therefore access was relatively easy, but at other times it had to be built outside the sea-wall on soft mud which was covered with sea-water at every tide. Viaducts were built in a few places. The ruins of one of these can be seen just a short distance from the town, where the rotting wooden timbers are all that now remain of a 345-foot long wooden bridge.

Today, the line of the old railway track provides an excellent stroll with far-reaching views, both inland across the meadows and across the River Colne to the low-lying marshes around Langenhoe, which are used for military training. Needless to say, the land around Langenhoe is closed to the public and this is probably the closest view that can be obtained of these coastal Essex marshlands. It is just possible to make out three tributaries of the River Colne on the opposite bank. The first is the Pyefleet Channel which separates Mersea Island from the mainland.

The other two channels are North Geedon Creek and South Geedon Creek, which flow either side of a small island called Rat Island. This inaccessible island, covering just 35 acres, has never been protected from the sea by earth embankments, but aerial photographs show that it is littered with the remains of oyster-beds which were presumably worked long before the Langenhoe marshes were acquired by the military. Today the island is wild and abandoned once again, and has now been designated a Site of Special Scientific Interest (SSSI). It has been leased from Colchester Borough Council to the Essex Wildlife Trust and is technically part of their Fingringhoe Nature Reserve, which we shall meet further round the coast, and yet, despite its inaccessibility, some birds' eggs are still somehow stolen every year. Rat Island has one of the largest colonies of black-headed gulls in Essex, with around 6000 birds regularly visiting the area. This particular gull, *Larus ridibundus*, is also known locally as the cob, a name which appears frequently around the coast. Another name for this bird is the peewit gull, though this should not be confused with the peewit (*Vanellus vanellus*), a more common bird also known as the lapwing or green plover.

The pleasant walk along the old railway embankment passes alongside open fields on one side, with the open waters of the River Colne on the other. An old map dating from 1805 shows that a farm called Dairy House once stood on these marshes, but all farm buildings have long since disappeared. About two miles out of Brightlingsea, the railway once crossed a 680-foot long viaduct called the Long Bridge. This was filled in during the early 1930s using gravel which was transported to the site by special night trains.

Just a few hundred yards further on, the sea-wall begins to veer slowly to the north. Several hardy plant species have colonised the mudflats around here and have formed a large area of saltings known as Aldboro Point. During the 1800s, a large portion of this rough land was used for grazing animals and was protected by a sea-wall, probably built around 1850. The ruins of a few low embankments still remain, and it is said that cylindrical drainage pipes can occasionally be found amongst the overgrown vegetation. As explained earlier, a great storm hit the east coast of England in 1897, and the land around Aldboro Point, like much of the low-lying Essex marshland, was abandoned to the sea during the ensuing floods. The railway survived the devastation of 'Black Monday' however, and despite further flooding in 1904 and 1928, during which parts of the track were washed away, trains continued to use the line until well after the Second World War.

In 1953, the Essex coast experienced the highest tide in living memory. For several hours on the night of the 31st January, the waves crashed against the embankments and the sea poured over the top. The sea-walls proved quite incapable of holding back a flood on this unprecedented scale. Like almost all of the coastal defences down the east coast, the railway embankment was badly damaged in the storm. The line fell under the notorious Beeching axe and was finally closed in 1964. The iron tracks were quickly pulled up and the opportunity was taken to build new stronger sea-defences, mostly incorporating the old railway embankment. At this stage, there still existed a few of the old original sea-walls which predated the railway, but even these were dug up and heaped onto the railway embankment for extra strength.

A large pool can be seen just inside the sea-wall near Aldboro Point. This is the site of an old Roman villa, possibly related to a Roman fort which once stood on the other side of the River Colne. The footpath continues northwards, past the remains of old embankments hidden amongst the saltings, until suddenly a creek bars any further progress in this direction. Known as Alresford Creek, the Brightlingsea railway used to cross this via a 430-foot long iron bridge. It is possible to follow the overgrown embankment for a further hundred yards to the water's edge and see the remains of the enormous pilings.

In order to allow boats with tall masts to sail up the creek, the central span of Alresford Bridge swung on a pivot through ninety degrees, and was usually left open for the two hours either side of high tide unless a train was due. The swing mechanism was operated manually by two men who had to row out from the far side of the creek, and in 1895 a cottage was built for the bridge-keeper just two hundred yards down the coast. Trains crossing Alresford Bridge had to observe a 10 mph speed restriction. This was later reduced to 5 mph because of the poor state of the ironwork, and the bridge was demolished in 1967, shortly after the railway's closure.

At the remains of Alresford swing bridge, the sea-wall heads eastwards, following the south bank of Alresford Creek. This narrow, winding waterway has an atmosphere quite different to the wide reaches of the River Colne. The surrounding landscape appears much more peaceful and remote, almost a forgotten corner of Essex, and yet the remains of a large wooden jetty on the opposite bank are an indication that industry is never far away.

Just a hundred yards upstream, a simple track crosses over the sea-wall and leads into the water. This is the ford which gave its name to the creek and also the nearby village of Alresford, and is pronounced "Arls-ford". The first part of the name may well be derived from the word "alor", the Old English name for an alder tree. If you wade

The tidal ford across Alresford Creek

out into the creek and feel around with a stout stick, you will find that the stony surface of the track continues to the far side of Alresford Creek where a few small dinghies can often be seen laying on the saltings. The ford is no longer maintained due to the creation of alternative roads, but it is still just possible to wade across the river at low tide, though a walking stick may prove extremely useful in locating the firmest route across the muddy bottom of the creek. Since the advent of the motor car, tidal fords have become something of a rarity because salt-water can be very corrosive to metal. However, in the days of wooden carts, the situation was quite the opposite:

"Men who used carts knew something about the advantage of a little moisture for tightening wheels. Not for the horse's sake alone was it that carters would drive through a roadside pond, or choose to ford a stream rather than go over a bridge beside the ford. The wheels were better for the wetting."

East of the ford, the sea-wall is wide and grassy, winding sinuously along the southern bank of Alresford Creek to its head, another mile upstream. Unfortunately, this delightful walk through undisturbed countryside is private. The right of way leaves the ford and heads inland up a gentle slope. The track passes the buildings of Moverons Farm and a couple of large ponds which appear to be the remains of flooded gravel pits, and eventually emerges onto the main Brightlingsea road near All Saints' Church. This was once very close to the centre of Brightlingsea, but it is said that the villagers left during the Plague to set up their own community by the waterside, a mile further south. Visitors can arrange to climb to the top of the church tower, which can be seen for miles around and provides a splendid view of Alresford Creek. The stairway up the inside of the tower is well-lit, but quite narrow towards the top.

From the landmark of All Saints' Church, the coastal footpath heads northwards along the busy B1029 away from the town of Brightlingsea. As you descend the hill, you can see Alresford Creek beyond the fields to the left. This was once the site of a small quay called Church Dock, though there is very little left to see today. A wartime pill-box stands at the foot of the hill, marking the start of an inland track which heads eastwards, leading in just over a mile to the head of Flag Creek, another quiet backwater described earlier. In this way, it is possible to make a round walk, almost 8 miles in length.

Continue up the road for a few hundred yards, looking out for a signpost on the left towards Thorrington Mill. Follow this track downhill until it opens out beside some farm buildings. At the foot of the slope, a tall weather-boarded building stands on the edge of Alresford Creek. This gaunt four-storey structure is Thorrington Mill, one of the country's few remaining tidal mills. Its machinery was recently restored to working order, and is open 2pm–5pm on the last Sunday of the month in summer.

The mill, which was originally known as Cooper's Mill, dates back to 1558, although the present building was built much more recently, in 1831. In 1974, it was sold to Essex County Council, and, with the help of volunteers, the mill was eventually re-opened as a working museum.

The machinery is powered entirely by the force of the tide. A dam has been built across the creek, thereby creating a large mill-pond upstream. As the tide rises, a sluice inside the dam allows the sea-water to flow through and fill up the mill-

The tidal mill at Thorrington

pond. When the tide reaches its peak and begins to ebb again, the sluice closes and the water escapes instead along a short mill-race, thereby turning the water-wheel. This can be seen alongside the mill, although it is easier to see the restored wheel from inside the building.

Beyond the mill-pond dam, the footpath around the Essex coastline continues to the left along the northern bank of Alresford Creek, soon joining the crest of a small embankment. The sea-wall meanders erratically downstream towards the ford, still overlooked by the prominent tower of All Saints' Church. At low tide, the creek almost dries out, leaving just a thin water channel coursing its way through the bare mud. At this state of the tide, the sleepy countryside appears to come alive as waders cover the mudflats.

Near Plumpton's Farm, the tiny Sixpenny Brook flows through the sea-wall into the main river, and the sea-wall forms a small inlet. It is now just half a mile to the ford. From the ford, a narrow tarmac road called Ford Lane heads up the hill towards the village of Alresford a mile away, where a railway station provides a useful link with the nearby town of Colchester. Meanwhile, the coastal path continues westwards along the banks of Alresford Creek, passing the ruins of a large wooden jetty. This was once linked to Villa Pit, a small gravel works operated by the Alresford Sand and Ballast Company just a hundred yards up the slope. The pit was named after the nearby Villa Farm, which had a decoy pond in this area. Decoy ponds were a traditional method of catching wildfowl around these marshy coasts. The Villa Farm Decoy was described as standing *"two miles and a half south-south-west from Elmstead, and one mile east from Wyvenhoe"*, and was disused by 1880.

You are not far now from the mouth of Alresford Creek, where a large iron swing-bridge used to carry the Brightlingsea railway across the river. The history of this railway and its demise after the Beeching report are described earlier. As on the southern bank of Alresford Creek, you can still see a short section of the railway embankment sticking out into the creek. A small boat-house has been built at the water's edge alongside the remains of the bridge pilings.

Beyond the site of the bridge, the narrow winding waters of Alresford Creek are left behind, and the coastline joins the River Colne again. Like the earlier stretch alongside this river, the footpath follows the line of the old Brightlingsea railway northwards, soon passing a small shingle beach called White House Beach. This was named after the nearby White House, a small building built near the river-bank here around 1900 on the site of the older Copyhold Farm. The route of the old railway continues in a north-westerly direction, and the wide embankment enables a fast walking pace to be comfortably maintained.

Just after a wood on your right, the coastal footpath leaves the railway-line behind, and instead follows a smaller sea-wall for the last mile into the town of Wivenhoe. Across the river, you can see a large gravel works on the outskirts of the village of Fingringhoe, but the scenery on the eastern bank of the River Colne remains undisturbed by big industry. However, it is clearly not far to the outskirts of Wivenhoe. The first sign that you are approaching the town is the sight of the new Colne Barrier.

Built between 1991 and 1993 at a cost of almost £15 million, the barrier now protects the upper reaches of the River Colne from surge tides. It also reduces the cost of maintaining sea-walls along the river-front at Wivenhoe and Rowhedge. There was initially some concern that the barrier would restrict yachting in the area, but the

National Rivers Authority eventually built a new club-house for the Wivenhoe Sailing Club just downstream of the barrier. The project also included new earth banks leading inland from the piers to higher ground.

From each bank of the river, a large pier has been built out into the middle of the river. The main navigation channel is not in the centre of the river at this point, and the piers are therefore of different lengths. If the piers had been built as solid constructions, they might have affected the tidal flow and interfered with the normal sedimentation patterns of the river. This would have threatened to obstruct the deep water channel, which has to be dredged regularly to enable large cargo ships to reach the quays near Colchester. The barrier was therefore designed so that water could flow underneath the piers. During a surge tide, a series of sluices can be closed to block this flow. There are ten of these sluices underneath the pier on the Wivenhoe side, and three underneath the Fingringhoe pier.

To allow shipping to pass through normally, a 30-yard gap has been left in the centre of the river. This can be closed at times of flood by means of a pair of mitre gates, like a pair of lock-gates. These mitre gates take seven minutes to close, and can hold back up to 26 feet of water. They are powered by hydraulic pumps underneath the main control building, which stands beside the river on the Wivenhoe side. The building also houses the shipping control room for the Colchester harbourmaster.

The whole barrier was built as low as possible in order to minimise the impact on the environment, but was designed so that it could be enlarged if the need should arise. This may be necessary sooner rather than later, because it was originally estimated that the barrier would be needed an average of four times per year. In practice, the barrier had to be operated eight times within just the first six months of its operation!

Leaving the barrier behind as you walk along the new access road, you finally leave the area of Tendring Hundred. Until relatively recent times, Essex was divided for administrative purposes into divisions known as 'Hundreds'. The entire coastal walk so far has been within Tendring Hundred, but during the upper reaches of the River Colne, you will be passing through the region called Lexden Hundred.

Wivenhoe

The town of Wivenhoe lies just ahead. Like Brightlingsea further south, this town was a member of the Cinque Ports group. Traditionally, the town has been closely associated with sailing and shipbuilding, and has produced many fine yachts over the last two hundred years. Unfortunately, when approached from the south, you first encounter the empty buildings of Cook's boat-yard, closed in 1986. However, the town still retains a strong nautical atmosphere, and is home to the Wivenhoe Sailing Club and the Colne Marine and Yacht Company. The river-front is a beautifully peaceful spot, with a row of houses (including an 18th-century pub called the Rose and Crown) overlooking the Colne, which is becoming quite narrow by this stage. At one time, there were attempts to turn Wivenhoe into a spa town with regular boat trips from London, but the plan soon petered out and the area remains quiet and undisturbed.

The Domesday Book referred in 1086 to the village of Wiunhov, a name which roughly translates as "Wifa's spur". The Old English word "hoh" usually meant a spur of land, probably referring in this case to the gentle slope to the north of the village. It is hard to believe that a tranquil spot such as Wivenhoe could be prone to earthquakes, and yet, in April 1884, a tremor damaged around 200 buildings in this area, including St. Mary's church.

At the end of The Quay, a timber yard forces walkers to make a short detour inland down a couple of side-roads. Just before the railway station, built in 1863, a small track leads to the left and allows access to the riverside again. The sea-wall heads westwards through open fields, leaving the town of Wivenhoe behind. Across the water are the buildings of Rowhedge, a small village which we will meet on the other side of the River Colne. As the path veers slowly to the north, a track joins the sea-wall. This was once the site of a passenger ferry which used to ply back and forth from Wivenhoe to Rowhedge, using a series of ropes and chains to pull the boat across the river.

Unfortunately, the ferry stopped working in 1964. In previous centuries, when roads were poor and almost everybody moved about on foot, ferries, sometimes as small as a rowing dinghy, provided an extremely useful link between riverside communities. In today's economic climate however, improved roads and the growth in car ownership have led to a decline in pedestrian and river traffic, and only the largest ferries can continue to operate.

Some old maps show a ford crossing the River Colne here. It seems extremely unlikely that people could have ever crossed the river at this spot because the river-bed appears to consist of very soft mud and silt, and even at low tide the water is still quite deep. The ford first appeared on a map in 1874, and it was again marked on Bartholemew's half-inch tourist map around the turn of the century, although all other maps of the region, including a reliable one of 1881 and another map dating from 1874, show a ferry instead. It is almost certain that, like at Brightlingsea Creek further south, one cartographer from that period was a little inaccurate, and that the mistake has been copied from map to map ever since.

At the beginning of the First World War, a temporary bridge was erected across the river here in order to help military supplies reach the ports around the Tendring peninsula. Old photographs show a visit by King George V to the area in 1917. The bridge was constructed so that one section could open to allow tall boats through, but the structure was demolished soon after the war.

You are now just a couple of miles from the town of Colchester, and during this stretch, the railway is never very far away. Construction of this line began in 1863, and it finally reached Walton-on-the-Naze and Brightlingsea a few years later, with an extra branch-line to the new resort of Clacton-on-Sea being added in 1882. Shortly after emerging from Wivenhoe Wood, a short section of the sea-wall has been eroded away by the sea. At high tide, water pours in through this gap and floods the marshy ground behind the sea-wall. This walk is therefore best attempted during the hours either side of low tide.

Colchester

For another mile, the coastal footpath continues in a generally north-western direction through open countryside, though constantly overlooked by the tall buildings of Essex University, built in the early Sixties. On the opposite bank of the River Colne, the buildings of the Whitehall industrial estate show that you are now on the outskirts of Colchester. This busy industrial region of town is known as The Hythe, a name which was commonly used for river-ports and quays.

Before long, the path leads to the first bridge across the River Colne. Known as Haven Bridge, it was built in 1996 to avoid the bottleneck at the older Hythe Bridge just upstream, and is only marked on the most recent of maps. This series normally describes the route to the tidal limit of each river, but for the River Colne this lies almost a mile further upstream just beyond East Bridge, and unfortunately there is no riverside path for this last stretch.

The town of Colchester has a long history, dating back even before the Roman occupation of Britain. It was the capital of the tribe of Britons known as the Trinovantes, until they were overrun in 10 AD by the Catuvellanian tribe. Their leader, a Belgic chief called Cunobelin or Cumbelin, was immortalised by Shakespeare as "Cymbeline". He was known as the "rex Brittonum" (King of the Britons), and ruled over most of southern Britain. In this way, Colchester is said to be the first capital city of the British Isles.

During the reign of Cumbelin, many Roman merchants settled in Colchester. In 43 AD, shortly after Cumbelin's death, the Romans invaded Britain and seized complete control. They also chose Colchester as their first capital, turning it into a garrison for their XXth legion. Indeed, it was in Colchester that the Roman emperor Claudius received the surrender of the British kings. The Romans knew the town as Camulodunum, a Latin name which translates as "fort of Camulos", a Celtic war-god. The modern name Colchester is derived from "castle by the Colne", the word "Colne" meaning simply "water" (as in the River Clun in south Wales), and not, as some people seem to believe, from Old King Cole!

Several tribes in the north of England continued their resistance against the Roman occupation. They were helped by a rebellious tribe in Norfolk called the Iceni. Led by Boadicea (or Boudicca), the Iceni staged a uprising in 60 AD, burning most of Colchester to the ground.

The town of Colchester has always had close links with the military and is still said to be the third largest garrison town in Britain, with around 4500 troops stationed in large barracks. The castle was built in the 11th century on the foundations of a Roman temple, and has the largest keep ever built in Europe. This is the site every year of the biggest military tattoo in Britain, a spectacular event usually held in the autumn. The castle also has a museum which opens daily (except Sundays in winter).

Nevertheless, the town itself is really outside the scope of this book, which is more concerned with the rural stretches of coastline. Readers who would like to find out more about Colchester and its history are directed towards the numerous books which have been written about the town, a couple of which are mentioned in the bibliography.

From Hythe Bridge in the centre of Colchester, a narrow grassy footpath heads downstream along the western bank of the River Colne. At first, the path is hemmed in by tall fences and buildings, but before long, it opens out onto King Edward Quay, a large concrete wharf which looks as if it has seen more prosperous days. Although shipbuilding ceased in Colchester during the 19th century, large vessels can still usually be seen along this stretch of the river.

After a few hundred yards, Whitehall Industrial Estate bars the way along the water's edge, and the public footpath is diverted inland along Haven Road for a short distance. This soon deteriorates into a rough track, often used by motorcycles for scrambling. The path passes alongside a sewage works and a few equally undesirable stagnant lagoons before finally leaving the last vestiges of Colchester behind and regaining a rural atmostphere. Once clear of the outskirts of the town, the walk down the River Colne is pleasant. The sea-wall follows the edge of the gently meandering river, giving pleasant views of Hythe Marshes, the name given to the unimproved grazing land inside the embankment. This upper stretch of the Colne is quite narrow for shipping, and for large ships is only navigable for a few hours either side of high tide. A series of powerful lights along the sea-wall allow the river to be floodlit if this is during the hours of darkness.

Just before a sharp bend in the river, a low earth embankment branches off to the right and runs roughly parallel to the footpath for nearly half a mile. Despite its height, it is quite possible that this subsidiary embankment was once the main sea-wall, and that the current embankment was built much more recently close to the water's edge. The narrow strip of land enclosed by the two embankments contains a few shallow rectangular pits, perhaps the remains of beds where oysters used to be cultivated.

Rowhedge

After passing a row of simple wooden jetties, the two embankments soon join up again on the outskirts of the village of Rowhedge. A building on the riverside forces the footpath to head inland and join up with the main road through the village, the name of which is simply a corruption of "rough hedge". Rowhedge used to be quite an industrial centre, with Daniel's Brewery (originally called the Donyland Brewery) and a couple of shipyards. Until 1989, many RNLI boats were brought to Ian Brown's boat-yard in Rowhedge for repair, but much of this industry has now moved elsewhere and the village is now quiet and off the beaten track.

In the middle of the village, the Anchor Inn stands alongside a public slipway where, until 1964, passengers could take a ferry across the river to Wivenhoe, described earlier in this book. However, there is no footpath along the river's edge until you get to the far end of the village. When the road ends, a signpost indicates a choice of two routes. To the left, a narrow path leads quickly back to the shores of the River Colne, and then proceeds along the river-bank.

This area of land was simple agricultural farmland until the Second World War, when gravel was extracted and used, it is said, for building aerodromes. Since 1973, the area has been developed as a wharf, and it now contains thirty acres of warehouses. Despite this industry, there is still a public right of way along the riverside. Do not be deterred by the warehouses – if you stick *rigidly* to the very last edge of coastline (skirting around one large container which has been left in the middle of the path), you will quickly find that the right of way leads to a grassy footpath with open views across the water to Wivenhoe.

Within a few hundred yards, the footpath turns sharply to the right and follows the northern bank of a small tributary of the River Colne. This narrow waterway has the unusual name of Roman River, possibly related to a man called John Romayn who was recorded in this area in 1377. The river is over ten miles long in its entirety, finally petering out near the village of Coggeshall. However, only the first couple of miles are tidal. The lower section of the river forms a series of contorted meanders, although a barbed-wire fence has been built across the last couple of these loops, without any obvious purpose, and the footpath takes a short-cut towards the prominent buildings of Fingringhoe Mill on the far bank.

Fingringhoe Mill was originally constructed in the early 16th century – some sources give the date as 1520, others say 1531. The mill was then driven by tidal power, like those near Thorrington and Walton-on-the-Naze. As the tide rose, a small pool behind the mill filled up with the incoming sea-water, and after high tide, this water was allowed to escape along a mill-race. This flow turned a large water-wheel for nearly eight hours as the tide dropped. The tidal mill at Fingringhoe was rebuilt around 1750, and was finally superseded by a neighbouring steam roller mill in 1893. Fingringhoe Mill used to grind flour, but when E. Marriage sold the site to C. Hitchcock around 1931, one of the conditions of sale was that flour was no longer to be milled here. This was stipulated in order to avoid competition with other local mills operated by E. Marriage. The new owners therefore changed to animal feed, largely steam-cooked maize, oats, barley and other cereals, a practice still continuing today.

Around 1936, the oil generators caught fire, and the mill was burned to the ground. The new owners managed to rebuild the mill and its silo using corrugated iron, a rare commodity during the years leading up to the Second World War. Since that date, electricity has provided all the power for the machinery, though during a power-cut around 1942, the operators reverted to the old tidal system for a brief period. The tidal wheel was removed in the 1950s, and today the only part of the original tidal mill remaining is the narrow mill-race.

There is a public footpath across the Roman River, passing through the mill and up the hill into the village of Fingringhoe itself, but the tidal limit still lies some distance upstream. Staying on the northern bank of the river, a simple track leads through a delightfully overgrown meadow to a quiet country road. Just a few yards to the left, Fingringhoe Bridge carries the lane over the river. This bridge was built in 1923, though it may have replaced an earlier structure on the same site. Once again, if you follow the lane to the south, you will quickly reach the village of Fingringhoe. The coastal route will eventually pass through the centre of this village, but first a pleasant three-mile detour is necessary to visit the tidal limit of the Roman River.

Heading northwards along the lane, named Fingringhoe Road, you pass the entrance to East Donyland Hall, a large building surrounded by a moat and with a set of fish-ponds nearby. Shortly after a bend in the road, which was once the site of a church dedicated to Saint Lawrence, you begin to enter an area known as Donyland Heath. If you were to continue along the lane past a pub called the Ipswich Arms, you would soon find yourself back at the outskirts of Rowhedge, but instead, after just a few hundred yards, a prominent footpath disappears off through the trees on the left. It is difficult to miss because of the presence of a large notice board which reveals that Donyland Heath is often used by the military as a training ground.

On days when the army are firing on Donyland Heath, prominent red flags can be seen all around the outside, and access to the heath is then forbidden. An unexpected detour around the perimeter involves a very long walk, and so it would be wise to check that the footpaths are open before setting out. The army usually announce in the local press the days on which they intend to be firing, and members of the local garrison may be able to provide extra information if you telephone them on Colchester (01206) 575121.

The idyllic footpath through the trees shows no signs of any military activity, and it makes a very pleasant change from the industrial environment along the upper reaches of the River Colne. There are, however, a lot of small tracks through Donyland Woods, and it is quite easy to get lost. In general, you should bear left at most of the junctions, finally emerging from the canopy of trees nearly a mile away onto the busy B1025 road. This is the main road from Colchester to Mersea Island and people with cars will find that a large lay-by along this Mersea Road is perhaps one of the most convenient places to park for a walk through the woods.

Just a short distance to the left, the road passes over Manwood Bridge, crossing the infant Roman River just a few yards downstream from the normal tidal limit. This bridge also marks the boundary between two of the original hundreds of Essex, the ancient districts into which the county was divided for administrative purposes. At Manwood Bridge, you leave Lexden Hundred and enter Winsted Hundred.

Some cars tend to drive quickly along the Mersea Road, and you should therefore take care when walking south along this road. Fortunately the coastal route soon leaves this busy road. Immediately after Manwood Bridge, a quiet country road known as Haye Lane heads up a gentle hill off on the left. About a third of a mile up this lane, a small unmetalled track forks off to the left. Public vehicles are not allowed along this track and it is therefore a peaceful haven for walkers, much more pleasant than the hazardous main road. It leads past the buildings of Upper Hay Farm to emerge half a mile later on Abberton Road, the main road through the village of Fingringhoe.

Fingringhoe

The centre of the village lies just a few hundred yards to the left along Abberton Road, and is centred around the Whalebone Inn, where a left turn at the crossroads leads back to Fingringhoe Bridge over the Roman River. Unfortunately there is no access to the southern bank of the river anywhere between Fingringhoe Mill and the mouth of the river. The nearest public route to the coastline is straight on at the crossroads along Abberton Road. This leads past St. Andrew's church with its traditional square tower.

The village appeared on documents in the year 975 as "Fingringaho", a Saxon name which probably means "dwellers on the cleared (or cultivated) spur of marshland". During the first half of the 11th century, the village was owned by the priory at West Mersea, nearly six miles away, but in 1046 Edward the Confessor granted the priory to the Abbey of Saint Ouen, at Rouen in France. The parish church of St. Andrew dates from this period, although it reverted back to the English monarchy when an act of parliament dissolved all foreign priories in 1414.

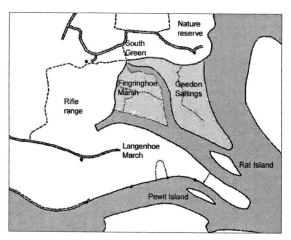

Continuing along Abberton Road, you get occasional glimpses of the Roman River winding to and fro at the foot of the slope. Along this stretch of the river, a low earth embankment follows the water's edge closely. At one time, this small sea-wall protected the adjacent farmland from flooding during high tides, but because the foot of the hill is at most a hundred yards further back, it was presumably decided that it was not worth maintaining this embankment for the sake of such a small area of farmland. Today, the sea has broken through in at least four places, and its rough top and muddy sides make it extremely difficult for walkers to follow, especially around high tide when you run the risk of getting stranded. In any event, this land is private and there is no right of way along the river-bank.

About half a mile from St. Andrew's church, Abberton Road reaches an important junction. The road to the left leads down the hill and across a narrow strip of tidal marshland to a prominent slipway into the River Colne. A ferry used to operate here to the village of Wivenhoe, whose picturesque waterfront can be seen just across the water. Although the ferry stopped some years ago, the track down the hill is still known as Ferry Road. From this viewpoint, the crumbling remains of an old sea-wall lead off in both directions around the coastline. To the north, the embankment turns left at the mouth of the Roman River, though it is not possible to follow it very far because a couple of stretches have been washed away by the tide.

A wartime pill-box stands on a prominent headland just a few hundred yards in the opposite direction, but once again a breach in the sea-wall makes access virtually impossible from the slipway. In order to reach the pill-box, it is necessary to retrace your steps back up Ferry Road. Just as the lane begins to climb up the hill, a delightful footpath leads off to the left through the woods. This track generally follows the foot of the escarpment, and soon emerges on a second road just outside the gates of a small gravel company. This area is called Ballast Quay, a name which would appear to indicate that the extracted gravel was used by sailors as ballast for their ships. During the late 1800s, a light tramway helped to carry gravel to the quayside. The name of the nearby Brickhouse Farm also suggests that this industry was once more widespread than today.

Unfortunately, you now have to make a detour back up Ballast Quay Road to the road junction near Fingringhoe, because the cranes and hoppers of the gravel works block any access to the open countryside downriver. Although the area inland is now largely covered with abandoned workings and flooded gravel pits, old maps show that this land was once good quality farmland, owned by Wellmans Farm. More recently, this was the site of Frog Hall, whose name can still be found in a small road nearby called Frog Hall Lane.

Just down the coast, a large nature reserve has been opened on the site of a second, disused gravel works. There are several ways to reach this Fingringhoe Wick reserve. The shortest route from Ballast Quay starts from the end of Brook Hall Road, but this involves negotiating a confusing maze of tracks through the gravel works. Most people arrive along a narrow lane which is signposted from Abberton Road half a mile west of Fingringhoe, although a much quieter back-street leads from the very centre of the village. All three routes eventually merge and lead to a visitor centre and a large car-park near the shores of the River Colne. The visitor centre sells leaflets which describe in excellent detail a selection of recommended walks, although you are warned that the reserve shuts early during the winter.

The story of Fingringhoe Wick really began in 1921, when the lands of Wick Farm were sold to a gravel extraction company. Not much is known about these early years, except that the area was taken over by the Freshwater Sand and Ballast Company in 1928. After the war, Brightlingsea Aggregates Limited began extraction on a large scale, scooping around 30,000 tons of gravel a year from an area known as the Freshwater Pit. Much of this material was used in the construction of a large oil refinery on the Isle of Grain in north Kent.

In 1959, the Freshwater Pit was finally exhausted. The gravel works were closed and the land was sold a few years later to the Essex Wildlife Trust for £4,000. The land around Fingringhoe Wick was the first to be acquired by this organisation, which had only been formed a few years earlier. (It was then known as the Essex Naturalists Trust.) The nature reserve was finally opened to the public in 1967. Today the trust owns many thousands of acres of land around Essex, and does a marvellous job protecting the local wildlife and creating new habitats for rare and endangered species.

The Fingringhoe Wick nature reserve has been laid out with two well-marked nature trails. The following description covers only the edge of the reserve, beginning at the north-eastern corner, near a small brackish pond known as Kitt's pond. This was once one of the settling ponds used by the gravel companies. Just outside the sea-wall here is a small area of rough saltings, intersected by hundreds of narrow channels which fill up with sea-water as the tide comes in. You may notice that amongst the long grass, a few large rectangular hollows can be seen. These were once used to grow oysters. The oyster industry reached its peak during the 19th century, employing thousands of people around the coastline, and oyster-beds of this kind can be seen all around the Essex marshlands.

Further south along the shores of the River Colne, past a couple of bird hides, the remains of the short jetty stand next to an artificial beach. When Fingringhoe Wick was a working pit, a small tramway carried gravel along this jetty to sailing barges which were moored out in deep water, though the jetty had to be shortened considerably after a ship collided with it in 1970. Today, a hide on the jetty provides an excellent viewpoint for bird-watchers, although visitors are asked to keep away from the beach during the winter months in order to avoid disturbing the wildfowl.

Jetty at Fingringhoe Wick nature reserve

At the far end of the beach, a disused boat-house stands on the edge of a small pond which was once used as a settling pool by the gravel companies. A good path leads past the Boathouse Pond, as it is predictably known, to Geedon Hide where the coastline turns sharply westwards. If you follow this meandering path for another two hundred yards, you will pass a couple of overgrown settling pools and eventually reach a second bird hide. This provides one of the best views in the Fingringhoe Wick reserve, overlooking an artificial brackish lagoon known as a scrape.

Beyond the scrape, stretching into the distance is an enormous expanse of marsh known as Geedon Saltings. Covered by thousands of tiny tidal channels, this is one of the largest areas of unspoilt tidal marshland in Essex. It is just possible to make out the remains of a thin earth embankment, snaking its way out across the saltings into the distance. This allowed the local farmer to graze sheep on Geedon Saltings, and during exceptionally high tides its extra height probably also provided a safe haven for the sheep when the saltings all around were covered with water.

From the scrape, a path leads inland past the remains of a few more settling pools to the car park and hence to the visitor centre. Opened in 1975, this centre provides useful books and leaflets describing the wildlife which can be seen around the reserve. The warden lives in the building directly across the road, once occupied by the manager of the gravel companies. According to a map in 1805, this is the site of Arch Hall farm. Although few details are known about this farm, it is known that the area has been occupied for thousands of years. In nearby gravel pits, two Stone Age flint axes have been found, dating from the Neolithic period (4500 to 2500 BC).

In 1928, the remains of a Roman house were uncovered near the jetty, and this was followed by the discovery of two more Roman buildings in 1936 and 1960, and a section of Roman Road was excavated in 1976. Indeed, William Wire, a 19th-century antiquarian from Colchester, included in his diary in 1847 a local tradition that a Roman settlement known as Bacon Town was sited close to Fingringhoe Wick. Although there is no evidence of a large Roman settlement here, it is interesting to note that the name in William Wire's diary is very similar to "Beacon Hard", the name once given to a nearby stretch of beach. This part of the foreshore consists of a layer of firm clay 40 feet wide and ten inches deep, and would have provided an excellent landing site for boats. The only other clue to Roman occupation is a raised mound out in Geedon Saltings. Although it has not been proved, it seems likely that this is an example of a "red hill". These "hills", which can be found all around the coasts of south-east England, appear to be sites where the Romans boiled sea-water to produce salt.

From the visitor centre, a narrow track called Wick Lane heads westwards along the top of a gentle incline, giving good views of the vast Geedon saltings. Mersea Island can be seen in the distance, and the high ground around Brightlingsea lies further to the left, beyond the Colne estuary. Aerial photographs of the slopes below Wick Lane show some signs of crop-marks, and remains of tiles and pottery have been found nearby, showing that this area was once occupied.

Wick Lane soons heads inland into an area of mixed woodland called Marshall's Plantation and joins up with the Fingringhoe Wick track. After passing Jaggers farm, the main road turns left and heads down the hill towards the buildings of South Green Farm. A little track leads off to the left here, weaving between a couple of sheltered houses. This was once the centre of a sizable village called South Green, and the name is still prominent on local road-signs.

At the foot of the hill, this track opens out onto the banks of North Geedon Creek. The geography here is quite confusing – almost as soon as it has branched off the main River Colne, Geedon Creek is split in two by Rat Island, which was described earlier. The channels join up again upstream of the island, but the creek soon divides again either side of an area of saltings, known as Fingringhoe Marsh.

During the early 19th century, large earth embankments were built around Fingringhoe Marsh to protect it from the rising waters. A separate sea-wall was built to enclose the south-western corner, and an east-west embankment divided the remainder of the land into two segments, though it is not clear why the marsh was split up in this fashion. It is possible that each section was owned by a different farmer, and that none of the landowners trusted his neighbours' sea-defences, or it may have been a simple way of limiting the flood damage if one of the embankments should happen to give way. In any event, the attempts to hold back the sea were in vain. Although some reports suggest that Fingringhoe Marsh survived the great tide of 1897, which devastated much of the Essex coastline, old maps clearly show that the sea-walls around Fingringhoe Marsh had been irreparably damaged by 1920. Salt-water poured in with every high tide, and the marsh slowly reverted back to its natural state.

Fingringhoe Marsh is today out of bounds to the public because the Ministry of Defence has taken over a large tract of land nearby for firing practice. Red warning signs have been posted around the boundary of the danger area, and prominent red flags are flown on days when the military are planning to fire. On a still day, the sharp sounds of gunfire can travel a long way across the flat marshes, punctuating the cries of disturbed birds. The close presence of the rifle-range means that members of the public are not normally allowed along the next stretch of coastline, although it has been known for the MOD to grant special permission when the firing range is not in use.

In order to rejoin the coastal path further south, you need to return to the Mersea Road, the same busy road which crosses Manwood Bridge near Fingringhoe. Although most people will return to the road at South Green and head for the twin villages of Abberton and Langenhoe, there is a little-used public footpath which skirts around the edge of the rifle-range. This can be used even when the military are firing. The route, indistinct at first, starts from the head of North Geedon Creek and follows the line of the prominent red warning signs inland. Beyond the buildings of South House Farm, the path opens out into a complicated series of woods and open meadows. Although there are very few footprints to follow, the warning signs are ideal markers, leading you unerringly and confidently along the correct route.

When no firing is taking place, this secluded path is so quiet that the range nearby is virtually forgotten, with only a few distant huts serving as a reminder of the close military presence. On such days, this path has much to recommend it, since it is infinitely more peaceful and rural than the sight of cars rushing at breakneck speed along the Mersea Road. In the distance to the east, beyond a line of concrete targets, it is just possible to make out the thin line of South Geedon Creek snaking its way across the marshes. Forming the southernmost limit of Fingringhoe Marsh, this creek comes to an abrupt stop at a low grassy dam which can be seen during the early part of the walk. The dam was constructed in the early 19th century in order to reduce the damaging effects of flooding during exceptionally high tides, but little effort was made to drain this low-lying farmland until fairly recently. Aerial photographs taken in 1954 still clearly show standing water inside the dam, marking the original route of the creek inland.

After nearly a mile, the right of way turns south crossing a military road known as Lodge Lane, originally a track leading to Langenhoe Lodge. The path becomes a little unclear after passing a line of trees known as Rising's Grove, but all routes southwards quickly lead to a second farmtrack. This track should be followed due west between cultivated fields to the farm buildings around Langenhoe Hall, and hence back to the Mersea Road. In the opposite direction, the track eventually peters out in the ungrazed expanse of Langenhoe Marsh. This undisturned marshland, protected from the rising waters by its own sea-walls, forms a long thin peninsula jutting out into the River Colne, but is usually closed to the public because of the nearby firing range. Near its eastern end, a short counterwall cuts across the peninsula, and a series of brackish-water pools have been created for wildfowl.

The Mersea Road heads almost due south, but about a mile before you reach Mersea Island, it is possible to rejoin the coastline. Just south of Pete Farm, small signposts show where a public right of way crosses the road. To the east, this footpath heads across a rather marshy field and rejoins the main sea-wall.

If you look at a detailed map of this area, you will notice that a parish boundary also crosses this field. Rather than following a straight line, the boundary meanders erratically to and fro as if it had been laid down by a drunken surveyor. This is because the boundary originally followed the line of a meandering creek. The construction of the sea-wall sliced this creek in two, and in the early 1900s, the inland half of the creek was filled in and replaced by a straight drainage ditch. Viewed from above, the line of the original creek is still obvious, and indeed it is possible to make out its route on the ground. The remaining half of the creek can still be seen outside the sea-wall, winding its way out amongst the saltings.

From the crest of the sea-wall, you get a good view of a small tidal bay. At high tide, only the highest patches of grass remain above water, but as the waters recede, an intricate network of muddy channels is revealed. The atmosphere in these quiet marshlands changes not just with the state of the tide – the scenery also varies with the weather, as the light of moving clouds is reflected in the swirling currents. The seasons also play a great part in shaping the environment. In high summer, the vegetation around the bay grows tall and lazy, whilst the return of winter also brings with it the noisy cries of the returning wildfowl.

Although the main coastal route heads southwards around the bay, it is possible first to make a short detour along the sea-wall to the east. For just over a mile, the tall embankment follows along the banks of a wide creek known as the Pyefleet Channel, and is bordered on the left by an area of unimproved grazing land known as Langenhoehall Marsh. This ground was probably reclaimed from the sea during the early part of the 19th century. A narrow ditch, running parallel to the sea-wall but a few hundred yards inland, appears to have been the original coastline. The footpath ends just after a wartime pill-box, where a barbed-wire fence has been placed across the path. Several signposts have been placed here declaring that the land beyond is owned by the Ministry of Defence and that visitors are not welcome.

The embankment around Langenhoe Marsh continues eastward, however, for another two miles before reaching the tip of a peninsula out in the estuary of the River Colne. This marshland was never fully drained and the winding creeks, although now inside the sea-wall and no longer tidal, create a feeling of remote wilderness. Eking out a living from this desolate land must have been a difficult task for the early farmers on Langenhoe Marsh, and their job was made even harder when the sea burst through the embankment around the 1850s.

Maps drawn up in 1838 and 1860 show the sea-defences holding up well against the tide, but by 1872 a large chunk of the southern sea-wall had been washed away. Salt-water now poured in through the gap at every tide. As a temporary measure, a new embankment was built inland around the edge of this breach. Within a few years, the original sea wall was restored, but even today, Ordnance Survey maps show a semi-circular drainage ditch following the route of this temporary sea-wall.

At the boundary of the MOD land, members of the public are required to turn back and retrace their steps back towards the inlet by the Mersea Road. Before you leave the end of the footpath, however, notice a short embankment heading inland away from the main sea-wall. If you follow along its crest, you will find that it dies away as soon as the ground gets a little higher. This appears to be classic example of a counterwall, built not as a primary defence against the rising tides, but as a precautionary measure to limit the damage that would be caused if one of the main sea-walls were to collapse.

After retreating back to the inlet near the Mersea Road, the footpath turns sharply to the left and continues past a large area of saltings. These are called Bonner's Saltings, and are named after a nearby farm. From the air, it is clear that several small tracks have been constructed across these saltings, weaving in and out of the clumps of vegetation and using simple earth bridges to cross the tiny channels. On the ground, however, it is virtually impossible to spot any sign of a path over the inhospitable terrain. One of the more visible examples can be seen leaving the sea-wall when the coastline makes a sudden turn to the right. From this point, a track leads far out into the saltings, and was once used for grazing cattle at low tide. A map from 1878 shows that this track was once well over half a mile long, but today it is so badly eroded that you risk becoming marooned if you venture out during the hours around high tide.

The sea-wall along this stretch of the coastline is relatively new. The original coastline, about fifty yards or so inland, is marked by a series of ditches and field boundaries. Meanwhile, on the seaward side of the embankment, the remains of a collection of oyster-beds can be seen as a line of rectangular hollows in the saltings.

The Strood

After a few hundred yards, you come across a wartime pill-box embedded in the sea-wall. A second pill-box stands just around the corner on the site of an old lime-kiln, but all eyes will probably be looking ahead at the prominent causeway crossing onto Mersea Island. This causeway, built by piling tons of stones and boulders onto the mudflats, is the only means of access onto the island. Despite significant improvements in the mid-1800s, the road is occasionally underwater at high tide. When this happens, a long queue of traffic builds up, patiently waiting for the waters to subside. This can seem frustrating these days when enormous bridges seem commonplace, but until the 18th century, the causeway was impassable for four hours at every high tide.

This causeway dates back at least to Roman times and is known as the Strood. Originally it was called the Strode, but this is probably a reflection of the old Essex dialect. The name is probably derived from the Old English word "strod", which was often used to describe an area of marshland overgrown with brushwood. The town of Strood in north Kent got its name in the same way, and the name also appears in an area near Maldon Quay.

The Strood onto Mersea Island, covered at high tide

In the 16th century, a "Strood-keeper" lived in a nearby cottage called Church House, though his work may have been related to the tidal mill which once stood at the mainland end of the causeway. The mill must have dated back to before 1551, because records show that the buildings were demolished in that year. It was rebuilt in 1560 and again in 1734. Part of the mill soon collapsed, and the whole structure had to be pulled down in 1769. However, the mill quay continued in commercial use for many years, and was used just after the Second World War to offload Kentish ragstone for sea-wall repairs.

Beside the road, you can still see the remains of the mill-pond. This pond was filled by the rising tide, and this head of water turned a water-wheel as the sea subsided again. The machinery could therefore only operate for a few hours after each high tide, and therefore, like the tidal mill described at Walton-on-the-Naze, there was an accompanying windmill to provide more power.

From the mainland to the edge of Mersea Island, the Strood is several hundred yards long. A couple of small slipways alongside are used by a local water-skiing club. Almost as soon as the Strood reaches dry land on the edge of Mersea Island, the road splits into two. The main road to the right continues to the built-up area of West Mersea, whilst a small branch to the left passes through quiet countryside, eventually reaching the small community at East Mersea. After half a mile up this side-road there stands a famous tumulus at Barrow Hill, dating from the first century AD, during Roman occupation. A local legend says that this is the burial site of twins who killed each other over their love for a local maiden, and it is said that their ghosts still haunt the area! When the thirty-foot high tumulus was excavated in 1912, a glass bowl inside was found to contain cremated human remains.

Mersea Island is sometimes incorrectly claimed to be the easternmost inhabited island in Britain, although this distinction is in fact held by Horsey Island near Walton-on-the-Naze. The shape of the island is close to an oval. Although it is never more than two miles wide, the distance from end to end is nearly five miles, and the complete cirumnavigation of the island involves a tough walk of over twelve miles. The following text describes its coastline in a clockwise fashion, starting from the Strood. Incidentally, the name Mersea itself comes from the Old English "meres-ig", literally meaning "sea's island", and hence the "sea" part is really the first half of the word and not the second. The name is unrelated to the Mersey at Liverpool, which comes instead from the Old English for "boundary river".

Just a few yards along the side-road to the left, the remains of an old embankment can be seen just across the ditch. An 1878 map shows that this was once part of the original sea-wall along the northern edge of Mersea Island, built in the early 1800s to protect a large area of reclaimed land. Towards the end of the 19th century, the tide broke through this embankment and a part of this land had to be abandoned to the sea. This was probably after the storms of 1897 which destroyed many sea-defences around Essex, though it is known that the sea-walls around Mersea Island were also damaged by the earthquake which hit Wivenhoe on the 22nd April 1884.

A new embankment was built further inland, protecting the farmland inside from the encroaching sea. The start of this second sea-wall can be seen on the left just a few yards further up the road. Ordnance Survey maps show a right of way along the line of the original sea-wall, but, because this has been washed away in places and is impassable, walkers have a right to get around the obstruction using the nearest reasonable alternative route. In this case, the nearest alternative route is obviously the new sea-wall, and so walkers can feel quite assured that they are acting within the law when walking along the new embankment, even though the Ordnance Survey map does not mark a right of way along its crest.

After winding its way eastwards through the salt-marshes for half a mile, the new sea-wall rejoins the route of the original coastline, and here you can still walk out along the old embankment to the point where it was breached. Although the tides have flowed in and out of this gap for around a hundred years, it is still possible to make out several straight lines in the vegetation. These were drainage ditches, dug when this land was still inside the sea-defences.

For the next mile or so, the sea-wall begins a series of wild zigzags, enclosing a wide area of open marshland. In choosing such an erratic course, the farmers who built the original embankment here two hundred years ago were probably following the best route across the saltings, making the embankment as stable as possible. From the grassy crest of the sea-wall, several unusual features can be seen in the wild saltings on the seaward fringe. In a few places, earth has been piled up to form low embankments leading away from the main sea-wall. These may have been made by local wildfowlers to help them catch their prey out on the marshes, or they may have led to small landing stages on the edge of the Pyefleet Channel, but it is difficult now to ascertain their real purpose.

After passing the buildings of Maydays Farm, the sea-wall follows a narrow creek which winds its way erratically through the marshes. After half a mile or so, where the creek turns sharply to the left, a series of low wooden barriers have been built across the creek in order to slow down the erosion of the saltings. These are groynes and consist of a wall of thin sticks and twigs held in place by pairs of strong posts. As the tide recedes, these groynes are designed to hold back the silt. This allows vegetation to grow back and stablise the mudflats.

Very soon, the saltings disappear and the path runs along the edge of the Pyefleet Channel. Although this part of Mersea island is known as Maydays Marsh, it is used today for intensive agriculture, and the view inland is mostly a simple panorama of enormous ploughed fields.

On the other side of the water, though, the tale is quite different, because the Langenhoe Marshes have been taken over by the military as a firing range. A tall embankment encloses an enormous area of unimproved marshland which has always managed to escape the plough and has only been drained in a very rudimentary fashion. The rough grassland there is criss-crossed by hundreds of meandering ditches, the remnants of narrow creeks which used to fill with sea-water at every high tide before the embankment was built. It is a great shame that the military authorities have decided to keep these unique and beautiful marshes closed to the public.

An easy mile's walk along the grassy crest of the sea-wall leads to the northernmost part of Mersea Island. Known as Reeveshall Marsh, it is also one of the newest parts of the island, only being reclaimed from the sea around 1850. Perhaps as a result of this, these sea-defences are amongst the best on the island, allowing a fast and easy stroll through some of the quietest countryside in the district.

It is nearly possible to walk past Pewit Island without noticing it. Standing on the far side of the Pyefleet Channel, this small island was once the centre of a thriving oyster industry. Until the early 1900s, hundreds of local men were employed in the trade, and although the popularity of oysters has steadily declined over the years, connoisseurs still consider the Pyefleet oysters to be amongst the best.

Pewit Island is littered with disused oyster-beds, and, standing at the head of a stony landing-stage, there still stands a large corrugated-iron building which was once used as a packing shed. Each year, in early September, the Mayor of Colchester used to visit the island to declare the start of the new oyster season. However, the shed has gradually fallen into disrepair, and the ceremony is now usually held on a nearby barge instead. This also marks the beginning of the Colchester Oyster Feast, an annual tradition dating back as far as 1667. On the far side of Pewit Island, there was once another pair of landing-stages, one on either side of the narrow channel between the island and Langenhoe Marsh. Although this cannot be seen from this walk, the remains of a hard leads out from Mersea Island towards the water's edge. A line of wide stepping stones has been laid out on the surface of the soft mud, presumably for easy boat access to Pewit Island.

With the buildings of Brightlingsea visible in the distance on the far side of the River Colne estuary, the sea-wall makes a sharp and unexpected turn to the south before resuming its generally eastward direction. This sharp meander was once the mouth of Pass Fleet, a deep inlet which used to flow in and out at this point. When the original sea-walls were being built around Mersea Island, the engineers did not have the resources to build a dam across a creek with such a strong current, and so for many years this was the northernmost limit of the island. It was only in the mid 1800s that a dam was finally built across Pass Fleet, at an easier point upstream. Now better known as Broad Fleet, the creek was finally tamed in the early 20th century by the construction of a second dam right across its mouth. This dam forms part of the modern sea-defences around the island, although the right of way marked on Ordnance Survey maps still crosses Broad Fleet using the original dam, four hundred yards inland.

Once past the dam, the sea-wall continues eastward in an almost straight line. At the end of this stretch, you can see an earth embankment heading inland towards a copse of trees. According to a map of 1807, this embankment was once part of the old sea-defences around Mersea Island. A right of way follows its original route as far as the trees, where a path leads up the hill to a back-lane near the village of East Mersea.

Just ahead, the buildings of the Colchester Oyster Fishery stand just inside the sea-wall. These are used as a base for the local oyster industry, and are open to the public on the first Friday of every month. Along with a few oyster ponds and a simple quay, these buildings were constructed only recently, although old aerial photographs show that a long hard has existed across the mud here for many years. From the fishery, a narrow track leads up the hill past North Farm to the centre of the village of East Mersea. This is not a right of way, however, and it may be better to wait for a second lane which heads inland just under a mile further on.

As you approach the eastern tip of Mersea Island, look out for the remains of a path across the saltings leading to the water's edge – it is rather optimistically marked as a public footpath on Ordnance Survey maps. This was once the landing-stage for a ferry which carried pedestrians across the mouth of the River Colne to Brightlingsea. One of the longest-serving ferrymen was Mr. Mole, who worked this route for 53 years, from 1880 to 1933. The stone path has today been cut in two by a deep channel of mud which is very difficult to cross. When the waters recede, two lines of wooden stakes can be seen further down, beyond the saltings. These used to support a platform which allowed access to the ferry at low tide, and was also used by the local coastguard.

East Mersea

A good footpath from the village of East Mersea provides the first proper access to the sea-wall since leaving the Strood four miles to the west. Parking space is very limited at the end of the road, and care must be taken not to block any of the farmtracks around the village. The village can trace its history back to the Domesday Book of 1086:

> *"Swein holds Meresaila in lordship, which Robert son of Wymarc held before 1066 as a manor, for 6 hides."*

Instead of being clustered around a central village green, East Mersea is spread out and scattered over several miles. Many villagers live towards the end of the road, near the eastern sea-wall, but a visit to the village pub, the Dog and Pheasant, involves a mile-long walk back along the main road.

It is now just a short walk to the easternmost tip of Mersea Island where the sea-wall turns sharply to the right and follows the southern side of the island, facing the open sea. At low tide, you can leave the sea-wall at this corner and cross a narrow stream using a line of stepping stones to reach a long shingle spit. Known as Mersea Stone Point, this has provided a natural harbour for boats right back to Roman times. The end of the spit is a very popular spot in summer, crowded with sunbathers, casual walkers and young children playing on the beach. It must be remembered, however, that the stepping stones are submerged at high tide, and although it is still possible to reach dry land safely, it involves a long detour along the coast.

Around the year 1540, a small military fort was built on these marshes. This blockhouse was triangular in shape, each wall being 300 feet long. Similar structures were also built around the same time at Brightlingsea and on Beacon Hill near St. Osyth, to defend the mouth of the River Colne. Like many blockhouses, they were only designed for short-term use, and were abandoned in 1552. When sea-defences were built around the island during the early 1800s, one source describes how the new sea-wall *"cut right through the ruins of the old Blockhouse, obliterating the remains of the two landward towers. Today, one must look very hard indeed to see where the old fort once stood."* The only remains of the fort are two grassy embankments just outside the main sea-wall, although the military presence is retained by a dilapidated pill-box from the last war.

Mersea Stone Point marks a significant turning-point in the walk around Mersea Island. Ever since leaving the Strood, the walk has consisted largely of an open stroll along the crest of a tall embankment which winds its way through undisturbed marshland. After turning the corner, however, you will find that the southern side of the island is relatively busy with boaters and holiday-makers making the most of the beaches. Just half a mile away from Mersea Stone Point, the land is high enough for an embankment against the sea to be unnecessary, and here the coastal walk changes its character completely, following along the beach with wide views out to sea.

Walking along the foot of a low cliff, you soon reach a small muddy inlet near Fen Farm. This is now the site of Cudmore Grove Country Park, opened in 1969 after an application for a caravan park had been turned down. Nevertheless, the seaside developers did have a certain amount of success just down the coast, where a small village of summer chalets has been built. Just past the last wooden bungalow, a track leads back to the East Mersea road, passing the cluster of buildings around East Mersea Hall.

For the next couple of miles, a low sea-wall stands

Low cliffs along the southern edge of Mersea Island

at the head of the beach, protecting the low-lying farmland during exceptionally high tides. The ground here is so flat that at low tide the receding waters reveal a strip of shingle beach almost half a mile wide, known locally as the Mersea Flats. In 1852, Sir John Rennie proposed a scheme to reclaim these flats, along with the neighbouring Ray Marshes. Once the salt-water had been drained away, this would have provided an enormous area of fertile land for his crops, but this ambitious project was soon abandoned.

Just after a tiny inlet, a couple of wartime ruins overlook the beach. From here, a track heads inland past a youth camp and towards the buildings of Rewsalls Farm. This eventually leads back to the East Mersea road, though it is probably just as quick to continue along the coastline to West Mersea.

Shortly after passing a large caravan site, a small pond stands just inside the sea-wall. Although at first sight it looks nothing out of the ordinary, it was in fact used for hundreds of years as a decoy pond to catch wildfowl. Tame ducks were used to lure passing birds towards the pond, which had five narrow offshoots, each covered with netting to trap unsuspecting birds. The most common catch was pochard (*Aythya ferina*), sometimes known as dun-bird (not to be confused with dunlin). These were sold locally for their meat. This decoy pond was so successful that the owners could afford to hire two permanent attendants, but it had to be abandoned around 1870 because of disturbance from nearby wildfowlers. More details on decoy ponds can be found later in this book.

West Mersea

Within a hundred yards of the decoy pond, a wartime pill-box stands on the edge of a small headland. With the track along the shoreline getting wider and busier, it is clear that civilisation is not far away. Once past a sewage works and yet another caravan site, you enter the residential area of West Mersea, a small town which occupies most of the south-western corner of Mersea Island. The centre of the town lies over a mile away, following the coastal path. It was first recorded in 1238 as "Westmereshaye", but it is known that the island was occupied centuries earlier because a number of Roman artefacts have been found here, including the remains of tesselated pavements.

West Mersea has always seemed slightly isolated even at the best of times, and locals have the added problem of the Strood flooding during exceptionally high tides. Numerous plans have been suggested over the years to improve communications to the island. In 1901, a rail link was proposed from Southend-on-Sea, using ferries to cross the Rivers Blackwater and Crouch, though nothing ever came of this ambitious scheme. Ten years later, a more modest plan for a direct line to Colchester was thwarted in its final stages by the outbreak of the First World War. After the war, a plan to link West Mersea to the main railway system at Stanway, just to the west of Colchester, was abandoned due to the increasing popularity of the motor-car. For people living on Mersea Island, the B1025 road to Colchester still provides the only land link with the outside world.

The town originally grew up around St. Peter's Well, a spring which used to supply the only fresh water on the entire island. Today, the town has a very nautical flavour, and the shallow channels of water leading off the River Blackwater provide an ideal haven for hundreds of yachts and small boats. Despite its small size, the town contains two sailing clubs, two boat-yards, and numerous marine engineers and sail-makers.

Oyster-beds

On the foreshore, however, the large rectangular pits testify to the industry which once dominated the town. Until its decline some seventy years ago, West Mersea was the centre of the local oyster industry. During the 19th century, oysters provided a thriving business, employing hundreds of men from Mersea Island and nearby villages such as Brightlingsea. The danger of poaching in some places also meant that nearly twice as many men could be needed to protect the layings than to actually harvest the oysters themselves. Since most people living in this region would have been employed or supported by the fishing trade, it is natural that the majority of their diet would have been based around locally-caught fish and shellfish, of which oysters would have formed a large part.

Many different types of oyster can be found around the world, all belonging to the genus called *Ostrea* or the much larger family of shellfish called *Ostreidae*. Around Essex, Ostrea edulis is the most common variety. Unlike tropical species, however, none of the Essex varieties produce pearls. Although there was intense debate as to whether the Pyefleet oysters produced around Mersea were inferior or superior to the Wallasea variety found further south in Essex, connoisseurs almost universally voted these two varieties to be unsurpassed anywhere else in the world. As John Norden wrote in 1594:

> *"Some part of the sea shore of Essex yealdeth the beste oysters in England, which are called Walflete* [the old name for Wallasea] *oysters... Ther is greate difference betwene theis oysters and others which lie vpon other shores, for this oyster, that in London and ells wher carieth the name of Walflete, is a little full oyster with a verie greene fynn. And like vnto theis in quantetie are none in this lande thowgh farr bigger, and for some mens diettes better."*

The life-cycle of an oyster spans several years, beginning when the mature oysters discharge their spawn into the water. The spawn of most shellfish is generally known as "spat". This spat is then drawn into the gills of nearby oysters where the eggs have already been produced. The fertilised eggs gradually develop hard black shells until they are strong enough to survive independently of the mother. At this stage, the eggs are ejected into the water by a sudden closing of the mother's shell.

The oyster eggs will then attempt to cling to a hard rocky surface where they can continue to mature safely. Around Essex, there is no surface rock and the fisherman need to deposit on the river-beds a special layer of debris to which the young oysters can attach themselves. This debris is known in the trade as "cultch" (or "skultch" according to some sources). Traditionally it was composed of broken oyster shells, but one observer described it as what *"an outsider would call rubbish, for it is composed of broken tiles, pots and pans, shards of all kinds, old boots even, all intermixed with empty shells."*)

The oyster season lasts from September through to April – months containing the letter R. A few oysters are sold out of season just to satisfy the market, but these will be of inferior quality. The river-beds are dredged and the oysters are sorted according to their age. The mature oysters, over four years old, are called "ware" and are ready for the market. From two to three years, they are known as "brood" or "broad" and are still immature. Those in between, from three to four years old, are called "half-ware" because they are sometimes sold on the cheap, but usually they are returned, along with the immature brood, to special oyster-beds along the shoreline. At this stage, the local Colchester Oyster Fishery sometimes also adds young oysters imported from the Outer Hebrides to this stock.

It is not known when the practice of oyster cultivation started, but the Roman writer Pliny (the elder) suggested that Sergius Orata first conceived the idea about two thousand years ago. At the height of the oyster industry during the 19th century, many thousands of rectangular pits were maintained all around the coast of Essex to protect the immature oysters, carefully nurturing them for between two and four years until they were ready to be sold on the open market. Virtually every bit of suitable foreshore was taken up with lucrative oyster-beds, and there was fierce competition for every stretch of shoreline.

During the peak of the industry, around 1850, around 500 million oysters passed through London's Billingsgate Market every year, and many millions more were consumed locally. However, the traditional oyster grounds were being severely over-fished, and by 1890 this number was down to only 40 million. During the First World War, the oyster-beds were further neglected, and in 1921 a mysterious disease swept across the country, decimating the shellfish population.

Although the oyster industry picked up between the wars, the harsh winter of 1939/40 killed most of the spat before the neglect caused by the Second World War. In 1947, just as the locals returned to their former professions, another harsh winter in 1947 destroyed most of the oyster stock, and the severe floods of 1953 covered many of the oyster-beds with mud and silt, suffocating the young oysters. The industry never properly recovered. During the 1960s, for example, less than one million oysters were cultivated annually, compared to around 2000 million in France.

As an indication of this decline, the River Crouch and the River Roach kept over 200 men busy during the 19th century. By 1972, this was down to two men. Although a handful of men still work a few of the oyster-beds around West Mersea, the vast majority were abandoned, and today you can just make out the remains of rectangular pits all around the Essex coast. In recent years, the industry has recovered a little, and around 10 million oysters are now enjoyed in this country every year, but it is unlikely that it will ever return to the levels of popularity of the 19th century.

Some of the greatest concentrations of oyster-beds are to be found on the small marshy islands off the point of West Mersea. The channel of water which flows closest to the town is known as Besom Fleet, and the largest of the islands lies just beyond. Covering nearly two acres, it is known as Cobmarsh Island. (The word "cob" is a local name for the black-headed gull, and appears in many place-names around the Blackwater Estuary, including the Cob Islands near Tollesbury.)

On the far side of Cobmarsh Island, the creeks form a confusing network of channels known collectively as the Mersea Quarters. As you head upstream, Little Ditch and Salcott Creek eventually veer to the west to reach the small village of Salcott, which is described later on. The remaining channels, called Thorn Fleet and Mersea Fleet, eventually head north-east to the Strood, separating Mersea Island from the mainland. At the mouth of the estuary, these two fleets flow either side of another low-lying island, known as Packing Marsh. Although it is only about a sixth of the size of Cobmarsh Island, aerial photographs show that the entire surface is taken up with rectangular oyster-beds. Because the landscape is so flat, it can be difficult to distinguish the separate channels and islands, but a large shed on the western side of Packing Marsh is always easy to spot. As its name suggests, this was originally used for packing oysters, but fell into disuse many years ago. In 1991, the building was leased to the Packing Shed Trust, who have restored it for occasional recreational use.

A short way beyond a lifeboat station, the buildings of West Mersea come to an abrupt end. Following the coastline around a small inlet containing the remains of more oyster-beds, you soon join the crest of a sea-wall which heads directly out into the open countryside. A caravan park on the outskirts of town soon gives way to large fields and a peaceful rural atmosphere quickly returns.

Looking inland, the ground does not begin to rise appreciably above sea-level until about a quarter of a mile inside the sea-wall. At the foot of this slope, a small drainage ditch probably marks the site of the original sea-defences around Mersea Island before this land was reclaimed. Along this stretch of the coastline, short groynes have been build out into the channel in order to protect the new sea-wall against tidal erosion.

Just across the Strood Channel, you can see the narrow peninsula of Ray Marshes. Although never more than a few hundred yards wide, this thin strip of saltings is over a mile long, separated from the mainland by the Ray Channel on the far side. In 1852, as mentioned earlier, Sir John Rennie proposed a scheme to reclaim these marshes, along with the Mersea Flats just around the coast, though his plan was never carried out. About half-way along, a slightly raised section of land has been colonised by bushes and trees. When the rest of the marshes are covered by very high tides, this section alone remains above the water, forming an isolated island known as Ray Island. The island was recorded as far back as 1376, as "La Raye".

Ray Island is owned by the National Trust and maintained as an important nature reserve by the Essex Wildlife Trust. It has also been designated a Site of Special Scientific Interest (SSSI). It is one of the few places around the Essex coast where the transition from uncultivated grassland to tidal salt-marsh is not interrupted by a sea-wall, and it therefore displays a rare combination of plant species. These vary in gradual steps from sea purslane and common saltmarsh-grass in the higher marshes to cord-grass, glasswort and common sea lavender down near the low tide mark.

The footpath onto Ray Island is not a right of way, but you may be able to arrange permission for a visit. The whole district is also described in detail in the novel "Mehalah" by Sabine Baring-Gould, the gentleman who wrote "Onward Christian Soldiers". As rector of East Mersea between 1870 and 1881, he gained a rare insight into the isolated Essex marshland communities of the 19th century, and, although his novel is written in the flowery language of the period and is based around fictional characters, the settings are accurate and it contains an excellent in-depth study of the marshland way of life.

After half a mile or so, the sea-wall begins to veer to skirt around the outside of a large inlet. The Strood is now clearly visible ahead, connecting Mersea Island to the mainland. Old maps show that a secondary embankment used to snake its way inland here, probably a counterwall designed to limit any flood damage.

Red hills

If you visit this area shortly after the fields have been ploughed, you may be able to spot one of the "red hills" that are scattered profusely around the shores of Essex. Standing about two hundred yards inland from the sea-wall, it appears only as a patch of earth with a slightly redder hue than the surrounding soil. Its exact position is marked on the Ordnance Survey 1:25,000 "Explorer" map of the area. It is in the rough shape of a circle about eighty feet across, though it is perhaps misleading to think of it as a "hill" since it is only very slightly raised above the rest of the field.

Red hills have been found in many places around the coast of south-east England, but Essex seems to have a particularly high concentration of them. More than 300 examples have been recorded, and excavations have shown that they often contain small shards of pottery. Many theories have been put forward over the years, but these days the consensus of opinion amongst archaeologists is that red hills are sites where sea-water was evaporated to produce salt. Salt was used to preserve meat and other foodstuffs, and was therefore a very important commodity until the modern era of refrigeration (even the word "salary" comes from the Latin word for salt). Although a few red hills have been found to date back to the Iron Age, most were formed during

Roman times, and it is known that there were many salt-works, or salinae, in Essex at the time of the Domesday Book.

Red hills are especially prevalent around the marshes near Peldon and Wigborough. When they are found inside the modern sea-wall, known as "dry" sites, the red hills have often been under the plough for many years. As a consequence, these sites have often been flattened and can only be detected by the red colour of the earth. In contrast, red hills discovered on the seaward side of the modern sea-wall are usually in an undisturbed condition. Several of these "wet" sites have been excavated, revealing several structures known as "briquetage".

Although their exact method of operation is far from certain, it is believed that red hills worked by allowing sea-water to flow at high tide into shallow tanks. These water-tanks were then heated by means of a large hearth which was fuelled with wood, possibly from coppiced trees nearby. As the water slowly evaporated away, crystallised salt was scraped off the sides of the tanks before being carefully dried and packed. The hearths and water-tanks were extremely fragile and would be liable to crack under the heat. It is thought that these parts were regularly discarded and replaced with new constructions, gradually forming the large piles of reddened earth which are visible today.

The footpath shortly joins the main road out of West Mersea. Turning left, it is now less than ten minutes' walk past an irrigation reservoir to the Strood leading off Mersea Island. This final stretch of Mersea Island is relatively high, and does not need a sea-wall to protect it from the tidal waters of the Strood Channel.

As you walk along the causeway, leaving Mersea Island behind, take one last look around you. At low tide, the receding waters reveal an eerie landscape of mud stretching into the distance on both sides of the road, with the Strood Channel to the west and the Pyefleet Channel to the east. At the far end of the Strood, where the sea-wall forks off to the right, you can see the remains of a tidal mill-pond, described earlier.

❋ ❋ ❋

Coming off Mersea Island back onto the mainland, the ground begins to get noticeably higher a few hundred yards to the north of the Strood. Pyefleet House stands beside the road here and the sea-wall disappears off to the left. From here, an extremely muddy path winds its way across the saltings towards Ray Island, but, as mentioned earlier, this is all private land. In fact, the next six miles of coastline are completely devoid of public footpaths. The route closest to the shoreline is back up the main road to a pub called the Peldon Rose, which was severely damaged during the earthquake which hit Wivenhoe in 1884. Taking a left fork, follow the main road straight through the villages of Peldon and Wigborough, where you can make a pleasant diversion inland to the bird reserve at Abberton Reservoir.

However, walkers who are particularly keen to enjoy this beautiful stretch of coastline may be able to get special permission to do so. For the benefit of walkers who are fortunate enough to be given permission, the following pages describe some of the features of interest around this coastline.

After leaving the main road near Pyefleet House, the sea-wall meanders around a small bay. This is the head of Ray Channel, and has a tiny quay which is now only used by a few private pleasure-craft, although in previous centuries it was almost certainly used by local farmers as an important dock to transport their goods. The embankment then heads due south-west into remote and unspoilt countryside, following the banks of the Ray Channel. In order to slow down the erosion of the coastline here, a few

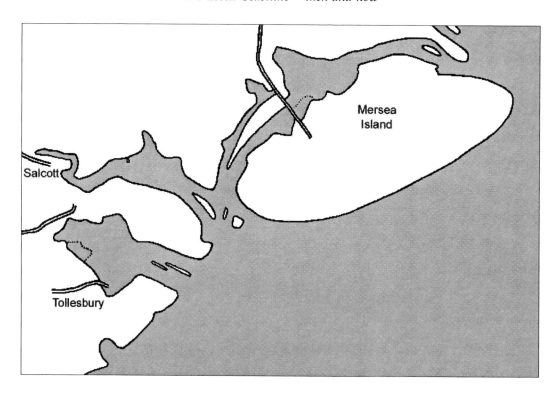

groynes have been constructed beside the creek. Each groyne consists of twigs and sticks woven around a line of vertical posts. These help to trap particles of silt and consolidate the shoreline to resist the scouring action of the tide.

Just before reaching the inlet of Sampson's Creek, an old map drawn up in 1860 shows that the sea-wall used to extend further into the creek than it does today. This embankment was breached, probably during the severe floods of 1897, and, instead of repairing the original sea-defences, a safer sea-wall was constructed a little further inland. Standing on this new embankment, you can still see the line of the old coastline protruding out above the level of the surrounding saltings.

The wreck of a wooden hulk indicates the site of Sampson's Creek. Until this creek was dammed, it was tidal as far as the hamlet of Little Wigborough, over a mile inland. Although you can still follow its route on a map, today it only carries fresh water, probably acting as a drainage ditch for the surrounding fields. A few older maps show some embankments which appear to suggest that the first dam to be built across Sampson's Creek was half a mile further inland, near the site of a "red hill".

It is a crime that this sea-wall does not carry a public footpath along its grassy crest, because this remote and undisturbed countryside would prove an excellent antidote to the stresses of modern life. Heading around the point of a long peninsula known as the Feldy Marshes, the raised embankment provides a marvellous view of the maze of tiny islands scattered around the Mersea Quarters. Packing Marsh and Cobmarsh Island lie to the east, just off the point of West Mersea, and the long thin strip of marshland known as Sunken Island can be clearly seen to the west. Even the saltings at the tip of Feldy Marshes are littered with the remains of oyster-beds, relics of the forgotten industry of these marshlands.

After rounding the tip of the peninsula, the sea-wall begins to follow the shores of a wide creek towards its head near the villages of Salcott and Virley. This creek is usually known as the Salcott Channel, though one map from 1805 names it the Verley Channel. The large arable fields of Feldy Marshes still provide the only view inland. This land was reclaimed from the sea only relatively recently, and Ordnance Survey maps still show the original sea-walls, a quarter of a mile inland.

The low-lying nature of this farmland is illustrated by the existence on Ordnance Survey maps of a short contour line marked with an altitude of 0 metres, i.e. at mean sea-level. Since the tidal variation around the Essex coast can be greater than 6 metres, this land would therefore be more than 3 metres underwater at high tide, if it were not for the strong sea-defences around the Feldy Marshes. This particular contour line marks the site of an old decoy pond, where wildfowl were once caught.

After following the banks of the Salcott Channel westwards for half a mile, you pass a large maze of saltings, known as the Copthall Saltings after the nearby hamlet of Copt Hall. Three "red hills" can be found just inside the sea-wall here. Like the red hill described earlier near West Mersea, these low mounds are believed to be the results of salt-panning activities dating back thousands of years. However, despite standing less than 200 yards away, the slightly reddish hue of the soil is virtually impossible to spot unless you know precisely where to look. This stretch of coastline was acquired by the National Trust in 1989, but only a few short footpaths are open to the public. Unfortunately none of these routes reach down to the sea-wall.

A narrow un-named creek branches off the main Salcott Channel and forces the embankment to make a long detour northwards. From the head of the inlet, the church of Copt Hall can be seen just a few hundred yards inland, but again there is no public footpath between the church and the coastline. Instead, the private sea-wall eventually turns south again, following the narrow creek back towards the waters of the Salcott Channel.

On this western side of the inlet, the saltings are even more extensive than before. This wide area of marshland is known as the Abbot's Hall Saltings, after the nearby farm of Abbotts Hall, though it is not clear why the Ordnance Survey use a different spelling for the two names.Thousands of tiny channels wind in and out of the tidal mudflats, creating a confusing jigsaw of isolated clumps of mud raised above the tides. Only a few plant species, such as sea purslane (*Halimione portulacoides*), are hardy enough to withstand both the dry atmosphere caused by the midday sun and the salty conditions of high tide.

A few years ago, a large legacy enabled the Essex Wildlife Trust to buy this stretch of coastline, including 700 acres of land around Abbotts Hall Farm. With a visitor centre to demonstrate the workings of a modern arable farm, the trust is also converting more than 100 acres of farmland back into salt-marsh. Heavy machinery was brought in to breach the sea-wall deliberately in five places, allowing sea-water to flood over the low-lying land inside. Within a few years, this land will gradually revert back to tidal saltings, providing extra habitats for endangered wildfowl. Instead of spending more and more money trying to protect vulnerable coastlines from erosion, this type of "managed retreat" is becoming increasingly popular.

In the middle of Abbot's Hall Saltings, two low grassy mounds stand out above the flat level of the marshes. These are obviously man-made and were probably constructed by local wildfowlers. Some sources have suggested, however, that these saltings also show relics of saltpans.

A more interesting feature, however, can be seen a few yards further on, where an unusual circular embankment has been built across the saltings at their narrowest point. Some historians have suggested that it might have been a Viking encampment. However, it is marked as "Ship's Lock" on detailed maps of the area, and this seems to give the best clue to its original purpose. The shape of the embankments suggests that it was used as a dry dock for boat repairs. At high tide, small ships in the Salcott Channel could be floated into the lock and moored up alongside a central jetty. As the waters receded, some form of gate would be placed across the entrance of the dock in order to keep the tides out whilst repairs were executed. Since Ship's Lock was not marked on maps before 1838, it appears likely that it was mainly used during the second half of the 19th century. Most commercial traffic died out before the 20th century, but farmers continued to use this site to load and offload boats until local roads were improved in the 1950s.

From Ship's Lock, it is about a mile and a half along the meadering shores of the Salcott Channel to the head of the creek in the tiny village of Virley, and this final stretch is a delightful stroll through unspoilt countryside. The grassy top of the sea-wall makes for easy walking, and provides a beautiful view of the upper reaches of the creek.

Virley

The twin villages of Salcott and Virley provide the first public access to the shoreline for six miles. A solid dam was built across the Salcott Channel just after 1948, but a wooden bridge across the creek originally provided the only link between the village of Virley, on the northern bank, and its larger twin Salcott, on the southern side.

The village of Virley gets its name from the Norman lord Robert de Verli. Today it only consists of a handful of houses, but this village holds a central position in the novel "Mehalah" by Sabine Baring-Gould, which, as mentioned earlier around Mersea Island, describes the surrounding marshlands in some detail. It was at Virley church that Mehalah, the heroine of the story, was married to the villain Elijah Rebow. The ruins of the Church of St. Mary can still be found in the gardens of the Old Rectory. The church held its last service in 1879, after which the building was declared unsafe. Following the earthquake which hit the area in 1884, the church roof had to be removed, and the walls of the building have gradually fallen into ruin.

During the 19th century, the village of Virley had its own public house. The White Hart once stood near the church, on a site now occupied by two houses. This was a popular haunt for smugglers, although, as Baring-Gould explained in his novel, at that time almost all the local people were involved in the smuggling trade:

> "The whole population of this region was more or less mixed up with, and interested in, this illicit traffic, and with defiance of the officers of the law, from the parson who allowed his nag and cart to be taken from his stable at night, left unbolted for the purpose, and received a keg now and then as repayment, to the vagabonds who dealt at the door far inland in silks and tobacco obtained free of duty on the coast."

Standing at the head of a long but shallow creek, whose navigation required some considerable expertise, Virley and Salcott were in an ideal location to benefit from the smuggling traffic. This was described in some detail in his novel:

> "Between Mersea and the Blackwater were several flat holms or islands, some under water at high-tides, others only just standing above it, and between these the winding waterways formed a labyrinth in which it was easy to evade pursuit and entangle the pursuers. The

[smuggling] traffic was therefore here carried on with an audacity and openness scarce paralleled elsewhere. Although there was a coastguard station at the mouth of the estuary, on Mersea Hard, yet goods were run even in open day under the very eyes of the revenue men. Each public-house on the island and on the mainland near a creek obtained its entire supply of wine and spirits from contraband vessels. Whether the coastguard were bought to shut their eyes or were baffled by the adroitness of the smugglers, cannot be said, but certain it was, that the taverns found no difficulty in obtaining their supplies as often and as abundant as they desired. The villages of Virley and Salcot were the chief landing-places, and there horses and donkeys were kept in large numbers for the conveyance of the spirits, wine, tobacco and silk to Tiptree Heath..."

Salcott

The village of Salcott is today much the larger of the pair, containing a village stores and the only remaining public house, the Sun. The name of the village is simply a contraction of "salt cottages", a reminder of the days when salt-panning was an important industry here. (The Old English word "cot" was frequently used to refer to a cottage or small hut, and appears in many place-names around Britain, such as the town of Ascot.)

Like its neighbour Virley, Salcott also has its fair share of smuggling history. Every farmer had his own horse and cart to carry contraband to clearing houses further inland. Smuggled goods were hidden in cellars, sheds or even outside in underground chambers concealed by vegetation. It was said that most villagers attended church not to pray to God but to keep an eye on their contraband hidden around the church building. Baring-Gould's novel includes a gruesome tale about a boatload of 22 excise men who were found off Sunken Island with their throats cut. Their bodies were apparently buried at Salcott Church, whilst another story tells how a group of Dutch smugglers stole the church bells!

The head of Salcott Channel has been truncated by a post-war dam almost directly behind Salcott church. On the south bank are the remains of a small quay, known appropriately as Church Wharf, but large boats would not have found it very easy to use because, even at high tide, the navigable channel is extremely narrow. At low tide, the creek almost dries out, leaving a tiny ribbon of water just a few inches deep.

Because the first part of Salcott Channel is private, the coastal route continues instead along the main road through the village of Salcott. At the end of the road, two footpaths head off in slightly different directions, but both routes quickly lead to the shores of Salcott Channel. From the top of the sea-wall, you then have a good view of the meandering creek heading into the distance in both directions. To the left, the channel upstream gets narrower as it approaches the tidal limit near Church Wharf, but unfortunately the footpath in this direction is stopped by a fence across the sea-wall. To the right, Salcott Channel heads out towards the open sea, bounded by the private estate of Abbotts Hall on the north and the Old Hall Marshes on the south, which forms the next part of the coastline.

Immediately beside the embankment here, a rectangular pit has been constructed on top of the saltings using a series of low earth walls. When filled with sea-water, this was probably used as a store for keeping fish. After following the southern bank of Salcott Channel for half a mile in a generally south-eastern direction, the sea-wall turns sharply to the left beside a small muddy creek which has the interesting name of Bull Bar's Creek. You can still follow the original route of this creek inside the sea-wall, along a line which now forms the boundary between the modern administrative districts of Colchester and Maldon.

Between Mersea Island and the River Blackwater, the coastline is broken up by a series of long creeks, some extending several miles inland across the flat coastal plain. This produces a chaotic labyrinth of long promontaries and deep inlets which can appear confusing at first. However, upon closer inspection, the arrangement is relatively simple. There are three main creeks to the west of Mersea Island, if you discount all the smaller tributaries. In order, they are called Strood Channel, Salcott Channel and Tollesbury Fleet. In between these three creeks, two long promontaries jut out towards the open sea. The first of these is the private peninsula around the Feldy Marshes, which has already been described in some detail. The second peninsula is known as the Old Hall Marshes, and it is around this promontary that the footpath now leads.

The Old Hall Marshes form an enormous peninsula, measuring over five miles in circumference. It was acquired in 1949 by Brigadier R. Colwin, who decided to leave it undrained so that the marshes could be used as a shooting estate. He leased it in 1978 to the Nature Conservancy Council. In 1984 the whole peninsula, along with the nearby farm buildings, was bought by the RSPB for the high price of £780,000. The Old Hall Marshes are now managed as a vast bird reserve, and some of the old arable land has even been converted back to grazing. Unfortunately a local dispute has been raging for many years over access to the site, but this peninsula is still the largest area of unimproved marshland in Essex, and a stroll around its perimeter is one of the highlights of the Essex coastline.

Although the Nature Conservancy Council designated this area as one of their first Sites of Special Scientific Interest (SSSI), this distinction no longer appears to be much of an obstacle to planning permission when councils come to consider new building proposals. Since our own elected authorities seem indifferent to our threatened landscape, it is therefore particularly pleasing to see that the RSPB has, at great expense, effectively taken on the job of protecting the Old Hall Marshes from the developers for the benefit of future generations.

At the corner of the sea-wall beside Bull Bar's Creek, a farmtrack heads inland towards the RSPB visitor centre. This track acts as a short-cut across the peninsula, bypassing nearly five miles of coastline, although it would be a crime to miss the Old Hall Marshes. You are also recommended to visit the site soon, because rising tides are threatening the sea-walls. When the sea-walls finally fail, the owners have planned to carry out a managed retreat, using new internal embankments to control flooding and minimise sediment loss.

You are requested to walk beneath the sea-wall, but note that the public right of way officially runs along the top of the sea-wall. This continues alongside Salcott Channel in a north-easterly direction. During the height of summer, this footpath can become quite overgrown with tall grass, but it does afford good views, both of the winding creek whose character changes constantly with the tide, and of the long grazing meadows inland.

Just over a mile from Bull Bar's Creek, the sea-wall reaches another sharp bend. This is known, for some long-forgotten reason, as Quince's Corner. From this point, you may just be able to make out, on the far side of the channel, the low embankments that make up Ship's Lock.

Wandering around the Old Hall Marshes, the stresses of modern life can be completely forgotten for a few hours, because this countryside is about as remote as you will find anywhere in the Home Counties. The walk should not be undertaken lightly however, since a complete circumnavigation of the promontary from the nearest road will be over six miles long. Most visitors tend to choose a warm summer's afternoon to tackle this walk, but sometimes it seems that much of the wildlife has retired to a quiet nook to fall asleep under the hot sun. It is therefore well worth considering a bracing stroll during the height of winter, when the skies will be filled with the cries of migrating wildfowl. In addition, fighting against the bitter northerly winds, you soon realise that the untamed marshes can provide a much more powerful experience during the harsh, short days of winter than the tame face which they display during the lazy summer. However, watch out for the early sunset – the walk may take longer than you suspect!

After faithfully following Salcott Channel since its outset in the village of Salcott-cum-Virley, the sea-wall finally leaves the shores of this creek behind about two miles after leaving Quince's Corner. Here the embankment veers sharply to the right, but the unprepared walker may be surprised to discover that this is just the entrance to a large inlet, and that the tip of the peninsula is still half a mile further on. This inlet marks the site where a large creek used to penetrate inland, dividing the Old Hall Marshes into two halves.

Pennyhole Creek, as it was known, was dammed from a very early date, probably when the sea-defences were originally constructed. This original barrage was built 500 yards inland, but before long it was superseded by the present dam, which was constructed across the mouth of the creek some time between 1771 and 1805. Even today, two hundred years on, you can still see the waters of Pennyhole Fleet inside the sea-wall, though obviously these are no longer tidal. The original dam is still visible 500 yards away, and it is possible to trace the line of the original sea-defences on either bank. The embankment along its southern side is now used as a firm pathway through the marshy terrain, but part of the northern embankment appears to have been dug up to make way for a boundary ditch. Many smaller embankments were constructed throughout the marshes, but their purpose was probably to provide dry pathways for grazing animals, rather than to hold back flood-water.

Unlike most of the low-lying coastal plains around Essex, the Old Hall Marshes have never been properly drained, and its surface is therefore still pitted with the scars of watercourses which once filled with sea-water at every high tide. From the air, it is easy to follow the route of these meandering channels across the marshes, many of them still carrying a thin ribbon of water, but from the ground the landscape is so flat that it appears to be just a chaotic jumble of water and dry land, akin to the Flow Country in northern Scotland.

Although these former creeks, known in marshland parlance as "fleets", no longer flow directly into the sea, the water is still so brackish that no trees can survive locally. Instead, the fleets have largely been colonised by plants such as lesser reedmace (*Typha angustifolia*) and common reed (*Phragmites australia*), and provide a wide variety of habitats for birds such as reed warblers and reed buntings.

The marshes also attract enormous numbers of wildfowl, including pochard and shoveler. In centuries gone by, the landowners took advantage of these winter visitors by constructing two decoy ponds on the Old Hall Marshes. These were designed to lure unsuspecting birds into one of the many offshoots from the pond. These narrow offshoots, known as "pipes", were covered with a fine net, and the trapped birds could then be either eaten locally or sent to one of the large markets in London. A detailed description of the operation of decoy ponds can be found later in this book, around Tillingham.

The remains of the two decoy ponds can still be found amongst the fleets of the Old Hall Marshes. The smaller of the two, known as Teal Pond, was located just to the south of Pennyhole Fleet, half a mile from the tip of the peninsula. With only four pipes, it was used primarily to catch teal, and was abandoned around the beginning of the 19th century.

The larger decoy pond, covering more than two acres, was constructed further to the north-west on a tributary of Pennyhole Fleet in order to ensure a regular supply of water. This decoy pond is one of the oldest around the Essex coastline, and was said to be extremely successful at catching duck, teal and pintail, though no detailed accounts were kept. During the 19th century, however, grazing animals began to disturb the wildfowl, and so the farmers tended to shoot around the surrounding marshes instead. The pond fell into disuse around 1890, though the remains are still clearly marked on modern Ordnance Survey maps. The detailed "Explorer" map also shows the eight pipes leading off the central pond.

From the inlet beside Pennyhole Fleet, it is only a few hundred yards to the eastern tip of the Old Hall Marshes. This promontary, known to sailors as Quarters Spit, stands at the mouth of both Salcott Channel and Strood Channel, looking directly across at the buildings of West Mersea. Because of the slopes of Mersea Island in the background, this is probably the best viewpoint for the the tiny islands scattered around the Mersea Quarters. To the right, at the very mouth of the river, stands the low-lying Cobmarsh Island. The tiny island of Packing Marsh is easy to distinguish because of the small oyster-packing shed, and the long strip of saltings on the far left is known as Sunken Island.

At one time, these scraps of saltings were much sought after, and went for vast sums of money. They were in great demand because they provided an ideal location for oyster-beds. Shallow pits were dug out of the marshes and used to cultivate immature oysters, as described earlier, around West Mersea. The remains of more rectangular oyster-beds can also be seen in some places around the Old Hall Marshes. One such example is on the edge of the saltings around Quarters Spit.

Leaving Quarters Spit behind, the sea-wall begins to head back towards civilisation again, skirting the southern flank of the Old Hall Marshes. The return path follows the shores of Tollesbury Fleet, the last of the quiet backwaters to be encountered before entering the enormous estuary of the River Blackwater. Just to confuse matters, however, this reach of Tollesbury Fleet is divided into two channels of water, imaginatively named North Channel and South Channel, by a narrow strip of saltings known as Great Cob Island. (A "cob" is a local name for the black-headed gull or peewit gull.)

Looking inland, the open pasture stretches far into the distance, a peaceful landscape with only the occasional ornithologist to disturb the herds of grazing cattle. After following the shores of Tollesbury Fleet for about a mile, the meadows are interrupted by another wide fleet. When the sea-defences were erected, Joyce's Head Fleet was cut off from the sea, and now provides a marvellous habitat for birds.

From Joyce's Head Fleet, the sea-wall winds erratically past an enormous area of saltings for nearly a mile before reaching the small cluster of red-brick buildings. These are the buildings of Old Hall, a farm which dates back to at least 1573. Old Hall Farm was once the centre of a sizable community, largely based around a local brickworks. When the bricks had been fired in a small lime-kiln, they were transported to their final destination by boat. At low tide, you can still see the remains of a wharf on the banks of the narrow creek, known locally as Old Hall Creek, where a few rotten timbers now stick up out of the mud.

This little community also had its own public house, probably stocked by the profits of smuggling. It was originally called The Hoy, describing a type of ship then commonly used around the marshlands, but the name was later corrupted to The Ship Ahoy. Sadly, the pub disappeared many years ago, probably at the same time as the brickworks.

This is probably the best starting-point for a walk around the Old Hall Marshes, though it should be noted that the farmtrack, known as Old Hall Lane, is too narrow for cars to park, and that visitors are therefore asked to leave their cars back near the main road. From the farm buildings, a stroll eastwards along the lane leads round a corner to the RSPB centre at Old Hall Marsh Farm. Here a prominent notice-board displays a helpful map of the marshes and gives up-to-date information on the birdlife. A footpath heading north-east then forms the beginning of a circular walk around the Old Hall Marshes, in a clockwise direction.

Pushing on with the coastal route from Old Hall Farm, the footpath quickly retreats back into remote and undisturbed countryside. The upper reaches of Old Hall Creek form a vast maze of tiny channels and creeklets, splitting up the saltings into isolated clumps of vegetation. After half a mile, the wide grassy sea-wall veers sharply to the east. This is the head of Old Hall Creek, although a ditch inside the sea-wall shows where it once continued further inland.

This ditch also marks the boundary between two of the ancient *"hundreds"* of Essex. Like many English counties, Essex was once divided up for administrative purposes into a number of districts known as "hundreds", notionally because each region was intended to contain approximately one hundred families. At Old Hall Creek, you leave the area known as Winsted Hundred and enter Thurstable Hundred, which includes most of the land on the north shore of the River Blackwater.

On the "Explorer" maps produced by the Ordnance Survey, the public right of way here is marked as diverting inland for a short distance before rejoining the sea-wall a hundred yards further on. However, as in several other such places around the coastline, this is just an anachronism dating from the time when the sea-defences were a little further inland. In reality, the actual footpath continues to follow the crest of the sea-wall, as shown on the Ordnance Survey's "Landranger" map.

Along this part of the coastline, several low earth embankments have been built on top of the saltings outside the sea-wall. Their original purpose is not clear, but one theory suggests that they were used to create pools of sea-water. When Tollesbury fishermen had a particularly good catch, the excess fish were stored here so that they could be sent to market at a later date.

From the head of Old Hall Creek, it is just under a mile around the coast to the village of Tollesbury. During this stretch of the coastline, the sea-wall used to meander wildly, with a uniformly flat landscape of saltings stretching into the distance. However, this is now the site of an important new experiment in sea-defences.

As well as rising sea-levels, there is also the problem that sea-walls are under constant threat of erosion, particularly from lapping waves. For many decades, the engineers' standard solution was to make the sea-defences stronger, usually with layers of concrete. Whilst this inevitably slows down the erosion, the embankments are often undermined after a number of years.

Engineers noticed that saltings are able to absorb most of the energy of the waves, and struck on a radical new solution to the problem. In August 1995, a short stretch of sea-wall was deliberately flattened with bulldozers, allowing the high tide to flow in and flood the land just inside. In its place, English Nature constructed a new sea-wall three hundred yards inland, using earth from a new borrow-dyke dug just inside. The abandoned farmland is rapidly reverting back to saltings, hopefully providing a natural buffer between the waves and the new sea-wall. Salt-marsh is a dwindling but important habitat for wildlife, and this type of scheme therefore provides the double benefit of replenishing this valuable resource.

This "softer" approach to coastal defence is becoming increasingly popular, as it provides a cheaper and simpler alternative to the traditional "hard" schemes where sea-walls are built ever higher, regardless of cost or aesthetic appearance. With sea-levels rising inexorably, it is very likely that we will see many more projects like this in the future.

The new sea-wall takes a much shorter route than the original coastline, which used to follow around the edge of a short promontary. There was once a stone "hard" at the tip of this promontary, but signposts ask you not to walk along the abandoned sea-wall because it is steadily eroding away.

The new embankment soon joins the original sea-wall again. In a few places, simple footpaths lead out across the saltings. These were probably constructed by local wildfowlers, but the paths are now generally in a poor state and are not to be recommended. The presence of a nearby sewage works is the first clue that you are nearing the village of Tollesbury, where Woodrolfe Road leads down to a large marina.

Recommended bibliography:

Shingle spits and salt-marshes – R. Butler
Smuggling villages of north-east Essex – George Pluckwell
The bawleymen – Derek Coombe
Brightlingsea : echoes of the past – Alfred Wakeling
Wivenhoe and Brightlingsea railway – Paul Brown
Wivenhoe – C. Dunn
The great English earthquake – Peter Haining
Colchester 1815-1914 – A. Brown
In search of Colchester's past – Philip Crummy
Essex River Colne – Vernon Clarke
Fingringhoe Wick – a gravel-pit nature reserve – Laurie Forsyth
Mehalah – Sabine Baring-Gould
The red hills of Essex – Colchester Archaelogical Group

Chapter four – the Blackwater estuary – Tollesbury to Dengie

This chapter is centred around the Blackwater estuary. During its last few miles before flowing out into the open sea, the River Blackwater is over a mile across. Although it is similar in size to most Scottish lochs, it is only in Essex that such an enormous inlet would be completely surrounded by a tall sea-wall.

Apart from a couple of minor diversions, a public right of way follows this sea-wall continuously around the whole of the estuary. Many little villages have built up around the River Blackwater. but they rarely encroach right down to the shoreline. For most of its length, therefore, the coastal footpath runs through open countryside, with wide views across the estuary. As a result, some of the walks can be rather long. In order to break up a long stretch into several shorter ones, this book mentions several useful points of access to the coastline. As well as its beautifully rural nature, the River Blackwater also has many items of particular interest. Decoy ponds and "red hills" are scattered around the estuary, and two unusual islands are also described in detail.

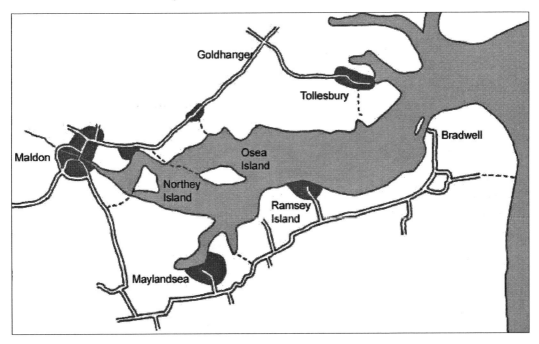

At the head of the estuary, the town of Maldon neatly breaks the chapter into two halves. This picturesque old nautical town provides an interesting contrast from the long miles of remote sea-wall. Just upstream, the area around Beeleigh also offers some pretty riverside walks.

The final part of this chapter is almost a section of its own, describing the unique countryside just beyond the Blackwater estuary. Known as the Dengie Flats, this landscape is completely different to the rest of this chapter. All of a sudden there are no villages, no country lanes – hardly any buildings at all. This part of Dengie contains arguably the most remote marshland to be found in the whole of Britain. A public footpath continues to follow the coastline, but the isolation is extreme. Visitors must be prepared for a long and often arduous walk. However, the wild scenery and unparalleled birdlife make this probably the most rewarding walk anywhere in Essex.

Tollesbury

The village of Tollesbury is well off the beaten track. Standing at the end of a narrow winding road, the original buildings were clustered around an old hall and church. Indeed the name itself means "Toll's fortified manor". Until the 20th century, most of the villagers earned their livelihood from sailing or fishing, but only one small road leads down to the water's edge. Known as Woodrolfe Road, this passes through a narrow gap in the sea-wall.

At one time, there were slots in the concrete wall on either side of this gap. During extremely high tides, wooden planks could be lowered into place to keep the flood-water out, but a new metal gate was recently installed here. This is closed two or three times a year, so you are recommended not to park beyond this gate. In any event, parking space is very limited outside the sea-wall, and should be reserved for local boat-owners.

Beyond the sea-wall, Woodrolfe Road continues for another hundred yards past a row of prominent white wooden buildings. These four sail-lofts are raised up off the ground on short stilts in order to protect them from sea-water. They were built in 1902 to dry the sails of local yachts.

Another four small buildings stood out on the saltings. These were used as packing-houses for the thriving oyster industry. The largest oyster business in this area was the Tollesbury and Mersea (Blackwater) Oyster Fishing Company, formed in 1876/77. At its peak, over 70 fishing smacks worked from Tollesbury. Even today, aerial photographs of the area show the remains of hundreds of oyster-beds scattered around the saltings. These appear as small pools, often rectangular in shape, which were dug out of the saltings. In these pools, fishermen would allow young oysters to grow and mature before sending them off to market.

Today, the oyster industry has all but disappeared, and the Tollesbury river-front is used primarily for recreation and leisure. A series of raised pathways now cover the saltings, providing access to around 100 moorings, mostly in the form of simple mudberths. The narrower channels of water have been bridged using long planks, but all the waterways eventually flow into one main creek. At one time, this was known as Woodrope Creek, presumably short for "wooden rope". The name is now marked on maps as Woodrolfe, but local people still refer to the area as "Woodrup".

Alongside the main channel of Woodrolfe Creek, there was once a small wharf. An old Trinity House lightship is now permanently moored here. Known as "The Trinity", this lightship has been used since around 1992 by a Christian trust called Fellowship Afloat. During the early 1900s, many local jobs were involved in the construction of racing yachts, as well as the royal yacht Britannia. Today, most of the Tollesbury villagers have turned their backs on the river-front and instead commute to nearby towns to work. However, there is still a strong nautical presence along Woodrolfe Road, with a number of specialised companies based in the area.

Most of the yachting at Tollesbury today is centred around Tollesbury Marina, near the end of Woodrolfe Road. Whatever the state of the tide, the marina is permanently in water, with pontoons that can take up to 240 boats. This is the home of Tollesbury Cruising Club, and there is a separate sailing club nearby.

Leaving Woodrolfe Road where it passes through the new metal gate, a good footpath follows the crest of the sea-wall past a row of modern buildings. Just beyond Tollesbury Marina, a second public right of way joins the coastline, leading down the hill from Woodrolfe Farm. At this junction, the sea-wall turns sharply to the left and you immediately head out into open countryside, quickly leaving the bustle of Tollesbury behind.

Tollesbury Wick Marshes

The footpath now heads around the edge of a long peninsula known as the Tollesbury Wick Marshes. Roughly a mile long, this peninsula contains some of the best scenery to be found anywhere around the River Blackwater. Most of the landscape has been designated a Site of Special Scientific Interest (SSSI). Starting from the centre of Tollesbury village, it is possible to make a circular walk around the peninsula. With a total distance of almost five miles, this route is highly recommended for strong walkers. If you use the Ordnance Survey's more detailed "Explorer" maps, this is a convenient point to switch over from map 184 (Colchester) onto map 176 (Blackwater Estuary) – fortunately there is a good overlap between the two maps!

At first, the sea-wall offers an excellent view of the saltings on either side of Woodrolfe Creek. This is one of the largest expanses of salt-marsh around the Essex coastline, supporting large numbers of wildfowl. According to official classification, the Blackwater estuary has ten species of birds in nationally important numbers, and four in internationally important numbers. This includes five per cent of the world's dark-bellied brent geese.

Inside the sea-wall, the land is mainly uncultivated. This has never been improved and drained for agricultural use, and has traditionally only been used for grazing. On old maps, a couple of small buildings were once marked, but even these have now gone. As a result, the scene is a remote wild landscape as far as the eye can see, broken only by pools and ditches of brackish water. Many of these are the remains of old creeks, long since cut off from the tidal river by the sea-defences. The marshes are also a botanists' heaven, with rough grassland dominated by plants with delightful names such as Creeping Bent (*Agrostis stolonifera*), Red Fescue (*Festuca rubra*) and Perennial Rye-grass (*Lolium perenne*).

Just over half a mile from the marina, Woodrolfe Creek flows into the main Tollesbury Fleet. As the sea-wall turns a gentle corner towards the right, you will see that Tollesbury Fleet is split into North Channel and South Channel. A long strip of saltings lies between these two channels. These saltings actually form two distinct islets, although this is not immediately obvious from the sea-wall. The smaller area of saltings, called Little Cob Island, lies closer to the sea-wall. As you walk further along the footpath, you may be able to spot the narrow creek that separates it from its larger neighbour beyond, Great Cob Island. The name "cob", incidentally, is an old local word for the black-headed gull or peewit gull.

The sea-wall continues along the shores of the South Channel of Tollesbury Fleet for two-thirds of a mile before reaching the tip of the peninsula. At this point, known as

Shinglehead Point, you finally rejoin the shores of the River Blackwater once again. At low tide, Shinglehead Point forms a narrow promontary of rough grassland and bare mudflats that projects for about a mile out to sea, forming quite an obstacle to navigation. Even at the highest point of the tide, an area of saltings almost three hundred yards long remains above the water. This provides an ideal habitat for a colony of little terns. These birds are relatively rare, and since they are very easily disturbed, you are requested not to stray away from the sea-wall here.

On the far side of Shinglehead Point, a wartime pill-box has been built into the earth embankment. This would have been a marvellous defensive position, commanding a wide view across the whole of the River Blackwater estuary. Immediately to the left, beyond the low-lying Cob Islands, it faces the sea-wall around the remote Old Hall Marshes. Beyond that, you can see the buildings of West Mersea. On a clear day, it is even possible to make out the hills around Colne Point and St. Osyth. almost eight miles away. Over to the right, you can see the buildings of Bradwell on the far side of the River Blackwater. The only thing to spoil the beauty of this panoramic view is the sight of the nuclear power station just across the water.

After the pill-box at Shinglehead Point, the footpath joins the shores of the main River Blackwater. This is a significant milestone in the coastal route, because you now begin an almost uninterrupted stretch of public footpath right around the head of this major Essex river, finally reaching the open sea once again at Bradwell, roughly 33 miles further on. Every section of this route is delightful, with easy walking and wide expansive views. Access to the sea-wall is very limited, but it could be argued that this minimises the disturbance and helps to preserve the tranquillity of the landscape.

Beyond Shinglehead Point, the footpath continues along the grassy crest of the sea-wall, now heading in a south-westerly direction. A series of groynes has been built across the mudflats here to try to halt the erosion of the sea-defences. These groynes, using lines of faggots interwoven with brushwood, aim to slow down the flow of the water, thereby promoting the deposition of silt. In this way, it is hoped that marshland plants will once again be able to take root and colonise the bare mudflats, providing a natural defence against the erosive power of the waves.

Shortly after the first set of groynes, the sea-wall turns sharply to the right to follow around the outside of a small inlet. If you are following the route on the more detailed Ordnance Survey maps (1:25.000 "Explorer" series), this is the point where you come to the end of map 184 (Colchester). However, even the next map in the series, 176 (Blackwater Estuary) fails to show that there is a second pill-box at the far side of the bay, closely followed by two more sets of groynes.

The most notable feature of Tollesbury Wick Marshes lies just ahead, as you come across the remains of an old railway pier. In 1904, a light railway extension was built from the main network to the village of Tollesbury, running the Crab & Winkle Express. By May 1907, the line had been extended down the hill and across the marshes to the coastline. A small wooden station was erected just inside the sea-wall, and a pier was built 1770 feet out into the River Blackwater in order to reach permanent water.

The aim of the light railway was to attract passengers away from the thriving ports of Brightlingsea and West Mersea. Unfortunately, the line was never very successful, and this extension was finally abandoned in 1921. During the Second World War however, the railway was temporarily re-opened to serve military shipping. Troops were also carried to the coastal batteries and mobile anti-aircraft guns. A pill-box was built alongside the pier, and a tower just inland was used to control electrically-operated mines.

In 1940, with the impending threat of German invasion, a short section of the pier was deliberately blown up, and parts of the walkway were removed. After the war, the railway fell into disuse once more and Tollesbury Pier Station was abandoned to the elements. Trains continued to run as far as the village of Tollesbury until 1951, when the whole railway-line was closed beyond Tudwich Road Station, just south of Tiptree. The track was pulled up for recycling, thereby ending any hope for the return of the Crab & Winkle Express.

Today, you can still clearly see the route of the old railway. From the sea-wall, a wide embankment runs in a straight line past the site of the old station towards the centre of Tollesbury, at the top of the hill. The remains of the pier are also evident, with two rows of wooden stakes heading out across the mudflats. The wartime pill-box still keeps its lonely vigil, although it has now settled into the mud at an awkward angle.

Mill Creek

Please do not walk along the old railway embankment – this land is private. To complete the circular walk from Tollesbury village, you should instead continue along the sea-wall a little further. The path soon turns a sharp corner and enters a large bay. This inlet is known as Mill Creek, a name which suggests that there was once a tidal mill nearby. There is no evidence now of its location.

At the head of Mill Creek, a public right of way leaves the sea-wall and heads inland, climbing diagonally up the hill. If you are making the circular walk around the Tollesbury Wick Marshes, then this path will take you back to your starting-point. The footpath soon turns left onto a farmtrack, which leads directly to the main road through Tollesbury. It is obviously a useful route of access to the coastline, but it is difficult to park near the end of the road without blocking access to Mell Farm. You are therefore asked to leave your car near the centre of the village, where it will not cause any obstruction.

From the head of Mill Creek, it is roughly six miles along the sea-wall to the village of Goldhanger. Along this length, several public footpaths lead down to the coastline, but these start so far inland that they do not generally help to break up this long stretch. As a result, these six miles are relatively quiet and unexplored, yet they form a marvellous introduction to the landscape of the River Blackwater.

In order to improve the sea-defences here, concrete panels have been erected vertically along the top of the sea-wall. In this cheap and simple way, the height of the sea-wall has been effectively raised by about a foot. Unfortunately, these panels also make it more difficult to sit down and enjoy the scenery. Looking across the river, it is still almost two miles to the far bank. At one time, this river was known as the River Pant, but this name now usually applies only to the uppermost reaches.

On either side of the river, a ridge of low hills slopes gently down towards the water's edge. As the tide goes out, enormous mudflats are exposed on either side of the main channel. In many places, large areas of marsh have been reclaimed from the sea, providing valuable acres of new pastureland. The land just beyond Mill Creek is a perfect example of converted saltings. If you look carefully, you can even see the remnants of tidal creeks winding their way amongst the rough grass. This reclaimed farmland is known locally as Mill Farm Marshes, and there is yet another reference to the old tidal mill just ahead.

Just a few hundred yards after rejoining the shores of the River Blackwater, the sea-wall diverts to the right around a tiny bay. The mudflats here are littered with clumps of saltings which form a short promontary known as Mill Point. On some old maps, the narrow channel of water which winds its way amongst these saltings was marked as Old Mill Creek. This creek originally ran roughly parallel to the main Mill Creek nearby. Unlike its larger neighbour however, Old Mill Creek was dammed when the sea-defences were built, probably around three hundred years ago.

Looking inland from the top of the sea-wall, you can still see the remains of the old tidal creek meandering across the reclaimed marshes. At one time, a second embankment followed the creek inland along its western bank. This may have been the original coastline, before Mill Farm Marshes were reclaimed from the sea. For many years this secondary embankment was maintained only as a precaution in case the main sea-wall failed, thereby limiting the damage caused by any flood-water. Protective embankments of this type were known as "counterwalls". With modern improvements in engineering, they are rarely needed these days, but old examples can still be found in many places around the Essex coastline.

Beyond Old Mill Creek, the sea-wall continues around the shallow inlet to rejoin the main river again. According to a map drawn up around 1880, this unusual location was the site of a bathing-house! Today, the scene is wild and desolate, with saltings on one side of the footpath and unimproved farmland on the other.

In the middle of this rough grassland, a large pool stands just a few yards inland. On the Ordnance Survey's more detailed maps, this pool is called Left Decoy, although it used to be known as Bohun's Hall Decoy, after a nearby farm. The names give a clue to the area's history, because this pool was artificially created as a "decoy pond" to catch wildfowl. During the 18th century, there were eight narrow offshoots leading away from the centre of the pool. These offshoots were known as "pipes", and were covered with a net in which wildfowl could be trapped.

This pond was particularly renowned for catching large numbers of pochard. A few of the birds were eaten locally, but most were sent away to markets. Left Decoy was abandoned around 1820, but many other decoy ponds continued in use until the end of the 19th century. More details about their operation are given later, during the description of a decoy pond near the village of Tillingham.

Beyond the pool of Left Decoy, the sea-wall continues in a generally westerly direction around a gentle headland. If you pass this way when the tide is out, you may notice a line of gravel and rough stones heading out across the mudflats. This causeway is called Thistly Hard. It leads across the soft mud to a tiny channel of water which never completely dries out, even at the lowest point of the tide. In this way, farmers were able to load and offload their boats at any time.

In order to take advantage of this useful facility, a wharf was built on this site, with a track leading to the farms inland. Today, there is no longer any sign of the old wharf, but the track remains in use as a public footpath. The path leads inland past Decoy Farm and then follows a farmtrack known locally as Thistly Road. At one time, it also connected with Lower Farm and Brickhouse Farm, but these have long since disappeared. The track eventually leads to the buildings of Bohuns Hall, just outside the village of Tollesbury. It is possible to park near Bohuns Hall and walk down Thistly Road to reach the sea-wall, but, at over a mile in length, this is clearly not as popular as the footpath to Mill Creek.

Whichever route you take to Thistly Hard, you will notice that the last few yards of this inland footpath are raised up on an embankment, like a miniature version of the main sea-wall itself. In some places, this would be an indication that the coastline has changed over the years with the construction of new sea-defences. However, this is not the case here. This low embankment is another example of a counterwall, built many years ago to protect Left Decoy Marshes from flooding if the main sea-wall is breached.

Beyond Thistly Hard, the sea-wall continues westwards along the shores of the River Blackwater. This part of the coastline is very vulnerable to erosion, because there are virtually no saltings to break the force of the waves before they hit the sea-defences. Instead, the embankment leads directly down onto a featureless plain of mudflats, known as the Tollesbury Flats. At low tide, these mudflats stretch out for almost a mile to a point called Thirslet Spit. They are split into two halves by a deep channel of water. This channel, named Thirslet Creek, is just the first of a series of creeks which fork off from the main channel of the river. This creates a confusing network of channels for sailors, but the problem is hidden at high tide as the water rises to cover the mud completely.

After half a mile or so, you reach a deep V-shaped inlet where the sea-wall is forced to make a sharp turn to the right for two hundred yards. At one time, a counterwall branched off from the head of this inlet to higher ground inland, but there is no longer any sign of it on the ground.

If you are following the route carefully on a detailed map, such as the Ordnance Survey 1:25,000 "Explorer" series, you will see that a red hill stands a hundred yards inside the sea-wall. The origin of these red hills is still very unclear. Some people believe that they were salt-making sites, but there is no conclusive evidence for this theory. It is known, however, that they date from at least Roman times. They are discussed in more detail earlier on.

The Ordnance Survey map shows three red hills in the vicinity. This first example is the largest of the three, with a diameter of around 100 yards, but all three have now been ploughed out and are very difficult to spot. The second red hill stands about half-way between the V-shaped inlet and the buildings of Rolls Farm, which you can see just ahead.

Following the coastal footpath, it is just over half a mile to Rolls Farm, one of the most remote in the district. The farm stands at the end of a long track called Prentice Hall Lane. This track provides the only useful access to the coastline between Tollesbury and Goldhanger. Prentice Hall Lane can therefore be used to break up the walk along this long stretch. Motorists can park just inland at Boreham & Profit's Farm, and it is then just under a mile down the lane to the sea-wall.

The scenery is bleak and wild, with a small area of ragged saltings just below the sea-wall. Far away to the east, you can still see the prominent power station at Bradwell, whilst just upstream lies Osea Island. This unusual island is described a little later on. Looking directly across the River Blackwater, you can see a cluster of houses and caravans on the far shore. These buildings belong to Ramsey Island, a small village near the road to Bradwell.

The sea-defences here have been built on the site of a third red hill. Some remains have even been found in the saltings outside the sea-wall, despite daily erosion by the tide. Continuing westwards, the embankment continues with a series of sharp bends until you reach the end of the saltings. From this point, the footpath takes a more direct route, running alongside Thirslet Creek. At low water, Thirslet Creek dwindles to become just a narrow tributary of the main river channel. At high tide, the River Blackwater expands to flood all the intervening mudflats, forming a continuous sheet of water nearly two miles across.

About half a mile beyond the saltings, a large pond lies just inside the sea-wall. This is another example of a disused decoy pond. Until the 19th century, there were many decoy ponds all around this part of the Essex coastline, providing large numbers of wildfowl for the local markets. This particular pond was known as Skinner's Wick Decoy, after a nearby farm of the same name. It originally had eight offshoots, or "pipes" as they are properly known. Around 1900, a local historian wrote that Skinner's Wick Decoy *"was formerly worked with great success, but was given up about thirty years ago."*

The farm is now known simply as Whyke Farm. From these buildings, a rough track leads down to the sea-wall, but there is no public right of way along the final few hundred yards. In any event, the track is very long and is therefore not much help as a route of access to the coastline.

It is not far now to the head of Thirslet Creek, where the remains of an old quay are slowly rotting away. Before the sea-wall was built, this creek continued inland for a further mile or so, stopping just short of the village of Tolleshunt D'Arcy. A narrow stream called Bowstead Brook still flows along this route, although it has been artificially straightened in several places.

From the head of the creek, the coastal footpath heads around the edge of a peninsula. In 1908, another red hill was discovered just inland at this point, about two hundred yards inside the sea-wall. With a diameter of roughly one hundred yards, this is one of the largest red hills in the district, but its height has been reduced by regular ploughing to around a foot.

Around this peninsula, there are many unusual features to look out for. The first appears just after a couple of sharp bends in the sea-wall, where a narrow bridge has been built across the mudflats to a clump of nearby saltings. Supported on short stilts, the wooden walkway even has a simple hand-rail, but the whole structure is extremely rickety and does not appear to be very safe.

Looking inland, one small area of scrubland has remained undrained and has escaped the plough. This unimproved marshland has turned into rough grassland, and now provides an important habitat for many endangered plants and animals. As a consequence, this is one of the few parts of the mainland to be included in the Blackwater Estuary SSSI (Site of Special Scientific Interest). It has not always been a haven for wildlife however – until the mid-19th century, a decoy pond operated on this site to catch large numbers of wildfowl. Known as Gore Decoy, the remains of the pond can still be seen today in the form of a large marshy pool about a hundred yards from the sea-wall.

The upper stretch of Thirslet Creek was sometimes known as Gore Creek, and modern maps still show the name of Gore Saltings nearby. These saltings lie just ahead, forming a thin promontary that projects out from the sea-wall. Beyond the saltings, an enormous plain of mudflats continues at low tide toward the middle of the river. Known as the Goldhanger Flats, these mudflats are bisected by a series of meandering channels called Upper Collins and Lower Collins. Eventually, after more than two miles, the mudflats finally peter out at a point known to local yachtsmen as Thirslet Spit.

Gore Saltings are cut off from the mainland by a narrow creek which flows just beneath the sea-wall. At low water however, it is possible to cross this creek by using a line of stepping stones. These can be found near the head of the peninsula, just beyond a sharp bend in the path. *Extreme care should be taken – these stones are very slippery!*

Rickety footbridge onto Gore Saltings near Goldhanger

Once across the stepping stones, you can walk along Gore Saltings for quite a distance. Along their southern edge, a sand and shingle spit has formed a low embankment. This phenomenon is quite common at the head of rivers in Suffolk, but is very rare around the Essex coastline. This unusual area, known as Bulham Beach, is well worth exploring.

Normally when exploring saltings of this type, it is vital to keep one eye on the clock, because the tide can come in very quickly and leave you dangerously marooned. At Bulham Beach however, there is no need to worry about the time. It does not matter if the tide comes in and covers the stepping stones, because the spit is joined to the mainland at its western end. *You are strongly urged to check first that this escape route is still available – shingle spits can change radically over time!*

Another unusual feature around this peninsula is the presence of a small cottage just outside the sea-wall. In order to avoid the damaging effects of salt-water, this building stands clear of the saltings on tall wooden stilts. Constructed using traditional weatherboards, it still appears to be well maintained.

The cottage is ideally situated – the interesting shingle spit of Bulham Beach is close by, and yet its isolated position means that there are very few visitors to disturb the peace. From the windows of the cottage, there is an excellent view of Osea Island in the middle of the river. This island is described in detail a few miles further on, just beyond the village of Goldhanger. The main deep-water channel of the River Blackwater flows around the far side of the island. To the north, there is a much narrower channel called Goldhanger Creek. At low tide, this creek almost completely dries out, and therefore almost all shipping keeps to the south side of Osea Island.

Beyond the cottage, the sea-wall continues around the peninsula, with a wide grassy path along its top. Before long, the path takes a sharp turn to the right. At this point, there was once another decoy pond. Standing just inside the sea-wall, it was called Widgeon Pond, although it was often known simply as Joyce's Decoy after the nearby farm. (Indeed, there is still a buoy out in the middle of the river known as Joyce's.) Some sources refer to the decoy pond as Solley's Decoy, but Richard Solly, a landowner based near Tollesbury, never owned this decoy pond, so this name is probably inaccurate. Until it was filled in, the pond had eight "pipes" or offshoots, in which wildfowl were caught using tapered nets. Widgeon Pond was finally abandoned around 1880. With Gore Decoy also being so close, it is little surprise that this peninsula was once known as Decoy Marsh.

Just a few hundred yards away, the head of a small inlet marks the end of the Decoy Marsh peninsula. Detailed maps show the position of another red hill just inside the sea-wall here, and archaeologists have found another four nearby. An excellent booklet was published in 1990 by the Colchester Archaeological Group, giving full details of all red hills known in Essex, describing the excavations and discoveries. This booklet is essential reading for anyone who is interested in finding out more about these strange relics.

At the head of this inlet, you cross the parish boundary between Tolleshunt d'Arcy and Goldhanger. The village of Goldhanger itself is now just one mile away. Walkers following the coastal route will probably be glad of the impending return to civilisation, because it is a very long stretch of coastline between Tollesbury and Goldhanger. Unfortunately it is not possible to break up this stretch into shorter, more convenient walks. A public right of way branches off inland from the head of this inlet. This footpath soon forks into two, both branches running roughly parallel to the coastline. Unfortunately, neither footpath helps to shorten the walk, and you therefore should continue to follow the sea-wall.

The final mile of footpath heads around another small peninsula. Until the middle of the 19th century, a small decoy pond operated near the tip of this promontary, but all traces have now disappeared. There are signs of another shingle spit forming along the edge of the saltings. By this stage, however, most walkers will now be looking ahead to the village of Goldhanger and the end of the long riverside walk.

For the last few hundred yards, the sea-wall runs alongside a deep inlet. This inlet gradually narrows until, at its head, a footpath leaves the crest of the sea-wall and runs along the edge of a playing field. Within two hundred yards, the footpath emerges onto a side-road in the middle of Goldhanger.

Goldhanger

The name of the village is said to mean "grassland where the corn marigold grows". Indeed, you would be hard pressed to find a more exciting name today, because Goldhanger is still a quiet rural village, lying just off the main B1026 Maldon Road. From the walker's point of view, it is an important milestone because Goldhanger offers the first access to the coastline for many miles. It also has a couple of pubs where walkers can refresh themselves –The Chequers and The Cricketers.

A small tidal creek flows into the inlet, and at one time the riverside must have been busy with fishing smacks unloading their catches. The remains of a Roman pier have been found nearby, and there are some suggestions that a tidal mill operated here during the 13th century. However, the creek gradually silted up, and by 1800 very few boats could reach the head of the creek. Today, the riverside is deserted once again and the village has now turned away from the river that once supported it.

Leaving Goldhanger, the coastal route follows the crest of the sea-wall along the opposite side of the long inlet. This time, however, you do not have to brace yourself for a long walk because it is only three miles to the Millbeach, the next point of access to the riverside. In addition, motorists can turn this into a circular walk by returning inland, using a useful footpath across the fields from Cobb's Farm.

The sea-wall runs past an area of land with the peculiar name of "Further Fish Pit Marsh", although at first sight the scenery may not appear to quite so interesting, with a sewage works standing just inside the sea-wall. However, this is the site of one of the most unusual red hills to be discovered around the Essex coastline.

Although it is not marked on the map, this particular red hill has a brighter colour than most. When it was excavated in 1906 and 1908, archaeologists uncovered a Roman settlement, along with signs of a kitchen midden (a primitive type of refuse site). Careful examination revealed the remains of a hearth with a series of nine flues, but surprisingly these turned out to be from a much later period. A human skeleton was also unearthed, leading to theories that red hills might be related to some sort of burial chamber. However, this seems unlikely because the skeleton was not found in a made grave, but was simply covered during the formation of the mound.

At the mouth of the inlet, the coastal footpath rejoins the shores of the River Blackwater and the sea-wall begins to veer to the south. At one point, the embankment unexpectedly juts out into the river for a few yards before resuming its original course. Old maps mark this as the site of an old coastguard station, but there are no longer any remains to be seen.

For the Essex coastline, the scenery is quite unusual. Instead of looking across an open river or a wide view out to sea, the wooded Osea Island takes up most of the horizon. At low tide, the River Blackwater dries out almost completely between the shoreline and the island, leaving just the tiny channel of Goldhanger Creek snaking its way across the wide plains of mud.

Close at hand, however, the surroundings are more typical, with a deep borrow-dyke closely hugging the foot of the sea-wall. Along this stretch, the seaward side of the embankment has been faced with concrete in order to minimise erosion. Indeed, the width of the path seems to suggest that this embankment has recently been improved. This part of the Blackwater Estuary has certainly had its fair share of major floods, dating back to at least 1736, when records show that a length of sea-wall was swept away.

Despite all this erosion and re-construction, archaeologists have discovered the remains of another red hill almost directly underneath the sea-wall, parts of it even extending out into the river. This red hill is relatively easy to find, because it is located where the footpath runs close to the buildings of Bound's Farm. A farm has stood on this site for many centuries, although the name "Bound's Farm" was originally given to a building that stood over a mile to the east, near Joyce's Farm. Like many large farms around these coastal marshes, a decoy pond was constructed nearby, although this had fallen into disuse by 1800.

For a mile beyond the buildings of Bound's Farm, the sea-wall makes a series of sharp zigzags around a couple of deep inlets. Keep a look-out for the site of yet another decoy pond – it is clearly visible just inland from the second inlet. This originally had five narrow offshoots or "pipes" for catching wildfowl, although one of these was filled in over the years. The local decoyman, an ingenious man called Mr. Cooper, also built large movable nets that stretched up between ten and twenty-five feet into the air. By removing a peg at the right moment, the net would spring up suddenly in front of the birds. In this way, he managed to trap large numbers of pochard in pens below the nets.

The pond operated until around 1870, but aerial photos show that even in 1954 the pond was still in almost pristine condition. Since that time however, the land has been radically altered. The four remaining pipes were filled in, and the surrouding fields were drained. During these changes, a counterwall was also removed. This embankment used to stretch from the head of the inlet for a third of a mile inland, protecting the farmland on either side from flooding in case the main sea-defences failed.

With modern engineering, sea-defences are considered to be relatively strong and safe, but over the centuries the sea-wall has been breached many times. Near the head of this second inlet, you can see the remains of one such incident where the creek, known locally as Gull Creek, burst through the embankment. Rather than repairing it, a new sea-wall was built just a few yards further inland. More recently, these sea-defences were improved by the National Rivers Authority.

Osea Island

Shortly after the second inlet, you approach one of the most unusual features around the Essex coastline – the long causeway across the mudflats to Osea Island. This causeway, said to have been built under the orders of a Roman governor of Colchester, is passable at each low tide for around four hours. This time varies considerably according to the tide and the direction of the wind, so you are warned not to take chances. When the tide is in, water covers the causeway to a depth of around 14 feet.

WARNING! On these flat plains of mud, the tide can come in much faster than you can run. This is a very dangerous route to follow without the benefit of a reliable tide-timetable. Cars have been lost to the sea after their occupants were caught out by a rapidly rising tide, and many people have come close to drowning on this causeway.

In any event, the island is privately owned and there is no public right of way onto Osea. The following description is only included for the completeness of this book, and to demonstrate the wide variety of landscapes that exist around these coasts.

Nearby Beeleigh Abbey was founded in 1180 by Robert de Mantell (some sources refer to him as Robert Martell). Documents show that he also gave the islands of "Ruckholme" and "Hardholme" to the abbey. This seems to relate to the islands of Osea and Northey, although it is not clear which is which.

Dropping down from the top of the sea-wall, the causeway leads down onto the mudflats and then turns sharply to the left to cross the narrow channel of Gull Creek. Swinging back to the east again, it then heads straight towards the island. It is only when you start walking along this stretch that you begin to appreciate how dangerous this causeway could be if the tide were to start coming in. This is because it is much longer than it appears – almost a mile from one end to the other – and the muddy surface makes it very difficult to run quickly.

For much of its length, the causeway lies almost level with the surrounding mudflats. Nevertheless, the track is maintained in remarkably good condition, with a firm surface up to eight feet wide. It is therefore quite easy to drive ordinary cars onto Osea. Indeed, this causeway used to be marked on maps as a 'cart road'. In order to prevent it from eroding away with each tide, the pot-holes are regularly filled with stones or gravel. As a result, maintaining this link with the rest of the world is by far the most expensive part of living on a remote island like Osea.

The track is bordered on either side by small boulders, all covered with slippery seaweed. Beyond these, the mudflats stretch out to the horizon in every direction. The mud is littered with small stones, giving the illusion of a firm surface. However, you do not have to stray far from the track before you realise that this mud is dangerously soft.

Walking along the causeway to Osea is one of the strangest experiences you are likely to encounter anywhere around the Essex coastline. The enormous plains of mud appear similar to the surface of the Moon, and indeed at times you feel equally remote and isolated. Back on the mainland, people watch from the safety of the sea-wall, just one hundred yards away, but with the intervening deep mud you might as well be on another planet.

Shortly before it reaches the island, the track veers slightly to the right. This is the lowest part of the causeway, crossing the channel of Goldhanger Creek. From this point, it is only a few minutes' walk before the track climbs up a gentle slope onto Osea Island. Incidentally, the word ending "ey" or "ea" used to indicate an island, and hence the name "Osea" originally meant "Osyth's Island". Technically therefore, it is a tautology to refer to Osea Island, since this would really mean "Osyth's Island Island". In practice, however, this is now usually overlooked!

Although Osea is over a mile in length, it is never more than a few hundred yards across. The causeway joins the island near its westernmost point, which has the rather unsurprising name of West Point. There used to be a heronry here, but the trees were destroyed by Dutch Elm Disease. At first, the track follows the northern edge of the island. This part of the island is relatively high, and does not need a sea-wall to protect it from high tides. But before long, the land drops away a little, and a low embankment soon runs alongside the track. From the top of this embankment, there is a beautiful view across a small inlet, full of saltings and winding channels of water.

Before long, the track turns sharply to the right and heads towards the higher ground in the centre of the island. Near this bend in the road, a few small yachts are usually moored amongst the saltings. For most of the time, they are effectively marooned in deep mud, but at high tide they can take advantage of the nearby channel of Earl Creek to reach the deep water of the River Blackwater. This bay is well protected from storms, and has been used as a mooring-place for many centuries. Indeed, there was once a small wharf here, served by a short tramway. The remains of three old tram-carts still lie nearby, half embedded in the mud of an oyster-bed. Around 1992, a new quay was built here, with a slipway alongside.

For such a small island, Osea has seen a lot of history. During the Middle Ages, the island had its own decoy pond to catch wildfowl. The precise location of this pond is not known, but it is known that it had become disused by 1890. In 1903, the island was bought by the brewing magnate Frederick N. Charrington. By this time, Charrington had become disillusioned with the brewing industry, and wanted to build a place for inebriates where they could *"live their lives free from the temptations of drink"*. He severed all links with the industry therefore, and moved to Osea. In 1910, he built a large convalescent home which he called Rivermere. Unfortunately, his plan never fully succeeded because large quantities of alcohol were smuggled in. Even today, hidden bottles are still regularly discovered by the inhabitants of Osea. The island was eventually sold, along with an unused building which Charrington had built as an orphanage.

During the First World War, Osea was used as a base for the Royal Navy Volunteer Reserve (RNVR). Large numbers of sailors were stationed on the island, and the navy even built a chapel for them. By 1916, the Navy began manufacturing Coastal Motor Boats here. These were specially designed for their speed, up to 55 knots, and were first used in January 1918. They were finally withdrawn from service in 1921, and the island returned to arable farming five years later.

In 1960, Osea Island was sold to Hilary and David Cole for the relatively low sum of £70,000. They sold it in turn to Cambridge University in 1968 as a property investment, but then bought it back in 1986. Under the new "set-aside" schemes for surplus farmland, much of the island was put to grass. In this way, the island attracts large numbers of brent geese during the winter, hopefully diverting them away from crops on the mainland nearby.

The Coles also planted 3000 new trees and began to renovate the buildings on Osea. Most of these are clustered around the high ground in the centre of the island, along a short stretch of road which is known as The Chase. The first building is the splendid old manor house. Just beyond a gate, the Island Estate Office stands just to the west of the track, with the black weather-boarded Pine Cottage just beyond.

Directly opposite the farm, a short length of track forks off from The Chase. Named East Street on local maps, a couple of small buildings stand on either side of this side-road. But all eyes are drawn to the imposing Edwardian building of Rivermere just a few yards further down The Chase. This is the convalescent home built by Frederick Charrington in 1910, and indeed is now more usually known as Charrington House.

For many years, this house stood unused and ruined, but it was recently renovated and converted into ten separate luxury apartments, which were put up for sale om 1989 with long leases. Just behind Charrington House, the old navy chapel has also been converted into two more flats, and they are all now occupied by journalists, literary agents and the like, using modems and fax machines to communicate with the outside world. As a result, the island now has over 20 inhabitants. A postman still visits the island every day, but life on Osea is generally dictated by the tides, with the causeway only passable for a few hours a day. At the time of writing, the island was up for sale again (with a price tag of around £6 million).

Beyond Charrington House, The Chase continues southwards past an old water-tower. It soon emerges on the island's southern shore beside a large shingle beach, with a panoramic view up and down the River Blackwater. Directly opposite you, the wide channel of Lawling Creek leads inland to the village of Maylandsea, whilst far off to the right you can see the trees on Northey Island.

In the middle of the beach, a large pier stretches out to deep water, although it has clearly seen better days. Parts of it have collapsed completely, but there are hopes that it will be repaired in the near future. At the end, a beacon is still used for maritime navigation. Just to the east of the pier, keep a look out for the remains of an old tramway. This tramway is not marked on maps, but you can still see a few rails leading down the shingle beach. It was built by the navy in the early 1900s to launch their Thorneycroft motor torpedo boats. You can also trace the stone foundations for some distance inland until the route of the tramway finally disppears into deep undergrowth, near a wartime anti-aircraft installation.

From the beach on the south side of Osea Island, most people return to the causeway by retracing their steps along The Chase. If you have plenty of time however, you can see more of Osea by making a circular trip around the eastern end of the island. This land is generally not so high above sea-level, and is therefore surrounded by a good sea-wall.

At first, overgrown bushes make it difficult to climb up onto the crest of the sea-wall, and you have to make a short detour along the beach instead. Once on the sea-wall however, it is not far to the south-eastern tip of Osea Island, where a wartime pill-box has been built into the earth embankment. From this point, there is an extensive view downriver. This is one of the narrowest parts of the River Blackwater, with the buildings of Stansgate Abbey Farm just half a mile across the water.

A shingle spit continues out beyond the sea-wall for another three hundred yards. Sailors call this East Point, although at low water the mudflats continue for another half mile or so. These mudflats used to be known as Goldhanger Spit, probably because they mark the entrance to Goldhanger Creek.

At the south-eastern corner of Osea, the sea-wall turns northwards alongside a small clump of saltings. Close to the foot of the embankment, you may notice the rectangular hollows in the saltings. These are characteristic of old oyster-beds. Until their decline in the early 1900s, oysters were so popular in Essex that virtually every available area of salting around the coastline was used to cultivate them.

Before long, you reach the north-eastern corner of the island, where another pill-box is embedded into the sea-wall. Some aerial photographs show signs that there was once another embankment running eastwards from this point. This suggests that Osea was once longer than it is today. This might explain why the shape of the island appears to be truncated at its eastern end. Indeed, it is quite possible that the island originally continued eastwards as far as Death Creek, a narrow channel that runs across the mudflats about five hundred yards out from the present sea-wall.

What is more certain is that Osea Island once had its own landing-strip for light aircraft! Two grass airstrips were built in the middle of the fields, crossing at right angles near the eastern end of the island. With a short track linking them to the buildings near the beach, they clearly show on aerial photographs taken around 1960. This suggests that they date from the Second World War, but in fact they were built after the war by the island's owners. The airstrips still exist today, but are no longer used.

From the north-eastern corner, the sea-wall heads back along the northern edge of the island towards the causeway. About a hundred yards from the pill-box, a small outfall stands next to a disused sewage works. This was once the site of an old jetty, and at low tide you can still see seven parallel planks of wood lying in the mud.

There are more signs of abandoned land just ahead, where the sea-wall veers slightly to the left. The original sea-wall continued on in a straight line at this point, before gradually curving to the left to rejoin the present sea-wall near the moored yachts. If you look carefully, you can still trace the start of its route amongst the saltings.

It is now just a short walk along the crest of the sea-wall back to the main track. All along this stretch, the remains of a few oyster-beds are clearly visible, in the form of rectangular pits in the saltings. Once on the main track, it is about two-thirds of a mile to the start of the causeway. *You are again strongly urged to check the state of the tide before crossing – the water can rise surprisingly quickly.*

Millbeach

Back on the mainland, we leave the Osea causeway behind. The coastal route continues along the crest of the sea-wall, soon reaching the end of a short peninsula. This was originally called Fauley Point, but today is more generally known as Decoy Point, after the large decoy pond that once stood nearby. An easy footpath then leads past a series of caravan parks, built on the site of The Round Tree. This was a large prominent tree marked on maps as long ago as 1900. All along this stretch, the sea-wall offers an excellent view of Northey Island. In contrast to its twin island Osea, Northey lies closer to the southern shore of the River Blackwater, and this time the deep-water channel flows around the northern edge of the island.

As well as the magnificent view, the owners of the caravans can also take advantage of a small natural beach which runs along the foot of the sea-wall. It is known as the Millbeach, and it gave its name to a pub just ahead (closed at the time of writing). The Millbeach also provides the first public access to a main road since leaving Goldhanger. Indeed, the volume of traffic warns you that you are now approaching the outskirts of a large town. During the summer months, the riverside here is very busy, a distinct change from the long undisturbed stretches of sea-wall lower down the river. In a few places, beach-houses have even been built on the foreshore.

Just west of the Millbeach, the River Blackwater turns very sharply to the south. This corner of the river, popularly known as Blackwater Bay, has always been a thriving area. This was the site of a large tidal mill called Barrow Mill, dating back to at least 1819. Indeed, this stretch of the river used to be known as Mill Reach. As the tide rose, water was allowed to flow into enclosed pounds. When the water-level began to drop again, sluices would divert the flow past the mill building itself, driving a large water-wheel. You can clearly see the remains of the two largest pounds, but the mill also made use of a third pound, just beyond The Millbeach pub. The three pounds were connected by a narrow ditch.

Barrow Mill also had its own wharf, on the site now occupied by the Saltcote Sailing Club. Like many mills around the country, it was eventually converted to steam. The buildings were finally demolished in 1892. Do not confuse Barrow Mill with the old traditional river-mill at Heybridge Creek, which is described a little later.

After rounding the corner, you enter a stretch of river called Collier's Reach, named after the coal-ships that used to offload here. These ships required large quantities of ballast in order to maintain stability during their long sail back to the northern coalfields. The sailors therefore filled the hulls with soil, dug from the river-bank. In this way, considerable areas of land were eroded away and eventually abandoned to the sea.

As a result, new sea-defences had to be built further inland to protect the farmers' fields. The present sea-wall therefore makes a series of sharp right-angled bends, although at low tide you can still see traces of the original coastline.

At one time, Collier's Reach was a busy industrial site. As well as the coal-ships, there was also a salt-making factory here. Until the invention of refrigerators, salt was in great demand as a food preservative, and Maldon was renowned as the salt capital of England for many centuries. More details are provided later on. This particular factory, the Essex Salt Works, finally closed down in 1839, although the area is still known as Saltcote.

Heybridge Basin

Walking southwards along Collier's Reach, you can see the buildings of Heybridge Basin just ahead. This is a popular spot in summer, with a large number of boats moored along the river-bank. A boat-yard is based in a low building which stands outside the sea-wall, just a stone's throw from The Jolly Sailor. This pub, built in 1798, once served beers that were shipped down by canal from Chelmsford. Today, the village has built up around Basin Road, but the community was originally centred on the Chelmer and Blackwater Navigation, an important canal whose entrance lock lies just beyond. Opened in 1797, this canal linked the thriving town of Chelmsford with the tidal reaches of the River Blackwater, enabling goods to be brought in by boat.

It was suggested as long ago as 1677 that the River Chelmer could be canalised between Maldon and Chelmsford, but it was not until 1766 that an Act of Parliament was passed to approve the plan. Unfortunately, this proposal was soon dropped because of local opposition, largely from millers on the River Chelmer. The council at Maldon also feared that a canal would harm trade at their own harbour.

According to maps of the time, such as the Essex map drawn up by Chapman and André in 1777, the River Blackwater originally flowed directly into Heybridge Creek. During the late 1700s, however, it appears that the river changed its course. Soon after passing through the village of Langford, it diverted southwards, joining up with the River Chelmer just upstream of Beeleigh Abbey. The original course of the river slowly dried out, although it is still possible to trace its old route today, just to the north of a dismantled railway.

In 1792, a short length of canal was dug alongside this new lower stretch of the River Blackwater, enabling boats to reach the village of Langford. With canal fever growing around the country, a new Act of Parliament was passed in the following year to start work on a much more ambitious project, canalising the River Chelmer itself. As a result, the Chelmer and Blackwater canal company was formed. This is now the oldest navigable waterway company in Britain. (The Stroudwater Navigation company had been set up in the West Country a little earlier, but this is now unnavigable, serving only as a water supply channel.)

The bridges and locks of the Chelmer and Blackwater Navigation were designed by John Rennie, and construction soon got underway. This involved canalising the River Chelmer upstream of Beeleigh Abbey, including several new cuts. From Beeleigh, a canal was dug northwards from the River Chelmer to join the new course of the River Blackwater. The navigation then linked up with the newly-opened Langford Cut before continuing eastwards towards Heybridge. A narrow basin was built just before the canal reached the tidal estuary of the River Blackwater. Here at Heybridge Basin, a broad lock was built to allow large boats to use the basin.

The Chelmer and Blackwater Navigation finally opened in 1797, at a total cost of £50,000. Between Heybridge Basin and the centre of Chelmsford, there were 14 miles of canal to negotiate, with 11 locks. It was capable of taking 30-ton boats up to 16 feet wide, but with a draught of only two feet, it was also the shallowest canal in the country. Its main trade was coal (hence the name of Collier's Reach nearby) but the canal was also used by many other businesses. One of these was The Old Ship, a new pub built alongside the entrance lock in 1798.

British canals suffered a slow decline over many years. During the 19th century, new railways sprang up around the country, often deliberately following the trade routes established by the canals. During the 20th century, improved roads introduced another form of competition, and many canals failed to re-open after the Second World War. The Chelmer and Blackwater Navigation fared better than most, but its last commercial trade, Baltic timber, finally disappeared in the early 1970s.

Since that time, the artificial waterways have become overgrown with weeds and are now very shallow indeed. The canal is still used by pleasure craft however. You can still hire narrow boats near Chelmsford, and there are a number of privately-owned craft in the lower reaches near Heybridge Basin.

The lock at Heybridge Basin is also rather unusual. The height of the tide varies widely in the River Blackwater, and so the two pairs of gates point in opposite directions. A third sliding gate has also been added, and this carries the main footpath across the mouth of the canal.

On the far side of the lock, the coastal footpath passes the lock-keeper's house and then quickly heads out into open countryside once more. However, there are still signs of past industry here. Between Heybridge Basin and the town of Maldon, the sea-wall passes a series of enormous gravel pits, most of which have now flooded. The area is remarkably peaceful, and is therefore very popular with local people.

At first, you get an excellent view of Northey Island just across the river, where a large house stands sheltered beneath a clump of trees. The footpath soon turns sharply to the right at a tight meander in the River Blackwater. At this corner, once known as Hering's Point, a small piece of land has been lost to the sea. At low tide, the original sea-wall is still visible, with a row of wooden posts sticking vertically out of the mud. Half a mile further upstream, a much larger area of land has also been abandoned. This second example is less obvious, though you may be able to spot the remains of an old embankment out on the far edge of the saltings.

Looking across the river, the right of way passes opposite the ancient quay at the heart of Maldon. As the crow flies, this is no more than three hundred yards away, but on foot there are three miles of walking to cover if you strictly follow the coastal route, as described in this book. These three miles include many different types of scenery, a welcome change from the bleak but beautiful wilderness of the Blackwater estuary.

Heybridge

The sea-wall soon begins to veer off to the right. Before long, it becomes clear that it is no longer following the course of the main river at all. Instead, the footpath is heading towards the banks of a smaller creek that flows into the River Blackwater from the north. This narrow tributary, known as Heybridge Creek, is tidal for only a short distance. Almost immediately after joining this creek, you reach a tall dam that stretches right across the channel. This was built around 1960 for flood protection.

In recent years, a small industrial area has built up on the far side of the dam, and there is therefore no public right of way along the far bank of Heybridge Creek. You must therefore divert inland for a short distance into the centre of Heybridge. It is possible to continue upstream along the eastern bank of the river, leading past Heybridge Hall and onto a small lane known as Hall Road. A better route is to cross the dam and follow a footpath up the western side of the river. This leads through a narrow strip of trees and bushes, eventually emerging on the main road near Heybridge Post Office.

From at least 1792 onwards, a water mill operated just upstream. Heybridge Mill, as it was known, was originally driven by a traditional water-wheel, although it was converted to steam-power around 1900. The machinery was housed in an enormous Dutch-style building, largely weather-boarded and standing three stories high. It operated until 1942, and the building was finally demolished soon after the Second World War, around 1954/5. There are numerous photographs of Heybridge Mill in local books, though be aware that it is sometimes incorrectly described as a tidal mill, and a few sources have confused it with the old mill at nearby Barrow Hill.

From the centre of Heybridge, there is an excellent circular walk. Just a hundred yards or so to the right, the Chelmer and Blackwater Navigation passes underneath the main road. If you follow the canal towpath to Heybridge Basin, you can then return to your starting-point along the sea-wall, a walk of two to three miles that includes a variety of contrasting scenery.

Around the Essex coastline, there are many occasions where you have to make a diversion inland. Whenever this happens, this book usually attempts to describe the route that most closely follows the coastline. From the centre of Heybridge, this would involve walking along the A414 towards Maldon, a busy road known as The Causeway. In this way, you can rejoin the River Chelmer and follow the northern bank upstream past a golf course. However, the noise of hundreds of vehicles does not make The Causeway ideal for pedestrians. A much more pleasant alternative is to walk along the B1018 for a hundred yards to reach a bridge over the canal. At this bridge, leave the road and follow the canal towpath upstream. This path is slightly shorter than the true coastal route, and it avoids the worst of the noisy traffic.

Upstream of Heybridge, the canal meanders wildly through the fields, completely ignoring the modern developments that have grown up nearby. Until recently, it passed underneath two disused railway bridges, although these have now been used to construct a road bypass around Maldon. Shortly after the second bridge, the towpath crosses over to the far side of the canal at a small footbridge. The Chelmer and Blackwater Navigation now passes through some beautiful open countryside, currently used as a golf course. Just beyond the club-house, the canal passes across an unseen boundary, entering the parish of Langford.

At the far end of the golf course, you enter a confusing area of interlinking rivers and canals. You may wish to read the following directions carefully to avoid getting lost! The first junction is with the Langford Cut, which flows in from the right. The lower reaches of the Langford Cut were soon filled in. However, you can still trace its route across the golf course.

Beeleigh

Just beyond the junction, the canal reaches the first of the two Beeleigh locks. This lock is unusually sited underneath a farmtrack, with one pair of gates on either side of a low stone bridge.

Immediately above the lock, you arrive at the waterways equivalent of a crossroads. The canal continues straight on, passing through a second lock before eventually joining the main River Chelmer. Meanwhile, the River Blackwater cuts across from right to left. To the right, it is only half a mile upstream to the village of Langford. The name of the village means "long ford", referring to an old bridge across the River Blackwater.

To the left of the crossroads, the River Blackwater flows over a large weir. The surroundings are rural and beautifully peaceful, and many people come here at weekends to admire the scenery. The countryside is particular attractive in the spring, and the gentle sound of tumbling water is extremely relaxing. The weir is also an important milestone, because it marks the tidal limit of the River Blackwater. Until this point, we have been slowly but steadily heading upstream along the river. From here on however, the walk is all downstream again. This also coincides with the ancient divisions or "hundreds" of Essex. As you cross the river, you are leaving Thurstable Hundred and walking into the Hundred of Dengy.

On the far side of the weir, the footpath reaches a small area of woodland. This marks the boundary between the parishes of Langford and Maldon. In effect, the woodland forms a tiny island, since it is surrounded by water on all sides. Indeed, it is only a few yards along the path to a second weir, this time marking the tidal limit of the River Chelmer. At one time, this weir was used to divert some of the water into a nearby mill-race. Beeleigh Mill was destroyed by fire in 1879, and the building was finally pulled down in 1960.

Beyond the weir, you are back on true mainland again and beginning the long trek downstream. But before you can reach the open stretches of the tidal estuary again, you have to negotiate a route through the busy but picturesque town of Maldon. At first, you follow a wide track called Abbey Turning. This leads past Beeleigh Falls House and begins to climb up a gentle slope. Beyond Beeleigh Grange Farm, the track continues uphill, but the coastal route soon turns off to the left along a minor farmtrack, known locally as Beeleigh Chase.

Despite its muddy surface, Beeleigh Chase has always been popular with walkers. These days, it acts as a footpath from Maldon to the beautiful wooded island between the weirs. Many years ago, it was used as a main thoroughfare to Beeleigh Abbey, which stood just to the north of the track. The abbey was founded in 1180 and dedicated to St. Mary and St. Nicholas. Like many monastic buildings, however, Beeleigh Abbey was destroyed after the Dissolution, and its remains were incorporated into a new house during the 16th century.

A road bypass has now been built around the western edge of Maldon. At one time, the town was served by two railways, but these have both now closed. The road was built along the line of a disused railway, even using the original railway cutting and bridge.

Beyond this busy bypass, there is a choice of routes. To the right, a footpath climbs steeply uphill towards a cluster of buildings on the outskirts of town. The coastal route chooses the second footpath, sloping gently downhill to the left. This wanders across open meadows to the banks of the river, and leads unerringly towards the centre of Maldon.

Maldon

A town stood on this site long before the Normans carried out their survey in 1086 for the Domesday Book. In the year 913, a document refers to a settlement called Maeldun, derived from the Saxon words "mael" (cross) and "dun" (hill). The name literally means "hill with a cross", although a cross usually implies a place of assembly. Maldon was clearly an important centre even in those early days, and the town received its first charter in 1171 from Henry II. If you are interested in finding out more about the history of Maldon, there are plenty of books on sale locally, such as The Book Of Maldon by Ian Linton.

At the centre of Maldon, the bridge provided the first route across the river. This was therefore an important crossing-point, although the current bridge is a rather unimposing structure of unadorned concrete. This is a useful starting-point for a circular walk, heading upstream to Beeleigh Falls along the northern bank of the river, and then returning to Maldon along the south bank, following Abbey Turning and Beeleigh Chase as described earlier.

Salt works

From the bridge, it is only a short walk up Market Hill to the main shopping area of Maldon. However, the coastal route does not climb the hill. Instead, it stays close to the riverside, following a narrow footpath through an area of small industries. Of these, the salt works deserve a special mention in this book. Until the 20th century, salt was widely used as a food preservative, and was a very valuable commodity. This is reflected in phrases such as "salt of the earth" or "worth his salt". Indeed, the word "salary" derives from the Latin word for salt, because it described the salt money paid to Roman soldiers. Its manufacture was a particularly important industry around the Essex coastline. In the Domesday Book of 1086, for example, 45 salt pans were recorded in the Maldon area alone.

Most households used a lot of salt, but it was also taxed heavily. By 1805, its price had risen to £30 a ton, an expensive burden to most families. Because of public resentment, this tax was finally abolished in 1825. The price fell dramatically, and salt therefore became much more widely available. With the expansion of the industry however, Maldon companies had to compete against competition in the north of England. The manufacture of salt, particularly from sea-water, was an expensive business. In Cheshire, on the other hand, enormous quantities of salt lay underground – it was only necessary to pipe it to the surface.

The salt industry around Maldon suffered badly, particularly when the railway era heralded a new method of bulk transport. The invention of the refrigerator also reduced the need for many food preservatives, and today there are only six salt companies left in the country. Of these, only one still manufactures traditional sea-salt, the Maldon Crystal Salt Company. It was built on the site of a 12th-century salt-pan, though the present buildings were first established in 1777. The factory was renovated recently, and now uses natural gas to evaporate off the water.

The footpath soon emerges on a small suburban street called Downs Road. Although it is often a busy area, this is a useful place for drivers to park their car before setting out on the next stage of the walk. The road ends at The Hythe, a small quay on the banks of the River Blackwater. Until the 19th century, The Hythe was the industrial heart of Maldon. For a few hours around high water, there would have been a frantic rush to load and offload boats before the tide dropped again. Today, the area has largely been landscaped for leisure use, and there is even a maritime museum nearby.

Just before a small boat-yard, the coastal footpath turns off to the right. Following the crest of a sea-wall, it gradually enters quieter surroundings and leaves the buildings of Maldon behind. You have not completely escaped from the trappings of civilisation however, because the footpath soon runs alongside a small refuse tip.

Northey Island

Once again, the estuary of the River Blackwater offers wide open views, and the peace of the surroundings is in great contrast to the busy town behind. Nevertheless, there are still plenty of points of interest to look out for. Just ahead, for example, you may be able to spot the tidal causeway leading across to the island of Northey. During the description of Osea Island earlier, it was explained that the word ending "ey" indicates an island, and hence it is technically a tautology to refer to "Northey Island". Nevertheless, most people now refer to it by this name.

The discovery of flint scrapers suggests that Northey Island has been occupied since the Stone Age. The island is also associated with the Battle of Maldon, a fierce clash that took place on 11th August 991 (although a few sources quote the year 993 instead). At that time, the island was being used as a base by a Viking army, controlled by Unlaf (or Olaf) Tryggvason. The invaders were preparing to attack an Anglo-Saxon stronghold in the town of Maldon nearby. Under the leadership of Byrhtnoth (variously also spelt Bryhtnoth or Brihtnoth), the Anglo-Saxons came out to meet the Viking invaders, and the two armies met at the Northey causeway. There are stories that Byrhtnoth allowed the Vikings onto dry land for a fair fight, but this may have been an embellishment added by later writers. In any event, Byrhtnoth was killed and the Vikings won the battle. The defeated Anglo-Saxon army agreed to pay the invaders up to £10,000 to keep the peace, and the Vikings moved away south to the Isle of Sheppey in Kent.

Over the next few centuries, very little is known about Northey Island, though it is likely that the higher ground was regularly farmed. During the 18th century, a decoy pond operated on the north-eastern edge of the island, trapping large numbers of wildfowl. Known as "the Decoy Piece", this pond became disused by 1800. Decoy ponds are described in more detail later on, during the description of the Dengie Flats.

By 1772, local maps indicate that embankments had been built around the edge of the island to prevent flooding. Since that time, the story of Northey Island has become a constant battle against the ever-rising sea-levels. In 1897, a major storm devastated many sea-defences around the Essex coastline, and Northey was no exception. Many sea-walls were swept away and most of the island was flooded. Basic repairs were soon carried out, but more storms hit the area in 1901 and 1903. As a result of extensive damage, the low-lying areas were finally abandoned to the sea. Today, only a small corner of high ground near the causeway remains above high tide.

In 1923, the island was bought by Sir Norman Angell, an enthusiastic man who spent a lot of money on improvements. He built a new house in the middle of the island, and installed mains water and electricity. Many of the remaining sea-walls were renovated, and the causeway was strengthened. In 1925, he also carried out a radical experiment by planting cord-grass amongst the tidal saltings. His plan was to consolidate the salt-marshes so that cattle could graze there at low tide.

For his experiment, he selected Townsend's cord-grass (*Spartina townsendii*), a fertile hybrid of the more common *Spartina maritima* (small cord-grass) and *Spartina alterniflora*, a species from America. *Spartina townsendii* was first spotted in the salt-marshes of Southampton Water, and is much hardier than the native varieties. The experiment was a great success, and this type of cord-grass was later used at other locations around the River Blackwater. Indeed, it is so dominant that some botanists fear that it may eventually wipe out the native species altogether.

In 1947, Northey Island passed to Sir Norman Angell's nephew, Eric Angell Lane. In April 1978, it was donated to the National Trust, and has operated as a bird reserve ever since. For almost seven years, the island was leased to the Essex Wildlife Trust, but it is now once again managed directly by the National Trust. One of the buildings is let as a holiday home, but otherwise the island is closed to the public unless you obtain a permit from the warden in advance – telephone Maldon (01621) 853142 or write to Northey Cottage, Northey Island, Maldon, Essex). There is a small charge for permits, but they are very simple to obtain, and a visit is strongly recommended.

Once a permit has been obtained, visitors approach Northey Island from the B1018, locally known as Mundon Road. A private farmtrack leads off the main road, passing through the yard of South House Farm. Cars are not generally allowed onto the island, so you will have to leave your car on the mainland. There is a tiny parking area just inside the sea-wall. Continuing on foot, the track climbs over the top of the sea-wall and across the salt-marshes. It leads to a causeway across a small branch of the main River Blackwater, called Southey Creek.

The causeway is covered for around five hours at every tide, and it is therefore vital to consult a tide-timetable before venturing onto the island. It is much shorter than the tidal causeway onto Osea Island, but both are believed to date from Roman times. The Northey causeway also requires frequent repairs to halt the constant erosion. As a result, the track has a very good surface, raised a foot or two above the surface of the surrounding mudflats. At high tide, the submerged causeway is a significant obstruction to shipping, and only the smallest boats are able to pass through Southey Creek.

The tidal causeway onto Northey Island

For the benefit of visitors who have gone to the trouble of obtaining a permit, the following text describes a walk around the island, heading in a clockwise direction. Once across the causeway, a good track continues along the western edge of Northey Island. This corner of the island is relatively raised, and there is therefore no need for a protective sea-wall. The track is lined with blackthorn hedges, although several varieties of trees have been introduced for diversity.

A small wooden hide has been built beside the track, offering spectacular views across the mudflats. You are asked to enter the hide as quietly as possible, in order to avoid disturbing the birds. Oyster-catchers are the most obvious, not least because of their prominent piping call, but there are usually also large numbers of other wildfowl, ranging from shelduck and curlew to much smaller birds, such as redshank or dunlin.

Before long, the track turns sharply to the right. At this bend, it is possible to continue around the edge of the island, following the remains of an abandoned sea-wall. You are warned that this path is extremely rough and uneven underfoot, and is only suitable for strong and agile walkers. The path leads past the rotting hulk of a barge called the Mistley, and eventually comes to an abrupt end at the northernmost tip of the island. By this time, visitors will begin to appreciate that Northey is an island of contrasts.

Shortly beyond this point, known as Hillypool Point, the sea-wall has been breached. Furthermore, on the eastern side of the island, the waters of Awl Creek have punched an even wider hole through the sea-defences. As a result, it is no longer possible to walk around the outer edge of Northey Island. However, if you are fit and agile, it is worth making the detour to Hillypool Point to enjoy a panoramic view across the River Blackwater. Directly ahead of you across the water, a row of caravans are lined up along the Millbeach, whilst to the left, the buildings of Heybridge Basin are clustered around the entrance lock of the Chelmer and Blackwater Navigation. Far away to the right, the flatness of the horizon is interrupted by the tall trees of Northey's sister island, Osea.

From Hillypool Point, you are forced to retrace your steps back along the eroding embankment. Just before you rejoin the main track again, keep an eye open for the remains of a few oyster-beds. During the 19th century, young oysters were stored here until they were ready to be sold at local markets. Today, the oyster-beds appear as large rectangular hollows in the saltings.

Back on the main track, it is less than two hundred yards to the island's only house. (An accompanying farmhouse and barn were destroyed by a bomb during the Second World War.) The sole remaining building is sheltered from the biting winter winds by a small copse of trees, marked on old maps as Ladies Grove. The house is tall and imposing, yet it is known as Northey Cottage. Visitors are asked to respect the privacy of the residents, and not to wander around the grounds of the house.

It was mentioned earlier that many of Northey's sea-defences were swept away by storms around the start of the 20th century. As a result, five-sixths of the island has been abandoned to the tide. A new sea-wall was built around the remaining one-sixth, principally the higher ground to the south-west near the causeway. There is a good footpath along the crest of this new sea-wall, and you can join this path just beyond Northey Cottage.

As it meanders back and forth, the new sea-wall provides marvellous views of the abandoned farmland, most of which has now reverted to salt-marsh, with a particular abundance of sea lavender (*Limonium vulgare*). These saltings are usually only inundated during a particularly high tide, such as a spring tide. In some places, there are rows of parallel ditches across the saltings. These are the remains of old farming ditches, showing the ridge and furrow method of soil drainage. With such a wide variety of landscapes, it is not surprising to find so many types of wildlife thriving here. Corn buntings and meadow pipits often rest on the overhead wires, and short-eared owls nest amongst the trees. A colony of herons disappeared some years ago, but brent geese are common during the winter months.

About half a mile from the house, a low embankment forks off to the left, snaking its way amongst the saltings. This was once the original sea-wall around the edge of Northey Island. It is still possible to follow its route for a few hundred yards, until you reach a section washed away by the tide. However, you are asked not to walk along this short spur to avoid disturbing nesting birds.

Shortly after this spur, the sea-wall turns sharply to the right. This is the site of an important experiment in flood protection. In the autumn of 1991, bulldozers pulled down the next stretch of sea-wall, filling in the borrow-dyke and flattening the ground. High tides are now held at bay by means of a second embankment, just a few yards further inland. By deliberately abandoning this narrow strip of ground, it was hoped that new saltings would form naturally and the new sea-wall would be protected from the worst of the wave erosion. Early results have proved very promising, and a much larger prototype has now been built north of the village of Tollesbury.

Beyond the site of the experiment, the footpath continues around the edge of a small field. You are now nearing the end of your walk around the island. This southern part of Northey is not as low-lying as the rest of the island, but it still requires the protection of a sea-wall. This was clearly illustrated during a flood many years ago, when a short stretch of this sea-wall was swept away. The sea-defences were repaired by constructing a new embankment a little further inland. As a result, the coastline now makes a quick detour to the right before resuming its course. When the tide is out, you can still see some remains of the original sea-wall. It is then only a short walk back to the tidal causeway across Southey Creek.

Back on the mainland, you now begin a long and lonely stretch of coastline around the edge of the Blackwater estuary. If you keep strictly to the sea-wall, it is over six miles to the next road, at Maylandsea. However, it may be possible to split this long haul into two shorter sections by making use of a private lane at Brick House Farm.

This walk is very typical of the River Blackwater – for most of its length, it feels extremely remote, shunning the local villages and hamlets. The coastal footpath seems forgotten and abandoned, and the area is rarely mentioned even in local books. Yet there are plenty of unusual items of interest, and the scenery is always wild and beautiful.

Leaving the Northey causeway behind, the sea-wall heads off into empty countryside. At first, it aims in a south-easterly direction, following the course of Southey Creek. Along the shores of this creek, a wide strip of saltings has built up, interwoven by a tangled web of deep muddy channels. Most of this foreshore is owned by the National Trust, as part of their Northey Island estate.

Away to the right, you may be able to spot a low grass-covered embankment, threading its way across the fields. Before long, this joins up with the main sea-wall. Probably without realising it, you have reached the site of Limbourne Creek, a small river that once flowed into the estuary at this point. The source of this river was just west of the village of Woodham Mortimer, almost five miles inland. The name Limbourne was recorded as long ago as 1327, when documents refer to a gentleman called John de Lymborne. Today, the narrow stream is known instead as Woodham Mortimer Brook, although there is still a narrow tributary nearby called Lime Brook.

When the first sea-wall was built around these coastal marshes, Limbourne Creek was dammed about half a mile inland. In the last thirty years, however, a second dam has been added at the mouth of the creek, as part of a general plan to improve the flood-defences. This new dam now carries the main footpath around the coastline, although technically the public right of way still follows its original route, heading half a mile inland. Limbourne Creek has virtually disappeared, but it still acts as the boundary between the parishes of Maldon and Mundon.

On the far side of the dam, the sea-wall turns sharply to the left. The countryside now feels very remote from civilisation. The only building for miles in any direction is the isolated Bramble Hall Farm, about half a mile inland, although old maps show that at least three other farm buildings once stood in this vicinity.

The Mundon Canal

The embankment soon makes a curious series of zigzags, forming an unusual "double promontary". At the second of the two points, an enormous sluice has been built into the sea-wall. It is difficult to envisage it today, but this area was once a hive of activity. In place of the sluice, there was once a navigation lock here, enabling barges to pass through the sea-defences and gain access to a short canal. Known as the Mundon Cut, this canal was just over a mile in length, finally ending at New Hall Lane near the buildings of White House Farm. Barges were then offloaded at a small wharf at the head of the canal, usually referred to as Mundon Wharf.

At one time, a track ran along the eastern bank of this canal from Mundon Wharf to the coastline. This track led to Mundon Quay, a small jetty that stood alongside the entrance lock. Both the track and quay have now disappeared, and the countryside is now quiet and rural once again.

The sea-wall now heads in a more easterly direction, following the channel of Southey Creek downstream. Looking inland, there are uninterrupted views across an open expanse of drained marshland, now carved up into a series of enormous fields. The flat coastal plain continues for about half a mile inland, before the ground begins to rise quite suddenly. Standing on the top of a prominent rise, the buildings of Iltney Farm were carefully sited above the floodplain, and now command a panoramic view of the estuary. As you get close to Iltney Farm, you may notice the remains of a few oyster-beds amongst the saltings.

As you gradually leave Northey Island behind you, the views across the river also open up. At high tide, the estuary appears as a single enormous sheet of water, and it is impossible to say precisely where Southey Creek merges with the main estuary. At low tide however, wide areas of mudflats constrict the water into narrow channels. You can then clearly see where the creek flows directly into the River Blackwater, at a junction known to sailors as "Latchingdon Hole".

Before long, the coastline turns sharply to the right and heads around the edge of a large inlet. A narrow channel called Cooper's Creek flows into the inlet somewhere, but it is virtually impossible to distinguish it from hundreds of other narrow muddy guts that wind their way in and out of the saltings. Along the base of the sea-wall, more rectangular pools indicate the site of old oyster-beds. Around this part of the Blackwater estuary, oysters were once cultivated along virtually the whole coastline.

At the head of the bay, the sea-wall turns left and begins a long trek to the end of a narrow peninsula. There are some signs that this land was reclaimed at a later date to the rest of the coastal marshes, but this evidence is not conclusive. Maps from around 1880 show a building sited in the middle of this peninsula, but the land is now desolate and uninhabited. The scenery is beautifully wild and undisturbed, but the detour adds another mile and a half to the coastal walk. It is clear that some people choose to bypass the peninsula completely by walking along a field boundary, but it must be pointed out that there is no right of way along this short-cut.

At the north-east tip of the peninsula, a narrow spit projects more than five hundred yards into the middle of the river. The spit is formed mainly of a narrow strip of saltings, although a tiny raised "island" stands proud of the waves at its farthest point. This is commonly known as Mundon Stone Point, although the stone from which it derives its name was originally sited half a mile to the west, at the north-western tip of the promontary. From the safety of the sea-wall, there is an excellent panorama of a stretch of the River Blackwater sometimes known as The Ware. Just across the water, the island of Osea is especially prominent, with its row of houses at the head of the beach.

Turning the corner at Mundon Stone Point, you begin a long haul down the eastern side of the peninsula. This is also the start of a long detour inland around the head of a major creek, originally called Latchingon Creek, but now more generally known as Lawling Creek. As the crow flies, it is less than a mile to the caravan park at Canney Marsh, on the far bank of the creek, but on foot it is almost six miles away. However, it is a very interesting walk with a wide variety of scenery. Almost immediately, Lawling Creek splits into two channels. The main branch, the western channel, is usually known as Mundon Creek, although some maps only apply this name to the uppermost stretch.

About two-thirds of a mile from Mundon Stone Point, a rough grassy embankment heads out from the main sea-wall to the edge of the saltings. At the end of this short spur, low earth walls have been built in the shape of a small rectangle. This appears to be the remains of a fish-pit, where live fish were stored in a pool of salt-water until they were ready to be taken to market. Before long, the sea-wall turns left at a sharp bend. At this corner, a public footpath heads off inland towards Brick House Farm, an isolated set of farm buildings at the end of New Hall Lane. Motorists may be able to arrange access to the coastline at this point. Brick House Farm is extremely remote, standing at the end of a long narrow country lane, but at one time there was a small cluster of farms near the shoreline here, with quaint names such as Sparrow Hall and Pockworth's Farm.

Along the shores of Mundon Creek, there is plenty of evidence that the coastline has changed considerably over the years. Old maps show short stretches of embankment inland, possibly the remains of the original sea-defences, and the sea-wall appears to follow a slightly different route to the modern coastline. If you look carefully, you can even see a few raised embankments today out amongst the saltings. These suggest that a narrow strip of coastal farmland was abandoned many years ago.

Perhaps the clearest example of this occurs where the footpath reaches a sharp bend, at the end of a short promontary. At this point, the modern sea-wall almost doubles back on itself, but you can see where the coastline originally continued on in a straight line for thirty yards or so. Shortly after this point, you enter a peculiarly-shaped inlet, also caused by the flooding of farmland. There was once a decoy pond just inland here. It is known to have operated in 1760, but it fell into disuse around the middle of the 19th century and is now impossible to trace.

Every time the sea-defences were breached by a storm or flood, a new embankment was built, usually just a few yards inland from the previous sea-wall. As a result, the modern coastline appears to meander aimlessly around the head of Mundon Creek, but the scenery is outstandingly beautiful at any time of year.

During the winter months, large numbers of migrating wildfowl collect around these marshes, and at low water the exposed mudflats are scattered with wading birds. The views may not be as dramatic as the Cornish coastline or the mountains of the Lake District, but the mood changes with every season and with every tide. No two visits are ever the same, and the simple peace of this wild landscape cannot fail to leave a lasting impression.

At a second, slightly larger inlet, you reach the true head of Mundon Creek, although this is not obvious from the footpath. At this point, a public right of way leaves the crest of the sea-wall and heads off inland, joining a network of public footpaths across the fields. Once again, these are not usually clear on the ground. One of these routes is known as "St. Peter's Way", an unofficial long-distance footpath leading to St. Peter's Chapel near Bradwell.

At one time, Mundon Creek continued inland for another couple of miles. After the building of the coastal sea-defences, this part of the creek became nothing more than a drainage ditch, but its meandering route still acts as the parish boundary between the neighbouring villages of Mundon and Latchingdon.

At the head of Mundon Creek, the footpath turns the corner and begins its long trek back towards the River Blackwater. Once again, there are remains of an old abandoned sea-wall leading out across the saltings, another reminder of the shifting nature of this coastline. On Ordnance Survey maps, you may notice that a right of way soon joins the sea-wall. Its route is not clear on the ground, but this was once a wide track leading from Lawling Hall to the riverside. In the days before modern roads and railways, small barges were widely used to transport goods from the local farms.

Maylandsea

Looking ahead, a cluster of moorings and modern houses indicates that we are nearing civilisation once again. This is the village of Maylandsea, a modern community standing just off the main Steeple Road. In 1924, the isolated Marsh Farm was one of the only buildings on this site, but the area has been gradually developed ever since. During the Second World War, Cardnells boat-yard employed over 80 people here, producing motor torpedo boats for the Naval base on nearby Osea Island. Today, the village is peaceful once again, and the bungalows are often used as holiday or weekend retreats.

Sailing is still the main industry in Maylandsea, and many yachts and dinghies are moored on the foreshore. The Harlow Blackwater Sailing Club and the Maylandsea Bay Yacht Club are both based here, and there are several other boat-yards and associated companies based along the river-front.

Maylandsea is often confused with its neighbour Mayland, a much older village whose manor dates back to the 12th century. The two villages lie in different parishes, even though they are less than a mile apart. However, there are more than two miles of coastline between Maylandsea and Mayland, mainly because of a long peninsula that splits Lawling Creek into two branches. Up to this point, this book has been describing the western branch, usually known as Mundon Creek, whereas the village of Mayland lies near the head of the eastern branch. You therefore have to make a long detour to the tip of this peninsula. This is a popular walk, although the footpath can be a little muddy in places.

At first, you pass a series of old stone "hards" before finally heading out into open countryside. Much of this land was reclaimed from the sea, and subsequently turned into farmland. It was once known as Sheep-pound Marsh, and there are even records of a decoy pond here. About a mile out of Maylandsea, you reach the tip of the promontary. The two branches of Lawling Creek meet here at a sharp corner in the sea-wall. After turning the corner, you are effectively walking upstream along the banks of the eastern branch.

On some old maps, this quiet backwater is marked as "Steeple Creek", but this appears to be a mistake. The cartographers seem to have confused it with a small inlet nearby. In any event, this eastern tributary is now known as Mayland Creek. Along the shores of Mayland Creek, the embankment meanders wildly, with a narrow borrow-dyke running alongside most of the time. Before long, however, encroaching buildings indicate that you are approaching the hamlet of Mayland.

Beyond a small sewage works, Mayland Creek narrows considerably. It is now just a short walk past a line of bushes to the head of the creek. There was once a tiny wharf at this site, known as Pigeon Dock, and maps show that a small building used to stand by the water's edge. The building has now gone, but yachts still occasionally moor in this sheltered haven. The area is delightfully peaceful, a welcome retreat from the frantic traffic nearby, and the picturesque scenery is also ideal for artists and photographers.

Two helpful footpaths join the sea-wall at the head of Mayland Creek. To the west, a track leads

Pigeon Dock, near Maylandsea

back to Maylandsea, taking a short-cut across the peninsula. This can be used to make an excellent circular walk. In the other direction, a footpath heads inland for two hundred yards towards the buildings of Bramble Farm, before finally emerging onto the main Maldon Road. This track provides the last useful access to the coastline for almost three miles.

Heading downstream again, you leave Pigeon Dock behind and begin the walk along the eastern side of Mayland Creek. This sea-wall is also the route of the St. Peter's Way, an unofficial long-distance path between Chipping Ongar and St. Peter's Chapel near Bradwell. The total length of the St. Peter's Way is about 46 miles, but it only joins the coastline for a short distance. After just half a mile, you reach a large inlet where the long-distance route heads inland again, following a farmtrack towards the village of Steeple.

Our coastal route continues along the crest of the sea-wall. The scenery is interesting and varied, but unfortunately this also includes a few caravan parks, one of which lies directly ahead. This is the Canney House Caravan Park, built on reclaimed land once known as Canney Marsh. At this point, Mayland Creek flows into the main channel of the River Blackwater. This marks the end of the long detour around the two branches of Lawling Creek, and you can once again look forward to an uninterrupted stroll along the wide, open river.

The walking is easy along the top of the embankment, although the grass can grow rather long during the summer. There are excellent views of Osea Island in the middle of the river, and you may just be able to spot the remains of Osea pier, standing at the foot of a small beach. There are also several unusual items back on the mainland. About half a mile from the caravan park, the sea-wall passes a narrow sand spit, curiously projecting out in a long arc. This appears to be artificial, perhaps built to slow down the erosion of the coastline.

The spit stands at the mouth of a large inlet, called Steeple Creek. The area is rich in birdlife, and several wooden hides have been built out on the marshes. The tidal mudflats are covered with various salt-tolerant plants, but it is clear that these are not typical saltings. For a start, there is not the usual abundance of sea purslane (*Halimione portulacoides*), a plant that is so characteristic of the Essex coastline. This is because the original sea-defences were swept away, and a large area of land has been lost to the sea here. Indeed, many of the old field ditches are still evident, forming parallel lines across the marshes. Local maps suggest that the farmland was abandoned between 1768 and 1840, although this evidence is not always reliable. There are also some reports that a water mill operated nearby, possibly even a tidal mill which required a large pound to drive the machinery. This may help to explain the peculiar arrangement of low earth embankments that are scattered amongst the saltings.

On the far side of Steeple Creek, the situation is reversed. Instead of losing farmland to the sea, a small area of marshland was reclaimed during the 19th century by the construction of new sea-defences. However, this new land was never properly drained, and remains as unimproved grazing land to this day. This sea-wall is perfectly walkable, but unfortunately it is not a right of way. At low tide, many people walk along the edge of the shoreline, but at high water you have to divert inland for a short distance. The landowners should be ashamed of denying the public a right of access. Let us hope that a permissive path will eventually be established here, thereby forming a continuous coastal footpath stretching uninterrupted over sixty miles around the estuary.

Stansgate

In the meantime, the coastal route has to leave the sea-wall at the head of Steeple Creek. A narrow lane called Stansgate Road runs parallel to the sea-wall at this point. It is possible for car-owners to park nearby, but the lane is narrow and great care should be taken not to cause an obstruction. The coastal route follows Stansgate Road to the left, past the imposing buildings of Stansgate Abbey Farm.

Around the 14th century, this isolated farmstead was home to a group of Cluniac monks. (The Cluniac order originated in 910 AD at Cluny, a small town near Lyon in France, and finally separated from the Benedictine order during the 11th century.) Their numbers gradually dwindled away, and by the time it was closed by Cardinal Wolsey in 1525, only two monks and a prior were left. The buildings fell into disuse, although the derelict chapel was used as a barn until the 1920s. Today, the only remaining part of the original abbey is a short section of wall, now incorporated into one of the farm buildings.

"Stanesgata" was recorded in the Domesday Book of 1086. Some people suggest that the name may refer to the "river gateway", since the River Blackwater is less than mile across at this point. Indeed this stretch of the river is still often known simply as Stansgate. However, the name literally means "stone gate", and may instead recall an ancient riverside entrance into the estate.

In more recent times, Stansgate Abbey Farm was the cause of an important polical battle. In 1961, Anthony Wedgewood Benn inherited the title of "Viscount Stansgate" upon the death of his father. Despite being an elected Member of Parliament, he was prevented from taking his seat in the House of Commons, on the grounds that viscounts are entitled to attend the House of Lords. Indeed, the High Court eventually annulled his by-election victory, and appointed his opponent as the local MP in his place.

After a prolonged battle, the government finally passed the Peerage Act of 1963. As a result, Tony Benn was allowed to denounce the title of Viscount Stansgate and return to the House of Commons. As an interesting footnote, it was only a few months later that Harold Macmillan was forced to resign as Prime Minister. Alec Douglas-Home was appointed his successor, but it was only because of the new bill that he was able to renounce his earldom and take up his new important position. Several other peers later followed suite, including Viscount Hailsham.

Passing the buildings of Stansgate Abbey Farm, the narrow lane eventually leads to the Marconi Sailing Club, where the public footpath rejoins the crest of the sea-wall. Once you move away from the background noise of the sailing club, the peace of the countryside quickly returns. This is typical Blackwater scenery – open fields on one side stretching uninterrupted into the distance, and the ever-changing river on the other side.

Ramsey Island

Looking ahead, you can see on the horizon a collection of houses. These belong to a small community called Ramsey Island. At one time, this village was separated from the mainland by a wide marshy creek, known as Ramsey Creek. Embankments ran along the banks of this creek, protecting both the mainland and the islanders from high tides. During the 19th century however, dams were built at each end of Ramsey Creek, thereby joining the island permanently to the mainland.

The remains of the creek can be seen about half a mile from the Marconi Sailing club. It appears as a series of marshy pools snaking inland, and is known as Ramsey Marsh or

Ramsey Fleet. (The name "fleet" is a common local word for a creek that has been cut off from the sea.) Ramsey Creek is now used as a drainage channel, and its route is therefore still obvious along most of its length. It is even possible to find the remains of a few of the old sea-defences, more than a hundred years after they became redundant. One of these embankments, along the south-western edge, is now used as a public right of way across the fields.

Beyond Ramsey Fleet, it is only a short walk to the centre of Ramsey Island. Like the village of Ramsey near Harwich, the name probably comes from the Old English word "hramsa", meaning wild garlic, with the traditional "-ey" ending to indicate an island. The community here is based around a central narrow street which leads straight down to the riverside, an area known as The Stone. This gives its name to the Stone Sailing Club, as well as to the nearby Stone Inn. For people walking the coastline, Ramsey is important because it provides the last public access to the sea-wall until you reach Bradwell, nearly four miles further on.

This long uninterrupted walk begins from The Stone, near the remains of some old oyster-beds. Passing a few houses, you approach the wide inlet of St. Lawrence Bay. Once again, this name is reflected in the St. Lawrence Inn, a large pub which stands just a short distance inland. Keep a look-out for the remains of Ramsey Fleet, which used to separate the island from the mainland.

Back on the "mainland" once again, a large caravan park has been built on the outskirts of the village. This is known as the Beacon Hill Farm Leisure Park. The farm itself stands, as the name suggests, on the top of a hill nearby. Beacons were often lit at times of celebration, or even as warning signals to other villages. However, older maps suggest that the name was originally Burkin, and could even have been a corruption of Barkham.

At the head of St. Lawrence Bay, you pass a small artificial lake before heading out into open countryside once more. The walking is usually very easy, because the sea-wall is very wide and topped with short grass. On the seaward side of the embankment, a concrete facing helps to protect against wave erosion. Just inland, a deep borrow-dyke runs parallel to the sea-wall, helping to drain the nearby fields.

After about five minutes' walk, just when you begin to think that you have left the trappings of civilisation behind, you encounter one last sign of modern development. A large slipway has been built leading down to the riverside, enabling boats to be launched from a convenient gravel beach. Beyond this point however, you are truly "away from it all". This stretch of the River Blackwater feels as isolated as anywhere in Essex. The only intrusion into this rural scenery is the ugly hulk of the nuclear power station which looms on the horizon ahead. This is still many miles away however, and it is easy to enjoy the tranquillity of this remote landscape.

At low tide, the water recedes over half a mile from the shoreline, revealing a large area of mudflats. At one point, about a mile from Ramsey Island, these mudflats are bisected by a deep channel. Known as St. Lawrence Creek, this channel is completely hidden at high tide, but its location is still obvious because of a small inlet it has carved out of the coastline. This inlet now forms the boundary between the parishes of St. Lawrence and Bradwell-on-Sea. You may also spot a short length of earth embankment amongst the saltings – this is probably the remains of the original sea-wall. At one time, there was also a decoy pond nearby, known as the West Wick decoy pond. This was used until around 1850, but all signs of it have now disappeared.

On the far side of the inlet, a caravan park stands on the side of a gentle hill. Beyond this, there is a long lonely stretch of coastline. The busy Maldon Road is never more than half a mile away, but down by the water's edge there are no signs of farm buildings or tracks for at least two miles. Along this remote river-bank, the sea-walls seems to wander aimlessly back and forth, making only slow progress towards the village of Bradwell.

Just past a deep V-shaped inlet, there was once an old jetty. However, this stretch of coastline suffered badly from erosion over the years. As a result, a decision was taken during the 1990s to deliberately abandon the original sea-wall. In its place, a new embankment was created a few hundred yards further inland. The old sea-defences were deliberately breached in two places, and the abandoned land is being allowed to flood and gradually revert to tidal saltings. In this way, it is hoped that this new salt-marsh will provide a buffer against the waves, rather than spending more and more money on expensive flood-defences. Examples of this kind of "managed retreat" are becoming increasingly common (see just north of Tollesbury for another example). The modern footpath follows this new embankment for almost a mile before returning to the original coastline once more.

Bradwell

After such a long and remote trek, most walkers will probably be glad to reach Bradwell and have an opportunity to rest their legs. The rural landscape ends abruptly at a large rectangular marina on the outskirts of the village. Around two hundred yachts are moored to the floating pontoons here. Even during rough storms, the entrance to the marina is well protected by Pewet Island, a thin strip of saltings standing just a few hundred yards offshore.

Bradwell village was recorded in the Domesday Book as Effecestra. The "cestra", or camp, may have been the Roman fort of Othona nearby (now the site of St. Peter's Chapel, described a little later in this book). The modern name of the village comes from the Old English "brad wella". This literally means "broad stream", a reference to the River Blackwater, whose channel is a mile and a half across by this point.

Today the village is sometimes called "Bradwell-juxta-mare", although the parish is properly called Bradwell-on-Sea, in order to distinguish it from another village called Bradwell, near Braintree, in north Essex. Just to confuse matters a little further, the village of Bradwell-on-Sea actually lies over a mile inland. The community that has grown up on the shores of the River Blackwater is technically known as Bradwell Waterside.

Bradwell Waterside is a small hamlet standing near the end of the B1021 road (locally known as Waterside Road). The road passes through the hamlet and leads directly onto a slipway on the banks of Bradwell Creek, a small offshoot of the main River Blackwater. The river has always been the life-blood of the local community, and even today there are several yacht clubs and associated businesses here. Bradwell also had the curious distinction of being one of the only ports allowed to trade with London during the Black Death. (The other was Burnham-on-Crouch.)

With a pub called the Green Man standing just inland, the riverside is always a busy area, particularly during summer weekends. However, the area would have been even busier under some of the plans proposed by the railway companies. During the 1890s, it was suggested that the Southminster line could be extended to Bradwell, connecting with a steam ferry to West Mersea. This would form part of a new through-route from

Southend to Colchester, using another ferry to cross the River Crouch at Creeksea. This ambitious plan was finally dropped in 1901 because of competition from road traffic. In 1919, another proposal to extend the Southminster line was suggested, this time just serving Bradwell Quay, but again the plan came to nothing.

Any ferry linking Bradwell with West Mersea would have to cross two miles of water. However, the river has not always been this wide. Over the centuries, the eastern half of England has been gradually sinking, and sea-levels have risen steadily. Two thousand years ago, during the Roman occupation of Britain, the river was much narrower and shallower, and there are serious suggestions that a road may once have crossed the river at this point. This would certainly help to explain the location of the Roman camps at Othona and Colchester. Many theories have been put about, but very little conclusive evidence has been unearthed. In 1906 however, after an exceptionally low tide, a police inspector from Colchester claimed to see two parallel rows of wooden posts crossing from Bradwell towards Mersea Island. Could this have been the remains of a Roman ford, or possibly the supports of an old bridge?

For official purposes, the mouth of the River Blackwater is defined by an artificial line drawn between Bradwell Quay and the Tollesbury marshes opposite. Beyond this point, the character of the coastal walk changes completely. As the river estuary slowly widens out into open sea, the sea-wall gradually changes from a river-bank to a true maritime coastline once again. Indeed, there are no more landing-stages until you reach the next river, at Burnham-on-Crouch. Between Bradwell and Burnham, there are sixteen miles of the wildest coastline to be found anywhere in Essex. Visitors who wish to explore this remote wilderness should be fit and capable of covering long distances on foot. There is a continuous footpath along these sixteen miles of sea-wall, but the ground is sometimes quite uneven and overgrown. There are great rewards for walkers who make the effort, because the scenery is quite unparalleled.

The first few miles, from Bradwell to St. Peter's Chapel, are quite easy underfoot. Parts of this sea-wall have suffered badly from erosion. In order to reduce the erosion, much of the embankment has been faced with concrete, and faggots have been constructed across the mudflats. These faggots consist of a line of wooden stakes embedded vertically in the mud, with long sticks interwoven amongst them. In this way, silt is allowed to settle, forming a natural protective barrier against the waves.

This initial stretch is deservedly popular, with wide views across the estuary towards West Mersea. Since 1956 however, the beauty of the area has been spoiled by the construction of a massive nuclear reactor nearby. Coming on stream in 1961, this unsightly hulk has dominated the skyline ever since. It is currently being decommissioned and as a result, despite this ugly eyesore, it is still easy to enjoy this coastal walk.

One of the most notable features of this walk is the enormous number of pill-boxes. Over the next three miles of coastline, you encounter at least 11 pill-boxes embedded into the sea-wall itself, and there are several more to be found inland. Looking out to sea, another unusual structure stands about four hundred yards from the coastline. This is the cooling-water intake for the power station. It also incorporates a "training wall", a quay made of steel and concrete where large tankers can moor, waiting for a high tide before coming inshore.

Beyond the training wall, the sea-wall heads eastwards, passing one pill-box after another. You are now approaching the end of the Dengie peninsula, a flat landscape of remote farmsteads and wild marshes. With views of open sea ahead, the scenery looks bleak and empty in every direction. Because of the powerful tidal current and the eroding force of the waves, saltings have only survived in a couple of shallow bays. At the first of these inlets, about a mile from Bradwell, a narrow track heads inland towards the buildings of Weymarks Farm. This track follows the route of an old earth embankment. This was an example of a counterwall, designed to prevent flood-water from spreading too far if the main sea-defences should fail. With recent advances in engineering, counterwalls are now considered unnecessary, but their raised routes along field boundaries makes them ideal for use as farmtracks today.

Continuing past the inlet, you soon reach a point where two pill-boxes stand just a few yards apart. At this point, the sea-wall turns sharply inland before quickly resuming its original course. A small strip of land has been abandoned to the sea here. If you look carefully, you can spot the remains of the original sea-wall, running along the edge of the saltings. Near the far end of this lost land, another track heads inland across the fields, once again following the route of an old counterwall.

Because of its remote location, the Dengie peninsula supports a wide variety of wildlife. In a few places, naturalists have intervened to support particular species. At the site of Easthall Outflow, for example, a series of ammunition barges from the Second World War are permanently moored just offshore. These provide extra nesting sites for birds, and also help to slow down erosion by dissipating the energy of the waves. Another unusual phenomenon is the presence of large numbers of cockle-shells nearby, many forming unusual banks and spits. The largest of these, the Bradwell Shell Bank, is owned by the Essex Wildlife Trust.

Just beyond the ammunition barges, the sea-wall makes a gentle curve to the right. This corner, known as Sales Point, was the site of a grand scheme in 1852 to reclaim all of the Dengie mudflats, and possibly the nearby Foulness Sands as well. If it had succeeded, this would have been the largest reclamation scheme in the country. Engineers began to build a new sea-wall across the mudflats from Sales Point, but the money soon ran out. Only a mile of the new embankment had been completed, and this was quickly swept away by the daily tides.

However, aerial photographs show signs of much earlier structures out on the tidal mudflats. Around the low-tide mark, lines of wooden stakes were once used to support a series of low wattle fences. These fences were in the shape of a rectangle, over three hundred yards long, in order to trap fish as the tide receded. When scientists studied the remains, the fish-trap was found to date from Saxon times, around the 8th century AD. These days, the remains are only exposed during the lowest spring tides.

Immediately after Sales Point, you may be able to spot the remains of a couple of piers just below the sea-wall. Maps show that the right of way here does not follow the crest of the embankment. Instead, it heads inland for a few hundred yards. This is because a new sea-wall was built in the 1970s, but the public right of way still officially follows the original coastline. However, nobody would reasonably expect visitors to stick rigidly to the old outdated route, and most walkers continue along the concrete top of the sea-wall, unaware of the anachronism.

St. Peter's Chapel

Looking ahead across the flat landscape, the tall building of St. Peter's Chapel can be clearly seen from miles away. At closer quarters, its simple structure belies the true history of this ancient building. The full story dates back around two thousand years, when the Romans built the fort of Othona on the coast here. Many centuries later, during the Anglo-Saxon era, the bishop St. Cedd arrived to convert the people to Christianity. Between 654 and 664 AD, he built a monastery on this site. It is believed that most of the stones for its construction came from the old Roman fort. Excavations have shown that the monastery was located on the top of the old Roman gateway, and hence the building is often known as St. Peter's-on-the-wall.

In its original form, St. Cedd's building was a simple rectangular shape with a rounded apse at its eastern end. This apse has now gone; large stones on the grass now mark its position. There is also some evidence of a tower, which some people suggest was used as a lighthouse.

The monastery operated for three or four hundred years, before eventually falling into disuse. For a long time, St. Peter's stood derelict, although it was restored as a simple chapel in the 1920s. One story from the Second World War tells how soldiers mistook it for a disused barn. They began using it for target practice, until it was pointed out that they were firing at the oldest cathedral church in England! Indeed, it is the only cathedral church in the country that still survives from the pre-Norman period.

For many years, St. Peter's Chapel was used only once a year, during an annual pilgrimage, but regular services restarted in 1954. It is now also the terminus of an unofficial long distance footpath, the St. Peter's Way, that stretches 46 miles across the Essex countryside from Chipping Ongar. But one mystery still remains – after powerful storms, the ruins of old buildings and tracks are occasionally revealed amongst the nearby saltings and mudflats. As long ago as 1594, John Nordern wrote:

"It appeareth to haue bene a town now greatly deuoured with the sea; and buyldings yet appeare in the sea."

Towards the end of the 19th century, a raised track was constructed across the marshes, leading to a small dumping ground on the edge of the saltings. As a result, this area is now known as Tip Head. Fortunately, the area is now protected for its marvellous wildlife. A nature reserve has been set up near St. Peter's Chapel, but the whole foreshore along the Dengie Flats has been designated a National Nature Reserve. It is ideal for marshland plants such as sea purslane (*Haliminione portulacoides*), as well as the various species of salt-marsh grass (e.g. *Puccinellia maritima*).

Dengie is now mainly renowned for its birds. A small wooden observatory stands on tall stilts just outside the sea-wall, providing an excellent viewpoint of the surrounding marshes. This is the Bradwell Bird Observatory, founded in 1954 and now run jointly by the Essex Wildlife Trust and the Essex Bird Watching and Preservation Society. Many types of wildfowl have been spotted here, including dunlin, knot and grey plover. This is also one of the best places in the country to see turnstone. Herons are common in the borrow-dykes, and the reedbeds also support smaller birds, such as reed warblers and reed buntings. Further out over the mudflats, brent geese can often be seen flocking in the winter to feed on the eel-grass (various *Zostera* species).

In 1971, the Shah of Iran held an international convention at his Ramsar palace to discuss wetlands around the world. In the Ramsar agreement, it was accepted that wetlands needed special protection because of their unique wildlife. Each nation agreed to set up a list of their most important sites, or "Ramsars" as they became known. The Dengie saltings are part of the Blackwater Flats Ramsar, one of the sites proposed by the British government.

This is all a far cry from the 19th century, when the marshes were viewed as a rich source of food. Wildfowlers spent many hours amongst the saltings, shooting large numbers of birds in order to supply the needs of the local villages. One of the last professional wildfowlers was Walter Linnett, who lived in a small black cottage just inside the sea-wall. He made his entire living with his punt and gun until he died in 1958. The wooden cottage, hidden amongst the trees, is now known as Linnett's Cottage in his memory.

Despite the dwindling number of wildfowlers, there has not been a corresponding increase in the number of birds. This is because man's modern developments have proved to be a far greater threat to wildlife than the old wildfowler's gun. In particular, intensive agriculture has destroyed many natural habitats. and sprawling towns and villages have swallowed up large chunks of countryside. Fortunately, the Dengie peninsula is not an attractive site for development, but it has suffered in other ways. From 1938 to the early 1960s, these marshes were used as a bombing range, and two tramways were even laid across the tidal mudflats. A series of brightly coloured pyramids were installed to guide planes to their targets. These red and yellow markers can still be seen today.

From St. Peter's Chapel, a footpath continues southwards along the sea-wall. Passing the last of the pill-boxes, the route then heads out into the middle of the wilderness. Until you reach the town of Burnham-on-Crouch, thirteen miles round the coastline, access to the sea-wall is very limited indeed. It is practical to reach the coastline in just two places – Grange Farm and Holliwell Farm. Visitors should therefore be prepared to walk long distances, and you are warned that the footpath can get quite overgrown.

This wilderness is sometimes known as the Dengie Marshes. The name dates back to at least 709 AD, when it was recorded as "Deningei". Some people have translated this as "forest-dwellers", whilst others believe that it may mean "island of Dene's people". The name was originally pronounced with a hard 'g', but a soft 'g' is now often used instead. Although rich in wildlife, the landscape has been radically altered by man. Until the sea-wall was built, this ground was rough marshland, inundated during only the highest of tides. During the Middle Ages, coastal marshes such as these were notoriously unhealthy and malaria was still rampant. After the construction of the first sea-defences, this disease slowly disappeared as the land dried out.

The marshes were not reclaimed in one go, however. The reclamation, or "inning" as it is sometimes known, was carried out over the centuries in a piecemeal fashion, typically 50 to 100 acres at a time. In order to "in" a strip of marshland, the landowner would need to build a new earth embankment along the seaward edge. The earth was obtained by digging a wide ditch nearby, often known as a borrow-dyke.

In this way, the Dengie peninsula has built up over the years as a series of long thin fields, each representing a single reclamation. Looking at a map, you can clearly see how the fields are separated by the old borrow-dykes, often aligned in a north-south direction.

About a mile from St. Peter's Chapel, there is a classic example of "inning". A new embankment was recently built across the saltings in order to reclaim a long rectangular area of marshland. In this instance, the old embankment is still in reasonably good condition, and indeed is still a public right of way. You therefore have a choice of routes. The new sea-wall is the true coastal footpath. It also offers better scenery, but the old embankment is slightly shorter in length, and this may be a important factor if you have a long walk ahead of you.

At the far end of this inning, the two routes meet again at Glebe Outfall, where a sluice passes through the sea-wall. This helps to drain the nearby farmland. At low tide, excess rainwater is allowed to flow through the sluice and along a deep muddy gully in the saltings. These saltings are hemmed in on both sides by recent innings, forming a large inlet almost completely enclosed by new sea-walls.

It is surprising to find military objects scattered around this inlet. The Ministry of Defence has taken advantage of the remoteness of this spot by erecting a collection of aerials in the middle of the saltings. If you look carefully, you may also find the remains of several barbed-wire supports, dating from the First World War. Another wartime structure stands on the mudflats nearby. This was used during the Second World War to launch missiles. It was originally built on the edge of the saltings, but most of this vegetation has since eroded away. As a result, the building now stands several yards out on the bare mudflats. In an attempt to halt this coastal erosion, a line of faggots has been laid across the mouth of the inlet. These wooden posts, sticking vertically out of the mud, are designed to slow down the tidal flow so that sediment has a chance to settle.

At the southern end of the inlet, a second sluice cuts through the sea-wall. This is known as Sandbeach Outfall, named after a nearby farm. Beyond this point, another area of marshland has been reclaimed, and as a result the embankment once again splits into two. If you continue in a straight line, you will miss most of the interesting scenery. This inning is nearly two miles long, and it is certainly worth turning left to follow the modern coastline.

As you reach the mouth of the inlet, the first thing you notice is another line of faggots heading away from the sea-wall. This time, the vertical posts are interwoven with small twigs in order to prevent sediment from being washed away. Further out to sea, just beyond the edge of the saltings, sixteen barges have been permanently moored to help slow down the erosion. The barges also provide undisturbed nesting sites for wildfowl.

In 1938, the army began to use the Dengie Flats as a bombing range. Some sources say that the wrecks of four boats were used as targets. From this point on the sea-wall, a tramway was built out across the tidal mudflats. About half a mile out from the shore, the tramway split into two branches, one in a north-easterly direction and the other heading south-east. The bombing stopped in the early 1960s, and the tramway has now completely disappeared. For posterity however, one section was rebuilt in the village nearby, in the playground of the local school.

Continuing southwards along the new inning, the raised embankment provides two contrasting views. Looking inland, featureless man-made fields cover the flat plain to the horizon. To the left, the mudflats and saltings carve out their own wild but natural scene. Meanwhile, the protective sea-wall stretches as far as the eye can see, not belonging to either of these environments, a sort of no-mans-land between these two distinct landscapes.

Just beyond the last of the moored barges, a small brick pumping-house has been built on the narrow strip of land between the sea-wall and the borrow-dyke. At one time, a small river flowed across the marshes at this point. A sluice, known as Hatsons Outfall, was built into the embankment to enable rainwater to drain off the fields.

To the north of the river, the last plot of marshland was probably reclaimed towards the end of the 19th century, and another area to the south was inned at around the same time. At first, the two innings were not joined together, and the river continued to flow along a narrow channel between the two. After many years, a dam was built across the mouth of this channel, thereby linking the two innings. This dam also has a sluice to drain the nearby fields, helped by the modern pumping-house. In this way, the old river has been reduced to just a drainage ditch, but it has not been forgotten – its original route still forms the boundary between the parishes of Bradwell and Tillingham.

Decoy ponds

The sluice is now known as Marshhouse Outfall, after the nearby farm of Marsh House. This farm has one of the oldest decoy ponds in Essex. The Marshhouse Decoy Pond was originally constructed around 1700, probably when the land was initially reclaimed. It was used to catch wildfowl until the early 1900s, and it is still in remarkably good condition. The pond lies on private land, but it is worth seeking permission for a special visit, for this is the best surviving example of a decoy pond in the county. You may find a few other decoy ponds still in working order scattered around the country, for example at the Slimbridge Wildfowl Trust in Gloucestershire, but these are usually maintained artificially for tourists.

Decoy ponds were built in a variety of shapes and sizes. Some ponds were as large as a hundred acres (half a mile across), but experience showed that smaller ponds were often more effective. The Marshhouse Decoy Pond is an average size at just over an acre in size (roughly 70 yards across). It was important to locate them in peaceful areas, away from villages and ploughed fields, so that the birds would not be disturbed. No shooting was allowed anywhere near a decoy pond because the sound of gunshot would frighten away the wildfowl.

To avoid disturbance, it was rare for anyone to see a working decoy pond other than the landowner and the decoyman himself. As a result, many descriptions of decoy ponds are wildly inaccurate. Furthermore, every decoyman had his own particular way of catching wildfowl. This book will try to strip away some of the myths, using Marshhouse Decoy to describe some of the techniques that were commonly used.

From the central pond, six offshoots lead away in different directions, like the spokes of a wheel. These offshoots, or "pipes" as they are properly known, are around 70 yards in length. Where they leave the central pond, they are around eight yards across, but they gradually narrow to a channel just a few feet wide. The whole pond is surrounded by tall reeds or rushes in order to shelter the birds. In some places, trees were also planted, particularly willow. Standing in the middle of bare marshland, the pond is clearly visible from the air, thereby attracting many passing birds. At Warmingford, north-west of Colchester, a decoy pond was built 12 miles from the sea, but most ponds were situated close to the coastline.

Wild birds came to feed at the pond, particularly around dawn and dusk. They were often attracted by tame ducks, or "decoy ducks" as they were known, that were bred in the neighbourhood. A screen was built around the pond itself, usually in the form of a fence, though sometimes a hedge was used instead. This screen enabled the decoyman to approach without being seen. It was important to approach from downwind so that the birds could not pick up the man's scent.

When enough birds had gathered on the pond, the decoyman would throw food to entice the tame ducks towards a pipe. As their confidence grew, a few of the wild birds would follow the decoy ducks into the pipe. Each of the six pipes was covered with a net, supported on large semi-circular hoops. Once inside the pipe, the wildfowl were effectively trapped. Indeed the word "decoy" itself probably derives from the old Dutch "de kooi", meaning "the trap or cage". It appears that the name "duck-coy" came over to Britain around the 17th century.

When a few wild birds had been enticed into a pipe, the decoyman would suddenly appear at a gap in the screen to scare the birds. The tame decoy ducks were quite accustomed to this, but the wild visitors would rise and try to fly away. Most birds take off into the wind, and therefore the decoyman would have to select the best pipe for the current wind direction. The birds would fly up the narrowing pipe, trying to escape the encroaching net. A curve in the pipe promised an escape, but inevitably the wildfowl would be trapped at the narrow end, where the decoyman would catch each poor bird and swiftly wring its neck.

The whole drive, catching as many as 50 birds at a time, could take as little as three minutes. If there were still plenty of birds on the central pond, the process could be repeated many times. Sometimes the decoyman would use a dog (known as "the piper") to entice birds into the net. The dog would appear at regular intervals up the pipe, and a few birds would follow through curiosity. This technique tended to trap hen birds, whilst cock birds were more attracted by food. In a few decoy ponds, a net was sprung suddenly into the path of oncoming birds. This was particularly successful at dusk, as the wildfowl left for the open marshes.

A day's take would typically be around 200 birds, although a good day would occasionally net over 1000. The numbers were extremely variable, depending on the wind, weather, time of day, and even the tide. The season ran from October to March, although it was difficult to operate a decoy pond in mid-winter, because the decoyman would only be able to break the frozen water at night, when there were no birds around to disturb.

At its peak, in the early 1800s, Marshhouse Decoy Pond managed to catch around 10,000 birds in the course of a single season. By 1900, this had dropped to about 2000 birds a year. Most of these consisted of wild geese, duck, teal and wigeon. Other common wildfowl included plover, curlew and dunlin (sometimes known as ox-birds or ox-peckers, although these names were often given to other birds as well). From time to time, the decoy pond would also trap tufted duck, pintail or pochard. The birds were mostly taken for sale at markets, such as Leadenhall Market in east London, but the prices would vary widely, depending on the season. A decoy pond was therefore an unreliable busines, and Marshhouse Decoy Pond stopped working in the early years of the 20th century.

Back on the sea-wall, the next stretch of coastline has few items of special interest, but the scenery is spectacularly wild. For a mile and a half, the sea-wall follows the eastern edge of a thin rectangular field. As you head further south, the saltings begin to build up, stretching further and further out to sea until eventually they extend for almost a mile across the mudflats. Looking inland, you can see another earth embankment running parallel with the coastline, just two hundred yards away. This embankment was the original coastline until this strip of marshland was reclaimed. Half-way along this field, a rough track heads inland across the Tillingham Marshes. The track leads to the farm buildings of Marsh House, but unfortunately it is not a public right of way.

If ever you want to escape from it all and find peace and quiet, this is the place to go. The Dengie peninsula guarantees solitude, and the cry of wild geese is in perfect contrast to the hectic congestion of the nearby towns. Because of the flat nature of the marshes, the wind blows uninterrupted across the landscape, carrying with it the fresh smell of the sea. The footpath can get quite overgrown, but the endless miles of sea-wall are a perfect way to exercise your body, clean your lungs and clear your mind.

At the southern end of the inning, you suddenly reach a sharp corner in the sea-wall, near the rotting remains of a wooden bird observatory. Turning right past an old wartime pill-box, the sea-wall soon rejoins its original course at Howe Outfall. As its name suggests, there is a sluice here, allowing water to drain off the fields and into the saltings. Incidentally, there is evidence amongst these saltings that land reclamation is not always a one-way process – sometimes the sea wins the battle, as demonstrated by some abandoned sea-walls nearby.

Grange Farm

At one time, a track led inland from Howe Outfall to the buildings of Howe Farm (originally known as Hoo Farm). The track disappeared a long time ago, but a public right of way heads inland just three hundred yards further on. This footpath leads to both Howe Farm and Grange Farm, providing the first useful access to the coastline since St. Peter's Chapel. However, the nearest road is still more than a mile and a half inland.

A second outfall lies a little further ahead, just beyond a bend in the sea-wall. This was once known as Potten Outfall, although it is now usually called Grange Outfall, after the nearby Grange Farm. This drains the largest watercourse around the Dengie coastline, a deep stream known as Asheldham Brook. The brook starts its life near the village of Althorne, seven miles inland, before snaking its way across the flat coastal plain. After heavy rain, the water-level in Asheldham Brook can rise dangerously fast. As a precaution against flooding, tall earth embankments have been built along its banks for the last few miles.

Until recently, a decoy pond stood close to the sea-wall here. Known as Grange Farm Decoy, it covered just over an acre and had six pipes. In an average year, the pond trapped almost 2000 wildfowl, mostly wigeon. In a single season however, it was occasionally known to exceed 10,000 birds. Grange Farm Decoy fell into disuse in the early 1900s, although aerial photos show that the pipes still had their hoops in 1957. Unfortunately, the pond has now been filled in, and all traces of its existence have gone.

There then follows another long lonely stretch of sea-wall. According to one old map, a track used to head out across the saltings, stretching for almost a mile to the edge of the mudflats. This track was probably used by wildfowlers, but it too has now disappeared. About twenty minutes' walk from Grange Outfall, you cross an unmarked boundary separating the parish of Tillingham from its neighbour, Dengie parish.

Eventually you meet a sharp bend in the sea-wall. Before this next piece of land was reclaimed, the coastline turned right here – you can still see the original borrow-dyke heading off inland. This was once the site of the Tillingham Coastguard Station, although boats could only be launched at high water. As the tide dropped, an enormous expanse of mud was exposed. The Ray Sands, as they were known, stretched two miles out from the coastguard station. Another tidal mudbank lies a little further out to sea. With only a narrow channel of water separating the two, this was a dangerous area for shipping. As a result, the Ray Sand Beacon was established at the low-water mark over a hundred years ago.

The sea-wall turns another sharp corner just a hundred yards further on, at a spot known as Bridgewick Outfall. As its name suggests, there is another sluice here, with a small pumping-house alongside. Getting its name from the nearest farm, Bridgewick is the sixth outfall along the Dengie peninsula. This long walk is renowned for its remoteness and seclusion, not for dramatic scenery, but it is helpful to have some features to aim for, if only to spur on weary walkers. The outfalls fit this category perfectly, as well as serving an important purpose for local farmers. The last of the seven working outfalls is known as Coate Outfall, almost a mile further south. Like most of the others, it too is named after a farm nearby, although Coate Farm has now changed its spelling to Court Farm.

Shortly after Coate Outfall, you reach the last of the new innings. An old embankment heads inland for a short distance, following the parish boundary for a short while. By this stage, the main sea-wall has been capped with a layer of concrete. This enables very fast progress to be made, but the hard surface can be very tiring on the feet.

Along most of the Dengie peninsula, saltings stretch out across the mudflats for quite a distance, but as you approach the mouth of the River Crouch, the saltings gradually dwindle away. Just beyond Coate Outfall, they disappear altogether, leaving the waves to lap directly against the sea-wall. These leads to increased erosion, and great efforts have been made to protect the sea-defences here. Lines of faggots have been laid out across the mudflats, comprising one of the largest such experiments around the Essex coastline.

Half-way along the faggots, the sea-wall swerves slightly to the left. This inconspicuous bend, now known as Shell Bank, was the site of Buxey Outfall. It is arguably the remotest point along the whole of the Dengie coastline. As the crow flies, it is around four miles to the nearest village, although it is much further if you follow public tracks and footpaths. At one time, the buildings of New Barn and Watch House stood near the sea-wall here, but these have now been demolished. Today, the nearest house is a mile and a half away.

Holliwell Point

Beyond the faggots, the sea-wall begins to curve gently round to the right, entering the mouth of the River Crouch. Passing a series of groynes, you eventually reach Holliwell Point, a sharp corner where a couple of pill-boxes have been embedded into the sea-wall within yards of each other. Looking across the estuary from this point, the military island of Foulness offers a tantalising glimpse of mysterious buildings. If you look carefully, you should be able to spot the spire of the island's church, almost hidden amongst a clump of trees. Several hundred people live on Foulness, but the island is usually closed to the general public because of its military installations.

The Dengie peninsula is bounded on its north and south sides by two major Essex rivers, the Blackwater and the Crouch. A sharp point stands at the mouth of each estuary, marking the transition between sheltered river and open sea. At the northern corner, Sales Point is popular and relatively busy. In contrast, Holliwell Point, nine miles further on, is remote and usually deserted. Nevertheless, it is an important milestone along this walk. Beyond Holliwell Point, the footpath leaves behind the open sea with its endless horizon, and instead begins the long trek up the River Crouch.

At first, the sea-wall heads around a large inlet of saltings, the first for several miles. On old maps, this is marked as Lubbers Hole, although this name has now fallen out of use. At the head of the inlet, you pass a third pill-box. On the Dengie peninsula, you could determine your progress by counting the outfalls. Along the next stretch of sea-wall, pill-boxes seem to act as milestones in a similar way. Between Holliwell Point and Burnham-on-Crouch, you pass eight of these wartime relics, and this is therefore a good opportunity to discuss them in more detail.

Pill-boxes

Pill-boxes were originally used during the First World War for defensive purposes around Europe. The early structures were mostly circular, which explains their name. However, some pill-boxes had a hexagonal shape, particularly in the Thames and Medway area. Only a few have survived to the present day, predominantly around Norfolk and Suffolk.

During the early stages of the Second World War, the War Office introduced various schemes to protect Britain against the growing threat of invasion. These included the re-introduction of pill-boxes, under the control of the Fortification & Works (FW) office. In June 1940, a department called FW3 was given the task of coming up with a series of designs, each suitable for a different type of terrain. Many of these designs were hexagonal in shape, because they were easy to construct and offered a strong and safe structure. Around the Kent and Essex coastline, the most popular type was the FW3/22, often known simply as the "type 22".

Over the next six months, over 5000 pill-boxes were built around the British Isles. These stretched from the Isles of Scilly to the northern tip of Scotland, although the south-east of England required the strongest defence due to its proximity to Europe. By embedding many of the pill-boxes into the sea-wall, a "coastal crust" was set up around this corner of the country. Fortunately, the threatened invasion never took place and very few of the pill-boxes saw active service. Nevertheless, they were so strongly built that it proved very difficult to demolish them after the war, and it is a testment to the people working at FW3 that almost all of their structures are still standing today.

Continuing around the inlet of Lubbers Hole, you come across the fourth pill-box near the far end of the bay. Accompanying it just a few yards inland, an old wartime tower stands in the middle of a field. In order to see over the sea-wall, this imposing concrete structure was built several stories high. At the top of the tower, narrow slits enabled soldiers to keep a look-out from behind its thick protective walls.

The walk along this stretch of the River Crouch is very typical of the Essex coastline. The sea-wall is tall and has a wide footpath along its crest, mostly covered with short grass. This is very easy on the feet, and allows fast progress to be made along the shoreline. A narrow borrow-dyke follows the sea-wall for most of its length, and enormous fields stretch across the flat plain into the distance. Maps of this district show not a single contour line in any direction for over four miles, and it can be quite an eerie feeling to experience this flat landscape for the first time. If you visit the area at high tide, you will also notice that the fields are considerably lower than the high-water level. During the devastating storms of 1895 and 1953, the local farmers suffered badly from the effects of flooding.

Looking in the other direction, disused oyster-beds line the edge of the saltings, their remains eroding away with each tide. On the far side of the river, strange military buildings can be seen on the island of Foulness. The inhabitants of Foulness lead a curious but peaceful existence, cut off from the rest of the country, and this closed island therefore holds a curious attraction to outsiders.

Before the military arrived in the early 1900s, Foulness was an extremely remote community, without even a bridge to the mainland. Ferries formed an important link with the outside world, and one of these operated across the river here during the 19th century. Leaving from a jetty known as Holver Stage, the boat crossed the River Crouch and led to a sharp promontary opposite called Crouch Corner.

Holliwell Farm

Shortly after the next pill-box, a good track heads inland towards Holliwell Farm, eventually leading to the main road beyond. This track is also a public right of way, providing the first useful access to the coastline since Grange Farm, almost six miles earlier. For many visitors, Holliwell Farm will mark the end of one of the longest and most remote walks around the Essex coastline. You are also warned that, at both Grange

Farm and Holliwell, you are not allowed to drive right down to the sea-wall. Car-owners should therefore plan for an extra mile of walking at either end of the walk.

From Holliwell Farm, it is just over three miles to the outskirts of Burnham-on-Crouch. This is a very pleasant riverside walk, with the scenery gradually changing from remote countryside to suburban sprawl. At first, the sea-wall makes a series of wild zigzags, with saltings in each of the inlets. During the 19th century, many of these saltings were used for cultivating oysters, and you can still see the rectangular remains of oyster-beds in a few places. At the tip of a gentle promontary, a pill-box marks the site of another ferry across the River Crouch. This led to a slipway on Foulness called Clark's Hard. No boats have run for about one hundred years, but Clark's Hard is still marked on Ordnance Survey maps as a public right of way, even though the public is generally excluded from Foulness.

There then follows a long lonely stretch of sea-wall. Even the pill-boxes seem to have deserted us, the next lying more than two miles away. Old maps show that several farmhouses used to stand near the coastline here, including buildings called Coleward and Pilehouse, but these have now disappeared as well. However the grassy surface is a pleasure to walk on, and the feeling of remote wilderness is gradually left behind.

The sea-wall also provides an excellent view of the creek that separates Foulness from its neighbouring island, Wallasea. This creek, known as Brankfleet, is regularly used as a short-cut to the River Thames. When the nearby military firing range is in operation, boats have to make a long detour around the Whitaker Beacon, many miles out to sea. But when the guns are silent, usually at weekends, sailors can cut many hours off their journey by navigating the sheltered creeks through to Havengore Bridge. At these times, Brankfleet becomes a busy throughway, and the final few miles of this walk pass a queue of brightly coloured yachts.

Recommended bibliography:

Some mesolithic sites along the rivers Blackwater and Crouch – S. Vincent
Some prehistoric sites along the rivers Blackwater and Crouch – S. Vincent
The book of Maldon – Ian Linton
Down the Chelmer and up the Blackwater – Vernon Clarke
The salty shore – John Leather
St. Peter's Way – Fred Matthews and Harry Bitten
Dengie : the life and the land – Kevin Bruce

Chapter five – the Rivers Crouch and Roach

At first sight, many people may consider this chapter to be a little unusual. In a book devoted to the Essex coastline, this chapter hardly describes any coastline at all. In fact, only about one mile of sea-wall actually looks out over the open sea. Instead, we head a little inland, covering the area around the River Crouch and the River Roach. Throughout this book, each river is covered as far as its tidal limit. The River Crouch is tidal for nearly twenty miles, one of the longest rivers around the Essex coastline. With a right of way almost continuous along both banks, there are plenty of excellent walks to choose from. The River Roach is only eight miles long, but this smaller tributary still has many points of interest.

There is a wide variety of scenery along the banks of both rivers, and each stretch has its own unique atmosphere. Near the mouth of the River Crouch, for example, the popular yachting venue of Burnham-on-Crouch overlooks a wide and busy expanse of water, and yet further upstream near Battlesbridge, the river is often deserted.

The Crouch runs through a shallow valley and is surrounded by a ring of low hills. At their highest point, these hills only reach 160 feet above sea-level, yet they are amongst the highest around the Essex coastline. This undulating landscape is well worth exploring, particularly near the villages of Althorne and Canewdon.

Down by the riverside, a large amount of low-lying land has been reclaimed from the sea. Over the centuries, the water-level has risen steadily, and strong embankments have been built to withstand the tide. However, man's efforts to hold back the sea have not always been successful. Along some stretches of the river, the embankments have been breached by vicious storms, and the sea has broken in and flooded large tracts of farmland. The farmers often abandoned the inundated land and retreated, building a new sea-wall further inland. In this way, the river-banks have changed frequently over the years. Despite the endeavours of many authorities, the battle against the sea continues today.

One of the best examples of abandoned land is at North Fambridge, although there are plenty of other sites up and down the river. The inlet at Brandy Hole is also well worth a visit. This inlet has some beautiful scenery, and is usually much quieter. These areas of lost farmland are always interesting to explore, although the lie of the land can sometimes be rather confusing without a detailed map.

In contrast to the rather hilly nature of the River Crouch, the River Roach flows through relatively flat landscape. Indeed. the Roach has a different atmosphere to its larger neighbour. It appears to flow aimlessly through the countryside, in no hurry to reach the open sea. There are several hidden inlets, and the walk along its northern shore is a well-kept secret.

The village of Paglesham Eastend, on the other hand, is a popular venue, particularly at weekends. During the summer, car-owners may find it difficult to park here. The village is renowned for its oysters, although this industry declined dramatically in the early 1900s. Many visitors walk down the lane to the riverside at

Paglesham, but very few people stray more than a few hundred yards from the boat-yard. For those who prefer a slightly longer stroll, there are excellent walks along the sea-wall in both directions, and you can even return by a different route inland.

Just downstream from Paglesham, the Roach and the Crouch flow along opposite sides of a large island called Wallasea. This island is utterly flat, with large sea-walls to keep out the tide. Wallasea is now almost exclusively used for growing crops, and it is a strange experience to gaze across miles and miles of endless fields, with no buildings or trees to break the view.

Wallasea is actually only one of a series of islands, collectively known as the South-East Essex Archipelago. This type of archipelago is unique to Essex, and it therefore has a special chapter of its own, later in the book. However, Wallasea is the only island in the group that is open the public, and it has therefore been included in this chapter.

The final part of this chapter describes the network of creeks that link the River Roach to the Thames Estuary. These hidden backwaters contain some of the most beautiful scenery anywhere around the Essex coastline. The geography can be confusing at time, so a good map is essential. In this corner of the county, the MOD is never far away. The last couple of miles in this chapter are actually inside a live military range, and are only open to the public when firing is not taking place.

Despite the difficulty of access, these narrow creeks are well worth exploring, and have many fascinating items of interest. The footpaths are generally in very good condition, and places like Little Wakering Creek and Wakering Stairs are deservedly popular in the summer. A walk along any of these sea-walls is strongly recommended, particularly in the winter months when the tidal mudflats teem with wildfowl.

Burnham-on-Crouch

The footpath reaches the town of Burnham-on-Crouch at the end of a back-street known as Belvedere Road. The name of the town is believed to come from the Old English "burna ham", which roughly translates as "homestead by the stream". This was not a reference to the River Crouch however, because the original settlement of Burnham was centred around a small stream nearly a mile inland. By 1840, old maps show that a separate village was growing up on the banks of the River Crouch, and this became known as "Burnham-on-Crouch" in order to distinguish it from its older neighbour. As the two communities expanded and eventually merged, the name "Burnham-on-Crouch" was used to describe the whole of the town.

As you enter the town, one of the first things to catch your attention is a prominent white building just outside the sea-wall. Overlooking the river, this tall box-like structure is home to the Royal Corinthian Yacht Club. This was founded towards the end of the 19th century. The town's other main yachting institution, the Royal Burnham Yacht Club, has its headquarters just a few hundred yards along the river-front.

Burnham-on-Crouch is renowned as a popular yachting venue, with hundreds of boats moored out in the river. A famous regatta is held every year during Burnham Week, usually the last week in August. The town has always had strong nautical connections, and is home to many small sailing clubs and yachting chandlers. Unfortunately the boat-yards now employ only a handful of people. Many of the inhabitants of Burnham-on-Crouch have jobs in the nearby town of Colchester, driving to work every day along the winding B1010 road.

During the 19th century, the oyster industry was an important source of local employment. In 1865, for example, one hundred men were involved in the cultivation of oysters along the River Crouch, mostly near Burnham, and many more people worked nearby along the River Roach and its tributaries. Although the oyster industry fell into decline many years ago, the town is still full of kiosks selling other types of seafood.

From the headquarters of the Royal Corinthian Yacht Club, with its large floating pontoon, the coastal route follows the river-front and soon emerges onto The Quay, a narrow back-street just off the main High Street. During the summer months, this is the landing-stage for a ferry to Wallasea Island. The boat originally led to Overland Point, a small promontary almost directly across the river from Burnham-on-Crouch. After the Second World War, most of the farms on Wallasea Island were demolished and the ferry was therefore diverted.

Burnham-on-Crouch is only a small town, and after passing the end of Coronation Road, the footpath soon heads out into open countryside again. However, just a short distance from the town, a large new marina has recently been built, and you therefore have to make a long detour inland around its edge. From the top of the sea-wall, you get a good view of Wallasea Island on the opposite bank of the River Crouch. This stretch of the river, known as Whale Shoal, is well sheltered from the North Sea storms and is therefore a popular mooring site for yachts. When the tide is out, you can see the remains of two stone causeways or "hards" leading out from the sea-wall towards deep water. These enabled sailors to reach their boats at low tide without having to wade through deep mud.

About a mile out of town, the footpath heads inland around the edge of a small inlet. During the 19th century, a series of oyster-beds were dug out of the saltings here. At that time, the cultivation of oysters formed one of the largest industries in these remote marshland villages, and the remains of their oyster-beds can be seen in many places along the River Crouch.

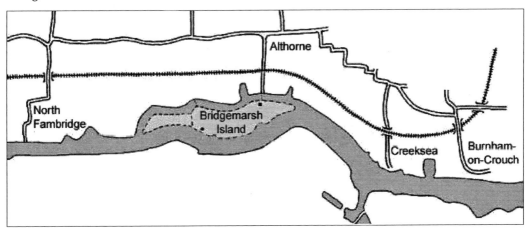

Creeksea

The coastal footpath is now approaching the tiny village of Creeksea. Around the Essex coastline, the suffix "-sea" in a place-name usually refers to an island (as in Wallasea nearby), but the name of Creeksea is instead believed to be a corruption of "creek hyth". A hyth is an Old English word for a landing place or quay, and is still in use in Colchester and Maldon. It has also been suggested that Creeksea gave its name to the River Crouch, although other sources say that the river's name is derived from the Middle English word "crouche", meaning a cross.

Whatever its derivation, the village of Creeksea dates back at least one thousand years. It was recorded in the Domesday Book in 1086 as Criccheseia, and is even claimed to be the site where King Canute attempted to turn back the tide (although many other coastal villages have made the same claim, such as Bosham in Sussex).

As you approach Creeksea from the river-front, the first building you encounter is called The White House, nestling in front of a row of trees. The building was originally known as The Ferry House, because a popular ferry service used to run across the River Crouch at this point to Wallasea Island. This ferry, which should not be confused with the Burnham-on-Crouch ferry to Wallasea Island, is mentioned as far back as 1625. At one time, you could summon the ferryman by ringing a bell which was attached to a post by the riverside. Unfortunately, the ferry stopped running in 1962. However, the narrow lane which leads down to the water's edge is still known as Ferry Road, and on the opposite bank there is still an old road-sign near Canewdon which indicates the original route to Creeksea via the ferry.

During the 19th century, while the ferry was running, an old half-timbered Tudor cottage was converted into a pub, probably obtaining much of its supplies through illegal smuggling operations. The Greyhound Inn, as it was known, ceased trading some time around 1900, but during extensive restoration work in 1929, a secret smugglers' den was uncovered.

Today, the riverside at Creeksea is peaceful and undisturbed, with only a single narrow lane leading up the hill to the main Burnham-on-Crouch road. This road passes the buildings of Creeksea Hall, partly dating from the 13th century. However, this village could have looked so different if plans in 1901 for a Southend to Colchester railway had gone ahead. It was proposed that a new railway-line from Southend to Wallasea would connect with a steam ferry across the River Crouch to Creeksea. A second new railway-line would then take passengers on to Bradwell where another steam ferry would cross the water to West Mersea. A third stretch of railway-line would then complete the journey to Colchester. Not surprisingly, this ambitious scheme was soon dropped.

From the old ferry hard at Creeksea, the right of way heads inland for a short distance, following the road away from the shoreline. However, after just a hundred yards, a footpath leaves the road to the left. This leads past a small building called Tideway and quickly returns to the sea-wall again. The scenery is typical of the Essex coastline, with high sea-walls providing a wide view over the surrounding landscape, and a low ridge of hills just a short distance inland on both banks of the river. Incidentally, it is at this point that the two Ordnance Survey "Explorer" maps begin to overlap – 176 (Blackwater Estuary) and 175 (Southend-on-Sea & Basildon). Once you reach North Fambridge, six miles further on, you will need to switch over to map 175.

Although this stretch of the river was originally called Birch Reach, it is now usually referred to as Cliff Reach. The reason for this unusual name is not clear from the Ordnance Survey's "Landranger" map, but is abundantly obvious as you walk along the river. Just over half a mile out of Creeksea, the sea-wall is replaced by a tall sandstone cliff, a feature you would not expect to find in this low-lying marshland. The Butly Cliff, as it was once known, was formed as the river gradually eroded its way through a low ridge, an offshoot of the main hills nearby. The right of way technically follows the top of the cliff, although at low tide it is much more interesting to walk along the beach below.

Leaving the cliff behind, the footpath resumes its usual course along the crest of a tall sea-wall. A railway-line runs quite close to the river at this point. Opened in 1889, this quiet branch line runs from Southminster to Wickford, where it connects with the main line. The Ordnance Survey map shows a small track leading inland from the sea-wall to a level-crossing. Beyond the railway, this track passes Stoke's Hall Farm on its way up the hill to the main road, but unfortunately it is not a right of way.

Bridgemarsh Island

Looking ahead, you can see the remains of Bridgemarsh Island in the middle of the river. Straddling the parishes of Latchingdon and Althorne, the island is now uninhabited and abandoned, but it once boasted its own farms and even a small brickworks. It is not known when the island was first occupied, but its earliest record refers to a flood in 1736 which washed away parts of its sea-defences, a problem which has dogged the island throughout its history.

The first detailed map of Essex was published by Chapman and André in 1777, and this clearly shows that the sea-defences around the central portion of Bridgemarsh Island had been repaired. Shortly after this map was produced, the island was enlarged by constructing a new sea-wall to the east, thereby providing another hundred acres of grazing land. A tidal ford was built across the creek to this new eastern section, and a large farmhouse was constructed just inside the sea-defences. Some remains of the farmhouse can still be seen today.

Around 1850, the island was extended to the west. This new part of the island, known as Raypits Marsh, quickly built up its own community, with its own shop and even a small school. As well as farming, many of the islanders made their livelihood at a new brick and tile works. The bricks were carried along a short tramway to a wharf where sailing barges could moor. You can still clearly see the remains of one of the chimneys.

In its heyday, Bridgemarsh Island had five wharves. Three of these were in the small creek to the north, and the other two were in the main deep-water channel, enabling large vessels to moor up. However, the brickworks soon closed, and the island fell into decline around 1900. In 1917, the island was put up for sale. It remained on the market for several years until the Bower family finally purchased it in 1920. They sold it almost immediately to the Harrison family.

Unfortunately the new owners failed to keep the sea-defences in proper repair, and many of the embankments were washed away during a very high tide in 1928. Because of the economic recession, the cost of repairing the damage was too high, and the island was abandoned to the tides. The carefully nurtured farmland gradually reverted to rough saltings, and subsequent storms destroyed more of the sea-walls. Indeed, after the 1953 floods, mud and clay were actually removed from the island in order to repair a major breach in the sea-wall on the opposite bank of the River Crouch, near the farm of Norpits.

In 1956, Bridgemarsh Island was designated as a Site of Special Scientific Interest (SSSI), and it was leased in 1960 to a wildfowling trust called the Bridgemarsh Island Trust. Three years later, they bought the island outright. The island now forms one of the largest continuous areas of salt-marsh in Essex, and is an important site for birds such as teal, redshank and brent geese. As a result, the salt-marshes are carefully protected from outside disturbance, and visitors to the island are strongly discouraged. A rough footpath is still maintained across the island for the wardens, but two piles of bricks are all that is left to remind people that this desolate marshland was once inhabited.

The River Crouch divides into two channels either side of Bridgemarsh Island. The main deep-water channel runs to the south of the island, whilst a much narrower creek winds its way around the northern edge. This smaller offshoot is Althorne Creek, named after the village of Althorne at the top of the hill. As you follow the shores of Althorne Creek, a small inlet forces the sea-wall to make a small detour. A public right of way leads from this inlet up the hill, but there is a much better access-point just half a mile further on, past a row of disused oyster-beds.

Althorne

Bridgemarsh Road provides the only access to the sea-wall for several miles, but if you drive right down to the sea-wall, you will probably find it difficult to park. This is because a boat-yard, Bridgemarsh Marine, has taken up most of the space along the river's edge. Most people therefore leave their cars at Althorne railway station. From the level-crossing there, it is about ten minutes' walk to the sea-wall.

At the end of the road, an old ford crosses Althorne Creek. This used to be the main route to the farm buildings on Bridgemarsh Island. You can still see a few remains of one of the buildings across the creek. The ford has not been in regular use for almost seventy years, and is no longer passable, although it is still clearly visible at low tide.

Leaving Bridgemarsh Marine behind, the sea-wall passes a collection of small chalets before making another small diversion inland. This inlet marks the boundary between the parishes of Althorne and Latchingdon. If you look carefully at the saltings here, you will find the remains of a few oyster-beds. The footpath then heads out into open countryside once more. There are no more roads, farms or buildings of any kind until you reach North Fambridge, more than four miles to the west, although the silence is occasionally broken by the sound of a nearby train on its way to Burnham-on-Crouch.

For the first mile or so, the sea-wall offers good views of Bridgemarsh Island. On the far side of the island, you can just make out the remains of a chimney. This was originally part of a small brick and tile works, one of many around the Essex coastline. The geology of the county consists almost entirely of thick clay, and therefore stone for buildings was in relatively short supply. Local communities had to manufacture their own building materials, until improvements in railways and roads enabled stone to be brought in from outside. One of the most popular imports was ragstone from Kent, known generally as Kentish rag. This was often used as a facing for sea-walls.

The brick and tile works, built on a part of the island called Raypits Marsh, had its own jetty in the main channel of the River Crouch. Goods were carried to waiting barges via a short tramway. Old maps also indicate that there were several farms at this end of the island. The main access route onto Bridgemarsh Island, as we have already seen, was over a mile away, near the buildings of Bridgemarsh Farm, but the workers on this remote western end had their own separate route onto the island.

Detailed Ordnance Survey maps show the remains of an old track on the mainland heading down the hill from Stamfords Farm towards the sea-wall. This originally led to a ford across Althorne Creek, aiming for the nearest point on the island. At low tide, the ford is still just visible if you keep a careful look-out when the sea-wall begins to turn to the left. If you have suitable footwear, walk out across the mud to the edge of the creek, where two lines of wooden stakes can still be seen. Unfortunately this ford, like its main counterpart to the east, is no longer passable.

Almost immediately after the site of the old ford, a series of groynes project out from the sea-wall across the mudflats. These were built as part of a government-funded experiment in coastal protection. Along this stretch of the walk, the name of the creek changes from Althorne Creek to Bridgemarsh Creek. Continuing along the coastline, you eventually reach the western tip of Bridgemarsh Island, where the creek finally rejoins the main channel of the River Crouch.

Originally, Bridgemarsh Creek itself had a small tributary, but it was dammed more than a hundred years ago. It is still in water, however, and you can see its narrow channel snaking away inland about half a mile behind the sea-wall. Two large embankments follow a parallel course, one on either side of the channel. These eventually join up again at an older dam, half a mile inland. An old map drawn up in 1768 shows only this older dam, and therefore these embankments effectively formed the coastline at that time. It also shows a farm along the northern edge of this tributary. Known originally as Bluemarsh, and later as Hydemarsh, this farm probably used the tributary as a means of transport. The buildings were finally pulled down about thirty years ago, but the track that once led to the farm is still in existence today, heading down the hill from Ulehams Farm and across the railway near a small barn.

Beyond the tributary, the sea-wall finally reaches the main channel of the River Crouch again. Turning the corner, you begin to leave Bridgemarsh Island behind, with the high sea-wall providing a marvellous last view of the island. This part of the mainland, known as Cuckow Marsh, was originally a thin peninsula, until the new dam was built across the mouth of the tributary nearby.

As with Bridgemarsh Island, there is plenty of evidence here that land can be lost to the sea, as well as reclaimed. Along this next stretch of the river, known locally as Longpole Reach, there are three places where a new sea-wall has had to be built after the original defences were swept away. The first instance appears almost immediately after you turn the corner onto the River Crouch, but the next two instances are much larger, forcing long detours inland. In each case, you can still see lines of wooden stakes marking the original route of the coastline.

At the last of these detours, the footpath leaves the parish of Latchingdon and enters the parish of North Fambridge. With a collection of moored boats ahead, it is clear that you are approaching civilisation again. Local maps indicate a public right of way heading inland from the sea-wall, but it is better to push on to the main road, a few hundred yards ahead.

North Fambridge

The twin villages of North Fambridge and South Fambridge are situated on opposite banks of the River Crouch. They are recorded in the Domesday Book in 1086 as both Fanbruge and Phenbruge. The name is said to mean "bridge over the foam", from the old English word "fam" meaning foam or froth. In 1066, a bridge across the river connected the two villages. The bridge had two spans, making use of a mudbank in the centre of the river. The bridge had gone by 1625, but a regular ferry had taken its place. The Fambridge ferry operated until just after the Second World War, and the road leading to the riverside is still known as Ferry Road.

The name is also maintained in the nearby Ferry Boat Inn, which dates from the 15th century and is said to be haunted by a ferryman. The most famous tale of the village, however, is based on the story of Thomas Cammocke, a servant of the third Lord Riche, who fell in love with Lord Riche's sister Frances. The lord disapproved, according to the story, and the couple decided to elope. As they fled on horseback, Lord Riche began to give chase. The couple reached North Fambridge, but the ferry happened to be on the wrong side of the river. Seeing that Lord Riche was rapidly catching up with them, the couple rode out into the deep water and managed to reach the far bank safely. Upon this act of courage, Lord Riche relented and gave his blessing to the marriage, saying: *"Seeing she has ventured her life for him, God bless them!"*

Along the riverside, there is a large floating pontoon enabling boats to moor up at all states of the tide. The North Fambridge Yacht Station dates back to the 1890s, although it was sold in 1981 to the owners of the nearby boat-yard at West Wick. The road leads right down to the water's edge, but the last two hundred yards are very low-lying and susceptible to flooding. A small embankment runs parallel to the road, enabling walkers to reach the main sea-wall at all times, but car owners are strongly advised not to park beyond the pub around the time of high tide.

Beyond Fambridge, the character of the river begins to change quite radically. Until this point, a range of low hills has confined the River Crouch into a single channel, with no major tributaries and clearly delineated river-banks. For the next few miles however, the hills die away, enabling the river to branch out into a series of major creeks and inlets.

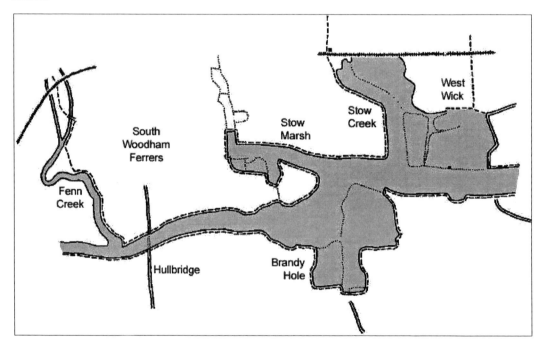

The low-lying nature of the land has also made it susceptible to flooding. From the riverside at Fambridge, you can see one of the areas of farmland that has been abandoned. This sea-wall was finally breached during the severe floods of 1897. Old maps show that a number of smaller embankments had been built further inland before that date, which suggests that flooding had been a problem during the 19th century. This marsh has now been designated as a Site of Special Scientific Interest (SSSI), and a large brackish pond has been built near the West Wick boat-yard to provide a habitat for winter wildfowl.

The remains of the original sea-wall are still clearly visible. Some stretches are still in a relatively good condition, although there is a major breach near the road-end. Some time around 1950, a small single-storey cottage was built on one of these remaining stretches of sea-wall. Known as Port Moor Cottage, this private building provides

Saltings near West Wick,
showing classic signs of old ridge and furrow

beautiful views across both the marshes and the open river. It is remarkably isolated, and can only be reached by boat.

Unfortunately, the breached sea-wall also means that walkers have to divert inland at North Fambridge. This is the end of the longest uninterrupted footpath around the Essex coastline. If you discount a small industrial estate on the outskirts of Maldon and a minor diversion near Stansgate Abbey Farm, the public right of way runs uninterrupted for over sixty miles from the village of Salcott-cum-Virley, near Colchester, around the estuary of the River Blackwater and the Dengie peninsula.

The diversion inland brings a welcome change in the landscape. Until this point, the walk along the River Crouch has involved long stretches of rural sea-wall, and the points of access to the coastline are often many miles apart. From North Fambridge to the tidal limit, the scenery is much more diverse, with farms generally much closer to the riverside. This means that the sea-wall is more accessible, and hence it is possible to divide the walk up into much shorter sections.

From the floating pontoon at North Fambridge, walkers will first have to follow the road back into the village. In the centre of the village, the main road turns off to the right to head back up the hill. This route eventually leads back to the main road from South Woodham Ferrers to Althorne. Alternatively, there is a public footpath across the fields if you turn left instead. This footpath reaches a level-crossing over the railway before heading westwards past The Old Rectory. It then heads up the hill past the buildings of Rookery Farm to rejoin the main road. If you are using the Ordnance Survey's more detailed 1:25,000 "Explorer" maps, you will need to ensure that you have map 175 (Southend-on-Sea & Basildon) to follow the next stretch of the coastal route.

At the beginning of this footpath, you will see signs pointing to the West Wick boat-yard, named after West Wick Farm which used to stand on the coastline at this point. The word "wick" was the name given by the Anglo-Saxons to any type of dairy farm. Around the Essex coastline, it usually referred to a farm that made cheese from sheep's milk.

At one time, a track led across the fields from West Wick Farm to Groom's Farm nearby. This land was devastated in the 1897 floods, and it is only recently that it has been restored properly. In 1972, a new stretch of sea-wall was built to link the boat-yard with the nearby railway embankment, which now doubles as the sea-wall. A small concrete munitions barge, which had been beached on the shoreline here after the Second World War, has now been left curiously stranded inside the new sea-wall. The construction of the new sea-defences should have enabled part of the coastal footpath to be re-opened, but unfortunately the local landowners still vigorously keep trespassers away.

To reach the sea-wall again after the diversion, look out for a small lane called Little Hayes Chase. This leaves the main road shortly after a couple of sharp bends. The lane heads down the hill towards Litle Hayes Farm. Drivers should park their cars just before the first of the farm buildings. A public footpath leads through the farmyard to a level-crossing over the railway-line. This side-line was opened in 1889, linking the towns of Southminster and Burnham-on-Crouch to the main railway-line at Wickford.

Beyond the level-crossing, a track leads across the corner of a field and towards the sea-wall. As you climb to the top, a large marshy inlet comes into view. At high tide, it appears almost like a wide lake, with the boats of West Wick marina visible near the far shore. As the waters recede, however, a myriad of narrow muddy channels are uncovered. This is the head of Stow Creek, a short offshoot of the River Crouch, whose enclosing sea-walls were washed away in the severe floods of 1897.

To the left, the sea-wall wanders around the head of the creek before merging with the railway embankment. You can still see some remains of the old sea-wall along the creek's east bank, but it has been breached in many places and is now only walkable for the first few yards. It is worth a short detour, however, for the views of the flooded marshland beyond. Where there was once a large area of arable farmland, saltings have now taken over, but rows of ditches still indicate the layout of the original fields about a hundred years ago. If you look carefully, you can also find the remains of a few bridges across the ditches.

From the head of Stow Creek, there is a public right of way past the buildings of Marsh Farm to the sea-wall. From here, an excellent path follows the crest of the sea-wall for nearly a mile until the creek rejoins the main channel of the River Crouch. Back at the main river again, the coastal route continues its generally westward course. With an easy grassy path along the top of a broad sea-wall, this is possibly one of the best short walks along the whole of the River Crouch. The scenery is delightfully remote and rural, with wide views across an area of undeveloped farmland known as Stow Marsh.

As you head further upstream, it will not be long now before you can cross the river and begin the long haul downtream on the south bank. However, in order to include some of the best parts of the Essex scenery, this book describes the coastline up to the tidal limit of each river. The tidal limit of the River Crouch lies a short distance beyond Battlesbridge, but another short tributary lies just ahead to slow down your progress upstream.

As the main channel of the River Crouch veers to the south, the narrow tributary of Clementsgreen Creek flows in from the west. The public footpath continues along the northern bank of this creek for nearly a mile, following the grassy crest of the sea-wall, before turning sharply to the north. As you turn the corner, you come across the end of the creek almost unexpectedly. A dam has been built across the creek, with a small sluice in the centre. Upstream from the dam, the creek has mostly dried out, but if you explore further, you can still trace the route of the original sea-defences.

Clementsgreen Creek originally continued inland for half a mile further. Before the days of good railway and road transport, this creek was used by boats carrying cargo around the coast. The name of the creek has been associated with a man called John Clement who lived at nearby Cold Norton in 1348, and there are records of a jetty here as long ago as 1519. The creek was also used by barges to reach a brick and tile works which operated nearby from 1896 to 1910. Although it is no longer part of the coastline, it is worth a quick detour to explore this interesting area.

Just a few yards north of the dam, the embankment makes a brief deviation to the right. It was built in this fashion in 1898 after the original sea-wall was breached. You will also notice that there is a second dam just ahead. This was built before the Second World War, and is a further sign that flooding has been a serious problem around this area for a long time. For a few years after the shortening of the creek, this older dam became redundant, but it is now back in use again. Ironically, it is now used to hold the water in, because the area upstream has been turned into a nature reseve. A small lake has been created, with raised paths leading out across the water.

The lake represents the original limit of Clementsgreen Creek. Old maps show that a large earth embankment once continued northwards for another 200 yards to join the railway embankment. This was probably a counterwall, built to limit any damage caused by a serious flood.

South Woodham Ferrers

On the western side of the lake, a large leisure centre indicates that you are now approaching the outskirts of South Woodham Ferrers. This modern town was built a couple of miles south of Woodham Ferrers, a tiny village that now stands almost forgotten on a back-road to Danbury. Records of the original village date back as far as 975 AD, when it was known as Wudaham. It was also mentioned in the Domesday Book of 1086 under the name of Udeham, an Anglo-Saxon name which means "settlement in a wood". The village was renamed after the land was acquired by a Norman knight called "de Ferrieres", from the village of Ferrieres at Saint-Hilare, 60 miles south of Paris.

It is known that the area has been occupied for at least two thousand years, because archaeologists have found a series of red hills and saltpans nearby. Woodham Ferrers was said to be the centre of the local salt-making industry, with references dating back as far as 1332. The salt business finally declined in the 18th century, but the connection has been maintained to the present day in the name of Saltcoats Park.

Despite its rural location, the local villagers were involved in many trades, often using the river to transport the goods to the appropriate markets. Centuries ago, John Cooke wrote that Woodham Ferrers had "*two wharves or creeks of the sea called Clements Grene and Woodham Fanne ... very fit and daily used for transporting and conveyance of wood, butter, cheese and corn to and fro from the city of London and elsewhere.*"

Since the construction of the new town of South Woodham Ferrers, and the opening of the pedestrianised town centre in 1981, the river has been largely forgotten. Whilst many Essex riverside villages have the old quay at their centre, most of these new houses face inland, away from the water's edge. The coastal footpath therefore offers an unusual view of the town, so close and yet virtually ignored.

From Saltcoats Park, the coastal route returns to the dam at the head of Clementsgreen Creek. Following the western bank of the creek, the footpath quickly leaves the town behind and heads eastwards back into open countryside. In the great storm of 1897, the sea broke through the sea-defences in several places along this short stretch. Attempts were made to repair the damage, but after the floods of 1953 three small areas of land had to be abandoned. The footpath therefore now makes a series of minor diversions, although you can still trace the route of the original sea-wall. Most of the old embankments can still be walked, but you have to take care not to get cut off by the rising tide.

As you head eastwards to return to the banks of the main River Crouch, you are effectively walking along one side of a long thin peninsula. This land is now kept as a nature reserve, and a series of pools and embankments have been built to create habitats for different forms of wildlife.

At one point, a small inlet called Hawbush Creek cuts deeply into the peninsula. Many years ago, the landowners built an embankment across the peninsula here, at its narrowest point. Known as a counterwall, it was designed to limit the damage caused by a flood if any of the main sea-walls should fail. Although the counterwall disappeared a long time ago, a short footpath now runs along its route. It is very tempting to take this short-cut in order to save almost a mile of walking, but the true coastal route goes right to the end of the peninsula. The point offers magnificent views down the River Crouch to the yachts at North and South Fambridge. Although it is only a mile and a half as the crow flies from this point to the jetty at North Fambridge, you would need to walk about seven miles on foot around all the creeks and inlets to reach this village.

From the point of the peninsula, the coastal route rejoins the main channel of the River Crouch once more. This stretch of the river, known as Brandyhole Reach, is delightfully rural and open after the suburban meanderings around South Woodham Ferrers, and is a deservedly popular walk for local people. A small isolated farm called Tiffens originally stood close to the sea-wall. Later known as Lower Barn, the last building was removed some years ago.

As you head upriver, the new houses of South Woodham Ferrers begin to encroach more and more upon the openness of the landscape. Despite this, Marshfarm Road is still the only point of access to the riverside. This road leads to the Marsh Farm Country Park, which was established by Essex County Council as an educational facility, showing visitors how a modern farm works. Aimed principally at children, the country park also has two picnic areas.

From Marshfarm Road, there is a ford across the River Crouch, offering the first opportunity to cross the river. At low tide, the water is shallow enough to wade across, although parents of young children should be warned that the flow can sometimes be quite strong. Until 1960, a ferry could convey pedestrians across to Hullbridge on the opposite bank. With the closure of the ferry, walkers can now only cross the River Crouch here at the lowest point of the tide, or continue upstream to the first bridge, at Battlesbridge.

With each of the major Essex rivers, this book describes the route as far as the normal tidal limit. In the case of the River Crouch, the tidal limit happens to lie conveniently close to Battlesbridge. These final few miles upstream have a character quite different to the rest of the River Crouch. Some stretches of the river-bank are privately owned, and the coastal route therefore has to detour a short distance inland to follow the nearest public footpath, but the walk offers a surprising variety of scenery.

Very shortly after leaving Marshfarm Road behind, a small creek flows into the River Crouch. Known as Fenn Creek, this little tributary causes the coastal route to divert northwards for a short while, the last of many such diversions on the northern bank of the river. The sea-wall along the banks of Fenn Creek is still a public right of way, but it is less popular than the footpath around the nature reserve, just a few miles to the east. This is probably because the landscape feels hemmed in by the suburban sprawl of South Woodham Ferrers. Indeed, it is not long before the houses come right down to the water's edge. At this point, the footpath leads onto a quiet backstreet called Gladden Way.

It is possible to continue along the sea-wall, around the edge of a small peninsula formed by a tight bend in the river, but this unfortunately is not a public right of way. The coastal route therefore has to turn left along Gladden Way, and soon rejoins Fenn

Creek on the far side of the peninsula. When the road dies away, a footpath continues to follow the eastern bank of the creek upstream.

Before long, Fenn Creek splits into two channels, with a low area of rough marshland in the middle. Known as Woodham Fenn, this is a delightful oasis of wildlife after the sterile housing developments that we have just passed through. Woodham Fenn has now been declared a nature reserve, although it seems a shame that these pockets of unspoiled landscape are only retained when the planners find it too expensive to develop the land for anything else.

When you reach a sewage works, an enchanting little stone bridge carries the footpath across the eastern channel of Fenn Creek into the middle of the marsh, close to a few small brackish ponds. If you are using the smaller-scale 1:50,000 "Landranger" maps, it is very difficult to follow the footpaths around Woodham Fenn, because their grid splits the marsh on two sheets. The confusion is not helped by the fact that, until just a few years ago, the map showed the public right of way following an impossible route! In practice, the footpath is clear on the ground, continuing northwards to a level-crossing over the railway line. (*Parents should obviously take great care with young children in this area.*)

Beyond the railway, footpaths spread out in all directions. Our coastal route forks off to the left, following around the edge of a pool to reach a small footbridge. This takes you across the western branch of Fenn Creek. You are now leaving behind the suburbia of South Woodham Ferrers for the last time, and entering into a region of grassy riverside meadows. Unfortunately there is no public right of way along the next stretch of coastline. This seems a shame, because these few miles would make a very gentle and pleasant walk, with no farmhouses to disturb.

Instead you must shortly leave the coastline and head inland. A footpath runs parallel to the railway, leading towards the busy A132 road. This road, known locally as Wickford Road, was built as a quick and easy route into the new town of South Woodham Ferrers. As a result, the traffic powers along at a terrifying speed. There is no pavement alongside the road, just a wide grass verge, and the coastal route follows this to the left.

With the roar of the traffic so close, this is not a walk to be savoured. After about three-quarters of a mile, your hopes of leaving the main road are raised by the sight of a side-road off to the left, passing through a railway bridge and signposted towards a caravan park. Unfortunately, this side-road, known as Hayes Chase, soon proves to be a big disappointment. Although it does lead back to the riverside, it is a private lane belonging to the owners of Little Hayes. There are no public footpaths from the end of this lane, and you must therefore continue along the busy Wickford Road for a little longer.

After another four hundred yards, a public footpath to the left offers a welcome relief from the noisy traffic. A stile leads almost directly onto a footbridge across the railway, and you immediately find yourself back in quiet countryside and open fields. You are unlikely to meet many other people on this short footpath, but the route of the public right of way is therefore not always obvious.

Within ten minutes, the farmland is left behind as the path reaches the edge of an area of uncultivated marshland, drained by a series of ditches. If you turn right past a small pond, the banks of the River Crouch are only a few yards away, and here the coastal route becomes clear once again. After a short stroll along the crest of the sea-wall, the footpath is diverted inland by a small inlet. From here, the public right of way follows Maltings Road, a quiet farm lane that leads from Gosse's Farm back to the main road at Battlesbridge.

Battlesbridge

During the early part of the Middle Ages, it was possible to cross the River Crouch using bridges further downstream, at Hullbridge and Fambridge. However, both of these lower bridges disappeared many centuries ago. In spite of a ford and the appearance and disappearance of ferries downstream over the years, Battlesbridge still retained its importance as the lowest permanent crossing-point over the River Crouch for many hundreds of years.

Some people try to claim that the name of the village is derived from a battle between King Canute and Edmund Ironside in 1016, but there appears to be very little evidence for this theory. It is much more likely that the name comes from a local man called Battle. It has been suggested that the bridge was maintained by a family called "Bataille". The accuracy of this information is hard to ascertain, but it is certainly known that a man called Richard Bataille lived nearby in 1327.

The current iron bridge was constructed using brick piers in the 1870s. However, the enormous increase in traffic since the war proved to be too much for this narrow bridge, and Battlesbridge soon became a major bottle-neck. A wider modern bridge was therefore built nearby, along with a short length of new road. Since the opening of this bypass, Battlesbridge has once again become a quiet little backwater. This peace is welcomed by many of the residents, but inevitably it also caused problems to some of the local businesses who relied on the passing trade.

The coastal route described in this book follows each river inland as far as the tidal limit. In the case of the River Crouch, the Ordnance Survey marks the tidal limit as being about a mile upstream of Battlesbridge, where the railway crosses over the river. At this railway bridge, the river is usually shallow enough to be fordable if you wear wellingtons, but the return walk along the southern bank is interrupted by another small river that flows into the River Crouch. This second river is too wide and muddy to cross, and walkers therefore have to make a long diversion down to the next bridge, near Rawreth on Church Road. If you use the Ordnance Survey's 1:50,000 "Landranger" series of maps, you will need to obtain map number 178 (Thames Estuary) to follow this extra diversion. Although it is clear that these few miles are occasionally walked, there are no public rights of way along any of the river-banks. These two rivers are of interest because they have marked important local boundaries for many centuries. They originally marked the edge of Chelmsford Hundred, Barstable Hundred and Rochford Hundred, and the same boundaries are still used for the modern council districts of Chelmsford, Basildon and Rochford.

Even if you are not allowed to walk along these rivers to the tidal limit, it is worth making a short diversion upstream from the bridge to see the remains of the old mill workings. The river is split into three channels at this point. The mill-race is on the left (as seen from the bridge), and an overflow weir to the right enabled excess water to drain away. The central channel was originally a flash lock, with a pair of wooden gates which could be opened to enable small boats to use the river.

It is known that a tidal mill was working on this site well before 1773, because records indicate that the mill was rebuilt in that year. This type of mill is described in more detail later in this book, at Stambridge. Despite minor damage from a fire in 1815, it continued working until the early 1800s, and the buildings were replaced some time between 1828 and 1836. Taking advantage of new advances in technology, a new steam mill was added just below the bridge, on the north side of the river.

The original tidal mill stopped working in 1902, and was demolished the following year. The steam mill continued to thrive however, and a new granary was built alongside in 1910. This is the enormous five-storey building that still towers over the riverside today. The owners also opened another new mill in 1933, this time on the opposite bank of the river. The two surviving mills were eventually bought by Unilever, and were for many years the area's main source of employment.

Both mills were closed in the 1970s, and for a while the site lay derelict. But around 1978, a yachtsman named Roy Hart bought the land around the old tidal mill, including the miller's cottage and drying kiln. He restored the lock-gates, rebuilt the mill wheel, and started a ski equipment business called Skeetex. Their sales office is now based in the miller's cottage. Battlesbridge has also become renowned as a centre for the antique trade, with over 60 dealers working from local premises such as the old granary. In addition to the marvellous Thames barge called "British Empire", the village also has a craft centre, a motorcycle museum and several pubs.

The River Crouch is the longest of all the rivers that punctuate the Essex coastline, and Battlesbridge is therefore a major milestone along the coastal route. Standing on the bridge here, you are about 19 miles from the open sea. However, the south bank and the north bank of the River Crouch are surprisingly different. The north bank has three major inlets – Stow Creek, Clementsgreen Creek and Fenn Creek – to slow you down, whereas the south bank has only one minor diversion. You will encounter this inlet shortly, near Brandy Hole. Progress downstream is therefore much faster than the walk upstream along the northern bank.

It is only a couple of miles down the River Crouch from Battlesbridge to the town of Hullbridge. The walk starts at a small road-junction at the southern end of the village, where a track leads down to the sea-wall. Unfortunately, this first stretch of the river-bank has no public right of way, and you therefore have to ignore the track and set off eastwards instead, along a quiet back-road called Beeches Road. After half a mile, where the road turns sharply to the right, a public footpath at last leads up onto the sea-wall.

This stretch of the River Crouch is known as Long Reach. Although it never strays far from farms and other buildings, the walk is very peaceful, and it is therefore a shame that only the south bank has a public footpath. In fact, if you look carefully at the Ordnance Survey map, you will notice that, even on the south bank, the public right of way officially leaves the sea-wall for a short distance and takes a short-cut across a field. In practice, it is much more sensible to continue along the crest of the sea-wall, enjoying the pleasant scenery offered by this raised viewpoint.

The river meanders wildly from side to side, and the sea-wall makes a series of corresponding zigzags. In one sharp corner, an extra embankment has been built in order to create a large pool for wildlife. Passing a small caravan site on the opposite bank, the footpath leaves the Chelmsford Ordnance Survey map ("Landranger" series, number 167) and moves back onto the Colchester map (number 168). Looking ahead, it is now not far to the outskirts of Hullbridge, but before you reach the first houses, look out for the remains of oyster-beds just below the sea-wall. These appear as short rectangular pits dug out of the saltings, and were originally used by local fishermen to grow oysters.

Hullbridge

Almost directly opposite the mouth of Fenn Creek, you reach the first buildings of Hullbridge. The town took its name from the river, because this stretch of the River Crouch was once called the River Hull. The word "hull" originally meant a vault or arch, and it is quite possible that this referred to the shape of the original bridge here. It is known that a bridge crossed the river here in the 13th century. Some sources indicate that the bridge collapsed around 1645, although others suggest there was still a bridge here in 1768. This may, of course, have been a replacement, but in any event there has not been a bridge across the river here for hundreds of years.

In its place, a ferry carried people and goods across the river. This stopped in 1960, but the main road down to the riverside is still known as Ferry Road. At low tide, there is a ford across the creek here. The water is usually less than a foot deep, and it is therefore just possible to wade across if you have a good pair of wellingtons. The best route is indicated by two rows of wooden stakes sticking up out of the mud from both banks. Indeed, this crossing is officially a public right of way, although you are likely to get strange glances from any onlookers who happen to be sitting on the patio of the nearby Anchor Inn!

Along the river-front, you will also find the Hullbridge Yacht Club and the Up River Yacht Club. These yacht clubs are the furthest upstream on the River Crouch. This part of the river is very shallow, and it is therefore very difficult for boats to get further upriver. The other main advantage of Hullbridge is that it provides car access to the riverside. This becomes increasingly important as you head down the River Crouch, because villages become further and further apart. As a result, you need to plan your walks carefully if you want to make the most of the excellent scenery along some of the more remote stretches of the river.

Fortunately, there is a small side-road that provides access to the sea-wall a mile east of Hullbridge. Known as Kingsman Farm Road, it passes through a series of caravan parks. You can usually park at the very end of the road, at Bartons boat-yard, although you should take care not to cause any obstruction because this land is all privately owned. Old maps indicate that there used to be a large brickworks nearby. It is almost certain that barges would have been used to transport material from this brickworks, and the site of this boat-yard therefore probably dates back hundreds of years.

It is also possible to walk along the riverside from the ford to Bartons boat-yard, overlooking the gardens of small cottages. Many homes have their own little wooden jetties. Whichever route you decide to follow, you will reach a large slipway at the end of Kingsman Farm Road. Beyond this point, the sea-wall was heavily overgrown until quite recently, but a good path has now been cleared through the trees and bushes. This scenery is quite unusual around the Essex coastline, because very few trees manage to thrive in the marshy conditions. There are high levels of salt a few feet below the surface of the soil, hindering the growth of trees and deep-rooting plants.

The new footpath winds back and forth through the trees, sometimes following the crest of the sea-wall and sometimes dropping back to a level gulley just inland. Soon however, you come out of the trees into more typical scenery – a wide grassy sea-wall separated from the open farmland by a shallow drainage ditch. At first, it is easier to walk along the foot of the embankment, where the grass has not grown too long. This can get a little muddy in places, but the footpath soons rejoins the crest of the sea-wall and the conditions improve underfoot.

This stretch of the river is known as Brandyhole Reach. The name is supposedly a reference to the smugglers who hid their brandy here until they could find a quiet moment to retrieve it. However, you will soon have to leave the banks of the River Crouch and divert inland again. If you look ahead a few hundred yards, you can see a huge gap in the embankment where the water pours through with each tide.

This sea-wall was originally breached during a storm in 1897. After the storm, the gap in the sea-defences was too wide and deep to repair, but the local landowners did not give up the fight. Instead of reconstructing the original embankment, they built a series of smaller walls on either side of the newly-formed creeks, much further inland. Using this method, they hoped to contain the flood to several narrow channels, but it appears that they were gradually losing the battle. Their new walls were swept away in a couple of places, and the surrounding fields were finally abandoned by 1924. At low tide, you can still see many of the original drainage ditches, forming rows of parallel lines across the saltings.

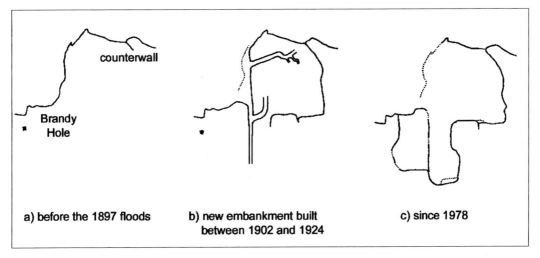

a) before the 1897 floods   b) new embankment built   c) since 1978
                                    between 1902 and 1924

Stages in sea-wall retreat at Brandy Hole

If you look further afield, you can also spot the remains of some of the failed embankments, built in the early 1900s in an attempt to limit the flood. They are now covered with a thick mat of long grass, and their light green colour stands out starkly from the darker green of the surrounding saltings. These embankments have gone unrepaired for over 70 years now, and many sections have been swept away by the force of the tides. This is clearly not a practical footpath therefore, but maps still clearly indicate that this is the official right of way.

In fact, this embankment had already been washed away when the public right of way was created! Public footpaths were drawn up as a result of the 1949 National Parks and Access to the Countryside Act. This law required each county council to prepare a definitive map of all public roads and footpaths in their area. However, most maps had not been updated for a while, since the country had more urgent concerns during the years of the Second World War. The detailed maps of Essex, for example, had not been revised since 1924, and did not show that this footpath was impassable. A new right of way was therefore drawn onto the definitive map, even though it had already been unusable for almost thirty years.

However, the law comes to our rescue. If you cannot follow a public right of way because of an obstruction of any kind, then you are entitled to follow the nearest reasonable alternative route. Although not enshrined in any statute from the Houses of Parliament, the British legal system also recognises case law, and this particular right dates back more than two hundred years. During the case of Taylor v Whitehead in 1781, Lord Mansfield declared that highways *"are for the public service, and if the usual track is impassable, it is for the general good that people should be entitled to pass into another line."* This important right has survived to the present day, and proves very useful at the Brandy Hole inlet.

As luck would have it, a new sea-wall has recently been built around the edge of this low-lying piece of land. This new embankment branches off to the right, past a sign saying "BWA Private". Do not be intimidated by this sign – the land may be privately owned, but, as explained above, you have a legal right to follow this route because of the obstruction on the official public right of way. The ground is quite uneven and the grass can grow quite long, but it is well worth persevering because of the wild and beautiful landscape ahead.

Heading southwards along this new sea-wall, you pass the site of Bartons Farm, which was demolished around 1950. At various points along the route, pipes have been laid through the sea-wall in order to help drain the nearby farmland. The sea-wall was obviously not designed with walkers in mind, and hence the earth is sometimes a little uneven around these pipes. This route should therefore be taken carefully and slowly. However, you are clearly not the first people to come this way because there are signs of a muddy footpath leading across a simple wooden bridge and out into the middle of the saltings.

Although you can be confident that you are legally entitled to walk along this new sea-wall, the lie of the land can be a little confusing because maps do not yet show the site of these new embankments. After turning a corner sharply to the left, you soon come to a junction in the sea-wall. The overgrown path to the left follows the remains of the early 20th-century embankments, and soon dies out in a sea of mud. Our coastal route instead follows the new sea-wall to the right.

From this point, a public footpath heads inland across a series of simple wooden footbridges towards a collection of mobile homes, built on the site of an old rifle-range. This footpath provides a useful link to the main road, and is popular with local people. It is a wonderfully wild spot, with desolate marshes stretching into the distance to the north. The area abounds with wildfowl in winter, and on still evenings the timeless tranquillity forms a perfect contrast with the impatient frenzy on the busy Lower Road nearby.

Continuing eastwards from the junction, a couple of fences have been placed across the crest of the sea-wall. The word "Private" has even been painted on one piece of wood, but, as explained earlier, you are quite entitled to walk this route because the official right of way has become impassable. Many people frequently walk this stretch of the sea-wall, and it provides a wonderful view across the marshes. Looking amongst the saltings, for example, you can see the remains of some earlier embankments, now breached in two places.

The footpath soon turns to head northwards once again, although there are still a couple of zigzags before you get back to the banks of the River Crouch. At one point, a smaller earth embankment branches off the main sea-wall to the right, and then quickly dies away as it reaches higher ground. This offshoot dates back to around 1920, and forms part of the coastal defences that were built after the devastating storm of 1897. When the new concrete sea-wall was built recently, this short length of embankment was retained as a counterwall, in order to limit the damage in case any of the main sea-defences should fail.

From this counterwall onwards, the crest of the sea-wall has been laid with a wide band of concrete. It is a pleasure to leave behind the rough grass with its dangerously broken surface, although the hard concrete surface tires your legs just as quickly. You can make much faster progress however, and you are free to look around at the scenery without fear of twisting your ankle in a hidden pothole.

Eventually, you reach the shores of the River Crouch once again. To the left, just across a narrow channel, you can still see the remains of the original sea-wall snaking off upriver. This short stretch of river-bank was known as Oyster Ledge, and some people still try to wade across to it at low tide. However, the mud is very soft and the channel is shallow for less than an hour at each tide. It would take longer than an hour to explore Oyster Ledge properly, and you are therefore almost certain to get cut off by the tide if you attempt this dangerous crossing.

Here you rejoin the route of the official public right of way. This embankment was strengthened and raised a few years ago, and as a result this is now one of the highest viewpoints along the river. From the corner, there is a marvellous panorama, and an ideal spot to take a last look back at the Brandy Hole inlet. The inlet shows a different face according to the state of the tide. At high water, the saltings are flooded to form a vast inland lake, with only the tops of the grass stems poking through the surface like a reed-bed. As the tide ebbs, the receding waters reveal a series of narrow muddy channels, often the remains of drainage ditches from the days when this land was cultivated. Whatever the state of the tide, the marshes are always bleak and desolate, but with a silent beauty that bewitches most visitors. Unfortunately the new concrete sea-wall does not make it comfortable to sit down and enjoy the peace of the landscape.

Almost directly opposite, you can see the masts of yachts moored at the West Wick boat-yard, just a short distance up a tributary of Fenn Creek. Looking upriver, the River Crouch snakes off to the left, whilst the smaller Clementsgreen Creek branches off towards the new town of South Woodham Ferrers. The view downstream is quite a contrast, because the river suddenly straightens out and heads directly eastwards for many miles. This stretch of the river is aptly known as Longpole Reach, and you can make very fast progress along the unswerving footpath. If you are using the more detailed Ordnance Survey "Explorer" maps, then you will find that the two maps start to overlap along this stretch – 175 (Southend-on-Sea & Basildon) and 176 (Colchester). The two maps continue to overlap until you reach Wallasea, seven miles further on.

At one time, a track used to head inland from the riverside to the buildings of Beckney Farm. No doubt the river was used to transport some of the farm goods, but the track has now disappeared, and the next contact with civilisation is at the small village of South Fambridge, now visible less than a mile away. About half way there, the sea-wall veers slightly around the edge of a tiny inlet. Amongst the saltings here, a series of wooden posts point vertically out of the mud. These posts, some standing around ten feet high, are probably the remains of an old quay.

In one corner of the inlet, a wartime pill-box is embedded into the sea-wall. From this point, a counterwall once led inland towards Beckney Farm. This low embankment would have helped to limit any flooding if the main sea-defences failed. With improved

Sea-wall near South Fambridge

standards in engineering, farmers can now place much more reliance on modern sea-walls, and therefore precautionary counterwalls are rarely needed today. In the opposite direction, you get a close view of Port Moor Cottage on the other side of the River Crouch. This isolated cottage can only be reached by boat.

South Fambridge

It is now only a short walk to the end of the road at South Fambridge. There is space immediately below the sea-wall for a few cars to park, but the main village lies about 150 yards inland along a narrow lane. South Fambridge is now a quiet village, well off the beaten track, although it was once on a busy trading route across the river with its sister village of North Fambridge. The ferries and the original bridge were described earlier in this book.

South Fambridge stands at the end of a long and winding road known, not surprisingly, as Fambridge Road. With the exception of boat traffic and a rarely-used footpath across the fields, Fambridge Road now provides the village's only link with the outside world. It also provides the last car access to the sea-wall until you reach the causeway onto Wallasea, six miles downstream. You can break this long stretch into two sections by climbing the hill into Canewdon, but this adds an extra mile to each part of the journey. Drivers also have the disadvantage of having to retrace their steps to their car. As a result, this section is not often walked in its entirety.

People rarely stray more than a few hundred yards from the end of the road, and most of the scenery is therefore extremely quiet and isolated. It is therefore perfect if you want to get away from the crowds. From a scenic point of view also, this walk has much to recommend it, particularly the views of Bridgemarsh Island. The ideal solution for drivers is probably to arrange for someone to pick you up at the far end of the walk and drive you back to your starting-point.

Setting out from the end of the road near South Fambridge, the Ordnance Survey's 1:25,000 "Explorer" map marks a "works" just below the sea-wall. This was once the site of a shellfish packing station, but in 1986 the council began to use this land as a landfill site. The refuse-dumping has now finished and the topsoil has been replaced. The area is now peaceful and green once more, and with a sea-wall almost thirty feet wide in places, it is unlikely to be breached by the tide in the near future. This sort of operation obviously causes some temporary disturbance, but there are great advantages in using landfill sites to strengthen our sea-defences since it performs two functions at the same time.

Half a mile from the road, a low embankment heads inland across the fields. This is another example of a counterwall. From this point, there was once a track inland towards the buildings of South Fambridge Hall. This fell into disuse many years ago, and has now completely disappeared.

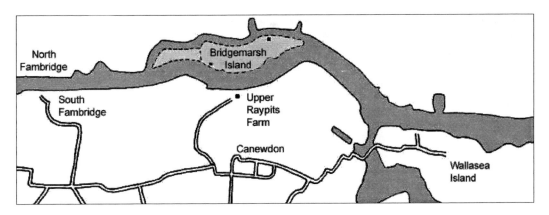

The walk downstream now heads in an almost straight line due east, aiming directly towards the open sea ten miles away. The grassy crest of the sea-wall allows for very fast progress, and there are wonderful views both up and down the River Crouch. For some unknown reason, this stretch of the river used to be known as Purfleet Shoal, although it is now more commonly known as Longpole Reach.

Keep a look-out for a large mound of rough grassland just inside the sea-wall. From this point, there was once another earth embankment heading inland. Although it may seem at first glance to have been just another counterwall, this was actually the original sea-wall. The drainage channel also veers inland at this point, indicating the old route of the coastline, but the embankment itself has now been ploughed into the fields.

The original sea-wall was in the shape of a semi-circle, forming a small inlet at this point. The new sea-defences were built in a much straighter line, cutting off the inlet and reclaiming the land. Within a few hundred yards, you meet the embankment at the far end of the inlet. A short section of the original sea-wall here has been retained for use as a counterwall.

Until about forty years ago, a row of farm cottages stood about a quarter of a mile inland. These cottages were originally called North Pitts, a name which was later shortened to Norpits. This farmland was very severely flooded in 1953, when a long section of the sea-wall was swept away. This area suffered probably the worst damage along the River Crouch, and it took months to rebuild the sea-defences. The "vile breach", as it became known, was finally plugged using gravel and clay from Bridgemarsh Island nearby. The buildings at Norpits were pulled down soon afterwards.

From the point where the embankment now branches off the main sea-wall, continue downriver for a further hundred yards. The sea-wall veers slightly to the right, and then back to the left again. At this second corner, a rough track heads inland across the fields. This once connected the Norpits farm to a little wharf on the banks of the river. Until the 20th century, farmers often used barges to transport their goods to the London markets. The track also marks the route of another counterwall. The counterwall may have gone, but its accompanying ditch still drains the fields. The track is now a public right of way, turning sharp left at the site of the Norpits cottages. It leads towards the buildings of Pudsey Hall, an ancient farm recorded in the Domesday Book of 1086 as Puteseia. It is possible to drive down the hill to Pudsey Hall, but this still leaves your car almost a mile from the main sea-wall. At the site of the Norpits wharf, the River Crouch begins to veer slightly to the north. This stretch is known as Shortpole Reach, and provides excellent views of Bridgemarsh Creek opposite.

Just ahead, you will find further evidence of past flooding. The main sea-wall was breached, and the landowners decided that it would be simpler to build a new embankment just inland, rather than repair the old one. As a result, the footpath now follows around the edge of a tiny inlet. At low tide, you can see the remains of the original sea-wall, now just a few boulders in the mud.

Before long, the coastal route rounds a gentle corner and aims instead in a more south-easterly direction. This corner, the first of two that you will encounter between South Fambridge and Wallasea, is known as Landsend Point. The name is quite appropriate, because this is one of the most remote parts of the River Crouch. It is not often walked, which seems a pity because it provides a marvellous view of Bridgemarsh Island across the river. Bricks and tiles were once made on the island, with a short tramway leading down to a jetty almost directly opposite Landsend Point. The jetty and its associated buildings disappeared many years ago, and the only sign that the desolate marshes of Bridgemarsh Island were ever inhabited is a solitary chimney off to the right. The island is described in detail earlier, during the description of the north bank of the river.

As you turn the corner at Landsend Point, you enter a stretch of the river known as Raypits Reach. Along the foot of the sea-wall here, a few oyster-beds have been dug out of the saltings. These have been disused for many years now, but a century ago oysters were a staple part of the local diet, and these saltings would have fetched a high price on the property market.

Before long, the coastal route takes a sharp bend to the right around the edge of a small area of saltings, and then another sharp bend back to the left to resume its generally eastward direction. At this point, a footbridge has been built across the borrow-dyke, with a footpath continuing across the fields towards the buildings of Bolt Hall. This has been designated as a "permissive path". This means that the landowner has voluntarily given his permission for people to walk along this path, but reserves the right to close it again. Since it is not an official right of way, the council and the landowner manage to avoid the legal bureaucracy normally involved in changing the route of a footpath. This permissive path helps the landowner because it diverts people away from the buildings of Upper Raypits Farm, and it is very useful to members of the public because it acts as a short-cut to Bolt Hall. From Bolt Hall, a farmtrack called Gays Lane heads up the hill to the village of Canewdon.

Canewdon

The hill on which Canewdon stands is quite pronounced, and although it is only 128 feet above sea-level at its highest point, this is one of the highest hills around the Essex coastline. It is one of a series of "bagshot" hills around the River Crouch, with other examples at Ashingdon and Latchingdon. These bagshot hills are the southern limit of the boulder clay laid down by glaciers during the last Ice Age. South of this line, there is only the older London clay.

With its excellent viewpoint, Canewdon was an obvious site for early settlers. The name of the village means "hill of Cana's people", referring to a Saxon from the 6th century AD. The idea that the name was derived from King Canute is therefore unfounded, since it predates the Vikings by many centuries.

The church was used for centuries as a lighthouse, with a bright light in the tower to guide sailors. Indeed, the hill is sometimes still referred to as Beacon Hill. In local folklore, Canewdon has accumulated plenty of eerie tales of witchcraft. Like many villages around the Essex coastline, smuggling was once rife around these parts, and local people would deliberately spread superstitious rumours in order to scare away outsiders.

Back on the river-bank, the buildings of Upper Raypits Farm lie just ahead. This represents the half-way point of the long walk between South Fambridge and Wallasea. From the farm, there are two rights of way inland. It is no coincidence that each of these footpaths represent the route of an old counterwall, because until the marshes were drained, raised embankments were usually the easiest method of getting from place to place.

Only one of the counterwalls still stands today. This follows the farmtrack to the south-west towards Bolt Hall. Indeed, this is the public right of way that is bypassed by the new permissive path. The other footpath heads across the fields in a south-easterly direction. It then turns sharply to the right and heads straight up a steep slope known locally as Butts Hill. It eventually reaches the centre of Canewdon via a quiet back-lane, and can therefore provide a useful way of breaking up the long coastal walk. This path also has historical interest, because the first few hundred yards follow a wide ditch called Old Fleet. This was once the borrow-dyke immediately inside the main sea-wall, until Dutch engineers reclaimed the Canewdon Marshes around 1700 by building a completely new sea-wall further to the north.

From Upper Raypits Farm, the coastal route continues eastwards along the crest of the sea-wall. A concrete path has been laid down, and it is therefore possible to make very good speed. However, this hard surface does leave your legs feeling very tired after a while, and there are still another three miles before you reach the next road, at the causeway onto Wallasea.

This stretch of the River Crouch, known as Easter Reach, is very remote and quiet, but has some of the best scenery along the river. For the first mile or so, you look across the river to Bridgemarsh Island, now just a series of abandoned salt-marshes. As the river begins to meander gently, the coastal route gradually veers to a more north-easterly direction. Then, about a mile out from Upper Raypits Farm, the sea-wall suddenly turns to the right as the river sharply changes direction. This used to be known as Easter Point, but now it is usually called Black Point. There is a second sharp point about 150 yards further on. This strange arrangement was created when a new sea-wall was built to reclaim a narrow strip of saltings here. You can still see the original sea-wall just inland.

Black Point provides an excellent view of the mouth of Althorne Creek opposite. Althorne Creek forks off here from the main River Crouch and flows around the far side of Bridgemarsh Island. You can also see the boats moored in Althorne Creek at Bridgemarsh Marine, and if you look carefully a little further to the left, you may even be able to spot a low brick structure on the island. These are the remains of Bridgemarsh Farm, the last building to be inhabited before the island was finally abandoned around 1930.

After you turn the corner at Black Point, look out for a row of rectangular pools amongst the saltings, just outside the sea-wall. These are disused oyster-beds, where oysters were cultivated during the 19th century. At that time, this stretch of the River Crouch was commonly known as Birch Reach. However, modern maps use the name of Cliff Reach instead, a reference to the low clay cliffs on the far bank of the river, near Creeksea.

Looking downstream, the yachts moored at Wallasea indicate that you are now on the home straight. It may not be far now to the Wallasea causeway, but you still feel as if you are in the middle of nowhere. The remote atmosphere is reinforced by the view inland – as far as you can see in every direction, the fields of pasture and crops appear to stretch to the horizon, only interrupted by the occasional hedge or solitary tree.

A tiny isolated barn stands a few hundred yards inland. This is recorded on local maps as Lands End, and the name seems very appropriate. However, the fact that it has a name at all, and the fact that it appears to have given its name to Landsend Point nearby, suggest that it may once have been a small farm in its own right. Today it is simply an outbuilding of the larger Lower Raypits Farm which lies in the distance.

As you head closer to Wallasea, the footpath veers slightly to the south. A large area of saltings has formed below the sea-wall at this point. Over the centuries, local fishermen have used these saltings to create a series of oyster-beds, and the remains of these rectangular hollows can still be seen.

Before long, the coastal footpath reaches the mouth of Lion Creek, and the sea-wall turns sharply to the south towards the main road. After a few hundred yards, the creek curves to the right. Originally, Lion Creek continued westwards across the marshes, eventually connecting with the ditch now called Old Fleet. Dutch engineers reclaimed the Canewdon Marshes around 1700, but they did not have the engineering skill to build a large dam. As a result, Lion Creek continued to flow inland for almost two miles. Canewdon Marshes effectively formed a long peninsula, joined to the mainland only by a narrow isthmus near Upper Raypits Farm.

Old maps of this area indicate that in 1805 there were two farm buildings on these marshes. One of these was Marsh Farm, now known as Lower Raypits Farm. Each farm had its own track leading across Lion Creek, probably via a ford or causeway that was only passable at low tide. Eventually, a dam was built across the creek about half a mile in from the mouth, and this is still the official right of way today. After the 1953 floods, it was decided that a second dam should be built closer to the mouth of the creek. This new dam now provides the quickest access back to the main road. Technically it is not a public footpath, but it appears that virtually everybody uses it today.

With the construction of the second dam across Lion Creek, a small lake was created between the two dams. In 1964, the Anglian Water Authority sold 12 acres of this land to the Essex Wildlife Trust for a nominal sum, and a further 8 acres of land were leased later. The trust converted the site into a nature reserve, which was finally opened in September 1986. The brackish water attracts large numbers of wildfowl, which can be viewed from a hide on the northern edge of the lake.

Beyond the Lion Creek nature reserve, it is only a short distance to Creeksea Road. This marks the end of the unbroken six-mile footpath from South Fambridge, and walkers who have successfully completed this long stretch will be glad that the end is finally in sight. If you are using the Ordnance Survey "Explorer" series of maps, here you need to switch over from map 175 (Southend-on-Sea & Basildon) to map 176 (Blackwater Estuary) for a few miles.

The main road leads from Canewdon towards Wallasea Island. There was once a small jetty here, known as Lion Wharf. At low tide, you can still see a few rows of wooden stakes poking out of the mud. At this road, our coastal route turns left, heading towards Wallasea. On the north side of the road here, a small square of land has been enclosed by a low earth embankment. The embankment is very rough underfoot and is not a public right of way. It appears that the enclosed land was never properly drained, and it still remains as rough marshland and saltings. A small turquoise boat-house stands beside the creek here, with concrete steps leading down into Lion Creek. A few yards further along the road, a rough path heads out across the marshes to the edge of the saltings, but all eyes will now be looking ahead at the causeway onto Wallasea Island.

Wallasea Island

The road onto Wallasea Island is metalled, but is occasionally covered at high tide. This road dates back many centuries, certainly before 1771, and there was probably a rough track here or many years before that date.

The road turns sharply to the left, with a muddy creek lapping at each side of the causeway. It then gently rises to cross over the top of the sea-wall onto the island. As you climb up to look across the wide expanse of farmland on Wallasea, the first impression is of an enormous saucer, with the sea-wall forming a gentle lip all around to protect the land from the tide. The island is almost four miles long in total, although it is never much more than 1½ miles wide.

General description of Wallasea Island

Wallasea is only one of a series of islands huddled together in the south-eastern corner of Essex. These islands are collectively known as the Essex Archipelago. Unlike most of the islands dotted around the British coastline, the islands of the Essex Archipelago could never be described as "offshore". Instead, they are in effect still part of the main British landmass, but separated from the mainland by narrow winding creeks. As a result, their outlines fit closely together, like the pieces of a jigsaw. The Essex Archipelago is therefore a special feature unique in Britain, and this close-knit group of islands is given special attention later in this book.

The creeks that separate each island from its neighbour are never very wide. Indeed, many of them almost dry out at low tide. In previous centuries, these creeks were criss-crossed by an ever-changing network of ferries, linking the island communities together. It is therefore rather ironic that today it is virtually impossible to reach any of the islands. All the islands are out of bounds to the general public, with the exception of Wallasea, and hence this island is treated separately.

Wallasea has always been very susceptible to flooding. In many places, the ground is below sea-level. The island is sometimes cut off from the outside world for an hour or so at high tide when parts of the causeway go underwater. However, in recent years, there has been some discussion whether to continue maintaining the sea-walls of Wallasea Island. It is expected to cost £2½ million to raise the embankments to a "1 in 100 year" standard, whilst some economists have claimed that the public benefit is only worth a fraction of this cost. It is quite possible that the authorities will decide to continue protecting only those sea-walls around the north-western corner of the island, where all the houses and marinas lie.

The island was originally called Wallis Ey, and is said to derive from the Old English word "wala". This was the plural of "walh", a word which translates literally as "foreigner", but was used by the Anglo-Saxons to describe any type of outsider, such as a Briton or a Viking. The same word can be seen today in the name of Wales, and also in the Essex town of Walton-on-the-Naze, where there was a Viking encampment. The "ey" is another Anglo-Saxon word signifying an island. This appears frequently around the south-east of England, some local examples being Canvey, Mersea and Sheppey. The modern name of Wallasea Island is technically a tautology therefore, because the word Wallasea already contains the sense of "island".

Driving onto the island, the main road twists and turns for almost a mile until it reaches the buildings of Grapnells Farm. On early maps, this was called Great Grapling (Little Grapling stood half a mile further east), but Grapnells may actually be a much older name, because the Domesday Book of 1086 recorded a local family called Grapinel. The road continues beyond the farm for just a hundred yards before you reach a gate across the road. No public access is allowed beyond this point, even though the road continues for several more miles across the island.

This is effectively the end of the road therefore, although it is worth having a good look around before you turn back. The scenery is completely featureless, with acres of ploughed fields as far as the eye can see. There are no trees or bushes to break up the surroundings, and the view is therefore quite desolate. Until the last century however, Wallasea was completely different, with more than seven farms scattered across the island. In 1899, there were so many families here that a school was built. Apart from a temporary closure around 1910, the school continued until the Second World War. It even attracted a few pupils from the neighbouring island of Foulness. A ferry between the two islands is clearly marked on maps dating from 1887 and 1920. This was only a rowing-boat, but it was a vital link between the two communities. By 1942, the attendance at the school had dropped to just four pupils, and the school was forced to close.

After the war, the small farms were bought out one by one until finally, in 1952, the whole island had a single owner. In the following winter, the Great Tide of 1953 devastated enormous areas of low-lying land down the eastern coast of England, and Wallasea was flooded very badly, with more than three-quarters of the land underwater. Furthermore, people were unable to escape the island at first because the causeway was flooded. Only a small area of land around Grapnells Farm remained above the flood-level.

Many of the sea-walls were completely swept away, particularly around the eastern end of the island. It was decided that this end of the island should be temporarily abandoned, and work immediately started to build new sea-defences. A new sea-wall was constructed north-south across the middle of the island, at a point where it was only 800 yards wide. Using 400 men to carry and arrange the sandbags, it took three weeks to re-secure the island, but it took much longer for the farms to recover because of the salt-water that had leached into the soil.

The sea-walls were eventually repaired, and the farms in the eastern half of the island were able to resume work. At this time, there were over 180 fields scattered around the island, mostly in a random pattern because of the haphazard nature of the original farms. Between 1960 and 1966, new drains were dug and the fields were re-arranged to form larger and more manageable areas. In this enormous undertaking, the traditional patchwork of the countryside was replaced by more functional, soulless strips. In total, there were now just 28 fields, each averaging about 85 acres. One by one, the old disused farm-buildings were pulled down. The last farm to be abandoned was Tile Barn, at the far south-eastern corner of the island. Wallasea currently produces large quantities of cereal crops and peas. The original field boundaries and ditches can still be made out on aerial photographs.

The sea-wall around the edge of the island totals about 10 miles. It is all walkable, but unfortunately there is only a public right of way along half of it. Only the northern and eastern edges are technically open to the public, with wide views along the River Crouch and part of the River Roach. It is a shame that the southern and western edges do not have a public footpath, because this follows some beautifully wild surroundings along the River Roach and Paglesham Creek. For completeness however, this book includes a description of the walk around the whole of Wallasea, beginning at the causeway and heading in a clockwise direction.

❋ ❋ ❋

Many visitors to Wallasea drive to the Essex Marina and begin their walk from there, but the natural place to start a walk around the island is at the causeway, where the road rises up to cross over the top of the sea-wall. This point is aptly named Wallasea Gate on early Ordnance Survey maps. Parking is not so easy though. There is an obvious spot beside the road just before you reach the causeway, but this occasionally gets flooded at high tide. You are strongly advised to consult a tide-timetable before leaving your car here.

As the road climbs over the sea-wall into Wallasea Island, the coastal route turns left along the crest of the sea-wall. Old maps indicate that there was once a small farm called Gore Marsh just inland here. Today, there is only a track leading into a caravan site. The view to the west is more pleasant, with saltings leading down to the banks of Lion Creek. A large number of oyster-beds were once worked here, and their remains can still be seen in the form of rectangular hollows amongst the saltings.

It is only a few hundred yards to the mouth of Lion Creek. At this point, you turn the corner and rejoin the River Crouch, now getting steadily wider as you head downstream. Just after the caravan site, you reach the Creeksea Ferry Inn. This was rebuilt quite recently after the original building was destroyed by fire. As its name suggests, this is the site of an old ferry across the river to Creeksea. When the tide is out, you can still see the slipway for the old ferry. Indeed, a few old road signs nearby still point this way to Creeksea. At one time, there were three ferries from Wallasea across the River Crouch, and a further two along the southern edge of the island across the River Roach. Only one of these still operates today, and even this is only seasonal.

Just east of the Creeksea Ferry Inn lies the Baltic Wharf with its large jetty. This was opened in 1928 to import timber, principally from countries around the Baltic Sea. As soon as you pass the jetty, the sea-wall bends to the right and you enter a shallow inlet. At low tide, you may be able to spot the rectangular remains of oyster-beds at the foot of the sea-wall.

This inlet used to mark the boundary between the parish of Canewdon and the parish of Paglesham. These days, the whole of Wallasea belongs to the parish of Canewdon, but when the island was farmed by a number of small communities, the land was divided up between five nearby parishes: Canewdon, Paglesham, Little Wakering, Eastwood and Great Stambridge. This form of fragmentation was common in coastal areas, particularly when there was no church nearby. During the 19th century, countryside like this was very remote and, at times, decidedly unhealthy. As a result, people who owned land on Wallasea rarely lived on the island, choosing instead to rent out the land to poorer local farmers. The choice of parish usually indicated where the landowners themselves lived, and parish information can therefore be very useful to historians.

There are 500 berths along the river-bank here, and the slipway is often busy at weekends. During the Second World War, large numbers of torpedo boats were built here, although the sea-wall had to be cut away in order to winch the boats into the water. After the war, a ferry operated from here to Burnham-on-Crouch, almost a mile downriver. This stopped around 1970, although a passenger ferry has now started operating again during the summer months. At the time of writing, this area was undergoing major redevelopment.

The Essex Marina provides the last public access to the sea-wall. From this point, it is almost four miles to the end of the island, at Wallasea Ness. The public right of way also continues for a further mile up the estuary of the River Roach, with wide-reaching views across the mysterious and inaccessible island of Foulness. The return trip is almost ten miles therefore, and will usually take over four hours, but the effort is well rewarded with magnificent views.

Setting off from the Essex Marina, you soon reach a floating pontoon. This pontoon acts as a mooring for hundreds of small boats, with many more anchored out in the River Crouch (sometimes known along this reach as Whale Shoal). As you continue eastwards along the top of the sea-wall, around a tiny inlet, you gradually leave civilisation behind. The boats get few and far between, and you eventually pass the last building on the island, Grapnells Farm, before heading out into open uninhabited countryside.

About half a mile from the Essex Marina, the sea-wall forks into two separate embankments. The left branch was the original route, leading out to a slight promontary known as Gardeness Point. This name is probably related to a local man called John att Garden, mentioned in records in 1578. This embankment has now been breached, and the coastal route therefore has to follow the newer right-hand branch instead. Ordnance Survey maps show that the official right of way still follows the outer wall, but, as this is clearly impassable, English law gives you the right to take the nearest convenient alternative. For more detail, see the notes around Brandy Hole, earlier on.

After a few hundred yards, the two routes join again. At low tide, you can see rows of wooden stakes leading down into the mud. These are the remains of an old slipway. It is possible that this was used by oystermen, because the nearby saltings contain the remains of several oyster-beds. Looking across the river, you are now almost directly opposite the town of Burnham-on-Crouch. The large white building that is prominent in the view is the Royal Corinthian Yacht Club. There was once a ferry across the River Crouch at this point. Records show that it operated from around 1927 until 1940, although it is almost certain that there had been a ferry here earlier, because one of the nearby buildings used to be known as Ferry Farm. The boat set out for Burnham from a sharp promontary just ahead called Overland Point.

After Overland Point, the sea-wall turns sharply to the right and makes a long detour around the edge of a deep bay. This irregular coastline is probably due to the land being reclaimed from the sea in several stages. From the head of the inlet, old maps show that an embankment ran in a westerly direction towards Grapnells Farm. This was probably the original edge of the island. When more land was reclaimed later to the north, around Overland Point, this old embankment was retained for use as a counterwall, to limit the damage caused by any floods. In many marshland areas, counterwalls were also used as the main trackways, and the modern farmtrack still follows the same route.

The coastal route continues up the far side of the bay. Before the drainage scheme of the 1960s, there was a small farm building just inside the sea-wall here. Originally called Acrefleet, it later became known as Grass Farm or Grasslands, and gave its name to the nearby promontary of Grasslands Point. The farm was renamed West Laws shortly before it was pulled down.

At the tip of Grasslands Point, you cross another old parish boundary. As mentioned earlier, the whole of Wallasea is today part of the parish of Canewdon, but the original boundaries give a useful historical insight into the old farm communities. Here you leave behind the old parish of Paglesham and enter a detached portion of Canewdon parish. However, it is only a hundred yards or so to a second promontary, Fleet Point, where you cross another old parish boundary. This next plot of land used to belong to the parish of Eastwood, a village that was over seven miles away.

Another farm building once stood just inland from Fleet Point. This was one of the oldest farms on the island. Although it was eventually called East Laws, its original name of Allfleets dates back to at least 1285, when it was recorded as Alfledenesse. From Fleet Point, the route settles down into a quiet walk along a large bay of saltings. About a third of the way around this bay, the sea-wall leaves Eastwood parish and re-enters land that was attached to the more local parish of Canewdon.

The scenery is positively serene along this stretch, an easy walk along the grassy crest of the sea-wall with only an occasional motor-boat to disturb the silence. Inland, enormous cultivated fields stretch into the distance, broken up regularly every three hundred yards by a drainage ditch that reaches right across the island. On the horizon, you can just make out the sea-wall around the southern edge of Wallasea, well over a mile away.

There are no buildings, not even as much as a single bush, to break up the monotonous view inland, yet this land was once home to several thriving farming communities. One of the farms was called Range Wood, a strange name since trees very rarely manage to grow in the brackish soil around these marshes. On more recent maps of the island, the farm is marked as Ringewood or Ringwood, and indeed this stretch of the River Crouch is still known as Ringwood Bar.

On the far side of the bay, the sea-wall once again forks into two branches. The left branch heads out towards a shallow promontary known as Ringwood Point, but this embankment has now been breached by the tide. Like Gardeness Point earlier, the coastal route therefore keeps to the new inner embankment. Once again, the official public right of way is still marked on maps as following the original coastline, but this is now completely impassable.

After three hundred yards, the two routes begin to join up again. Old maps indicate that there was once a counterwall leading inland here to a small farm called Lower Barn. It was mentioned earlier that counterwalls were often used as trackways, because of the marshy nature of most of the land. This counterwall is a good example, providing access from the farm to the river, where a small landing-point was built beneath the sea-wall. This stretch of the river was originally known as Horse Shoal. A "horse" is a local word for a mudbank or small island in the middle of a river, although no such island exists today.

Almost as soon as the two branches meet, the embankment splits once more. The outer sea-wall, leading to a promontary called Barrington Point, has again breached, probably during the floods of 1953. Walkers must therefore stick to the inner embankment again. After a few hundred yards, this arrangement is repeated for a third and final time. Indeed, it is not until you reach the north-eastern corner of the island that the two embankments finally join up again.

This corner, known as Wallasea Ness, is a very important milestone on the coastal route. At this point, you turn right to begin the long walk up the banks of the River Roach. The neighbouring island of Foulness is not open to the public, and therefore this is effectively the end of the walk along the banks of the River Crouch. There are three main rivers that punctuate the Essex coastline – the Crouch, the Blackwater and the Colne, but the River Crouch involves the longest detour by far.

At Wallasea Ness, the sea-wall turns sharply to the right, but saltings and rough grassland continue beyond the sea-wall for another hundred yards or so. A thin peninsula of deep mud then continues for a further two hundred yards, forming a hidden obstacle to boats heading down the River Roach. It is marked on nautical maps as Brankfleet Spit (this lowest stretch of the River Roach used to be called Brankfleet). Indeed, this region has taken many different names over the years. On detailed Ordnance Survey maps, for example, you will see this river junction marked as "Ness Hole", but in earlier centuries the area used to be known as Wallfleet. As a result, local oysters were often referred to as Wallfleet oysters, and at times the name has even been applied to the island of Wallasea itself.

Many people turn round at Wallasea Ness and head back towards the Essex Marina. This is a pity because the public right of way continues for another mile southwards along the banks of the River Roach, with some of the the most interesting views to be seen anywhere around the island. This last section of the footpath is therefore strongly recommended if you can make the extra distance.

Starting from the corner of the sea-wall at Wallasea Ness, the sea-wall heads southwards with wide views across the River Roach to the island of Foulness. This island is owned by the MOD and is used by the Defence Testing & Evaluation Organisation (DTEO). It is also the headquarters of their Environmental Test Centre. As a result, Foulness is closed to the public. Nevertheless, a few hundred people still live on the island, with their own church, shop and even a pub, sealed off from the outside world. Foulness is described in detail later on, along with the other islands that make up the Essex Archipelago.

About five minutes' walk from Wallasea Ness, a few saltings begin to form along the foot of the sea-wall. At this point, there used to be a counterwall heading due west towards a small farm. This was marked on various maps as either Shire Farm or Underbarn. The counterwall has now been ploughed up, but a break in the borrow-dyke indicates where it originally left the main sea-wall.

As you continue southwards along the shores of the River Roach, the saltings outside the sea-wall gradually grow wider and wider. It is known that these marshes were occupied during Roman times because archaeologists have found the remains of a red hill nearby. Red hills are found in many places around the Essex coastline and are thought to be the remains of ancient saltworks. (More information about red hills can be found earlier in this book, during the description of Mersea Island.)

Looking inland, the endless landscape of enormous fields is broken only by the concrete track from Grapnells Farm. This farmtrack eventually ends right at the foot of the sea-wall, very close to one of the old parish boundaries. At this point, you would have left Canewdon parish behind and moved instead into a part of the island that belonged to the parish of Great Stambridge. This is only for a few hundred yards however, because the sea-wall soon begins to veer sharply round to the left. The unusual shape of this part of the island is the result of later reclamations of land, or "innings". This south-eastern corner of Wallasea was "inned" in two separate stages later than the rest of the island. The new plot of land became part of the parish of Canewdon.

The public right of way ends at a sharp corner in the sea-wall. This is the easternmost point of the island, and provides a magnificent panorama of Foulness. Looking due east, the village of Churchend lies just over a mile away. It is is easy to spot because of the tall church spire nestling amongst the trees. This village is the main centre of population on Foulness, with a church hall, shop, and a small pub called the George & Dragon. Beyond Churchend, the hamlet of Courtsend lies near the end of the road. This was once home to a second pub called the King's Head, but it closed a few years ago. Further to the south are the buildings of two of the oldest farms on the island, Priestwood and Rugwood.

Looking just upstream (to the right), a large slipway from Foulness leads down into the water, near the farm of Monkton Barns. This slipway is known simply as The Quay, and indeed this stretch of the River Roach is often called Quay Reach.

Back on Wallasea, this corner of the sea-wall represents the end of the public right of way. The land is private beyond this point, but the sea-wall remains in a walkable condition around the entire southern edge of the island. For completeness, this book contains a description of the next section of the coastline, in the hope that one day it will be open to members of the public. In the meantime, it may be possible for individual walkers to get special permission from the landowner.

From the easternmost point of Wallasea, the sea-wall heads due south at first, but very gradually it begins to veer around to the west. This stretch of the river is known as Whitehouse Hole, after a building that once stood nearby on Foulness. The bend in the river continues until the coastline once again runs east-west. At this point, there used to be an old farm just inside the sea-wall. It was recorded on maps as Tile Barn or Tyle Barn. Other old maps show a building in this area called Devil's House, although is it not clear whether this was simply a different name for the same dwelling. Over the years, it has been spelt in several different ways, such as Davil's and Duvals, probably named after the original owner. Local folklore includes colourful tales of a woman called Mother Redcap who was believed to be a witch. As a result, the building gradually became known instead as Devil's House. The building disappeared many years ago, but this stretch of the river is still known as Devil's Reach.

The sea-wall makes a couple of sharp turns around a small bay of saltings. This marks the end of the more recently reclaimed corner of the island. Before the Second World War, this was a busy part of Wallasea, with a floodgate leading through the sea-wall to a small wharf. A private ferry operated from this wharf across the river to the island of Foulness opposite. Every day, children would cross from Foulness to attend the school on Wallasea. A track led in a north-westerly direction across the island towards a small community centred around the school, including the farms of Sherwoods and Tilletsmarsh.

Continuing westwards past a series of oyster-beds, you come to a second slight indentation in the coastline. This was once a wide inlet where a large creek penetrated deep into the island. The inlet has now been cut off by the construction of new sea-defences, but the creek still survives today in the form of a meandering drainage ditch which winds its way inland. Indeed, this is one of the few ditches that was not diverted and straightened during the massive reworkings of the early 1960s.

Looking across the river from this point, you have a good view of the channel that runs southwards between the islands of Foulness and Potton. This channel was originally called Yokefleet, or sometimes Yokefleet Creek. Some sources refer to it as The Gore Channel, but today it is usually known as The Middleway. Amongst this confusing network of creeks, it is clear how these various islands fit together tightly like a jigsaw. They form a group of "inshore" islands that are unique around the British coastline, and were once all closely interconnected by a series of small ferries. As mentioned earlier, they are collectively known as the Essex Archipelago, and are described in more detail later.

The sea-wall continues due west in an almost straight line, with sinister glimpses across the river of military buildings scattered across Potton Island. Back on Wallasea, there used to be tracks leading inland to a couple of farms.

Eventually, the sea-wall turns sharply to the right and follows a small tributary of the River Roach called Paglesham Pool. Around 1900, a small ferry operated across the mouth of this creek to Paglesham Point on the mainland. Standing on the sea-wall today, it is hard to imagine that a small community once thrived here.

Just after turning the corner into Paglesham Pool, you enter a large inlet of saltings. This was once used for cultivating oysters, and the rectangular oyster-beds can still be seen all around the inlet. After about half a mile, the sea-wall begins to veer to the left. At this point, old maps show a counterwall heading inland. This has now been ploughed into the fields, but the modern farmtrack still follows its original route. Counterwalls were built to protect a farmer's land from flooding in case the main sea-defences failed, and so they usually represent the boundaries of a landowner's property. This means that parish boundaries often follow the route of counterwalls as well, and this is no exception. At this point, you leave behind land that was once tied to the parish of Great Stambridge, and move onto land that belonged to Canewdon parish instead.

For the next couple of miles, the sea-wall meanders back and forth beside saltings along the edge of Paglesham Pool. The number of wild zigzags suggests that this part of Wallasea was gradually reclaimed from the sea piece by piece, each new sea-wall following the drier parts of the marshes.

The sea-wall passes close to the farm-buildings of Grapnells, and then continues in a more westerly direction. Eventually you reach the causeway once more, though a large fence has been built across the crest of the embankment here to discourage walkers. This is a shame because it stops people from enjoying marvellous scenery along Paglesham Pool and around the southern edge of the island. It also seems quite pointless, since there are no farm buildings or machinery anywhere near the route to worry about. Indeed, the deep borrow-dyke along the foot of the sea-wall makes it virtually impossible for walkers to stray from the edge of the island. Nor is there any livestock to be disturbed, and so this route seems an ideal candidate for a new public footpath.

※ ※ ※

From the Wallasea causeway, the coastal route now begins to follow Paglesham Pool southwards to the shores of the River Roach. In the Middle Ages, boats sometimes used this route as a short-cut from the River Crouch to the Roach, and hence to the River Thames and the London markets. However, after the causeway was built, it effectively formed a barrier between Lion Creek and Paglesham Pool.

Paglesham Pool

This upper reach of Paglesham Pool is often known as Paglesham Creek. Over the centuries, farmers in this area have fought a constant battle against the sea. On the

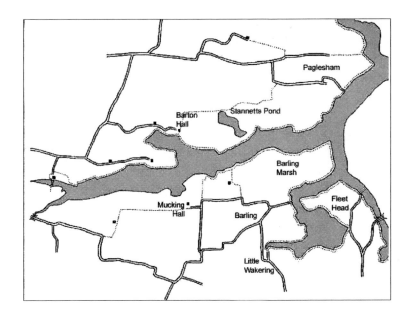

The River Roach

mainland side of the creek, large areas of salt-marsh have been reclaimed from the sea, only to be abandoned later after devastating floods. This has happened on two distinct occasions, and the remains of the failed sea-defences can still be traced amongst the saltings.

From the air, the route of the two embankments is immediately obvious, but it is not so clear when you are on the ground. The earlier embankment can be seen on either side of the causeway, roughly half-way between the mainland and the island. If you look in the direction of Paglesham Pool, you can follow the line of the earlier sea-wall, heading across the marshes towards a modern telegraph pole.

You can rejoin the coastal route back on the mainland, where a concrete fingerpost indicates the public right of way down Paglesham Creek. It is possible to park a car beside the road here, but be aware that this part of the road can be flooded during very high tides. You are advised to check a tide-timetable before leaving your car here.

From the roadside, a footbridge carries the path over a wide ditch. The path soon turns sharply to the right, but if you were to continue on in a straight line, you would actually be following the second of the abandoned sea-walls. This more recent embankment originally stretched for another 300 yards across the marshes, crossing the route of the older sea-wall about half-way out. It is not clear when this land was finally abandoned, but old maps show that the embankments had been breached by 1876.

With a series of small fishing lakes just inland, the modern footpath wanders through a sort of no-mans-land, without a sea-wall to define the edge of the tidal marsh. The plantlife is unusually varied because the transition from freshwater scrubland is more gradual, through a region of brackish soil, to pure salt-marsh with its carpet of sea purslane (*Halimione portulacoides*).

Most people believe that Paglesham Creek starts at the Wallasea causeway, but in fact the true head of the creek lies half a mile further to the south. You are, in reality, still heading upstream. Before long however, the footpath reaches a wide dam, now the head of Paglesham Creek. This dam was built over two hundred years ago, but the creek originally continued inland for another mile or so, and the parish boundary still follows the same route today. For a short distance, the channel of the old creek is still used to drain the fields, with a sluice built into the dam to allow excess water to flow out to sea at low tide.

Paglesham Churchend

At the far end of the dam, a public footpath leaves the sea-wall and heads southwards across the fields. This provides the last access to the coastline for almost three miles. The footpath inland leads to the village of Paglesham Churchend, coming out onto Paglesham Road just alongside the Punch Bowl Inn. As its name suggests, the village of Paglesham Churchend contains the local parish church, dedicated to St. Peter. This is the first of two villages that bear the name Paglesham – its twin village stands just over a mile to the east and will be described in more detail a little later.

From the dam, the coastal route follows Paglesham Creek downstream, with a wide grassy footpath along the top of the sea-wall. Old maps show that there was once a small wood nearby, known as Hobley Grove, but this has now disappeared. About half a mile from the dam, you encounter an old wartime pill-box just outside the sea-wall. From this point, a track heads inland. This is now a private farmtrack, but it used to provide access to a small wharf beside the creek. Again, all signs of the wharf have now gone.

You eventually reach a corner where the sea-wall turns sharply to the south. The creek is very narrow at this point, but all you can see of Wallasea Island opposite are the buildings of Grapnells Farm visible over the top of the sea-wall. Beyond the corner, a narrow inlet of saltings has accumulated on the banks of the creeks. Another private farmtrack heads inland towards the buildings of East Hall. This track indicates the route of an ancient counterwall which disappeared many years ago.

About fifty yards further on, a second counterwall can still be seen today where the sea-wall veers to the left. This counterwall was once the original coastline, but then a new sea-wall was built, reclaiming a large area of marshland. Old maps show that it belonged to the parish of Hockley, with the boundary once again following the line of the counterwall. This new plot of land used to be known as North House Marsh, after a nearby farm. The farm changed its name to Clements Farm, and this plot of land is therefore more commonly known today as Clements Marsh. The name also appears in Clements Point, a small promontary about a third of a mile downstream.

Beyond Clements Point, the sea-wall continues to follow the gentle meanders of the creek, which is known along these lower stretches as Paglesham Pool. As you walk along the footpath, keep a look-out for the remains of abandoned oyster-beds – they appear as large rectangular pits dug out of the saltings.

About half a mile from Clements Point, the sea-wall veers to the right around the edge of a small inlet. Across the saltings here, a muddy footpath leads out amongst the oyster-beds, with a tiny footbridge crossing the deep channel. At the head of the inlet, a public footpath heads inland towards a building once called Finches, but now known as Well House. The footpath follows an old counterwall. This was the original coastline before Clements Marsh was reclaimed from the sea. If you look carefully at the local Ordanance Survey map, you will notice that the official footpath makes a quick detour across the fields to the north. This extra loop is because the public right of way follows the precise route of the original embankment, but the landowners later re-arranged the field boundaries and straightened the counterwall.

It is now only a few yards to the mouth of Paglesham Pool, where you will find a pill-box embedded in the sea-wall. At this point, the creek flows into the main channel of the River Roach. This is a significant milestone around the coastal route of Essex, because the River Roach is the last major obstacle to be overcome before we reach the final leg of the journey up the River Thames.

From Paglesham Point, there was once a ferry across the mouth of the creek to Wallasea, serving the communities that used to live on the island. After the severe floods of 1953, it was even suggested that a permanent dam should be built here, so that there would be fewer miles of sea-wall to maintain. This plan was soon shelved, although many similar schemes were carried out around the Essex coastline, such as Lion Creek nearby.

At Paglesham Point, you begin the long walk up the banks of the River Roach. This river offers some of the most varied walks around the Essex coastline. Most of the time, public roads are close enough to make access relatively easy, whilst keeping far enough away from towns and villages to give it a remote dreamy atmosphere.

Below the sea-wall here, rows of oyster-beds stand parallel to each other amongst the saltings. The River Roach Oyster Fishery was at its peak around 1878, with around 200 employees, but most of the oysters were killed off by a mystery disease in 1921. The 1953 floods caused many of the beds to silt up, thereby suffocating the oysters. As a result most of these oyster-beds were abandoned long ago, but a few are still used today and continue to supply a dwindling oyster market.

Paglesham Eastend

Beyond the oyster huts, two large sheds indicate that you have arrived at Shuttlewoods Boat-yard. This lies at the end of Waterside Road, a pot-holed track that leads to the village of Paglesham Eastend. It is just possible to drive cars along this track, but there is nowhere to park at the boat-yard, particularly on a warm summer weekend. You are therefore advised to leave your car in the village and walk along the track to the sea-wall.

Paglesham Eastend lies about a mile to the east of its twin village, Paglesham Churchend, and has long been connected with the sea and smuggling. Many of the smuggling stories centre around a former churchwarden called William Blyth (1756-1830), who managed a grocer's shop here. He was even suspected of wrapping his contraband goods in leaves from the parish register. Another story tells how his boat was boarded by a revenue cutter in the River Crouch nearby. Whilst his illicit goods were being confiscated, he managed to get the King's Officer drunk. He then recovered all his booty, along with plenty of goods that had been confiscated from other smugglers, before escaping up the River Crouch to Paglesham. More stories are contained in an excellent booklet on Paglesham, written by Rosemary Roberts and first published in 1972.

Crop-marks near East Hall and South Hall Farm indicate that this area has been settled since at least the Bronze Age. The village was recorded in the Domesday Book as Pachesham. Place-name specialists say that this was a corruption of "Pachelham", and believe that the name means simply "hamlet of Paccel". By the time John Norden compiled his famous map of Essex in 1594, it had changed to the more recognisable name Packelsham.

If it was originally renowned for oysters and smuggling, the village today is known to outsiders for two reasons: a large pub called the Plough And Sail, and walks out along the River Roach from Shuttlewoods Boat-yard. Things could easily have turned out so different though. In 1919, there were proposals for a railway from Rochford to Paglesham, but this was eventually abandoned because of competition from roads. And then, in the 1950s, it seemed that a nuclear power station might be built on the riverside at Paglesham. However, because of the need for more cooling water, the site was transferred in 1955 to Bradwell. The village has therefore managed to retain its rural tranquillity, standing almost isolated at the end of a long winding road. The atmosphere of the place is well summed up by a poem written in 1888 by a local landowner called James Wiseman:

If ever you should chance to stay at Southend,
Hire a cab or a horse, or a donkey, where 'ere
You fancy – drive to Paglesham, where
The three pollard elms are still standing – When there
Climb up one, and look down its cavernous trunk,
Or descend if a man of good mettle and spunk,
You may – mind, I don't say you will – chance to find
Some "Schnapps" or cigars, left by smugglers behind,
If you don't – 'tis no matter – Go then without fail
Some half-mile on, to the pub – Plough and Sail,
At East End you'll find it – When there don't forget,
Order oysters, bread butter with stout (heavy wet).
As often 'tis called there by both of the sexes –
'Tis Courage brewing, and marked with XXX's;
When before you – the stout, bread and butter – they set 'em,
Then ask for the oysters – I wish you may get 'em!

Most walks around the Essex coastline require you to retrace your steps back to your starting-point. Circular walks are quite rare, but here you have a choice of two. From the boat-yard at Paglesham Eastend, you can walk back along the sea-wall to Paglesham Churchend, returning to the boat-yard along a combination of inland footpaths, tracks and main roads.

The second circular walk is slightly shorter. This starts off in the other direction from Shuttlewoods Boat-ard, heading westwards along the banks of the River Roach and coming inland at Stannetts Pond. This route, which rejoins the main road at South Hall Farm, also has more varied scenery, and amongst the saltings are constant reminders of the old oyster industry. This stretch of the River Roach is called Paglesham Reach, and there are wide views across the river, first of Potton Island and later Barling Marsh.

About a mile out from Paglesham Eastend, you reach a gentle promontary called Blackedge Point. Until relatively recently, the marshes just inland were littered with brackish pools. Known as Eastend Marsh, these pools are still marked on a few out-of-date maps. One of the pools was used as a decoy pond for catching wildfowl, although it became disused around 1800.

Beyond Blackedge Point, the sea-wall turns sharply to the right around a small bay filled with saltings. Once again, characteristic rectangular hollows indicate that oysters were cultivated here. As a result, these saltings would have fetched a high price a hundred years ago. After the oyster industry collapsed, a boat-builder chose this remote spot to set up business, at the head of a sharp inlet ahead. This disappeared many years ago, and the area is wild and desolate again, although a row of modern electricity pylons spoils the view a little.

Just after the inlet, you reach Stannetts Pond, a pool that stretches inland for almost half a mile. At one time, this was just a short offshoot of the main River Roach. Known as Stannetts Creek, it marked the boundary between Paglesham parish and Stambridge parish. The creek was dammed in the first half of the 19th century, though the boundary remained unchanged. It is possible that this early dam was swept away by the tide, because maps from 1887 and 1897 show the creek still flowing directly into the river. However, it is more likely that the maps were simply out of date.

Stannett's Pond is a beautiful site, lined with reeds and usually thronging with swans or wildfowl. Sited well away from nearby villages and roads, it is always peaceful, though the overhead power cables once again tend to intrude into the scenery. There is a good footpath all around the pond, and this links up with an inland footpath from South Hall Farm, thereby completing a circular walk from Paglesham Churchend.

In the other direction, the inland footpath heads west towards the buildings of Barton Hall. Note that the "Explorer" map is a little inaccurate – instead of cutting diagonally across the field from corner to corner (as marked on the map), the actual path follows the technical right of way, i.e. around the edge of the field. This footpath can be used to make another circular walk, and has the added distinction of a contour line on the map! At the dizzy height of ten metres above sea-level, this slope is the first contour line to be encountered along the coastal route since Canewdon. The raised position offers a good view of the River Roach.

Back at the dam on the shores of the River Roach, further signs of oyster cultivation are visible amongst the saltings. At one point, a rough earth embankment heads out across the saltings to the edge of the mud. This was once a landing-stage. If the tide is out, you can also find the remains of an old "hard" to the left.

From the dam, the coastal route continues westwards, gradually heading upriver. The footpath soon reaches a small promontary where a pill-box has been built into the sea-wall. On the far side of the River Roach, you can see the modern brick buildings of Roper's Farm. Further to the left, the spire of Barling church rises above a cluster of trees. Back on the north bank of the river, there was once another farm building just inside the sea-wall. It was known as Finches, possibly after a man called William Ffynche in 1403. The building was pulled down several years ago, but the site is still clearly visible.

Beyond the pill-box, a large area of saltings has built up along the edge of the river. This gradually increases in size as the sea-wall veers gently to the right, until it is clear that you are entering a large bay. Known as Bartonhall Creek, it is a maze of narrow muddy channels that almost completely dries out at low tide. In winter particularly, the exposed mudflats are quickly covered with a plethora of wading birds, such as oyster-catchers.

Some sections of this embankment have become quite overgrown, and it is easier to drop down off the sea-wall and walk along the saltings below. You are therefore advised to avoid this stretch around high tide. Remember also that the ground can remain waterlogged for a few hours afterwards. The problems soon disappear once you reach a clump of trees.

At the far end of this copse, a small cluster of buildings shelters beneath the trees. These are the buildings of Barton Hall, once known as Breton Hall. The name is said to derive from its original owner, Richard Brito, one of the four knights who murdered Thomas Becket at Canterbury cathedral in 1170. The house was later occupied by Captain John Harriott, who is generally known as the founder of the Thames River Police. In the south-eastern corner of Essex, he is also known for his enterprises on Rushley Island, which are discussed later.

At Barton Hall, the sea-wall disappears for a short distance, and the footpath instead heads inland for a while. This continues until you reach a track near a brightly-painted farm. In 1549, this building was recorded as Hampton Barons, but it is now known as Hampton Barns. From this farm, there is a public right of way along a track to the village of Great Stambridge, just under a mile inland. However, it is possible to park much closer to the sea-wall just a little further ahead, and so this farmtrack is rarely used by walkers.

At this farmtrack, the coastal route rejoins the crest of the sea-wall. This is the head of Bartonhall Creek, overlooking acres of saltings on one side, and fields of horses on the other. If you drop down from the sea-wall at the next corner, there is a path along the edge of a field towards the buildings of Waldens. This path effectively acts as a short-cut, cutting half a mile off the coastal route. It is clear that it is frequently walked, but there is no public right of way along it.

The proper route continues along the crest of the sea-wall, heading back towards the shores of the River Roach. Before long, you emerge from the bay of Bartonhall Creek and reach the main channel of the River Roach once again. This part of the river, originally known as Broomhills River, usually has short grass along the top of the sea-wall, and this makes for very easy walking.

The scenery is quiet and rural, with the occasional line of trees to break up the view. The land is very flat, and in winter it is often quite windswept. In order to provide some shelter, farmhouses were usually built amongst a cluster of trees. Looking around at the surrounding countryside, you will notice that almost every copse has a small building hidden inside. Another example lies just ahead. This is the farm of Waldens, a common place-name in Britain. It is usually a corruption of Wall Ends, a name given by the Romans to a weak point in a defensive system. In this case, it is said that Caesar's navy used this area as a first point of attack on Britain.

From Waldens farm, a side-road closely follows the sea-wall for a short distance before veering inland. It eventually joins the main road near Great Stambridge church. Although it is technically a private road along most of its length, walkers often use it to reach the sea-wall. The local farmers appear to tolerate cars so long as they are carefully parked and do not cause any obstruction to farm vehicles.

Back on the river-bank, the footpath continues past another series of old oyster-beds, their rectangular shape clearly showing at the foot of the sea-wall. A prominent line of trees lies just ahead, and once again this indicates that a farm-building lies sheltered nearby. This is the farm of Great Stambridge Hall, built on the site of a short tributary of the River Roach. The creek was dammed many years ago, and a small pond now stands on the same spot.

Continuing upriver, the footpath approaches a large building known as Broomhills. Indeed, this upper part of the river was originally known as Broomhills River. Before you reach the building however, the public right of way diverts inland along a track. This marks the end of one of the longest continuous coastal footpaths in Essex. Leaving the island of Wallasea aside, there has been an unbroken right of way around the coastline all the way from Battlesbridge, almost twenty miles away. The footpath follows the track inland for just over a hundred yards before turning left. This is the current right of way, despite prominent notices which might suggest otherwise. After another 300 yards, it emerges onto a small side-road called Mill Lane.

Stambridge Mill

The coastal route now turns left along Mill Lane, heading back towards the River Roach. Following a recent diversion, the footpath leaves the lane and follows around the back of a row of houses. This is the site of a post windmill, built in 1816. However, Mill Lane gets its name from a much older mill that stood at the end of the road, on the shores of the river. It was driven by tidal power, and you can still see the remains of the old tidal pound. In its heyday, the pound covered three acres. As the tide rose, it was filled with sea-water through a pair of canal-type gates, which then closed as the tide fell again. The water then escaped along a short mill-stream, turning a large wheel.

A tidal mill has worked here since at least 1500, and it is known that the mill was rebuilt in 1762, but the details of Stambridge Mill are unclear until the 19th century. In 1809, the owner built a completely new four-storey wooden structure here. It was leased in 1824 to William Hugh Rankin, whose family were to run the business for 138 years. Rankin enlarged the mill-pond, and finally bought the mill outright.

Tidal mills can only run for a few hours at each tide, and were gradually superseded by more modern methods. Here at Stambridge, a more powerful steam mill was built alongside the old tidal mill, although this new structure burned down in 1878. Its replacement was a tall five-storey brick structure which formed the mainstay of the business. By this stage, the old tidal pound was rapidly silting up. It therefore held less water, and the tidal mill became less efficient. Despite this, it continued to work as recently as 1951. A detailed description of its machinery can be obtained from the Education Department of Essex County Council.

In 1962, the business was sold to Associated British Foods, and the old abandoned tidal mill burned down just a couple of years later. The steam mill continued working however, although this has since been replaced with a series of enormous modern buildings. Only the tidal pound remains to show the humble origins of this important industry. The coastal route crosses the dam at the head of this pound.

This dam marks the site of one of the oldest bridges across the River Roach. Indeed, the name Stambridge itself comes from the old Saxon "stone bridge". This derivation is also clear from the Domesday Book, which records the nearby village as "Stanbruge". Today, the dam still effectively forms the first bridge across the river. For the purposes of this book therefore, this is the point where the coastal route reaches the head of the river and begins its long eastward journey along the southern bank.

From the south end of the dam, a public right of way heads southwards towards a small modern industrial estate. It is possible to walk through the estate, following the roads of Millhead Way and then right into Rochehall Way, but this route is not exactly pleasant. It is no surprise to learn that this was once the site of a hospital for infectious diseases! Instead, the recommended route enables you to explore the old mill-pond. A good footpath follows it inland from the southern end of the dam. This leads to the main Southend Road, emerging near a pub called the Horse and Groom.

By this point, the River Roach is not much more than a ditch, but the name of Salt Bridge, where the road crosses, suggests that salt may have originally been an important industry here.

Rochford

At Salt Bridge, you are only a few hundred yards from the centre of Rochford. The name of the town indicates that this was originally the site of a ford across the River Roach, but it is less well known that the river took its name from the town, and not the other way around. The "Roach" part of the name comes from the Old English word "raecc", which referred to a type of dog used for hunting. Indeed the word "rache" was regularly used for a hunting-dog as recently as the 16th century, and is still occasionally used in Scottish dialect today.

The village was mentioned in the Domesday Book of 1086 as Rochefort, presumably mis-spelled because the Norman writers confused it with the French "Rochefort". On John Norden's map of Essex in 1594, the town was correctly indicated as Rocheford. The town's main historical claim to fame is that Anne Boleyn was born at nearby Rochford Hall. This story has been passed down from generation to generation, though it is not clear whether it is actually true. Either way, there is now a large pub called the Anne Boleyn, just a few hundred yards south of Salt Bridge.

The pub stands beside a busy roundabout, where Sutton Road forks off the main B1013. Leading off to the east, Sutton Road is the key to the next stage of the coastal route. Less than half a mile down this road, you pass Purdey's Industrial Estate, a development which is only marked on the most recent of maps. Shops and warehouses have been built here, destroying the old footpath which used to cut across the peninsula from Stambridge Mill. One of the side-roads leads to a boat-yard on the shores of the River Roach. Unfortunately, this lane is closed to the public. It is possible to visit a short stretch of sea-wall alongside one of the large DIY stores here, but the area is littered with rubbish and is not worth the detour.

Leaving Purdey's Estate behind therefore, our coastal route continues eastward along Sutton Road. Almost immediately, the road crosses over a tributary of the River Roach. This is known as Sutton Ford Bridge. The name Sutton was in use by the year 1200. It is short for "south town", presumably meaning south of Rochford. The name of the bridge also reveals that there was once a tidal ford on this site. Because this was such an important river-crossing, the local council financed a plan around 1780 to build a bridge here. The money was given to John Harriott, an influential landowner who lived nearby at Broomhills. (His attempts to reclaim Rushley Island are described later on.)

Harriott's original bridge was very narrow and formed quite a bottle-neck. Around 1903, it was replaced with a much wider structure, although the current Sutton Ford Bridge dates from around 1950. Upstream of the bridge, the river remains tidal for only a hundred yards or so, with a pair of sea-walls zigzagging wildly across the fields. The route of the river was changed after the banks burst in the 1953 floods, and extensive works have been carried out for many miles upstream.

Today, it is still possible at low tide to wade across the river at Sutton Ford Bridge, but unfortunately there is no right of way along the river-bank here. The coastal route therefore has to head inland for almost three miles. The route begins by following Sutton Road eastwards, past Sutton Bridge Farm. This was originally known as Sutton Ford Farm, but the present building was built as recently as 1923. It is said that the concrete floors were reinforced with railway-lines because the owner was afraid of earthquakes. In any event, the building was severely flooded in 1953, and also suffered later from vandalism. As a result, it lay derelict for many years until it was finally restored in 1978.

From Sutton Ford Bridge, it is only a few hundred yards to a sharp bend. On this corner, Shopland Road branches off to the left. The name of this road is a reminder of the old village of Shopland. At one time this was a small but thriving village, but the houses were demolished one by one. The village gradually dwindled, and only Shopland Hall remains today.

As you head eastwards along Shopland Road, a lane soon branches off to the left. This lane quickly leads to Fleet Hall Farm on the shores of the River Roach. As with many of the Essex marshes, the farmers originally transported most of their goods by boat, using a small wharf nearby called Sutton Wharf. This would be an ideal starting-point for a walk along the southern bank of the river, but unfortunately there is no public right of way. This seems a shame because the countryside is virtually unspoiled. There is some beautifully wild scenery, both inland and looking across the river. Many of the saltings have eroded away, and groynes have been built across the mudflats to protect the remaining sea-defences. The low sea-wall is still in a good condition however, and it is clear that some people regularly walk along its crest.

Unless you have the permission of the landowner therefore, you should continue along Shopland Road. About half a mile further on, the road turns sharply to the right. At this bend, a narrow track branches off towards Butler's Farm. A public bridleway follows this track, offering a welcome opportunity to get away from the narrow and busy country roads. The atmosphere changes almost immediately to a quiet rural scene, and the frantic pace of speeding cars is quickly forgotten.

The track turns a sharp corner and passes a collection of farm-buildings. At first, the track heads straight towards the banks of the river again. At one time, it led to the edge of the water, where another small jetty was used by the local farmers. During the late 19th century however, these marshes underwent a major change as a whole stretch of new sea-defences were built. These completely replaced the old sea-walls, which had been built piece by piece over the centuries. In some places, tidal saltings were enclosed by the new embankment, and this reclaimed land is mainly used today as unimproved pasture. In contrast, further to the east, a small area of farmland was abandoned to the sea. Even though this land was lost more than 100 years ago, it it still possible to trace the route of the original sea-wall amongst the saltings.

Today, the public bridleway no longer reaches the shores of the River Roach. Instead, it turns to the right and runs parallel to the coastline for almost a mile. At its lowest point, it crosses over a narrow ditch. This was once a significant creek, snaking its way inland across the marshes for several miles, past the hamlet of Stonebridge. Creeks of this type were often used to mark important boundaries, and this is a typical example. Even today, when you cross the ditch you are stepping from the parish of Sutton into the neighbouring parish of Barling.

Mucking Hall

Shortly after crossing the ditch, you reach the farm of Mucking Hall. This was the site of a Roman villa, and there are still traces of an ancient moat. Just beyond the buildings, a good farmtrack branches off to the left. This leads to a small inlet on the banks of the River Roach. The farm once had its own wharf here, but today the only signs of past industry are the remains of a few oyster-beds.

Although walkers often come this way to reach the sea-wall, there is no public right of way along this track. Instead, our coastal route has to continue inland, following the bridleway eastwards. Before long, it comes out onto a quiet country road near Mucking

Hall Cottages. From this point onwards, the nature of the route changes completely because it is now possible to rejoin the sea-wall.

From the row of cottages, follow the road northwards. This is known, perhaps not surprisingly, as Mucking Hall Road. Within a hundred yards, it turns very sharply to the right at Bolts Farm. At this corner, a public right of way continues northwards past the buildings of Roach Farm and along a narrow track. Within half a mile or so, it leads to the sea-wall, and it is indeed a pleasure to climb up to the top of the embankment and admire the picturesque view of the River Roach once more. Looking across the river, the large inlet of Bartonhall Creek lies just to the left, but the scenery is otherwise unspoilt countryside, with just an occasional isolated farmhouse to break up the horizon.

The sea-wall is wide and generally flat, and the walk along its crest is easy. At first, you head around the outside of a shallow inlet. Amongst the saltings here, you can still see the rectangular remains of derelict oyster-beds. This is classic Essex coastline – a grassy sea-wall running alongside a wide borrow-dyke, with low-lying farmland stretching inland into the distance. Unlike many of the larger rivers around Essex, the River Roach remains relatively unknown, and visitors are virtually assured of a relaxing and undisturbed walk. The tranquillity of the landscape is in marked contrast to the popular sea-front at Southend nearby.

Shortly after the shallow inlet, a small jetty has been built out from the sea-wall, with a narrow track leading inland towards Roper's Farm. These brick buildings are relatively recent, but a farm has stood on this site for many centuries. The first Ordnance Survey map, in 1801, showed a building called Gladwins Farm with its own jetty nearby. Known at the time as New Quay, this original jetty stood just over a hundred yards to the east of the present construction. Indeed, if you look carefully at modern Ordnance Survey maps, you will notice that the official right of way joins the sea-wall at the site of this original jetty. On the ground though, it is clear that the actual footpath follows the track, in a straight line all the way up to the sea-wall.

This footpath provides the last access to the coastline for just over two miles. After the jetty, you begin to head around the edge of a narrow peninsula known as Barling Marsh, and it is quite easy to make this into a circular walk, leaving the car at Barling church. However, this peninsula is currently being used as a large-scale refuse tip. The coastal footpath is expected to remain open during this work, but the thundering lorries tend to distract from the peaceful atmosphere.

It is almost a mile and a half from the jetty at Roper's Farm to the end of the peninsula. The promontary comes to a surprisingly abrupt end at a point known as Barling Ness. At this point, the River Roach is joined by an offshoot of Potton Creek. This offshoot, known as The Violet, separates Potton Island from the mainland. From the top of the sea-wall at Barling Ness, you can see a few low brick buildings on the island, but most of the time the place looks deserted.

Barling Ness also marks an important milestone in our route around the Essex coastline, because this is where you leave the River Roach for the last time. The river actually continues downstream for another four miles before it finally flows into the River Crouch, but these lower reaches of the river flow past the islands of Potton and Foulness. These islands are both out of bounds to the public, but they are described later in this book.

The Roach Backwaters

Turning the corner at Barling Ness, you leave behind the River Roach and enter a different type of landscape. The south-eastern corner of Essex comprises a series of interlocking islands, separated by a maze of narrow creeks. Indeed, it is only half a mile to the first of many confusing junctions. Here the sea-wall veers to the right to follow a tributary of The Violet known as Barlinghall Creek. This tributary is named after the buildings of Barling Hall which lie a mile ahead. This is a very enjoyable stretch of footpath, with easy walking and excellent views of creeks and quiet farmland. When you finally arrive at the inlet for Barling Hall, you will discover a small wharf that has been constructed out of a large barge.

If you are making the circular walk around Barling Marsh, a rough road heads inland from the wharf to your starting-point at Barling church. Meanwhile, the main coastal footpath continues along the top of the sea-wall. Just south of the wharf, the sea-wall turns sharply inland around a small inlet. Like most of the coastline in this part of Essex, oysters were cultivated here during the 19th century – you can still see the remains of rectangular hollows dug out of the saltings.

Alongside this inlet, the creek splits into two channels at a junction once known as "Hell Hole". Away on the opposite bank, the smaller of the two branches is called Fleethead Creek, whilst the main channel changes its name to Little Wakering Creek from here onwards. As this name indicates, you are approaching Little Wakering, the first coastal village for almost six miles. This whole area is today dominated by a small gravel works.

Little Wakering

Now in its upper reaches, Little Wakering Creek gets narrower and narrower at every bend. Before long, just around a sharp corner, the creek suddenly comes to an end at a large sluice. This is clearly of modern construction, but it is likely that there has been a dam on this site for many centuries – old maps show there was once a farm called Dam Farm here. It is even possible that a wharf was built nearby, although only the smallest of craft could have negotiated this narrow waterway.

The name "Wakering" is of Anglo-Saxon origin, referring to a person called Walchel or Walcher. The village has grown steadily over the years, and today the sluice stands at the end of a side street called Kimberley Road. Whilst this is a very useful point of access to the creek, parking space is often limited, and visitors should be careful not to cause inconvenience to residents.

From the end of Kimberley Road, another public footpath follows the sea-wall along the south bank of Little Wakering Creek, gradually heading downstream again. This path offers an interesting walk through very enjoyable countryside. During the first part of the walk, a low concrete wall has been built along the crest of the embankment, providing a little extra protection against flooding. However, this wall soon disappears as you leave the village behind and head out into open countryside once again.

Within about half a mile. you pass close to the farm buildings of Little Wakering Wick. At this point, the sea-wall begins to veer to the right and the creek widens out noticeably. There is some evidence that this wide stretch was created artificially many years ago as a tidal mill-pond. The local historian Hervey Benham believed that a tidal mill stood in 1420 *"on the stream that flows north of the common,"* probably a reference to Little Wakering Creek.

He added that, in the village of Great Wakering, the road now known as Chapel Lane was once called Old Mill Lane. In 1597, *"the lane followed the stream at a point where there is still a wider stretch some sixty yards long, with a barn nearby known as the Mill Barn."* Today, it is difficult to trace the original route of Chapel Lane, and there are no visible remains of a tidal mill on the ground, but the evidence does seem compelling.

Continuing downstream, the sea-wall now heads in an easterly direction through a quiet and undisturbed rural landscape. The soft grassy nature of the footpath makes for very easy walking, and the tall embankment provides an excellent viewpoint for the surrounding countryside. Looking inland across the borrow-dyke, cultivated fields stretch into the distance towards the village of Great Wakering. The buildings far off to the right date from the 17th century. Known as Little Wakering Hall, this was once the home of the local historian Philip Benton.

On the other side of the sea-wall, the forces of nature have moulded a wilder but more natural scene, a view that changes with every tide and with every season. In the no-man's-land between Little Wakering Creek and Fleethead Creek, a large mass of saltings has formed, with narrow muddy channels winding their way amongst the raised clumps of vegetation. A more inhospitable terrain would be hard to imagine, but, if you look closely, you may spot a raised track zigzagging its way across this tangle of saltings. After almost half a mile, this rough footpath leads to a large circular mound, right in the middle of the saltings.

Over the years, this mound has had many different names, such as Hell Hill, possibly related to the nearby creek junction of Hell Hole. It has also been known as Smugglers Hill, but the most common name appears to be Brimstone Hill. This might just be an elaboration of the "hell" idea, although some historians suggest a connection with a local man who lived in the area in 1240.

One fact that is indisputable is that Brimstone Hill is not a recent construction. It was mentioned over a hundred years ago by the local historian Philip Benton, and it has even been suggested that it is the remains of a red hill, dating back to Roman times. Certainly it is known that other red hills exist in the vicinity – one was found on the mainland nearby, although this was destroyed when the farmland was levelled in 1969.

Whatever the history, Brimstone Hill is now used occasionally by wildfowlers, but it must be pointed out that the footpath across the saltings is badly eroded and very rough underfoot. *Furthermore, the tide comes in extremely fast in this area, and the saltings are often underwater at high tide. It is therefore extremely dangerous to venture out across the saltings.*

Just after a sharp zigzag in the sea-wall, you pass close to a remote farm called Halfway House. The track that serves this farm also continues right up to the sea-wall, thereby providing a useful point of access. The Halfway House track can even be used to make a circular walk around the next stretch of coastline, returning inland from the inlet at Mill Head.

Before long, the concrete-lined sea-wall turns sharply to the left. This corner is sometimes known as Fleet Head. In the south-eastern corner of Essex, the name "fleet" was used specifically for the "inned" part of a creek, inside the sea-defences and cut off from the tide. Originally however, the name was generally applied to any river or creek.

There is some confusion about the "head" part of the name. Ordnance Survey's 1:25,000 "Explorer" map places the words "Fleet Head" a little distance inland, next to a promontary. This suggests that the name may once have referred to the "head of land". However, older versions and other scales of Ordnance Survey map all print the name directly alongside the corner in the sea-wall. This supports the view that the "head" refers not to the head of land at all, but to the head of the creek nearby.

Either way, this corner marks the start of a long journey around the edge of a large peninsula. Just inside the sea-wall, the Halfway House track continues across the farmland, cutting across the peninsula to the far side in less than five hundred yards. This track is still a right of way, but the true coastal route follows the embankment around the outside of the peninsula, taking almost a mile and a half to reach the same point.

This walk is one of the best in Essex. The path is good underfoot, and passes through some beautiful but wild countryside. Indeed, this peninsula is the first Site of Special Scientific Interest (SSSI) to be encountered along the coastline for about 45 miles. A farm called Layfleet disappeared many years ago, but the land is still farmed. The irregular fields are separated by large patches of open water, the remains of the original tidal creeks.

At first, the path follows Fleethead Creek downstream, with wide views across the saltings. After about fifteen minutes walk, you reach the tip of the peninsula, where Fleethead Creek merges with Barlinghall Creek. At this junction, the raised sea-wall provides an excellent view of a picturesque wharf on the far bank. This is an isolated spot, with rural scenery in all directions. Looking inland, there is an interesting contrast between flat featureless fields and winding channels of brackish water.

Most people tend to walk around this area during the summer, but they miss one of the greatest attractions of these coastal marshes. During the winter months, the area comes alive as thousands of wildfowl flock around the Essex creeks. At this time of year, battling against bitter winds, a long and hard walk around this wild peninsula will reward you with memorable views of a dramatically bleak landscape.

After another half a mile, Barlinghall Creek meets the larger channel of Potton Creek. Unless you have a map, it is easy to be confused by this network of interconnecting creeks. Potton Creek can be used by boats at high tide as a useful "short-cut" between the River Roach and the River Thames. This route can cut over twenty miles off the journey, largely because the military firing-range on Foulness forces an extra-long detour around the Whitaker Beacon. This short-cut is also better protected from the weather, but the narrow channel and shallow waters require more specialised skills. Furthermore, boats are only allowed to pass through Havengore Bridge when the military are not firing.

Potton Island

As mentioned above, the coastline now begins to follows Potton Creek upstream. This stretch of the creek, sometimes known as Bullmans Reach, flows between the mainland and Potton Island. This large deserted island, two miles in length and roughly a mile across, is owned by the Ministry of Defence and is out of bounds to the public. The buildings of Potton Farm are clearly visible, sheltered just behind the sea-wall. This is the only farm on the island, although you can see several other low brick buildings in the distance, the remains of a mysterious military past. Potton Island is described in more detail later, along with the other islands that make up the Essex Archipelago.

The original route onto the island was by means of a tidal ford across Potton Creek. At high tide, this is completely hidden underwater. As the tide drops however, a large stone causeway is uncovered, sloping down from a removable gate on the mainland to the muddy bed of the creek. At this point, a series of narrow pipes have been incorporated underneath the surface of the track, allowing water to continue to flow along the creek. Without these pipes, the causeway would act as a low dam, with the build-up of water weakening the structure.

Tidal causeway onto Potton Island

On the far side, the track climbs up the bank towards a similar floodgate on Potton Island. It is possible to walk across the ford, although you will need good boots because in places the track is buried under several inches of mud. It was improved in 1946 by Italian prisoners of war, but the surface is often covered in seaweed and can be extremely slippery. *The MOD does not allow you to set foot on Potton Island itself.* A new military bridge was built across the creek many years ago, but the ford is still in good workable condition.

Heading southwards from Potton Ford, the footpath continues along the crest of the sea-wall. This is classic coastal scenery – a wide grassy embankment with a simple farmtrack running along its base. The original sea-defences were constructed out of simple earth, leaving a deep ditch just inland. This "borrow-dyke", as the ditch is properly known, is often covered with reeds, forming a haven for insects and other forms of wildlife. A detailed survey in 1956 also revealed the presence of a "red hill" in this area. These red hills are believed to date back to Roman times. There is still some discussion about their original purpose, but this particular red hill shows signs of pipes running through to a simple oven or hearth.

Looking out across the creek, the sea-wall is protected in several places by small patches of saltings, the clumps of vegetation helping to stabilise the mudflats and reduce erosion. On the far side of the creek, a second set of buildings can be seen on Potton Island. These low brick-built cottages stand on the island's main road, called Farm Crescent. This road links the farm with the military swing-bridge, which is clearly visible just ahead.

The bridge is quite an impressive structure. Constructed from a mixture of metal and concrete, it stands on three piers that have been sunk into the bed of the creek. At high tide, the central section of roadway can be swung through 90 degrees in order to let boats sail up the creek. The bridge, along with its associated barriers and warning

The swing-bridge onto Potton Island

lights, is controlled from a brick building that doubles up as a military checkpoint. Note that the access road leading up to the bridge is owned by the MOD and is not open to the public.

Beyond the bridge, the coastal route continues to follow the sea-wall along the shores of Potton Creek. Along this stretch, the MOD has erected a series of notices to warn members of the public to keep off their land. Some people feel intimidated by these notices, but this concern is unfounded – the sea-wall itself is a long-established public right of way.

A short distance beyond Potton Bridge, you can see the masts of numerous yachts, some moored along the banks of the creek and some resting on dry land. This large boat-yard, with its own cranes and slipway, was once owned by a man called Bill Sutton, and is still known as Suttons Boat-yard.

Just south of the boat-yard, the sea-wall turns sharply to the right into a large inlet. A wooden jetty was, until recently, the site of the Wakering Yacht Club. This inlet is known as Mill Head, a name which dates from the 16th century. At that time, this was a tidal pound, powering the machinery in Lord's Mill. All signs of this small tidal mill have now disappeared, but this history may explain why the inlet now has such an unusual shape, almost in two separate sections.

More recently, the shallow waters of Mill Head were used as a mud-dock for the nearby brickworks. Until the 20th century, very few roads were in a condition good enough to carry heavy building materials. As a result, many coastal villages had their own small brickworks, transporting their goods around by boat. At its peak in the mid-1800s, the Great Wakering brickworks employed over 1000 people. This particular factory closed many years ago, and the site is now covered by a large landfill site, but the village still has a small brick-making industry further to the west.

Circular walk near Great Wakering

After several miles of remote coastline, Mill Head finally marks the end of the long trek around the edge of the Fleet Head peninsula. At the innermost point of the inlet, a public footpath heads inland towards Common Road, a quiet back-lane alongside Great Wakering Common. Perhaps the most enjoyable route is a circular walk around the Fleet Head peninsula, three miles of beautiful and interesting countryside. For this circular route, it is best to start near the end of Common Road, where the road splits. (Note that, at this junction, the road straight ahead leads to Potton Island. It is privately owned by the MOD and is closed to the public.) Through a gate to the left, a public footpath follows a track past the buildings of Halfway House, leading eventually to the sea-wall at the corner known as Fleet Head. Turning right at the corner, it is easy to follow the sea-wall around the peninsula (as just described) to the Mill Head inlet. From this inlet, a footpath brings you back inland to Common Road again.

Common Road is therefore an important access route for most walks in this area. The road begins near the parish church in Great Wakering, a quiet village which has the distinction of being the driest place in the United Kingdom. In a typical year, Great Wakering experiences around 18 inches of rain, less than half the national average of 43 inches.

The next stretch of coastline, from Mill Head to Oxenham Farm, is full of interest and is a short but popular walk. On the far side of the Mill Head inlet, you head out into open countryside again. This sea-wall was strengthened a few years ago, and gives an excellent raised vantage-point over the surrounding scenery. On your left, the width of the channel varies enormously according to the tide. Indeed, at low tide the channel is actually narrower than the borrow-dyke that runs along the foot of the embankment. It is around this point that Potton Creek merges with the upper reaches of Havengore Creek. From here on, you are effectively heading downstream again, with the open sea just two miles away.

About five minutes' walk from the Mill Head inlet, you pass a small boat-house, with its own slipway leading down into Havengore Creek. This boat-house stands directly opposite the entrance to The Middleway, a wide creek that is often used as a short-cut by boats from Burnham-on-Crouch. The Middleway separates two mysterious islands – Potton on the island, and Rushley on the right.

Rushley Ford

It is often said that Rushley belongs to the Ministry of Defence, but in fact the island is privately owned by a local farmer. All the same, there is no public access onto the island, although it does have an interesting history. This is described later on, along with the other islands of the Essex Archipelago. Rushley is the only island in the archipelago without a road link to the mainland. At high tide therefore, it is only accessible by boat. However, the usual means of access is at low tide, using a rough ford a few hundred yards further on. This ford is uncovered for just four hours at low water. People who venture onto the island must therefore be careful not to get cut off by the incoming tide.

Tidal ford onto Rushley Island

The ford onto Rushley Island is much more rudimentary than the Potton causeway to the north. Many tons of stones and gravel have been applied over the years, but each tide brings an extra layer of silt. As a result, the ford slowly becomes buried under the mud. Near the sea-wall, this mud can be up to a foot deep. Contrary to most people's expectations, the surface of the ford is much firmer near the centre of the creek, probably because the strong current does not allow silt to settle. Tractors still regularly use the ford to cross onto the island, and it can take vehicles with a single-axle weight of ten tons. However, the soft mud makes it difficult to cross on foot.

Just beyond Rushley Ford, the buildings of Oxenham Farm stand just inside the sea-wall. This area has been farmed for over 600 years (records refer to Oxonhamme in 1358) though the current buildings are relatively modern. One of the newer houses is Rushley Cottage, built in 1974/5.

Oxenham Farm provides the last access to the coastline for a mile or two. A narrow lane leads up to the farm from Landwick Cottages, but this is only a right of way on foot – only authorised vehicles are technically allowed to drive up to the sea-wall. Ordnance Survey maps show a second public footpath heading westwards across the fields from Oxenham Farm. Do not be tempted to try this route – it is blocked in several places by wide drainage ditches.

From Oxenham Farm, the coastal route continues around a small inlet. Looking across the creek, you can just spot a small barn on Rushley Island, its prominent black roof just poking above the sea-wall. Rushley is the smallest of the islands in the archipelago, and you only have to walk a few hundred yards, just beyond an unsightly sewage works, before you reach the end of the island. From this point, you can look directly up a creek known as Narrow Guts, which separates Rushley from its neighbour, Havengore Island.

Havengore Bridge

By this stage however, most eyes will be drawn to the sight ahead. In 1988, the MOD built an impressive new bascule bridge onto Havengore Island, linking up with their installations on Foulness. These islands are out of bounds to the public, and are therefore described in a special section of their own, but it seems appropriate to describe the bridge here because of its obvious impact on the scenery.

The original Scherzer rolling lift-bridge across Havengore Creek

This is actually the second bridge to stand on this site. The first bridge was started in 1915, along with two light railways to help with the construction. Many people believe that the bridge was brought over from Germany as part of wartime reparations, but there is no truth in this story. The structure was actually built by a Scottish company as part of a larger project to link the island of Foulness with the mainland. The bridge and its connecting roads were finally opened in 1922.

The War Department had agreed on a design known as a Scherzer Rolling Lift Bridge. This enabled a long stretch of roadway to lift up to allow tall yachts to pass underneath. Rather than using an ordinary hinge to take all the strain, this type of bridge is hinged around a pair of enormous wheel-like structures, roughly thirty feet across. These wheels could then roll slowly along metal platforms to lift up the bridge. At first, the mechanism was operated entirely by hand, but an electrical system was later added. The weight of the roadway was counter-balanced by a large metal tank overhead.

The original bridge included a railway track. The structure was largely made of metal and suffered from corrosion and subsidence. Over the years, it generally deteriorated and traffic was eventually limited to a single lane. A weight limit of ten tons was also imposed, forcing farmers to carry

The original Havengore Bridge, opening for boats

their goods across the bridge in several trips. In 1982, engineers were asked to design a replacement bridge. Construction of the new bridge started in 1987, and it was finally opened on 10th November 1988, at a total cost of £5½ million.

The new Havengore Bridge

The new concrete bridge is both wider and higher than the original, but it still has an opening section for boats. However, the MOD have slung a boom underneath the bridge, thereby controlling all boat access along the creek. This boom is hinged so that it drops out of the way when the bridge is raised. For two hours either side of high tide, road traffic can be stopped and an enormous stretch of road can lift to an almost vertical position. Unlike its predecessor, the new bridge no longer carries a railway track.

On a more general point, it is interesting to note that Scotland has only two islands that are connected to the mainland by a bridge (Skye and Seil), whilst Wales has just one (Anglesey). In contrast, Essex has no fewer than four, yet the county is rarely associated with islands and coastlines.

As you approach Havengore Bridge along the sea-wall, the footpath is surrounded by a series of tall wire fences. The land beyond the bridge is part of the military range, and is closed to the public when firing is taking place. At such times, a locked gate bars any further progress around the coastline, and you have to retrace your steps back to Oxenham Farm. The ranges are more likely to be quiet at weekends and Bank Holidays, but you are advised to check at the military checkpoint near Landwick Cottages before setting out on a long walk, because the MOD police sometimes fail to unlock the gate.

Beyond the gate, walkers are channelled through a narrow tunnel underneath the bridge. When you emerge on the far side, the footpath quickly rejoins the sea-wall, now just half a mile from the open sea. Keep a look-out for strange markings leading out across the saltings – these mark the site of the original bridge.

Before the military took over this land, old maps show a coastguard station on the banks of Havengore Creek here, with a private ferry onto Havengore Island. Going even further back in time, this was once the base of a customs ship, patrolling the nearby creeks on the look-out for smugglers. This ship was called The Beagle, later to become famous through the voyages of Charles Darwin.

Three hundred yards from the bridge, navigation charts show the remains of a ford across the creek. From the sea-wall, the saltings are too extensive for you to see the bed of the creek, but from Havengore Bridge stakes can be seen sticking out of the mud, crossing the creek in two parallel lines. The charts are correct to warn shipping of an underwater obstruction, but this is not the remains of a ford at all. In practice, these metal stakes once supported pipelines across the creek, carrying water and telephone cables onto Havengore Island.

However, if you were to venture down to the bed of the creek and explore more closely, you would find pairs of wooden posts embedded in the mud just a few yards to the right of the pipelines. It is not obvious from the bridge, but from the edge of the saltings it is clear that these posts form a direct line across the creek. This appears to be the site of a raised walkway across the creek, perhaps not used for over a hundred years.

Heading south-eastwards from Havengore Bridge, the footpath soon reaches the mouth of Havengore Creek, where the channel finally opens out into the Thames Estuary. This corner, known as Haven Point, is an important milestone. Here you leave behind the Essex Archipelago with its intricate network of narrow creeks and mysterious islands, and begin a long but fascinating walk along the shores of the River Thames.

For the first two miles of this walk, the land is very low-lying. This area was reclaimed from the sea many years ago, and is still marked on a few maps as Newlands. Today, the peninsula is part of a firing range known as the New Ranges. Various military buildings are scattered around the ranges, although some parts are still reserved for farming.

This stretch of coastline is always popular with bird-watchers. In winter, the mudflats teem with wildfowl, particularly brent geese. However, the sea-wall is exposed to the wind, and winter visits are often bitterly cold. Because of the firing range, walkers are reminded that they should not stray from the sea-wall.

About a hundred yards from Haven Point, the path bends slightly to the right. Because of its excellent vantage-point, a pill-box was built into the sea-wall here during the Second World War. The pill-box remained in good condition for many years, but unfortunately the authorities saw fit to demolish the structure just a few years ago. Not far beyond this point, the surface of the sea-wall changes from grass to concrete. This allows walkers to make faster progress, but is much more tiring on the feet.

Wakering Stairs

The path eventually leads to a point called Wakering Stairs, where an access-road climbs up onto the sea-wall. On most weekdays, red flags are raised around the perimeter of the range, indicating that firing is taking place and all footpaths are closed to the public. But when the military are not firing, you are allowed to drive right up the sea-wall at Wakering Stairs. This narrow road, known as Stairs Road, starts from a barrier beside the MOD checkpoint at Landwick Gate (at the end of New Road). It then winds its way across the ranges, with two level-crossings over the MOD's own railway system.

Various military tracks branch off Stairs Road, with names such as Catherine's Walk, Benn's Way and Sally's Walk. They have a barrier across each entrance, and are clearly out of bounds to the public.

Just before the shoreline, there is a small car-parking area and Stairs Road then climbs up on to the top of the sea-wall. Until around 1990, a large pill-box stood on the top of the embankment here, with a ladder leading up to a short tower. This was built during the war to support an anti-aircraft gun. This raised platform acted for many years as a useful viewpoint for bird-watchers, but was eventually demolished by the military authorities. At around the same time, a new control tower was built just inland. This is just one of a series of towers recently constructed along the coast by the MOD, all with prominent yellow features.

Stairs Road pre-dates the firing range by many centuries. Indeed this was the original route onto Foulness Island. Once the track reaches the top of the sea-wall, it then drops down the far side and heads out across the tidal mudflats in an easterly direction. The mud is usually very soft close to the shore, and hence the first few yards of the track have been improved with a rough stone and concrete surface. In the 1920s, Ordnance Survey maps show that the route temporarily split into two tracks for a hundred yards before joining again. This may have been a cartographer's mistake – there is certainly no sign of this bifurcation today.

After a third of a mile, the tidal track suddenly veers to the left and runs parallel to the coastline for five miles, eventually reaching a similar headway on the remote island of Foulness. This ancient track was known as the Broomway, after the bunches of twigs or "brooms" that were used to mark the route across the mudflats. More details are given in the description of Foulness Island, but it seems appropriate to mention the landward section here.

Wakering Stairs was only one of a series of headways leading out to the Broomway. Over the years, different headways came and went, including one known as Kings Head, a mile and a half to the west of here. In 1867, for example, the historian Philip Benton described the re-opening of Wakering Stairs:

"The passage through Wakering (by Landwick) to Foulness was disused for many years, being impassable, and those having business therein were obliged to take the sands from Pigs Bay in South Shoebury (opposite Suttons), but the importance of having the old road restored becoming apparent, the repair was undertaken about 25 years ago by subscription, and the onus of keeping up the highway is now borne by Great Wakering."

Wakering Stairs eventually became the preferred headway, although the dangerous tidal route along the Broomway became redundant in 1921 when the new road across Havengore Bridge was finally opened. Today, the Ministry of Defence still occasionally uses the old track across the mudflats to retrieve shells that have been fired from the mainland. The Broomway is also a public right of way and therefore is technically open to the public when firing is not taking place. However, the route is no longer marked and the track is therefore now more dangerous than ever. (Note that the mudflats are littered with marker posts for tracking shells – these do NOT indicate the route of the Broomway.)

At weekends, Wakering Stairs is often a popular spot. Some people drive here to walk the dog, others come for the birdlife, whilst many people enjoy it simply for the fresh air and unusual views. However, most visitors tend to follow the concrete sea-wall to the east of Wakering Stairs. In contrast, the grassy footpath to the west is usually deserted and is ideal for a quiet undisturbed walk in the countryside.

Following the crest of the sea-wall in this westerly direction, the path veers slightly to the right just a few yards after leaving the road. Many years ago, the coastline turned left at this corner, but a long strip of farmland was abandoned to the sea during the 19th century, possibly after the storms of 1897. At low tide, you can still see the route of the original sea-wall, and the remains of field ditches are occasionally visible amongst the saltings.

Along this stretch of coastline, the countryside has mostly been left undeveloped, with only occasional signs that this is a military range. A long grey building houses an indoor firing-range, but otherwise the footpath passes some beautifully undisturbed countryside. There are also wide views out to sea, an area named on maps as the Black Grounds.

About fifteen minutes' walk from Wakering Stairs, the footpath along the sea-wall comes to an end at a tall wire fence, a spot called Morrin's Point. The next few miles of coastline include the headquarters of the Shoeburyness New Ranges, and the public right of way therefore has to detour inland. With the fence to your left, there are no problems following the correct route. At one point, the footpath crosses over a railway track, built in 1888, before joining a centuries-old path known as Cupid's Chase.

It is interesting to note how this area has changed beyond recognition over the last hundred years. Until the arrival of the military, there were many routes of access to the coastline. Stairs Road has already been mentioned, and Morrin's Point was named after the nearby Morrin's Chase, which now leads instead to the indoor firing-range.

The route of Cupid's Chase has also been diverted over the years. As its name might suggest, it originally led to a small promontary called Cupid's Point. This promontary was part of the farmland that was abandoned to the sea in the late 1800s. Further to the west, tracks like Cherrytree Chase and Poynter's Chase have now been absorbed into the closed military zone, but the name of Poynter's Point is still marked on detailed maps.

Some of these tracks may have been used over the centuries to reach the mudflats and travel along the Broomway to Foulness. Certainly it is known that Kings Head was a popular access route. This was a small headland to the west, in an area known as Pig's Bay. In 1922, the Ordnance Survey map even shows two separate headways leading out from Kings Head, joining up again 150 yards from the shoreline. Another track nearby was known as Suttons Head (occasionally also called Kennets Head). This is still marked as a tidal causeway on the modern "Explorer" maps.

Back on Cupid's Chase, the footpath leads through the fields and across a second level-crossing before finally emerging on Suttons Road. This is a private military road, linking the Shoebury headquarters with the rest of the firing range. Directly opposite you, a gate leads out of the military range and onto Victoria Drive, a quiet suburban street just off Poynters Lane. From time to time, the military police fail to unlock this gate, so it is worth checking in advance if you want to make a circular walk.

Poynters Lane heads south towards the military town of Shoeburyness. Beside the road, a tall barbed-wire fence runs around the perimeter of a large military establishment. The New Ranges have been built along the coast here, thereby forcing us to make a long detour inland. However, the next access to the shoreline is only half a mile further on, down a side-street called Blackgate Road. Passing the main entrance to the New Ranges, this road passes over a small level-crossing and leads directly to Shoebury East Beach.

Shoebury East Beach

Only about half a mile of this beach is open to the public. The grass verge is sometimes covered with parked cars, and the whole area can get very crowded during the summer. The eastern end of the beach is marked by a row of tall posts, erected during the Second World War to hinder any attempted invasion. This boom now forms the boundary of the military firing range, and you are therefore ordered not to go beyond this line.

The boom originally stretched out to permanent water, over a mile from the shore. Since the war, it has been shortened by a few hundred yards, but it is still easy to follow the remaining posts out across the mudflats. *If you do venture far from the shore, great care should be taken, as the incoming tide can cross the mudflats faster than you can run, and it is obviously essential to consult a tide-timetable.*

To the south-east, low embankments form an artificial island, which is described in more detail later around Foulness. On a clear day, the shores of Kent can also be seen far away to the right, over seven miles away across the Thames estuary. This area of water is known to sailors as The Nore, from the Old Norse word "nor" which was used to describe a sea inlet. Ever since London established itself as an important trading port in the early 18th century, The Nore has been a vital and busy shipping lane.

Shoebury East Beach is quite popular with local families. For small children, a wooden flight of steps leads down to a shallow paddling pool, and a large café provides refreshments during the summer months. However, it is not long before the coastal route has to retreat inland again along a side-road known as Rampart Street. This leads to the end of the High Street in Shoebury. On the left here, a large gateway stands at the entrance to the site of Shoebury Garrison. Until recently, this garrison played an important part in the history of the area.

Shoebury's military connection began in 1805, when Lt. Gen. Henry Shrapnel conducted a few experiments here. This led eventually to the development of the shrapnel shell, though it was not until 1848 that the War Department bought its first land in the area. Following two years of building and preparation, an experimental range was opened on the 1st April 1851. Five years later, a permanent School of Gunnery was authorised, and this began operations in 1859.

The military establishment took over most of the land near the promontary at Shoebury. This promontary was originally called Black Tail Point, but it soon became known just as Shoebury Ness. Today, the town is frequently referred to as Shoeburyness, although this is technically a misnomer. At the tip of the promontary, a short barge pier was constructed in 1859 in order to transport heavy goods to the ranges, though the present pier dates from 1909. The pier makes use of a convenient deep-water channel which crosses the Maplin Sands at this point. The channel is known as The Knock, a name which occurs in several other channels in the vicinity, such as Knock Deep, West Knock and Knock Swin.

The testing site quickly flourished and expanded. When the railway was built at Shoebury, an extension was constructed into the ranges. The New Ranges were then opened in 1890, and the War Department continued to buy up land to the north-east of the garrison. This led ultimately to the purchase of Havengore, New England and Foulness islands.

There was a bad gun accident in 1885, but the worst disaster to strike the ranges occurred in 1918, when a serious fire and explosion caused £3 million damage and resulted in the complete evacuation of the civilian population of Shoebury. Since these incidents, however, the safety record of the ranges was commendable, and local residents became quite used to the distant sounds of gunfire and explosions.

However, during the 1980s and 90s, military operations were scaled down, and the large number of soldiers gradually dwindled to just a handful, leaving the buildings to fall slowly into disrepair. The MOD eventually sold the site, and the area is currently undergoing extensive redevelopment. Some of the historic buildings are being renovated, and many new homes are being built. It is hoped that the developers honour their plans to re-open access to this stretch of coastline, after being denied to local people for so long. Much more development is planned, including a business park, and so, until work is finished, our coastal route has to skirt the garrison.

From the gateway at the bottom of the High Street, the nearest public route to the coastline is along Campfield Road. A large area of land here is taken up by factories and warehouses. About half a mile along the road, an inconspicuous signpost indicates the entrance to Gunners Park. This was once used as a firing range, but, after being leased to Southend Borough Council, it was finally opened to the public in 1986. One small section of Gunners Park has been set aside for wildlife. Most of this "countryside" has been artificially laid out, though it seems odd that many conservationists spend so much of their time and effort building up a tiny area of artificial landscape when most of the genuinely wild countryside nearby is under threat.

A good track leads through Gunners Park almost as far as the shore. Here, the park is bounded by a concrete sea-wall, with a narrow beach on the seaward side. To the east of the park, the land starts to rise slightly, and the coastline around the rest of the garrison consists of low sloping cliffs, covered with vegetation. Dotted around the site are a number of old disused military buildings, some dating back to the Napoleonic era. Unfortunately, at the time of writing there is no access along the coastline, and you need to retreat from Gunners Park back onto Campfield Road. However, the major redevelopment of this area is almost certain to lead to substantial changes over the next few years.

Continuing to the west along Campfield Road, you soon reach a junction with the main Ness Road. To the right, Ness Road is the name given to the last section of the A13, a main trunk route which leads right through Southend-on-Sea and all the way into central London. To the left, however, Ness Road becomes the B1016, leading back to the coastline within just half a mile. This is the start of a long stretch of beach which continues westwards for many miles, although the construction of a low concrete sea-wall has meant that the sandy foreshore can no longer be seen from the road. If you are using the Ordnance Survey's 1:25,000 "Explorer" maps, it is worth noting that from this point onwards there is a large overlap between map 176 (Blackwater Estuary) and 175 (Southend-on-Sea & Basildon). The overlap continues until you reach old Leigh, almost six miles along the coast.

Thorpe Bay

These are the outskirts of the up-market dormitory town of Thorpe Bay. Like the village of Thorpe-le-Soken in north-east Essex, the name of this district is probably derived from the Old English word "throp", or its Old Norse equivalent, "thorp". This name was often given to a secondary settlement or an outlying village, although in this case the parent town was almost certainly not Southend-on-Sea but the nearby village of Prittlewell.

Lawns and large gardens sweep down from the houses at the top of the hill to the road-side, where cars jostle in the summer for the last few parking spaces. If the sun comes out at the weekend, the beach can get quite busy, though the area is popular with windsurfers regardless of the weather. There are also a couple of yacht clubs, and drivers should watch out for yachts being slowly carted across the road.

At high tide, the sea covers most of the beach, and on occasions it has been known to top the sea-wall, flooding a few low-lying sections of the coastal road. As the waters recede however, it becomes clear that the sandy beach only forms a narrow strip along the coast. Below the beach, an enormous area of mudflats is revealed by the tide, stretching over a mile out to sea.

Standing near the low tide mark, a large ship appears to have broken its back on the mudbanks and is now lying in two separate parts. These are in fact the remains of a section of Mulberry harbour, a floating concrete platform built during the Second World War to help with the Allied landings at Arromanches in Normandy. *Although people have managed to reach the wreck by walking out across the flats at low tide, it must be stressed that any attempt to emulate this feat can be dangerous. As explained with the boom on Shoebury East Beach, the incoming tide can cross these mudflats much faster than you can run. There are also various water-channels which can cut off your retreat, and their positions tend to change from year to year. If you want to wander around the mudflats, be sure to stay within a safe distance of the beach and always consult a tide-timetable.*

On a clear day, a pair of binoculars will give a good view of another wreck on the opposite bank of the River Thames. In 1944, a Liberty ship called "The Richard Montgomery" sank on a shallow sand-bank whilst sailing past the mouth of the River Medway. At the time, the ship was carrying 4000 tons of bombs for the war effort, and these were considered to be too unstable to recover. Instead, the wreck was carefully marked by a series of prominent buoys to ward off passing ships. Although various plans have been suggested over the years, it is still believed that the wreck is too hazardous to disturb, and there are many scare stories about the tidal wave and destruction that any explosion might cause. Specialist divers regularly check the wreck, and it is hoped that the explosives will eventually decay enough to become harmless.

Recommended bibliography:

A discovery of old Essex – Richard Pusey [Crouch & southern Blackwater]
That time o' day (memories of Burnham-on-Crouch) – John Booth
Burnham-on-Crouch in old picture postcards – European Library
A short history of South Woodham Ferrers – Floyd Wentworth
Where's Woodham Ferris? – Les Holden
A history of Rochford – L. Cryer

Chapter six – the Essex Archipelago

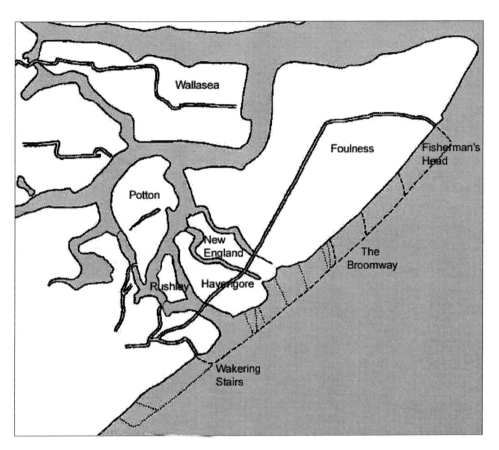

This chapter describes the Essex Archipelago, a special group of six marshy, onshore islands, surrounded by sea-walls, which lie at the south-eastern edge of Essex. Remote, relatively isolated and prized for their agricultural value, they are separated by tidal creeks and form an interlocking pattern, like a jigsaw puzzle. There is no comparable feature anywhere else in Britain and the archipelago offers some of the wildest and most beautiful scenery in the area. Unfortunately public access is extremely limited, but this book describes the landscape, features and unusual history of this unique corner of the country.

Of the six islands, Foulness, New England, Havengore and Potton Islands are owned by the MOD. Most of them have a civilian population, but access to the general public is not usually permitted. The MOD have built road bridges to these islands which can open up for water traffic. Wallasea is perhaps the stranger in this group, and is described separately in the previous chapter. Both Wallasea and Rushley Islands are privately owned.

Potton Island

Potton Island is a perfect example of why the Essex Archipelago is unique. Despite being an island, Potton has no coastline overlooking the open sea. Instead, it is surrounded by land in all directions, separated only by deep rivers and tidal creeks. It is connected to the mainland by a good road-bridge, and yet Potton Island remains largely unknown, even to people who live locally. Nor is it one of the smallest islands in the archipelago – Potton is more than two miles in length and, at its widest point, is about a mile and a half across.

Potton Island is criss-crossed by a network of narrow drainage ditches, dividing the land into a series of irregularly-shaped fields. A tall sea-wall encircles the island, much of the earth taken from a wide borrow-dyke that runs along the foot of the embankment.

Like the other islands in the archipelago, the land is extremely flat and low-lying. Indeed, some people say that the word "Potton" means a deep hole, particularly in a river-bed. Another source says that the island may have been named after one of its owners – records show that a family called Potton were living on the neighbouring island of Foulness in 1799. However, it is more likely that the family were named after the island, not the other way around, because the area was recorded as Magna Potting as far back as 1244.

The place-name "Potting" appears to be of Anglo-Saxon origin, meaning "land of Potta". This might refer to an Anglo-Saxon landowner. There is certainly evidence that the Romans lived here – in the 1950s, two red hills were discovered during the construction of the new road across the island. (Red hills are discussed in more detail earlier in this book, during the description of Mersea Island.) The red hills on Potton were found to contain pieces of Roman pottery, now kept in the museum at Southend-on-Sea.

Potton was originally bisected by a narrow tidal creek. When the first sea-defences were built around the edge of the island, this channel was blocked off at either end. As a result, the water no longer ebbed and flowed with the daily tides. In south-east Essex, this type of channel is often called a "fleet". Old maps of Potton Island show that this channel was known as the Great Fleet, although the name "Boundary Fleet" is sometimes used instead.

The Great Fleet divided Potton Island into two parts. The southern end of the island was the smaller part. Known as Little Potton, it belonged to the parish of Little Wakering, which was later absorbed into Barling parish. The northern part of the island, called Great Potton, was much larger. The soil here was generally of better quality, although it was more low-lying and prone to floods. Great Potton was originally part of Great Wakering parish, although it too eventually transferred to Barling parish.

The parish information is important to historians, because it strongly suggests that Great Potton and Little Potton were owned by different landlords, just like Wallasea and Two-Tree Island. Old maps show further evidence of this, in the form of an earth embankment on the northern bank of the Great Fleet. This was a counterwall, a precautionary measure to limit the damage caused by any floods.

Each part of the island even had its own farmhouse. Little Potton Farm and Great Potton Farm stood just a hundred yards apart, on opposite sides of the Great Fleet. Some maps show a third building called Newhouse. This stood just a little further to the west, near the head of the tidal ford. (This ford was the original route of access onto the island, and is described in more detail earlier.)

From Great Potton Farm, a track called Pasture Lane headed northwards across the island. This led to an area of farmland known as Newlands. As its name suggests, this land was reclaimed from the sea at a much later date, some time between 1805 and 1860, by the construction of a new length of sea-wall across the saltings. The addition of Newlands brought the total size of Potton Island up to 1024 acres. The original sea-defences disappeared long ago, but the accompanying borrow-dyke still survives. This ditch is clearly marked on modern Ordnance Survey maps, in the north-western corner of the island.

Potton Island remained a quiet backwater until after the Second World War. The MOD already owned the neighbouring islands of Foulness, New England and Havengore, and were looking to buy Potton as well. However, during the night of 31st January 1953, the eastern coastline of England was devastated by one of the highest tides ever known. The sea-wall around Potton was breached in eleven places, leaving the island flooded for many months. Eventually the sea-defences were repaired, and on 27th April 1955, the MOD compulsarily bought the island.

The MOD moved the Armament Research Establishment (ARE) from Foulness onto their newly-acquired island. One of their first actions was to improve access onto Potton by building a bridge at the southern end of the island. The new bridge, described in more detail earlier, was designed with an opening section in order to allow sailing craft to pass through. From the bridge, a new road was built up the west of the island to Great Potton Farm. Known as Farm Crescent, this road was just the first of a series of new tracks, linking together the various military buildings scattered across the island. Most of these tracks were simple concrete affairs, often just a single lane wide.

Despite the arrival of the MOD, 80% of the island was leased back for farming. Some of the fields were used for pasture, whilst the more fertile land was used for growing crops. The Farm Cottages were probably built around this time to house the farm workers. These three brick houses were located just inside the sea-wall, alongside Farm Crescent. Being two storeys in height, they are clearly visible from the mainland.

The ARE was renamed the Blast and Fragmentation Range, and later became part of RARDE. Since around 1977, the MOD has largely abandoned the island. Indeed, it is not even part of their aircraft exclusion zone. The Farm Cottages are now the only inhabitable buildings on the island. All the original farmhouses have gone, although a few barns are still used at the site of Great Potton Farm, near the old tidal ford.

These days, the island is almost deserted. The counterwall that once divided Great Potton from Little Potton has gone, but the Great Fleet still exists as a wide ribbon of water, snaking its way across the middle of the island. From the mainland, you can see where the Great Fleet originally flowed out into Potton Creek – this appears as a small inlet just south of the ford.

The Great Fleet was much wider on the far side of the island, an area once known as Rainbow Marsh. Here it flowed out into a channel usually called The Middleway (sometimes also known as Yokefleet or the Gore Channel), forming a large bay of saltings. During the 19th century, these saltings were used for a number of oyster-beds. Although they have not been used for around a hundred years, these oyster-beds are still clearly visible to passing sailors in the form of large rectangular pits. Indeed, the Middleway is a popular route for local yachtsmen, because it acts as a useful short-cut between the River Crouch and the River Thames.

Half a mile further north along the Middleway, there is another inlet of saltings, named on old maps as the East Salts. This inlet was originally the mouth of a second creek that cut across the middle of Potton Island. The Old Fleet, as it is known, was also blocked off from the daily tides by the sea-defences. It is now very shallow and overgrown, but visitors to the island can trace its route across the fields.

At its northern end, the Middleway joins the River Roach. This river, which forms the northern edge of Potton Island has virtually no saltings along its banks. As a result, the sea-defences are very susceptible to wave erosion. This stretch of embankment has been reinforced with a concrete facing, but it is nevertheless gradually being undermined.

The future of Potton Island remains unclear. Over the years, there have been many ideas for its development, either for new houses or for recreational use, perhaps as a nature reserve. It has even been suggested that Potton could be turned into an enormous refuse tip, rather like the massive works near Mucking on the banks of the River Thames. But for now, the MOD continues to keep Potton firmly closed to the public, leaving an air of mystery hanging over the island. Visits are not normally possible, and outsiders can only obtain glimpses of this forgotten island from a few vantage points on the mainland nearby. The best views can be obtained either from the Fleethead peninsula, or across the River Roach from Paglesham Eastend.

Rushley Island

Rushley is by far the smallest of the six islands that comprise the Essex Archipelago. From north to south, the island is about a mile long, but it is rarely more than a few hundred yards in width. As we shall see shortly, it is also one of the newest islands in the group, yet it is not clear where the name comes from. The word ending "ey" is often found around the Essex coast. This comes from the old Anglo-Saxon language, indicating an island. However, in this particular case, it is possible that the name originally ended with the word "ley", which instead signifies a field or pasture. This theory is also supported by the original Ordnance Survey map, surveyed around 1800, which spells the island "Rushly".

Until the late 18th century, Rushley was a low-lying tidal marsh. As a consequence, it is not surprising that the island has little early history. In an auction in May 1780, the marshes of Rushley were sold at an auction for £40. John Harriott, the new owner, had an ambitious plan to turn the saltings into rich farming land by building a sea-wall around the edge of these marshes. His first task was to build a shelter for the workmen, raised on wooden stilts above the saltings to protect it from the tide.

Between July and December 1781, Harriott's men built an enormous embankment around the perimeter of the island, a total of 2½ miles. The construction of the new sea-wall was a massive undertaking, thirty feet across at its base and with an average height of eight feet. The last gap was closed on Christmas Day, but unfortunately the workmen had ignored Harriott's suggestion to strengthen the embankment with timber. As a result, the new wall was swept away by a high tide just three days later.

In early 1782, the wall was repaired, this time under Harriott's direct leadership. In addition, he built a comfortable new farmhouse on the mainland nearby. He tried to plant crops on his new island, but the sea-salt did not leach out of the soil as fast as he had expected. For the next six years, his attempts to grow wheat, barley, beans, oats and peas all failed. He had a little success with rape, mustard-seed and rye-grass, but Harriott still made an enormous financial loss. Nevertheless, the Society for the Encouragement of Arts and Sciences awarded him their gold medal for his endeavours.

John Harriott also tried digging to find fresh water for his new island. He sunk wells up to 40 feet deep in three different places around Rushley, but without success.

However, this digging did unearth various archaeological artefacts, including iron spear-heads, human bones and pieces of Roman pottery.

In 1790, fire destroyed the farmhouse on the mainland. This was rebuilt before the next winter, but Harriott was left short of money. In order to cut down on his expenses, he postponed his plans to heighten the sea-walls. As a result, Rushley Island flooded again on 2nd February 1791. He wrote in his diary:

"I looked down on the raging watery element swelling itself to a height that had never been known before, and over-topping my walls as if in search of what I had formerly wrested from its dominion."

One source of information says that no walls were breached during this flood, whilst another says that the embankments were swept away along the western edge of the island. Either way, a new western sea-wall was built around this time. Being further inland, this also meant that around ten acres of valuable farmland had to be abandoned to the sea. Furthermore, the floods had left new deposits of salt in the soil, and Harriott realised that no useful crops could be planted for several more years. Financially destitute, he heightened the sea-defences one last time and sold out, emigrating to America.

Rushley's chequered history continued under the new owner, Francis Bannester, who renewed the search for fresh water on the island. At that time, people living in these remote marshes had to arrange for all fresh water to be brought in by boat, an expensive and time-consuming process.

Francis Bannester began digging in 1828, but encountered problems after 200 feet. During his second attempt, he struck solid rock at a depth of 455 feet. Not to be defeated, he used an arrangement of iron pipes to chisel through this rock layer, which turned out to be just 8½ inches thick. Bannester later described his success:

"Early on the morning of the second day, 1st of January 1829, the iron rods suddenly dropped down a distance of thirty feet below the rock, into what I supposed an immense body of water."

After Bannester's success on Rushley Island, wells were sunk on the other neighbouring islands. A plentiful supply of cheap fresh water was the solution to many health problems, and was therefore one of the most significant events in the history of these isolated communities.

A few years ago, Rushley Island came onto the market, described by the estate agents as:

"An island farm in the Thames area of some 207 acres, comprising 115 acres of arable land, 27 acres of sea-wall and grass and 65 acres of saltings and ditches... The island is easily accessible by rowing-boat and at low tide across a small causeway and affords excellent bird-watching facilities. Good moorings are available, the River Thames is quickly reached by boat via Havengore Bridge and the River Roach is within a few minutes' sail leading to the River Crouch. There is also excellent wildfowling available."

The wildfowling rights alone are said to be worth £2000 every year, though it is always difficult to place a value on the arable land itself. In 1976, the sea-walls were strengthened in order to protect this fertile soil from flooding again. The Anglian Water Authority carried out more work in 1979 to drain the land, and several of the ditches were removed in 1983.

Details of the tidal ford are included earlier, just before the description of Oxenham Farm. This also mentions Rushley's only building, a small barn close to the ford. There is no supply of electricity on the island, although a narrow pipe now brings mains water onto the island. Other than these small points, the interior of Rushley contains just open fields and little of interest to visitors. However, the sea-walls around the edge of the island command some excellent views of the surrounding creeks and saltings.

The island is bounded to the south by the channel of Havengore Creek. Whether arriving by boat at high water, or on foot at low tide, Havengore Creek is the usual means of access from the mainland. Rushley is also sandwiched between two smaller creeks that run roughly north-south. To the west of the island, The Middleway flows along the edge of a large area of saltings. These saltings were once part of the farmland, standing inside the island's sea-defences, but they were abandoned to the sea after the original sea-wall was damaged. On the eastern side, drainage water flows through a large sluice into a creek called Narrow Guts.

Contrary to popular opinion, Rushley Island is not owned by the MOD. Indeed, it is the only island in this southern group that is not occupied by the military. However, being privately owned, it is still not open to the public, and it therefore shares the same remote and "out-of-bounds" atmosphere as its neighbours.

Havengore Island

The southernmost island in the Essex Archipelago is known as Havengore Island. Almost two miles in length, but rarely more than half a mile across, Havengore has always been one of the least developed islands in the archipelago. Certainly the name of the island hardly sounds inviting – the word "gore" was an old English name for mud, and the "haven" was simply the creek alongside.

Nevertheless, Havengore Island has been inhabited for many centuries, with several farms scattered around the island. Until around 1970, for example, Marsh Farm stood just inside the sea-wall, two hundred yards north-west of Havengore Bridge. Old maps also show that there was once another building to the north of the island, on a thin peninsula originally called Middle Haven. Over the years however, these various buildings have disappeared one by one, leaving today only the buildings of Havengore Farm in the centre of the island. The island is relatively fertile, growing a range of crops such as wheat, beans, peas and linseed.

At its southern end, the island has been extended on two separate occasions by the construction of new embankments across the saltings. The newly-enclosed marshes were then drained to create more grazing land. On Ordnance Survey's more detailed 1:25,000 "Explorer" maps, you can still see the lines of drainage ditches marking the original outlines of the island.

Until the early years of the 20th century, these farms were very isolated. Indeed, Havengore was the last extra-parochial land in Essex (the last piece of land to be allocated to a parish). At high water, the only means of access was by boat. As the tide receded, however, it was possible to reach the mainland using an ancient track known as the Broomway, which crossed the tidal mudflats south of the island. This was a tricky and dangerous route, and was only passable for a few hours around low tide. The Broomway is discussed in more detail later on, during the description of Foulness.

Over the years, there have been three distinct routes out across the saltings to the Broomway. The mudflats are constantly shifting, and it is possible that each track was abandoned as the mud became too soft. The last of these tidal tracks fell into disuse around eighty years ago. Two of the three headways, however, are still named on modern maps. The oldest was probably Havengore Head, to the west, which dates back to at least 1805. Sharpsness Head to the east was named after Sharps Ness, the easternmost tip of the island.

Life on Havengore Island changed radically with the arrival of the military. As described earlier, they constructed a new bridge across Havengore Creek. In 1922, a connecting road was opened, linking the islands of Havengore, New England and Foulness to the mainland for the first time. Today, this road is used by hundreds of cars on their way to Foulness. Hardly a single vehicle stops at Havengore Island these days. Indeed, most people now associate the name "Havengore" with the Havengore bridge, and the island itself has almost been forgotten. Indeed, ever since the adjoining creeks were partly drained, there is no longer any obvious distinction between Havengore and the neighbouring islands of New England and Foulness.

New England Island

Most of the islands of the Essex Archipelago are closed to the public, and they all have a remote and isolated character. However, every one is visible from the mainland to some extent or other, with the sole exception of New England Island. Tucked away between Havengore and Foulness, New England remains hidden from the mainland, a small secret island just 364 acres in size.

New England Island has a long thin shape, running from north-west to south-east, although its boundaries have changed many times over the centuries. Storms have repeatedly damaged the sea-defences, and the owners of New England have had to fight a constant battle against the sea. The history of the island is sometimes unclear because local maps were often inaccurate, and sometimes inconsistent. As a typical example, one map drawn up in 1536 shows "Watercreek" running along the southern side of the island, whilst a second map published later that century shows this name to the north instead.

Despite the confusion, it is clear that New England originally consisted of two separate islets, linked by an earth embankment. All the farm buildings were on the southern islet. The northern islet was much the smaller of the two. One map shows that in 1587 this northern islet was divided into two by another raised embankment. This may have been a counterwall, designed to limit the damage caused by any floods. These two parts were marked as Sherwood Fresh Marshes and Sherwood Salt Marshes. It is possible that the cartographers had mistaken the name, since all other features around this area were known as "Shelford".

During the 17th century, parts of New England were owned by St. Bartholomews Hospital in London, including the main house on the island. It is likely that the land was mainly used for grazing animals. A hundred years later, in 1768, Rev. Philip Morant wrote a detailed history of the area, noting simply that *"New England and Rushley have nothing remarkable."* Flooding was already becoming a serious problem by this time. One map shows that the sea-defences had been breached in three places, leaving "Sherwood" Salt Marshes open to the ravages of the tide.

By 1791, maps started to show important changes around New England. The landowner, a man named Christopher Parsons, repaired the sea-walls around the northern islet, and major work was also carried out on the saltings just to the south. The creek here originally divided into two branches, but Parsons managed to build a dam across the smaller of the two branches. Although permanently cut off from the sea, this stretch of water was never fully drained, and can still be seen today. Around this part of Essex, creeks of this nature are often locally referred to as "fleets" – this particular example is often known as The Big Fleet.

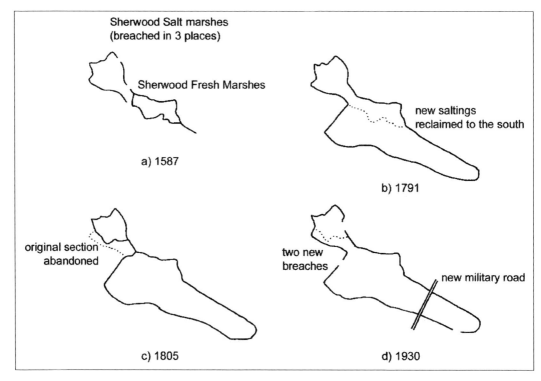

Sherwood Salt marshes
(breached in 3 places)

Sherwood Fresh Marshes

a) 1587

new saltings
reclaimed to the south

b) 1791

original section
abandoned

c) 1805

two new
breaches

new military road

d) 1930

Stages in the development of New England Island

In this way, Christopher Parsons reclaimed a large area of saltings and enlarged his grazing land considerably. These new embankments effectively joined the two islets together for the first time to form one single island. However, flooding continued to be a constant problem for later owners. In 1815, for example, several stretches of sea-wall were swept away, and had to be rebuilt.

Between 1830 and 1870, a series of diaries were kept by Chris Parsons, presumably a son or grandson of the previous owner. These describe his treks around New England, Havengore and Foulness and give a good indication of life on these remote islands. New England Farm consisted of a collection of buildings to the south of the island. It is unlikely that the surrounding land was ever properly drained for agriculture, because the sea-defences were constantly failing. Every time this happened, sea-water would pour into the island, leaving salt in the soil. This salt would kill off most crops, taking several years to leach away.

The creeks and saltings around New England Island were a haven for wildfowlers, and oysters also brought in a little income. Young oysters were reared amongst the saltings of Shelford Creek, and also to the north of the island, around a peninsula known as Yokelet Point. (Yoke Fleet was the old name for the creek that yachtsmen call The Middleway.) This northern peninsula was particularly prone to flooding, and its sea-walls were breached at frequent intervals. If you look carefully at a modern Ordnance Survey map, you can still see a small inlet just east of Yokelet Point where a small area of the island was abandoned to the sea.

On 29th November 1897 (a day that later became known as "Black Monday"), a severe storm struck the south-east corner of Britain. Up and down the coast, sea-defences were swept away, leaving 30,000 acres of land underwater. New England Island was hit very badly, with several breaches in its sea-walls. The sea poured through the gaps, flooding the island at each high tide. The owners could not afford to repair the damage, and the island was left to fall into disrepair.

New England Island would therefore have been consigned to the history books had it not been for the arrival of the military. Between 1900 and 1917, the War Department bought up Havengore Island, New England Island and most of Foulness. Their intention was to use the nearby tidal mudflats as an enormous new firing range. (Further details are given later in this book, during the description of Foulness.)

In late 1915, the War Department began constructing a major road across their new islands. New England presented them with a problem however, because the land was still often underwater. As part of their project, the War Department decided to repair the island. To the south of the island, the sea-wall was still breached in several places alongside New England Creek. Instead of repairing the embankment, the War Department blocked off the creek from the sea entirely by building a dam at either end. In this way, New England Island was permanently linked to its neighbour, Havengore Island. The engineers were then able to build their new road across the two islands, using a causeway to cross the remains of the intervening creek.

On the northern side of the island, facing Foulness, the sea-walls were in much better shape. The engineers decided to build a road-bridge across Shelford Creek at this point. This road between the mainland and Foulness was finally opened in 1922. The road completely changed the lifestyle on these islands. Until 1922, all goods were brought in by boat or carried along the Broomway at low tide, a tricky and sometimes dangerous route across the mudflats. With the arrival of the road, the remote island communities were permanently linked to the outside world for the first time. Despite the improved communications, the military owners soon restricted public access onto the islands, and the area therefore retains much of its remote and isolated character.

Over the years, Shelford Creek gradually silted up. Following the disastrous floods of 1953, the coastal defences were improved all around the country. As well as strengthening the sea-walls, many tidal creeks were blocked off entirely. Shelford Creek, for example, was dammed at its seaward end, and a second dam was erected half-way along, just south of the sleeper bridge. A new section of road was built immediately inside the dam, where it would be safe from flooding. The old bridge has been disused ever since, but it is still in good condition today. Unfortunately it can only be seen by climbing up onto the sea-wall. From the road, it is hidden behind the tall dam, and most people now drive past unaware of its existence.

Around 1963, the southern half of Shelford Creek was drained. In this way, Havengore and New England islands were permanently joined onto Foulness. All three islands are now controlled by the MOD and are normally closed to the public. New England Farm disappeared some years ago, its place taken by a collection of new military buildings, known as the Avocet Demilitarisation Facility.

New England Creek has been cut off from the sea for over eighty years, and now just forms a shallow pool of reeds on either side of the road. However, the northern half of Shelford Creek is still tidal, and is a haven for many types of birds. Many people are disappointed that the MOD does not allow greater public access to the beautiful countryside around New England Island, but it is worth remembering that it was their arrival that saved the island in the first place.

Foulness Island

It is often claimed that Mersea is the largest island in Essex. Some people dispute this, claiming that Canvey Island is slightly larger. In fact, the record is actually held by Foulness, at the eastern end of the Essex Archipelago. Indeed, Foulness is the third largest island in the whole of England (beaten only by Sheppey and the Isle of Wight). Foulness is more than five miles in length, with an average width of around two miles. Furthermore, when the tide goes out, it goes out a very long way indeed. At low water, the mudflats stretch for another six miles off the tip of the island.

Today, the suburbs of Southend-on-Sea have encroached to within two miles of Foulness, and yet, despite its size, the island is virtually unheard of outside the immediate area. Many have heard that the island is used for military experiments, but even people living nearby are rarely able to offer any more information than that.

Beyond the military fence and the guarded check-point, you can clearly see the church spire on Foulness, along with a few military buildings and curious structures. The island is often viewed with a mixture of fascination and suspicion. A lot has been written about Foulness over the years, and this unfortunately includes a fair amount of half-truths and gossip. Perhaps this book will help to clear up a few facts about Foulness. There again, it is quite possible that it will inadvertantly perpetuate a few myths. Either way, we hope that this book will encourage you to take the trouble to visit this special island – it is a unique experience, and is not as difficult as you might think!

In the 1970s, some pieces of ancient pottery were discovered on the island at Little Shelford. These were found to date from around 190 AD, so it is clear that Foulness was inhabited during Roman times. However, very little is known about the early history of Foulness. The island was first recorded as Ethurlarness, apparently named after a local Saxon called Ethular. In 1215, it was referred to as Fughelness, from the Old English words "fugol" (bird) and "ness" (promontary). This gradually developed into the modern name Foulness, therefore meaning "a promontary of birds".

Foulness has always been one of the most inaccessible islands in Essex. During the early years of map-making, it was so difficult to reach the island that most cartographers didn't even bother trying. Instead, they drew their maps based on what they could see from the mainland, along with (unreliable) information from nearby residents. As a result, early maps were very inaccurate, with the island often drawn the wrong size and shape. The Ordnance Survey tried in vain for around seventy years to visit Foulness in order to update their information, and it is only in the last few years that they have been given permission. The very latest maps openly depict a few military buildings, but many of the smaller details are still hopelessly out of date.

The Broomway

Until the 20th century, the only ways to reach Foulness were by boat at high tide, or across the mudflats at low tide. The route across the tidal mudflats was notoriously dangerous. Around this part of Essex, the mud tends to be very soft along the shoreline. The tidal route therefore stayed further out, running parallel to the sea-wall up to half a mile out, where the surface of the mud was firmer. In such a bleak and featureless landscape, it was easy for travellers to get lost on the mudflats, particularly in fog. The track was therefore marked with a series of stakes on the seaward side. These were said to resemble upturned brooms, and hence the route became known as the Broomway. They were described by Herbert Tompkins in 1904:

"Of the brooms there are nearly 400; they are placed 30 yards apart, and are sunk two feet into the sand. Every year they are renewed; but it is necessary to repair many of them at shorter intervals."

The upkeep of these brooms was an important task for the people of Foulness. In his book of 1867, the local historian Philip Benton wrote:

"The sum of £15 (five of which was contributed by Mr. Finch [the lord of Foulness manor], and ten by the parish out of the Church Rate), is annually paid for keeping up and renewing the brooms on the shore, which indicate the road leading to the island."

The Broomway was an extremely dangerous track, and many people have died attempting the route. Many travellers timed their passage incorrectly and got caught out by the incoming tide. The mudflats are virtually level, and the tide can therefore sweep across the landscape faster than you can run. Some people are said to have sunk into unexpected soft mud. Near Shelford Head, for example, old books refer to a hole in the saltings known variously as Snagsby's Edge or Shagsby's Hole where a man of that name perished.

Perhaps the greatest danger is simply getting lost. Apart from the brooms, there were no other landmarks to indicate the route back to safety. Even the incoming tide gave no clues: the mudflats are so flat that the water swirls randomly around the slight undulations, and can arrive from any direction. Once they lost their bearings, it was only a matter of time before unfortunate travellers succumbed to the rising tide. Fogs were not uncommon either:

"These fogs at a distance appear to be a bank, and upon turning round you lose all idea of north, south, east or west."

The Broomway had a total length of more than eight miles. Every mile or so along the track, an offshoot would head off towards the land to link up to one of the nearby farms on Foulness. Since the mud tended to be softer close to the shoreline, a firm "headway" usually had to be built out from the sea-wall. The main headways were made of Kentish ragstone, whilst the smaller routes consisted simply of gravel laid across the mud. Some headways, such as Fishermans Head and Wakering Stairs, have survived for many centuries, whilst others have come and gone. Many of the headways are marked on modern Ordnance Survey maps as rights of way, but this is only an anachronism – they are usually impassable, and always dangerous (see later). For the record, the following list describes all the major headways that have been used at one time or another:

- Suttons Head, in Pig's Bay, just a few hundred yards from Shoeburyness East Beach (sometimes also known as Kennets Head). This fell into disuse when Wakering Stairs was re-opened in 1867. The causeway is still marked on Ordnance Survey's 1:25,000 "Explorer" maps, and still appears to be used occasionally by the MOD.

- Kings Head, also in Pig's Bay, where the modern military jetty now stands. This has not been used for many years.

- Wakering Stairs, the main approach to the Broomway for over a hundred years. It is described in more detail earlier, and is open to the public when firing is not taking place.

- Havengore Island. Three different headways (including Sharpsness Head) are mentioned earlier. They all fell into disuse long ago, but an MOD track was built out from the shoreline more recently.

- New England Island. This headway appears to have been relatively short-lived.

- Shelford Head. This was the westernmost headway onto Foulness itself (although the MOD have built a newer track across the saltings). Old maps show that this was in use in the late 1800s, and it is still just possible to make out its route today.
- New Burwood Head. One track led directly out to the Broomway, whilst another branch joined up with Asplins Head just to the north. It was only marked on one map, in 1872, and was probably abandoned in favour of another headway nearby:
- Asplins Head, probably associated with Charles Asplin who lived in Rochford in 1805. Previously known as Great Burwood Head, this headway dates back to at least 1805, and is still in reasonably good condition today. In recent years, it was used to reach an installation on the mudflats where tests were carried out on liquefied gas fires.
- Rugwood Head. This first appeared on local maps in 1867. It is still marked on modern Ordnance Survey maps as a "public byway open to all traffic", but in practice it is almost impassable. If you stand in exactly the right location, it is just possible to make out its route.
- Eastwick Head, previously known as Pattisons Head. This has been used on and off since at least 1867, and remains in reasonable condition today.
- Fishermans Head, the last headway along the Broomway, and still occasionally used today. The concrete surface is badly pitted, but it is still possible to negotiate this headway in a four-wheel drive vehicle with care. Indeed, this is the only way of carrying heavy loads onto the island – it was used, for example, to transport a supersonic TSR2 plane onto Foulness.

WARNING!

When the MOD are not firing out on Maplin Sands, it is possible to walk out from Wakering Stairs and across the mudflats to re-trace the ancient route of the Broomway. However, *it cannot be stressed enough that this is a serious undertaking.* You need to wait two hours after the tide has gone out to allow the sands to dry out, but a tide-timetable is not sufficient by itself. The tides can vary with the wind, and you should be aware that low pressure zones out at sea can also affect the tides.

Once out on the mudflats, the brooms have not been replaced for many years, and the entire route is now unmarked. There are many short posts sticking out of the mud, and observant visitors may note that some of them form straight lines. Note that these were installed only recently by the MOD as "range pegs"; they do NOT mark the route of the Broomway, nor do they lead back to the shoreline. It should therefore be clear that anyone intending to follow the Broomway must be an expert navigator, or you will find yourself either slowly heading out to sea or floundering around helplessly in the deep mud close to the shoreline. In such completely featureless surroundings, it is inevitable that you will lose all sense of direction, and a magnetic compass is absolutely essential.

Furthermore, remember that there is nowhere to sit down and rest during the entire six-mile route, and, since you are not allowed to land at Fisherman's Head, walkers must be fit enough to cover the 12-mile round trip without a break. Once you are out on the mudflats, there is no way of abandoning the walk, because almost all of the original headways are now abandoned and impassable – the deep mud close to the shore can be treacherous.

In spite of all these serious warnings, anyone that makes the trek along the Broomway is assured of a memorable experience. Perhaps it is not surprising that a lot of rubbish has been written over the years about this ancient track. The surroundings are utterly devoid of landmarks. Flat plains of mud stretch as far as the eye can see in every direction, with just a thin line of a sea-wall visible along the northern horizon. In such a mysterious and barren landscape, you quickly become disorientated and the mind soon starts playing tricks.

Underfoot, the sands are relatively firm, but often covered with a few inches of water. As a result, it was quite easy to take a horse & cart along the Broomway, and four-wheel drive vehicles can easily negotiate the ground provided that you know the correct route to follow. The terrain is accurately described in one book from 1865:

"Looking a little ahead, you fancy that there the ground is quite dry, but come to the place and you find all alike plashy: everywhere ripples and pools and millions of worm-casts."

The most critical point in the walk is at the mouth of Havengore Creek. Here, you may have to wade across a shallow ribbon of water that snakes across the mudflats. It should be no more than six inches deep. If it is much deeper, this may be a warning that the tide is coming in early. Further on, travellers originally had to wade across the mouths of New England Creek and Shelford Creek, but these were both dammed during the 1920s, and have now silted up completely.

In 1971, the government gave the go-ahead to build a new Maplin Airport nearby. This would have involved the reclamation of several square miles of tidal mudflats. In order to check that the plan was feasible, engineers constructed a small circular "artificial island" a few miles south of here, close to the low tide mark. However, complaints about the proposed airport soon poured in from all quarters. Some people suggested that air corridors would become too congested, whilst others were concerned about disruption as far afield as the cockle industry at Leigh-on-Sea. Because of the firing-range, it was also noted that the area would need to be meticulously cleared of all unexploded shells. Many people were worried about the effect on local wildlife, and risk of planes being damaged by bird-strike. In addition to the land reclamation and the construction of the buildings and runway, the airport would also have required major new roads to London.

Remains of the artificial island

In 1974, the project was abandoned because of the costs involved. Instead, new terminals were planned for Heathrow airport. Over the years, the idea of building a new airport on the Maplin Sands was resurrected several times, but most of the uncertainty was lifted in November 1989 when the Transport Secretary, Cecil Parkinson, decided on a massive expansion of Stansted Airport instead. Despite this, developers still occasionally mention the potential of the Maplin Sands from time to time.

The artificial island rapidly became a haven for wildlife, with a colony of little terns, sandwich terns and common terns. Because of its remote and difficult position on the edge of the tidal mudflats, the local warden uses a hovercraft to get there safely.

However, many years of erosion have taken their toll, and the circular embankment was eventually breached. Despite the claims of BP Oil about major engineering works to re-build the island and preserve it as an official bird sanctuary, the island is now reduced to just a small fraction of its original size. The last remaining section is being rapidly washed away, and is not likely to survive above the waves for much longer.

Recent developments on Foulness

Following the Cold War, there was a radical shake-up in Britain's armed forces, and Foulness did not escape the changes. For many years, the Ministry of Defence was able to maintain a wall of silence about the secret work carried out on these islands, but government departments were eventually forced to account for the way they spend our taxes. A wave of privatisations swept through the MOD, and the organisations that now run our military installations are much more open and visible to the public. Indeed, a large number of organisations have been involved in Foulness over the years. The land was technically owned by the Proof and Experimental Establishment (P&EE), who leased various parts of Foulness to other government bodies such as:

- The Environmental Test Centre (ETC). Opened in 1963, this tests the effects of natural and man-made environments on various products. It is particularly renowned for Highly Accelerated Life Testing (HALT), where products are exposed to extreme temperatures, humidity and vibration in order to ensure that they will survive the conditions out on a real battlefield. It is still a division of the MOD but has been operated by various private companies.

- The Atomic Weapons Research Establishment (AWRE), a division of the main facility at Aldermaston. In 1987, the AWRE joined with the Royal Ordnance factories at Cardiff and Berkshire to become just "AWE" (Atomic Weapons Establishment). The management was sub-contracted first to a private company called Hunting-Brae, and then to a consortium led by British Nuclear Fuels.

In 1995, the P&EE itself was also privatised, and the Defence Testing Evaluation Organisation (DTEO) took over the island, as well as the neighbouring ranges at Shoebury. The island is still frequently used for munitions tests, but the AWE gradually scaled down their operations on Foulness, moving much of their work to Aldermaston. Control of the island passed to DERA (Defence Evaluation Research Agency) and then to yet another organisation, Qinetiq, but by 1997 most of the AWE personnel had left the island. However, a token presence still remains, and it would be surprising if the AWE buildings remain vacant for long – it is likely that there will be more organisational changes in the future.

Geographical description of Foulness

This section describes Foulness in more detail, starting from the south-western corner (alongside New England Creek) and progressively moving towards the north-eastern tip of the island. It is inevitable that there will be large gaps in this description because many military installations are deliberately omitted from the text. If you want a more complete view of Foulness, you will need to visit the island for yourself. Despite the imposing military checkpoint, it is relatively easy to get permission. Perhaps the easiest way is to telephone the landlord of the local pub, the George and Dragon (01702 219460). Note that this permit only entitles you to drive directly to the pub – people who stray from the main road will be thrown off the island by the MOD police, and will jeopardise future goodwill.

From time to time, a few organisations arrange walks around the island. Do not take much notice of the "public rights of way" that are marked on Ordnance Survey maps – these footpaths still require special permission from the military, and this is rarely granted. The footpaths can provide useful information to historians because they tend to indicate the route of long-forgotten tracks around the island. A good example is the "road used as a public path" zigzagging up the middle of the island to Churchend. This was once the main thoroughfare on Foulness, connecting together many of the remote farmsteads. It fell into disuse after the new military road was constructed in 1915. However, this old track is a useful way of describing the layout of the island, and this book therefore follows its route, from south to north.

The track starts at the southern end of the island, alongside Shelford Creek. A signpost stands below the sea-wall, indicating the route of a "Public Bridleway" inland. In practice, this section of the track (once known as Dengie Road) has been closed to the public for many years. This southern corner of Foulness is today a forgotten wild expanse of open fields. Large parts of the island are still farmed, mostly by Belton Farms and the Burroughs family. Indeed, the island has won prizes for its winter wheat, and also produces large quantities of barley, rape and linseed. However, this part of Foulness is less fertile than the rest of the island.

Despite this, the land alongside Shelford Creek was extensively farmed for many centuries. The buildings of East Shelford Farm and Great Shelford Farm have now gone, but in places you can still see regular parallel lines in the fields, a sign that this land was once used for more intensive agriculture. Indeed, there is evidence that this part of the island has been occupied since Roman times. Fragments of ancient pottery have been uncovered in several places, and two red hills were discovered in 1848. These "red hills" can be found all around the Essex coast, and are believed to be Roman sites where sea-water was evaporated in clay vessels to produce salt.

Until around 1900, a few isolated farms were scattered around the westernmost tip of Foulness. At the mouth of Shelford Creek, the promontary of Smallports Point was named after a nearby farm of the same name. Old maps showed another building called West Shelford not too far away. This part of the island was divided into two by a wide stretch of water known simply as The Fleet. (A fleet was a local word often used to describe a creek that has become cut off from the sea.)

On the far side of The Fleet, there was a remote farm called Smallgains. From this building, a track once headed due north to the edge of the island, a spot marked on detailed maps as Smallgains Point. In practice, this is hardly more than a slight bend in the sea-wall. According to one book, a railway carriage stood on the sea-wall here until the 1940s and was used for summer holidays. The accuracy of this story is difficult to determine, but Smallgains Point was certainly important for another reason. If you were able to walk just 300 yards west from the point, you would see the remains of a "hard" leading down into the bed of the creek. Until around 1920, this was used by a rowing-boat as a private ferry, linking Foulness to the neighbouring island of Wallasea.

Getting back to the old track known as Dengie Road, the original route headed eastwards away from the sea-wall. Beyond the buildings of Little Burwood Farm, it continued in a roughly easterly direction, meeting the modern military road near Jerry Wood. It is quite rare to have tall mature trees in marshland because of the salty soil, but long-eared owls have successfully made their nests here for many years. According to old maps of the area, the buildings here were originally known as Pond Marsh, named after the large area of marsh to the west. At one time, there was also an alehouse here.

A second farm stood just a few hundred yards away, called Old Barn (also once known as Small Ports).

Standing beside the trees at Jerry Wood, it is eerie to look around at the surrounding landscape, flat and exposed to the elements. Although the sea-wall is at least a mile away at its closest point, the embankment appears to surround you and enclose the fields, as if you were standing in the centre of an enormous saucer. One author wrote in 1865:

"You will fancy the isle to be a big muddy dish, of which the bank, running all round about twenty miles, represents the brim."

At Jerry Wood, the main road is closed by barriers when firing takes place. From here onwards, the original track was known as Turtlemarsh. At first, it veers across to the eastern side of the island, passing the isolated farms of Great Burwood and Bethlehem Row (now demolished), before rejoining the route of the modern road. The buildings of Rugwood and Priestwood have stood on this site since the 13th century, although the current weather-boarded buildings only date from the 18th century.

Along with the nearby buildings of New Burwood and East Wick, most of these ancient farmsteads had their own headways onto the Broomway (see earlier for more details). These headways have all now silted up, but a quote from 1865 describes the barren view from Eastwick Head:

"I saw a prospect which looked anything but pleasant: a vast expanse of brown sand, rough with ripple marks, whereon no dry spot was visible, while the track for the first furlong at least seemed to be sludge."

In contrast, the western side of Foulness was much more sparsely populated, with only one farmstead along the entire western edge of the island. Known as White House, this stood half a mile north-east of Horseshoe Corner near a bend in the river. Today, even this last solitary building has gone, although the name lives on – this stretch of the River Roach is still called Whitehouse Hole. Because of its isolated location, this remote part of Foulness is a haven for wildlife, and several small islets have been constructed in the middle of the borrow-dyke to provide safe nesting for birds.

Churchend

The main road leads in a straight line towards the village of Churchend, at the northern end of the island. This is the heart of Foulness, with around 30 buildings clustered around the Church of St. Mary. Records show that a chapel was built on this site as early as 1386 by Lady Joan de Bohun, but this was later abandoned, probably during the reign of Henry VIII. Around the time of the king's death in 1547, a new church was built and Foulness was turned into its own separate parish. It seems likely that this new church left the Lord of Foulness short of cash, because the church bells were sold in 1552 in order to pay for essential sea-wall maintenance. The church itself was re-built between 1848 and 1850. In such a flat landscape, the church spire stands out as a prominent landmark for many miles around, and is clearly visible from the mainland. Unfortunately, it has not been regularly used since 1999. A tall windmill also stood nearby, but this was demolished in 1915.

For many years, the village of Churchend had a tiny grocery shop on the main road. With fresh meat supplied once a week by boat from Burnham-on-Crouch, it also acted as the village post office. In 1998, this moved to a small building beside a pub called the George & Dragon. Foulness used to have several pubs, such as the Rochford Hundred

Volunteers, an alehouse just outside the village. One by one, the pubs have closed over the years, leaving the George & Dragon as the last survivor. It has been licensed since the 18th century, housed in a large white weather-boarded house that itself dates back to around 1650. Over the last few decades, various other island amenities have dwindled and closed, one after the other. The primary school was forced to close in 1988, the 15 remaining pupils being then required to take a daily bus to a nearby school on the mainland. In this way, yet another link with the local village community was broken.

Churchend still has a village hall, but the pub now acts as the main focus for the isolated inhabitants of Foulness. Even the future of the George & Dragon must be in some doubt, and it would be difficult to maintain a close-knit community in Churchend without any local amenities.

Outsiders who take the trouble to visit the island will find an unfamiliar atmosphere on Foulness. Beyond the MOD barrier, life is quiet and rural, running at a slower pace. For example, the islanders only got mains electricity as recently as 1952. The sheer inaccessibility of Foulness helps to provide an easy-going atmosphere for the few remaining inhabitants, cut off from the unwelcome pressures of modern life outside. The island retains a relaxed atmosphere, where everybody knows everybody else and crime is virtually unheard of. However, this was not always the case. During the early 19th century, for example, this remote island was a lawless place, a refuge for wanted criminals, and bare-knuckle fights were often held around the churchyard.

The main road forks at the centre of the village of Churchend. To the left, a lane heads westwards towards the River Roach, passing the site of the old island school and aiming for the farm of Monkton Barns. Old maps also show the buildings of Smoky Cottages alongside, but these were pulled down. The lane finally reaches the edge of the island near the mouth of the River Roach. A jetty and slipway has stood for many years on this site, imaginatively known as The Quay (indeed, this stretch of the river is often referred to as Quay Reach). By tradition, The Quay has been a popular stop-off point for passing sailors who want to take the opportunity to walk into Churchend for a drink at the village pub.

Just one mile north of The Quay, the waters of the River Roach join the River Crouch, a junction sometimes marked on sailing charts as "Nase Hole". At high tide, this junction offers a short-cut from Burnham-on-Crouch through narrow winding creeks to the River Thames. During the 19th century, sailors also had to beware of Horse Island, a small bank of saltings that partly blocked the mouth of the River Roach. This small islet has now eroded away completely.

Back on the lane between Churchend and The Quay, another track forks off towards the remote farm of Nase Wick, where a large pond has been created in front of the buildings. This is a quiet and undisturbed haven for wildfowl, with relatively rare species such as mandarin duck, wigeon and tufted duck being frequent visitors. Beyond Nase Wick, the track continues northwards, finally reaching the sea-wall near a promontary called High Corner. During the 19th century, a coastguard ship called The Dove was regularly moored here in a shallow bay off the River Crouch, fighting a hopeless battle against the smugglers who frequented the area.

From the centre of Churchend, the other fork in the road leads off in the opposite direction towards the eastern side of the island. Until the early 1900s, this track ran along the top of an earth embankment, meandering between the scattered farmsteads. When the War Department took control of the island during the First World War, they built a new road which was much straighter and more direct. However, the route of the original track is still marked on maps as a "road used as a public path".

The road leads eastwards past the isolated buildings of Lodge Farm. Old maps also show a building called Middlewick about half a mile further on, just before a slight bend in the road. This was once the edge of the island, with only saltings beyond, flooded at every tide. Over the centuries, landowners have reclaimed large sections of these saltings by building new sea-walls out across the marshes. In this way, the island of Foulness has been gradually extended, piece by piece. If you look carefully at the more detailed Ordnance Survey maps of the island, you can see evidence of these reclamations, or "innings" as they are known. This is particularly true along the eastern side of the island, where parallel rows of ditches indicate where the original sea-defences once stood. The earliest known "inning" took place here at Middlewick before 1420. The island was soon extended several more times. Beyond New House Farm, for example, the land now known as Arundel Marsh was "inned" during a second phase, some time between 1424 and 1486.

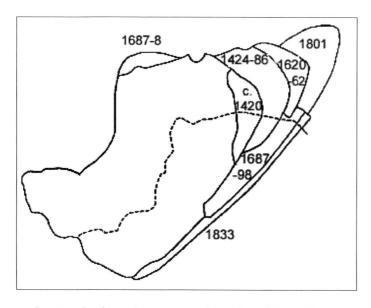

Stages in the enlargement of Foulness Island

Coming back to the present day, New House Farm now stands beside a junction in the main road. Straight on, the road leads within less than a mile to the edge of the island, at a spot known as Fisherman's Head. However, the road does not stop here. Instead, a track climbs over the top of the sea-defences and down onto the tidal mudflats beyond. At first, the track is raised above the soft mud on a short concrete causeway, but this soon peters out once the mud gets firmer, away from the sea-wall. Fisherman's Head now provides the main access onto the Broomway, the ancient tidal route described earlier on.

Courtsend

From the junction at New House Farm, a second road turns left, heading northwards into the hamlet of Courtsend. In order to provide a firm and dry surface underfoot, most of the original roads and tracks tended to run along the top of earth embankments. This road is another good example – indeed, this was once the sea-wall around the edge of the island.

Courtsend is little more than a disjointed scattering of houses, though it used to have its own public house. The Kings Head pub was first licensed in 1589, and was said to be the oldest building on Foulness. However, the island's population has steadily dwindled from a peak of almost 800 people (in the 1871 census) down to a current estimate of less than 300. As a result, the Kings Head finally closed in 1989.

On the far side of the village, the road passes Ridgemarsh farm, built around 1700. The building's earlier name of Brick House is a reminder that this was claimed to be the first brick building on Foulness. The road eventually comes to an end at the edge of the island, at a short promontary known as Crouch Corner. This is a desolate windswept spot, looking out over the wide estuary of the River Crouch. Old maps of the region show that a hard originally led down into the water here, and it was therefore sometimes referred to as "Crouch Loading". The hard has long since gone, as has a row of buildings that used to stand just inside the sea-wall here (imaginatively called Crouch Cottages).

The view from Crouch Corner is particularly empty and bleak. The River Crouch is more than half a mile across by this stage, and there is little to see on the far bank other than yet another sea-wall. The land across the river consists of yet more reclaimed marshes, and is therefore as flat and featureless as Foulness itself. A quick glance at an Ordnance Survey map shows that you would have to travel another three miles inland before reaching even the first contour line, at the dizzying altitude of five metres above sea-level! Looking upstream, the bustling town of Burnham-on-Crouch is prominent in the distance, whilst the open sea is visible to the right, within a couple of miles.

Before you reach the open waters of the North Sea, the last mile of Foulness forms a broad headland called Foulness Point. The land here, also known as East Newlands, was "inned" around 1801, one of the last parts of the island to be reclaimed from the sea. This was also the site of the last coastal battery to be built during the Second World War. Erected in July 1940 to house six-inch and six-pounder guns, it was also the most short-lived, being closed early the next year.

Today, only a small area of tidal saltings remains outside the sea-defences at Foulness Point. Further out, a number of cockle-beds lie in the shallow waters, and their discarded shells are carried in on the tide here, forming one of the largest shell-banks in the country. This was once home to a colony of little terns, although the birds have abandoned the site over recent years. Seals are often spotted around this area, and there are regular boat-trips during the summer months from Wallasea and Burnham to see the seals. At low tide, the mudflats continue for around six miles beyond Foulness Point. A large buoy has been permanently moored at the tip of these mudflats. Known as the Whitaker Beacon, it is an important marker for yachtsmen, indicating the safe entrance into the River Crouch.

Recommended bibliography

Fowlness, the mystery isle 1914–1939 – John S. Dobson (limited edition 1996 by Baron)
Foulness – John Smith
The ecology of Maplin Sands – L. Boorman
Eastern England from the Thames to the Humber (volume two) – Walter White

Chapter seven – the Thames estuary

This chapter describes the final part of the Essex coastline, along the River Thames. As the crow flies, it is less than thirty miles from the mouth of the estuary to the border with London. However, following the meanders of the river and all its tributaries, the true distance is almost twice this figure. When you also include the walk around Canvey Island, this chapter covers a total of eighty miles of coastline.

These eighty miles fall naturally into three sections. The first section starts in the built-up area around Southend-on-Sea, with busy promenades along the sea-front between Thorpe Bay and Leigh-on-Sea. This book is aimed primarily at the more rural parts of the Essex coastline, and so this first section is only described briefly, for completeness.

The central section of this chapter explains the confusing network of creeks and channels around Canvey and Coryton. In the minds of many, this area conjures up an image of oil terminals and refineries. These people will probably be unaware that these creeks also contain some of the most beautiful countryside along the tidal River Thames. If you know precisely where to go, there are some wonderful walks in this area, and you are almost certain to have the sea-wall to yourself. The north-western corner of Canvey Island is particularly recommended for strong walkers, and Vange Creek is also worth exploring.

Beyond Coryton, the last part of this chapter describes the riverside walk upstream of Coryton. This long stretch alternates between small towns and open marshes. In this way, you are never far from civilisation, and the riverside path is very popular with local people. Tilbury also has the attraction of two large Napoleonic forts – these provide a fascinating insight into the history of the river and are well worth a visit.

The last few miles of the Essex coastline have been taken over by large factories, and most people therefore prefer to visit the countryside further downstream. East Tilbury is one of the most popular spots for day-trippers, but visitors will find many other good walks described in this book.

✳ ✳ ✳

Southend-on-Sea

Records of a hamlet called "Southende" date back to at least 1481, standing on the outskirts of the nearby ecclesiastical town of Prittlewell. Even as late as 1800, it consisted of only a tiny cluster of buildings huddled together on the top of the hill overlooking the sea. In the early 19th century, Southend was developed as a seaside resort, and the suffix "-on-sea" was added for commercial reasons to make the area sound more attractive. The town was still relatively small however, since only rich people could afford the time and money to visit the resort, and it wasn't until 1842 that it was made into a separate parish.

When the Tilbury railway opened in 1854, Southend-on-Sea suddenly became within easy reach of thousands of day-trippers from east London, and the town began to expand rapidly. In June 1888, the direct route from Fenchurch Street was opened, and a second line, from Liverpool Street via Wickford into Southend Victoria station, was completed in the following year. The railways played a major role in transforming Southend-on-Sea into the popular resort you see today.

Southend's most famous landmark is undoubtably its pier. Although it is not the longest pier in the world (this record being easily held by one of the enormous oil installations in the Middle East), Southend Pier does hold the record for being the longest *pleasure* pier in the world. From the mainland, it is nearly a mile and a quarter to the small cluster of buildings at its head.

Construction of a wooden pier began in 1829, but because of financial difficulties it was not completed until 1846. In the early days, horses and donkeys were often used to pull cart-loads of visitors out to the pier-head, and tramlines were eventually laid down to make the job easier. When the pier was rebuilt between 1887 and 1889, the tramlines were doubled up, thereby allowing a constant stream of trams to carry visitors up and down. The new trams were also powered by electricity, the first system of its kind in Britain.

The site of Southend Pier had been deliberately chosen so that the pier-head was always in deep water. As a result, ferries and cruisers were able to moor here, even at the lowest point of the tide, and a lifeboat station was also built near the end. During the Second World War, Southend Pier proved to be an extremely useful staging post for the navy, though this did mean that the pier was temporarily out of bounds to the public. Once the war was over, a new set of electric trains was commissioned. In 1959, the Victorian pavillion close to the shore burned down, but it was replaced within three years by a 10-pin bowling alley. A more serious fire on the 29th July 1976 destroyed almost all of the buildings at the pier-head. Although firemen quickly reached the blaze, the inaccessibility of the pier-head made their job extremely difficult. Fire-boats were hindered by the low tide, and by the time the flames were eventually extinguished, the fire had caused damage estimated at millions of pounds.

Without the financial revenue brought in by the pier-head attractions, the whole future of the pier was in serious jeopardy. The electric trams were declared unsafe in 1979 and had to be abandoned, and for many years it looked as though Southend Pier would be allowed to fall into ruin. The situation was not helped when a large ship collided with the pier in 1986, damaging the lifeboat station and causing more damage to the substructure. The bowling alley suffered another serious fire in the 1990s. Today, the pier's future is still far from secure, but new electric trams have started carrying passengers again, and boat trips to the town of Strood in north Kent have restarted from the pier-head.

A broad promenade runs all along the sea-front, providing excellent views of the beach and the boats far out in the River Thames, still some five miles wide at this point. This promenade makes for a marvellous stroll along the shore, although such a walk can hardly be described as quiet and relaxing because the seaside is naturally popular with thousands of day-trippers. There are already plenty of publications on the market which describe the towns and coastal resorts of Essex (consult the bibliography for some recommendations). This book concentrates instead on the hidden scenery and relaxed atmosphere to be discovered around the more rural stretches of the coastline. Only the major features along the Southend sea-front will be described here.

The Nore

Out at sea, far off to the east, lies an area of water known to sailors as The Nore, from the Old Norse word "nor" which was used to describe a sea inlet. Ever since London established itself as an important trading port in the early 18th century, The Nore has been a vital and busy shipping lane.

With an increasing volume of traffic using the River Thames, a large number of ships were wrecked on the treacherous shoals and sand-banks which are scattered around the Nore. Because sand-banks tend to shift position from year to year, sailors soon learned that they could not rely on old navigation charts. A gentleman named David Avery struck upon the idea of marking the entrance to the River Thames with a bright lantern, which could be installed on a ship permanently anchored out in The Nore. Avery managed to obtain finances from Robert Hamblin, a seaman from Lynn, and the Nore Lightship was finally built in 1732. This was the first lightship to be established in English waters, and it proved immensely successful. It was described by one author as the *"beacon of hope that soothes his sorrows past and marks the home that welcomes him at last."*

This is only the start of the story however. Trinity House became anxious that too many lighthouses and ships were falling into private hands, and so they arranged a 61-year lease on the Nore Lightship. The scheme allowed David Avery to collect the bills for the lightship, provided that he paid an annual sum of £100 to Trinity House. This gave Avery the financial security that he wanted, and when the lease ran out in 1794, Trinity House obtained complete control of the lightship.

The Nore Lightship was replaced in 1796, but trouble was now brewing. The country was in economic chaos after four years of Napoleonic war. All foreign allies had either surrendered or defected under the might of the advancing French armies, and even Ireland was on the point of rebellion. At home, there was a run on the Bank of England, and William Pitt the Younger was struggling hard as Prime Minister in the face of growing discontent over food shortages. The only obstacle to a full-scale invasion from France was the British navy, and even they were clamouring for better working conditions. The ships in which they served were cold and cramped, and they had no medical facilities to deal with the frequent outbreaks of disease. Wages had not been increased for over 150 years, and were rarely paid anyway.

In February 1797, a group of sailors serving at Spithead near Portsmouth approached a retired admiral called Lord Richard Howe. The seamen held him in high regard, and asked him to press their case in Parliament. When March had passed without a reply, the Spithead sailors decided to take more explicit action. They directly petitioned the House of Commons and began a campaign of disobedience. Although they were offered more pay, they decided to hold out for better working conditions. At first the Admiralty agreed, but the sailors discovered that secret plans had been drawn up to deal harshly with any mutineers. The Admiralty completely lost control as the sailors took over their ships and went on strike, leaving the south coast of England vulnerable to Napoleon's navy.

The government acted immediately. On the 8th May, an Act of Parliament was raised to satisy the sailors' demands, passing through both Houses and getting Royal Assent all within 24 hours. Since the Spithead rebellion had now achieved all its aims, the navy there quickly returned to normal. Because of poor communications, however, this news took too long to reach the sailors who were stationed out in the Thames Estuary. On the 11th May, the Nore sailors mutinied in sympathy with their Spithead colleagues, and seized control of the flagship "Sandwich", unaware that the government had already given in to their demands. This left the Nore seamen in a very difficult position, because they now required Royal Pardons for their mutiny. The authorities were growing impatient with mutineers however, and decided not to concede to the new rebellion.

Many of the Nore sailors deserted, and the uprising became extremely disorganised. Having achieved no progress by the 28th May, the rebels decided to gamble by blockading the River Thames. In retrospect, this was probably a bad decision, because local traders were scared of the effect this would have on their business. The mutineers began to lose their popular support, and this was probably the turning-point of the whole revolt.

The government passed another Act of Parliament to make mutiny a capital offence, and Trinity House deliberately sank all buoys and beacons around the Thames estuary. This meant that the rebels were now unable to escape. On 12th June, with dwindling supplies, they realised that their position was hopeless and decided to surrender. The Nore mutiny had been quashed. The ringleader, Richard Parker, was hanged from the yard-arm of his ship, and with the Admiralty back in control, the navy began its long struggle against the French forces which led ultimately to Napoleon's downfall. Britain had been saved from the brink of defeat, though it is worth reflecting that if the unnecessary mutiny at The Nore had continued a little longer, the history of Europe could have taken a completely different course.

In 1839, the Nore lightship was again replaced. The new ship, known as "No. 14", or "Old Stormy", faithfully served sailors in the Thames for a century. At the outbreak of the Second World War, it was withdrawn in order to hinder any possible invasion. In 1944, the lightship was towed out to sea near Dover as part of a secret mission, but it was sunk by enemy action. The lightship was never replaced. After the war, a simple beacon was placed at The Nore, and to this day this marks the haunt of Old Stormy.

Maunsell Forts

Although the Second World War caused the demise of the faithful lightship, the war did leave its mark on the Thames estuary in the form of the Maunsell forts. On a clear day, two of these enormous structures can be seen from Shoebury East Beach. If you look carefully at the south-eastern horizon, you may just be able to spot a compact cluster of large mushroom-shaped towers about six miles out to sea, known collectively as the Red Sand Towers. About ten miles away to the east, a second group, called the Shivering Sand Towers, is often hidden by haze.

During the early years of the Second World War, German aeroplanes found that the River Thames was the Achilles heel of the British defences. German bombers were able to fly a long way up the Thames estuary towards London before they were detected and attacked. In order to remove this weakness, a civil engineer called Guy

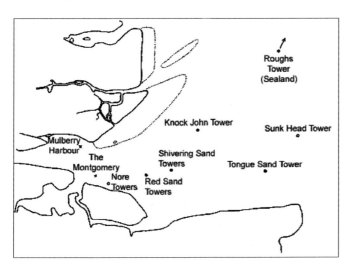

A. Maunsell was asked to design a large platform which could be quickly and cheaply constructed in the middle of the Thames estuary. His first design proved too costly, but construction based on a second design began in earnest in July 1941. The first structure was towed out to sea the following February. By October 1942, four of the navy forts were in place. A further seven were planned for the army, but a decrease in German aircraft activity meant that only three were ever built. They were installed the following year:

Army forts (June-Dec 1943)	Navy forts (Feb-Oct 1942)
Red Sand Towers	Knock John Tower
Shivering Sand Towers	Tongue Sand Tower
Nore Towers	Sunk Head Tower
	Roughs Tower

As well as acting as vital anti-aircraft posts, they were also invaluable for the extra radar cover they could provide. All information on approaching enemy planes was passed via an underwater communications cable to bases on the mainland. As a back-up, the Maunsell forts probably also had a radio link to the mainland, though they generated their own electricity in order to avoid power failure at a crucial moment. By the end of the war, they had between them managed to shoot down 22 planes, as well as 25 V1 flying bombs (some sources say as many as 30).

Two different types of Maunsell fort were built during the war. The forts visible from Shoebury East Beach were operated by the army. Each fort consisted of seven metal towers, each standing above the water on four long legs. One of these structures was mounted with a powerful searchlight, and a second unit acted as the radar and command centre. The remaining five towers were fitted with anti-aircraft guns (four 3.7" guns and a single 40mm Bofors gun). They were connected by a network of overhead walkways, but each tower was able to operate as a self-contained unit, providing accommodation for 120 soldiers and sufficient storage space for up to six weeks without re-supply.

The army abandoned the forts in 1956. During the 1960s, these army forts were used by a series of pirate radio stations. The Red Sand Towers, for example, were home to Radio City and Radio Sutch (1964-67). Today, these army forts are in a poor condition. In the case of the Red Sand Towers, only one of the overhead walkways remains, and even that is probably now too dangerous to use.

The Shivering Sand Towers are in an even worse state. All the walkways have been removed and one of the seven towers was knocked over when a ship called the Ribersborg collided with it in fog in 1963. Four people were killed in the accident – the only casualties suffered during the lifetime of the forts. Today, only a short stump remains above the water-line from this seventh tower.

Remains of the Shivering Sand Towers

There was once a third army fort standing just off the Isle of Sheppey in north Kent. Known as the Nore Fort, it was badly damaged during the war when a ship collided with it. In later years, it became a major obstruction to the shipping lane, and was finally pulled down in 1959/60.

The second type of Maunsell fort was operated by the navy. Situated much further out to sea than the army forts, each navy fort consisted of two large concrete drums standing vertically on the sea-bed. The drums were nearly 40 yards tall and were made up of seven levels. The three lowest floors contained fresh water, magazines and general stores, whilst the sailors lived in the upper levels so that they would always be ready for immediate action. The navy forts were manned by 120 servicemen, each required to do a six-week stint before returning to the mainland for a ten-day rest. A long concrete platform was built across the top of the drums to support the radar units and a large control room. In addition to a pair of Bofors guns, the 70-yard long platform also provided enough space at either end for two powerful 3.7" anti-aircraft guns.

After the war, the navy forts were occupied for a few years, but were finally abandoned in 1956. For many years they maintained a lonely vigil at the mouth of the Thames estuary. Because of their distance from the shore and the low-lying nature of the land around Shoebury, they were usually beyond the horizon and therefore invisible from the mainland, no matter how clear the weather. These forts were therefore purely the prerogative of keen sailors, though they could sometimes be glimpsed far below if you flew from Southend Airport.

The first of these navy forts is known as Knock John Tower. For a brief period in the 1960s, this tower was used by pirate radio stations, such as Radio City and Radio Essex, later renamed to BBMS (Britain's Better Music Station). In August 1967, the Government introduced the Offshore Broadcasting Act in an attempt to curtail the burgeoning number of unlicensed radio stations. Today, despite fifty years of neglect, the anti-aircraft guns still stand proudly at each end of the platform, but the building units look burnt out and appear to be in a poor state.

Knock John Tower

The second navy fort was called Tongue Sand Tower. It was built, as its name suggests, on a shallow sand-bank out in the estuary, and therefore stood much higher out of the water. Unfortunately, the platform collapsed during a storm in 1996. Although Tongue Sand Tower was nearly 23 miles out to sea from Shoebury East Beach, it was only eight miles out from the town of Margate in Kent. The distinction of being the most remote fort therefore belonged not to Tongue Sand Tower but to another navy fort which stood about twelve miles off Walton-on-the-Naze. It was known as Sunk Head Tower, an appropriate name as it turns out, because the fort has now largely fallen into the water. The reason for this state of affairs has a lot to do with the last of the seven Maunsell forts, the Roughs Tower which was built some seven miles off the Suffolk town of Felixstowe.

Sealand

In 1966, Roughs Tower was boarded by Ronan O'Rahilly (the head of the pirate station Radio Caroline) and Roy "Paddy" Bates (an ex-major who had previously run Radio Essex and BBMS). Unlike the temporary squatters before them, the two Southend businessmen planned to turn the fort into a permanent home. However, the two men soon fell out, and after a minor scuffle Roy Bates took full control of the tower. Since it stood outside the 3-mile limit for British territorial waters, the law entitled him to declare it as a self-governing nation. And so, on 2nd Sep 1967, Roy Bates set up "Sealand", a state completely independent from Britain. With Prince Roy and his wife Princess Joan as heads of state, Sealand soon began passing its own laws. The principality has its own currency, printing its own notes and coins. Sealand also operates its own system of passports and stamps, and in recent years has also issued driving licences!

The British legal system was, needless to say, somewhat shaken by this unexpected declaration of independence. Roy Bates had already been fined for radio piracy, but much more important legal wrangles continued for many years over the status of Sealand. Although it appeared that Roy Bates had indeed found a genuine loophole in the law, lawyers pondered for years over arcane problems such as whether Sealand had ever been formally abandoned, or whether the fort, being constructed entirely out of British materials, was automatically part of Britain.

In order to avoid more independent territories like Sealand, a military helicopter in 1967 carried a group of Royal Engineers out to Sunk Head Tower. Despite their expertise, it took them a whole week and more than a ton of explosives to damage the fort so that it could never again be safely occupied. On 1st Oct 1987, the government also changed the law so that territorial waters extended out for 12 miles. Sealand therefore appears to have escaped the net, but there is no chance of the controversy being repeated on any of the other Maunsell forts. At a conference on the laws of the sea in December 1982, the United Nations laid down new international rules about artificial islands. Article 60 requires such structures to be removed immediately after use.

The principality of Sealand has seen several nasty incidents over the years. In 1968, for example, Trinity House men were working on some buoys nearby when a row broke out with the occupants of the tower. Starting with verbal abuse and foul language, it quickly escalated to a full-scale confrontation. Roy Bates's son Michael fired a gun into the air in order to ward off the Trinity workers. As a consequence, Michael was taken to court on gun charges. However, the magistrates at Chelmsford Assizes court had to concede that Sealand was an indepedent nation and did not come under the jurisdiction of British law. According to one source, Roy Bates told a British official: *"This has nothing to do with you. I can tell them to murder someone if I want to. I am the person responsible for the law in Sealand."*

In 1977, Roy Bates accused customs of breaking international law by holding up vital supplies bound for Sealand, but more serious trouble was on the way. During 1978, a consortium of businessmen and international lawyers from Holland, Germany and Belgium were involved in discussions for developing the tower further. Unhappy with the proceedings, "Prince" Roy broke off negotiations. In August of that year, whilst Roy Bates was away with his wife on business, two of the German businessmen arrived by helicopter and forceably seized control of Sealand. They kidnapped Michael Bates, and after holding him for a few days, dumped him on the Dutch coast.

When Roy Bates returned, a vicious battle ensued between the two factions. Prince Roy soon regained control and imprisoned the German raiders. One of the two men was sentenced to clean the decks, but the invaders were eventually pardonned, and peace returned once again to the principality. Sealand has been tranquil ever since, and was even used for a friend's wedding in 1979. Engineers are regularly brought in to check that the structure is safe. Far from being eroded by the sea, it seems that the sea-water has actually helped to strengthen the steel-reinforced concrete, and Sealand looks set to survive another hundred years or so.

Most supplies are brought in by boat, although helicopters are used very occasionally. Otherwise, the occupants are very self-sufficient, with their own electricity generator in the tower. (The underwater communications cable was lost soon after the war, probably dredged up by fishermen because of its valuable copper.) Sealand continues to thrive, with several hundred "associate" citizens (despite attempts by Spanish fraudsters to sell false passports via the Internet). The principality has its own website, and there are even plans to construct new buildings on the sand-bank alongside Roughs Tower. The water is often only a few yards deep, so it is possible that the engineering problems would actually be relatively easy to handle, at least compared to the legal issues that would undoubtedly arise!

Back on the western side of Southend Pier, below the prominent buildings of the Alexandra Yacht Club on the cliff-top, a large area of land has been reclaimed from the sea. In 1922, an amusement park was built here and it later expanded to the eastern side of the pier.

As you progress further westwards, the road-side is still packed with parked cars, but it is clear that the town centre is now gradually being left behind. The promenade continues westwards for several miles, overlooked by a steep grassy slope. At one point, an electrically-powered Cliff Lift carries pedestrians up to Clifton Terrace at the top of the hill. Most of the ground at the foot of the escarpment was reclaimed from the sea around 1910 for the construction of the coastal road. This was an expensive operation, costing around £100,000 and requiring hundreds of barge-loads of gravel.

Below the road, the beach is popular with families, particularly during summer weekends. The beach is mostly comprised of soft sand, but as the waves break, the strong uprush of water carries small pebbles and coarse gravel further up the beach. The weaker backwash then drags the finer material seawards again. This eventually leads to a grading effect, whereby the larger grains and pebbles are usually found near the top of the beach and the finer sand is lower down near the water's edge. Wind and sea erosion can cause serious problems for a seaside resort such as Southend-on-Sea, but long wooden groynes have been constructed to hold the sand in place.

At first sight, the large expanse of bare sand appears to be completely devoid of any natural life-forms, but this is largely because all the small animals burrow down into the sand as the tide recedes in order to avoid predators and the drying effects of the sun and wind. The coarser particles of sand will dry more quickly than the fine grains of the mud, and hence there is less life towards the top of the beach. In this higher region, you will usually only find abandoned shells, which will eventually erode to become part of the sand structure itself.

In contrast, the lower reaches of the beach are often full of animal life. Although most birds are frightened off by large crowds of people, plenty of smaller animals can be found near the low-water line. These generally fall into three categories. The deposit-feeders, such as lugworms, are often dug up by fishermen for bait, and you frequently find the abandoned shells of suspension-feeders such as cockles. The third group contains the scavengers and carnivores, including crabs which scurry around the mudflats. The surface is relatively firm underfoot, and the open mudflats out beyond the sandy beach make for a pleasant and interesting stroll. The tiny holes which can be seen in the surface of the mud are the burrows of sand-hoppers. These animals emerge at night to feed on any available plant or dead animal material they can find among the debris.

Westcliff-on-Sea

Continuing westwards along the coastal B1016 road, known here as Western Esplanade, you enter a district called Westcliff-on-Sea. Along this stretch of the coastline, several stone tracks lead out across the mudflats towards the low-water mark. The first of these "hards" stands a few yards west of the Cliff Lift. They are often used to reach boats moored out on the tidal flats, but they are also frequently used by local bait-diggers.

A few hundred yards beyond the Westcliff Leisure Centre, a prominent building stands at the top of the slope. This is the Cliffs Pavilion, the town's major concert hall and entertainment centre. It has a marvellously wide-reaching view of the sea-front and the Thames estuary. Almost directly below it, a second hard heads out from the shore towards the water's edge, and a third hard can be found half a mile further on, next to a small jetty.

Out in the deep water channel of the River Thames, large container ships regularly pass by on their way to Tilbury, but from time to time you may also spot an old Thames sailing barge. These distinctive ships, with their large reddish-brown sails, were once common around the estuary, carrying hay, straw and coal up and down the river. They were also used around the River Medway, often with a cargo of Kentish ragstone.

Around the Essex coast, local boatbuilders have developed their own traditional designs, and the unique style of the Thames barge has likewise evolved over the centuries. Brightlingsea was particularly noted for building some of the largest examples, up to 120 tons net weight. A few Thames barges were as large as 150 tons, and yet they could still be manoeuvred by just two men. Their flat-bottomed shape made them very versatile, capable of crossing the North Sea as well as navigating along narrow creeks and rivers. In most cases, the mast could be lowered for low bridges. Some designs had an overhang at the stern (or "swim"), and were therefore known as swim-headed. Later versions also included an extra diagonal mast, called a spritsail, in order to extend the sail even further.

The use of Thames barges declined rapidly after the Second World War, although it was not until 1971 that the last one left active commercial service. They are now lovingly maintained, and there is even an annual race, starting and ending at Southend Pier.

Chalkwell

Beyond a shallow paddling pool, you start to enter another suburb of Southend-on-Sea. This area is known as Chalkwell, suggesting that chalk was dug out of the ground here many years ago by local farmers in order to neutralise the acidic alluvial soil. This is very similar to the ancient "dene-holes" which were once dug around the south-western corner of Essex.

Just beyond another stone "hard", a prominent landmark can be seen on the tidal mudflats about a hundred yards out from the shore. This tall obelisk is called the Crow Stone, and at low tide it is safe to walk out from the promenade to read the inscription on its side. A similar stone, known as the London Stone, stands on the far side of the River Thames off the Isle of Grain. The two stones were erected to mark the seaward limit of the City of London's jurisdiction over the River Thames from the year 1197 onwards.

The Crow Stone was placed on the foreshore around 1285. It was superseded by another obelisk in 1755, but this new marker was soon found to be cracked and had to be replaced with the current 16-foot high granite obelisk. The old stone was removed and is now on view at the Prittlewell Priory museum in Southend-on-Sea. The jurisdiction of the City of London ended in 1857, but the Crow Stone remains a familiar landmark to local residents.

Chalkwell Esplanade continues westwards for another half a mile, but this road has been a dead-end for vehicles since the construction of the railway nearby, and most traffic now turns north up Chalkwell Avenue, suddenly leaving the seaside quiet and relaxing. Although the promenade gets much narrower as you pass a shallow paddling pool and approach Chalkwell railway station, the absence of cars makes this stretch of the coastal path extremely popular. It leads past the moorings of the Thames Estuary Yacht Club, founded in 1947, until it eventually emerges nearly a mile later beside the buildings of Bell Wharf in Leigh-on-Sea. Incidentally, it is along this stretch that you reach the edge of the Ordnance Survey "Explorer" map 176 (Blackwater Estuary). If you are using this series of maps, then you must now change to map 175 (Southend-on-Sea & Basildon).

Leigh-on-Sea

Unlike the districts of Westcliff-on-Sea and Chalkwell, Leigh-on-Sea was once a large village in its own right, and it is only in recent years that it has been swallowed up by the rapid expansion of Southend-on-Sea. In the Domesday Book, the village was recorded as Legra, but by 1254 it had become known as "Leye". The name probably comes from the Old English "leah", a word referring to a meadow, from which we also get the modern English word "lea". Like many other towns around the coast, the suffix "-on-sea" was added during the 19th century to make the area sound more attractive as a seaside resort.

In the Middle Ages, Leigh-on-Sea was the largest port between Harwich and Gravesend, and its boat-yards built some of the largest ships of its time. The craftsmen helped to repair ships damaged in sea-battles in the North Sea, such as those during the wars against Holland. There is also some evidence that the Pilgrim Fathers' ship, the Mayflower, was either built or kept here, and several historians have said that the fore-runner to the shipping company Trinity House was formed from the merger of the Guild of Pilots at Leigh-on-Sea and Deptford. Although there is no conclusive evidence to back up these suggestions, it is certain that Leigh-on-Sea was a major shipping port until around 1650. Over the years, Leigh Creek has slowly silted up, causing a steady decline in shipbuilding, and today only small boats can make their way up the tidal creek to reach the harbour-side at Bell Wharf.

Leigh-on-Sea still has a strong nautical atmosphere today, with several chandlers and boatbuilders based in the High Street. The narrow strip of land on the south side of the railway-line is often referred to as "Old Leigh". This area of town has managed to retain a quaint olde-worlde atmosphere with narrow lanes and a delightful jumble of closely-knit old houses which, apart from a couple of unforgiveable modern buildings, contribute to the charming feel of this picturesque fishing village.

Old Leigh is also well served with pubs. Near the eastern end of the High Street is The Smack Inn. Further along, the Peter Boat is also named after an old type of small fishing boat. When the original 17th-century building burned down in 1892, it is said that secret smuggling rooms and tunnels were discovered underneath. To the west, the Crooked Billet is one of the oldest buildings in the town, dating from the 16th century. If you do want to wander around the old town or visit one of the pubs, be warned that the High Street is very narrow and that space for cars is extremely limited. It is much easier to leave your car in one of the large car-parks near the bridge.

Over the centuries, Leigh-on-Sea built up a reputation as a thriving fishing village. The trade in oysters grew rapidly during the 17th century, and eventually much of the foreshore from Leigh-on-Sea to Thorpe Bay was taken up by oyster-beds. The importance of the industry at that time is well demonstrated by an incident in 1724 when Leigh-on-Sea was raided by a crowd of around 500 fishermen from Queenborough in north Kent. They seized as many oysters as they could carry and took them up to London to sell them. As well as the depletion of their stock, the Leigh-on-Sea fishermen were devastated by the resultant drop in prices because of the sudden glut of oysters on the market. The invaders were eventually taken to court and had to pay damages of around £7000, an enormous sum in those days.

Until the beginning of the 19th century, most of the fish caught at Leigh-on-Sea were taken to the London markets by boat. Any excess fish were stored locally in specially constructed ponds until they could be sold. From the top of the hill overlooking Leigh-on-Sea, you can still see the remains of seven fish-ponds off the eastern tip of Two-Tree Island. These will be described in more detail a little later in this book when you reach Two-Tree Island.

Although the new railway-line provided Leigh-on-Sea with a good link to the London markets, its location close to the wharves tended to restrict the growth of the village. For many years, the old part of the town could only be reached by using one of the two level-crossings over the railway. One of these was beside the original railway station, and only a few traces remain of the second level-crossing, behind the Crooked Billet. It was not until relatively recently that the situation was eased by the construction of a modern concrete bridge across the railway-line, though some locals argued that this tall structure destroyed the quaint olde-worlde charm of the sea-front.

Shellfish

From the large car park underneath the bridge, a narrow lane continues westwards along the shore, following a row of wooden cockle-sheds. On the far side of these sheds, a large artificial beach has built up over the years from discarded cockle-shells. Leigh-on-Sea is renowned for its shellfish, but the industry did not really take off until around 1830. This is perhaps surprising because the cockle-beds out in the Thames estuary are amongst the largest around Britain, being over 47 square miles in area, and the richer beds can contain over a million cockles per acre.

The cockle industry has expanded rapidly, and today more than a quarter of all Britain's cockles are landed here at Leigh-on-Sea. The beds are dredged by suction, and although some boats are still offloaded using the traditional Dutch-style yoke and bucket, most firms now use labour-saving conveyor belts to transfer the fresh cockles into dumper trucks. Despite fierce competition from Belgium and the Netherlands, the Thames cockles are often considered to be of a higher quality, and the industry in Essex continues to this day.

The cockle-sheds also sell a variety of other shellfish, including whelks, crabs and lobsters. Of the winkle family, only the common periwinkle (*Littorina littorea*) is edible, and this is very popular around Leigh-on-Sea. There is also a growing demand for other shellfish such as prawns, although people often confuse these with shrimps. A prawn has two pairs of feelers projecting from its head, whilst the shrimp has only one pair.

When walking around on the sea-bed, shrimps and prawns are both translucent. They only obtain their vivid colour during the boiling process. The common edible shrimp (*Crangon vulgaris*) also comes in two different colours. Although the word "shrimp" is often used to describe a pink colour, it is believed that the true shrimps are brown. The two varieties have a noticeably different taste, and fortunately they prefer slighly different habitats. Their shoals therefore rarely overlap on the sea-bed and fishermen have little difficulty in separating them out.

Beyond the cockle-sheds, a narrow lane follows the muddy foreshore to a large boat-yard. A flight of steps here leads up to the main road beside the railway station. This is also a significant turning-point because here you leave the built-up area around Southend-on-Sea and enter open countryside once again. Apart from the modern housing estates on Canvey Island, this is the last major conurbation you will meet around the Essex coastline before entering the suburban sprawl in the east end of London.

A large sea-wall has been built around the next stretch of coastline to protect the land inside from flooding. The embankment is mostly made of earth, but a protective layer of concrete has been laid along its crest for the first few yards. Although this sea-wall is not technically a right of way, the land appears to be used as an area for general recreation, and this walk is extremely popular at weekends.

Unfortunately the land just inside the sea-wall contains many of the undesirable trappings of town-life, such as a large car-park for the railway station, a depot for domestic refuse, and even an area set aside for skate-boarding, but the view on the seaward side is much more interesting. The embankment overlooks the upper reaches of Leigh Creek, a wide but shallow waterway punctuated in several places by raised areas of saltings. These are capped with a swarth of marshland plants such as sea purslane (*Halimione portulacoides*) and common sea lavender (*Limonium vulgare*), both of which are hardy enough to withstand the salty conditions during high spring tides. On the far side of the creek, the shrubs and bushes are part of the nature reserve on Two-Tree Island, which will be described shortly.

Beyond a small car-park, three playing-fields take up a lot of the open space. At the end of the first field, a concrete slipway leads down from the top of the embankment into Leigh Creek. A small wooden landing-stage stands on the edge of the saltings here, and as the tide drops, the receding waters reveal the sad remains of a wooden hulk embedded in the mudflats nearby.

Two-Tree Island

Continuing westwards along the sea-wall, just past the moorings of the Leigh Motor Boat Club, a narrow and flimsy-looking bridge carries the road across the creek onto Two-Tree Island. The island is over a mile in length but rarely more than a few hundred yards wide. It got its name from two elm trees which stood towards its eastern end until a storm blew them down in 1965. A photograph from 1930 shows that they were the only tall trees on the island, and because most of the other vegetation was composed of low-lying shrubs and bushes, the trees were one of the most prominent features of the island.

The history of Two-Tree Island is at best sketchy. It is known that it was reclaimed from the sea some time around 1640, and that it was divided into two portions. The western end of the island was known as Haughness, whilst the larger eastern section was called Oxfleet. Like Skipper's Island near Walton-on-the-Naze, the two portions were probably owned by different farmers, because each half of the island had its own separate link to the mainland and it seems that the two plots of land were allocated to different parishes. Even today, Oxfleet is under the jurisdiction of Southend-on-Sea Borough Council whilst Haughness belongs to Castle Point District, with the district boundary neatly bisecting the island.

Two-Tree Island, along with a couple of farm cottages, was bought by the Salvation Army in 1890 as part of their new estate around Hadleigh, but there is no evidence that they developed the island. This may have been due to its inaccessibility, which at that time could only be reached by a tidal ford at low water.

In 1936, the Salvation Army sold the island to Southend-on-Sea Borough Council for use as a refuse tip. Although their plans were initially interrupted by the outbreak of war, a bridge onto the island was finally built, and the dumping of domestic refuse began in earnest in 1953. Beginning with Oxfleet to the east, a constant stream of lorries raised the level of the ground by up to fifteen feet. Within twelve years Oxfleet was completely full. After laying down a final capping of earth so that vegetation was able to recolonise the site, the council turned their attention to the western part of Two-Tree Island. By 1985, this region had been filled to the same level as Oxfleet, and the council was forced to look for sites elsewhere.

From the bridge, a public road cuts right across the island to the southern shore, where a large slipway leads into the channel known as Hadleigh Ray. A large boat-yard has been built alongside the slipway. In 1974, an enormous earth embankment was built alongside the road as part of a scheme to construct a flood-protection barrier across Hadleigh Ray. Needless to say, this ambitious scheme eventually proved to be too expensive, and a cheaper alternative was built instead, further upstream. Very little of the embankment remains to be seen today.

A small wildlife reserve was established in 1968 on the edge of the island. By 1974, the area known as Oxfleet, on the eastern side of the road, had become recolonised enough to be added to the reserve. Today, the Leigh National Nature Reserve contains a wide range of plant species and has even regained several thriving animal communities, such as badgers, foxes, weasels, voles, lizards and grass snakes.

However unsightly they may be, the need for refuse tips is an inescapable result of our modern throw-away lifestyle, but as long as they are properly landscaped, Two-Tree Island illustrates how the land can still provide enormous pleasure afterwards to the local community. As an additional bonus, refuse tips can also raise the level of low-lying land, reducing the risk of flooding.

In 1966, the Government issued a White Paper entitled "Leisure in the Countryside" which recommended that country parks should be deliberately sited on derelict land near towns. Although this seemed to be a welcome move to regenerate surburban waste-ground, it missed the opportunity to protect genuine countryside from being swallowed up by inappropriate development. Surely prevention is better than cure? Even today, when we like to believe that we are more environmentally aware, our open countryside is still treated with the lowest of priorities. Nature reserves are usually only established after the land has been desecrated and abused, and can no longer give financial benefit to anyone else.

As an example, the nature reserve in Gunner's Park at Shoebury was only created when the military authorities handed over the land to the council. The Wat Tyler Country Park near Pitsea is built on the site of a disused explosives works, despite the presence nearby of a large area of unspoilt but threatened marshland. There are many more examples, demonstrating that the designation of "nature reserve" or "Site of Special Scientific Interest" (SSSI) holds no real value. A review commissioned by Wildlife Link found that 40% of SSSIs were suffering from significant "deterioration or damage". Genuine environmental protection requires real sacrifices, not lip-service, and it is sad that our remaining countryside will never be safe from inappropriate development until the authorities reassess their priorities.

A large gate half-way across Two-Tree Island indicates the main entrance to the nature reserve. From here, a marked track leads eastwards through the undergrowth. About five hundred yards from the road, the path drops down a gentle slope to a much lower section of Two-Tree Island. The land at this eastern end represents the original ground-level of the island, as this part was never used as a refuse-tip. This is because of a sewage treatment works, constructed here in 1910.

The marked trail through the nature reserve eventually reaches the eastern tip of Two-Tree Island. Whilst admiring the view of Old Leigh from the top of the sea-wall, you overlook a wide area of tidal grassland and rough saltings. Although the managers of the nature reserve do not encourage people to stray over the saltings because of the disturbance to nesting birds, you can follow a raised path eastwards across these marshes for a further six hundred yards. *For obvious reasons of safety, this route must always be avoided during the hours around high tide.*

At regular intervals along this raised path, square concrete blocks have been constructed on the saltings. These are shafts leading vertically down to a large underground pipe, and are probably related to the nearby sewage works. However, the path is much older than the sewage works. It was raised above the level of the surroundings in order to provide access to a series of fish-ponds which were constructed out in the saltings. (The use of these ponds was described earlier in this book during a discussion of the fishing industry of Leigh-on-Sea.) You can still trace the outline of six fish-ponds which form a straight line just to the left of the path, and a seventh can be found a short distance to the north of the first pond. Unlike oyster-beds, which are usually dug below the level of the surrounding marshes, these fish-ponds have been built above the ground by constructing a rectangular embankment on top of the saltings. Since the seven ponds were abandoned, each embankment has been breached, and at high tide they all fill up with the swirling waters from Leigh Creek.

The raised path continues eastwards to the very edge of Leigh Creek. The saltings here are being slowly eroded away, and the embankments around the sixth fish-pond have been almost completely washed away by the tide. Beyond the saltings, the Marsh End Sands have largely been colonised by long strands of eel-grass (*Zostera*), giving the mudflats a subtle green colour when viewed from a distance.

This marine plant, also sometimes known as grasswrack, has slender grass-like leaves which trail across the surface of the mud. There are two main varities of eel-grass. *Zostera noltii* is usually found on the top of muddy hummocks, and is more prevalent during the summer, whilst *Zostera marina*, closely related to *Zostera angustifolia*, grows more strongly during the winter in the wetter depressions. These grasses help to stablise the mudflats, and together with the abundant green macro-algae (mainly *Enteromorpha* species), they provide food for the enormous flocks of up to ten thousand dark-bellied brent geese which invade these shores during the winter months.

Back at the eastern end of Two-Tree Island, you have a choice of directions. The main route around the island follows the sea-wall southwards, but it is worth making a quick detour to the north. From the top of the embankment here, you can clearly see inland the remains of the sewage settling pools, but a much more interesting feature can be found near the north-eastern corner of the island. As mentioned earlier, each half of Two-Tree Island had its own separate link to the mainland. The eastern half was joined to the mainland by a tidal ford across Leigh Creek, which is nearly three hundred yards wide at this point. Although few details are available, it appears that a track made of gravel and stones was built on top of the mudflats here, giving access to this end of the island for just a few hours around low tide.

Around 1867, the local historian Philip Benton wrote that the Oxfleet ford was no longer maintained and that the stones had become completely covered with mud. Its route is still clearly marked on the detailed "Explorer" maps published by the Ordnance Survey, although it has not been properly used for more than a hundred years.

Standing at the north-eastern corner of Two-Tree Island, you can still just make out the route of the old Oxfleet ford leading across Leigh Creek towards a prominent red life-belt. Although the ford is no longer used to cross Leigh Creek itself, local people still occasionally use parts of the route to reach boats moored at the edge of the water.

Returning to the eastern end of Two-Tree Island, a wide footpath leads southwards along the top of the large sea-wall. Within a few yards, it reaches the south-eastern corner of the island, where the remains of a wartime pill-box are now almost hidden behind a small tree. With its roof beginning to cave in, the pill-box is now in a very dangerous condition, and its entrance has been blocked off.

On a clear day, Two-Tree Island offers a wide view across the mouth of the River Thames to the gentle hills of north Kent, more than four miles away. To the right, you can also see the roofs of modern housing estates hidden behind the massive sea-defences of Canvey Island. Closer to hand, another expanse of saltings stands at the foot of the sea-wall. This area is now called Leigh Marsh, although the name originally referred to this entire coastal region, including the whole of Two-Tree Island. In order to slow down the erosion of these saltings, faggots have been laid across some of the narrow muddy channels. These lines of sticks and twigs are designed to trap the fine grains of silt which would otherwise be washed away by the strong currents. This helps to consolidate the banks of earth and also promotes the growth of marshland plants such as sea purslane.

After the nature reserve was set up, this corner of Two-Tree Island rapidly became overgrown, but in the last few years the land has been completely transformed. Several scrapes, or brackish ponds, have been created to provide more wildlife habitats, and the earth which was excavated was then used to strengthen the sea-walls around the eastern end of the island.

From the pill-box, a footpath follows the crest of one of these enlarged sea-walls along the southern flank of Two-Tree Island past the new ponds. Where the land rises up to rejoin the central raised portion of the island, a path branches inland to a small wooden hide which overlooks the scrapes. Meanwhile, the main route continues westwards towards the road. Along this stretch, the refuse tip did not encroach right up to the edge of the island and you can still see the original borrow-dyke just inside the embankment. This wide ditch was dug out centuries ago to provide material for the original sea-wall.

About seven hundred yards west of the pill-box, aerial photographs of the marshes reveal a disused path heading out from the sea-wall in a straight line across the saltings. Like most of the old marshland paths around the Essex shore, it was almost certainly built by wildfowlers from the nearby villages, but unfortunately the tide has now eroded away the first few yards of the path. It is no longer walkable and even its route is now very difficult to find.

Continuing westwards along the sea-wall, you eventually reach a wooden stile over a wire fence. This is the boundary fence of the nature reserve, and from this stile it is only a few yards back to the main road. The road is rather narrow here, and visitors are therefore recommended to leave their car in a small car-park a hundred yards down the road to the left, near a small boat-yard. Old maps show that this area of land was once the site of a small farm building which was known (using the old spelling of Leigh-on-Sea) as Lee Marsh Farm.

At the end of the road, a large concrete slipway heads down into the waters of Hadleigh Ray. The road acts as a convenient dividing line for Two-Tree Island. The eastern half of the island has been turned into a nature reserve, whilst the western half is part of the Hadleigh Castle Country Park, named after the famous local landmark which can be seen a few miles away to the west at the top of a hill. The name of the country park is a bit of a misnomer, however, since Hadleigh Castle itself is not actually within its boundaries. The park was opened on 18th May 1987, and is managed by a division of the Essex County Council.

On Two-Tree Island, there are three main entrances into the country park. In the centre of the island, a gravel track leads through a gateway into an open area of land used by model aircraft enthusiasts. On the northern and southern edges of the island, wooden stiles give access to an enjoyable footpath which circumnavigates the western end of the island. As mentioned earlier, this half of the island was used as a refuse tip much more recently than Oxfleet, and although it has now completely grassed over, it has not yet had enough time to become fully overgrown, and it therefore makes a much more enjoyable stroll than than the neighbouring nature reserve. The following text describes the walk around Haughness in a clockwise direction, beginning at the boat-yard on the southern side of the island.

From the boat-yard, a wide path leads past a second, much smaller slipway and follows the southern edge of Haughness, heading towards the western end of Two-Tree Island. A couple of wooden picnic tables overlook the waters of Hadleigh Ray, an ideal spot for a quick rest. However, you are warned to watch out for adders, particulary if you are with dogs or young children. The adder is the only poisonous snake found in Britain, emerging between April and September. They grow up to two feet in length, and have a distinctive black zigzag running along their back. They are very timid, and will usually disappear into the long grass when people approach, but during hot weather they are more sluggish and it is possible to come across one by surprise.

At the western end of the island, a small triangular plot of land was reclaimed from the sea nearly two hundred years ago. In the last twenty years or so this was allowed to fill up again with brackish water, apparently creating a haven for migrating birds. A small wooden bird hide has been placed beside the water's edge, but the nearby footpath provides exactly the same view, and during the summer months, only the tamest birds will not be frightened away by the constant stream of walkers. The ideal time of year for bird-watching is during the cold winter months, when very few visitors are around to disturb the large flocks of wildfowl which descend upon these shores.

The walk around the outside of the pond has a completely different atmosphere to the rest of Haughness, and is well worth the extra distance. At the very tip of the island, a rough path leaves the sea-wall and heads out a short distance across the saltings, using a variety of dilapidated wooden bridges and rotting planks to cross the channels of deep mud.

From the tip of Two-Tree Island, you can walk back along the northern flank of the island. A few years ago, parts of the

Remains of footbridge
off the western end of Two-Tree Island

sea-wall around the pond were being rapidly eroded away, though it seems odd that this did not occur on the seaward side of the island, where one might expect the force of the waves and tidal currents to be greater. However, an effort was recently made to repair this stretch of embankment using hundreds of sand-bags. At the same time, a large pipe was embedded in the sea-wall, thereby allowing sea-water to flow freely in and out of the pond with each tide.

The height of the pipe has been arranged so that, as the tide drops, there are always a few inches of water left behind. At this state of the tide, you can see that a deep ditch runs around the edge of the pond just inside the sea-wall. This was once the island's borrow-dyke, a ditch artificially dug out to provide earth for building and maintaining the sea-wall. Borrow-dykes can be seen inside many of the sea-walls around Essex, and are particularly noticeable around the Hadleigh Castle Country Park.

It has already been mentioned that each half of Two-Tree Island originally had its own separate link to the mainland. A tidal ford onto Haughness can be seen just a few yards ahead, where the sea-wall around the pond rises up to join the main section of the island again. At low tide, the creek here almost completely dries out, and a layer of gravel and stones has been laid across the mud to provide a dry route across to the mainland. Unlike the long tidal ford onto Oxfleet at the eastern end of the island, which was apparently abandoned some time during the 19th century, this Haughness ford is much shorter and is still in relatively good condition. It appears that, even in recent years, some care is being taken to maintain it by laying down fresh layers of hard-core, particularly on its southern bank.

The ford is quite easy to cross, but the large stones require a reasonable sense of balance, and infirm people would probably be best recommended not to attempt it. The raised layer of stones and gravel acts as a small dam, holding back the water upstream to a depth of nearly a foot, but the ford itself is generally quite dry and free from mud. It is even used occasionally by motorcyclists who enjoy scrambling around the island, though in recent years a wooden fence has been erected across the track, probably with the aim of discouraging such activites.

The Haughness ford became redundant soon after the Second World War when the more practical road bridge was built onto Two-Tree Island, but it is pleasing to see that the ford has remained in such a good state of repair. These ancient tidal routes provide a lot of interest for walkers who wander around the Essex coastline today, and they give an interesting insight into the history of the coastal marshlands.

If the tide is out, this ford provides an excellent link in an interesting coastal walk between Leigh-on-Sea and Benfleet. From Leigh-on-Sea, walkers can cross the road bridge onto Two-Tree Island and wander through the country park. Then, by using the ford to cross back onto the mainland, it is possible to continue westwards along the shore to Benfleet. Returning by train, this makes an ideal walk of just less than four miles. However, it seems that most visitors to Two-Tree Island are just out for a short stroll, and from the western tip of Haughness they will need to return to the road. A good footpath follows the northern edge of the island, leading unerringly back to the road bridge, just over half a mile away.

❋ ❋ ❋

Back on the mainland again, a golf driving range stands close to the bridge. The range is surrounded by a tall wire fence to stop golf balls going astray, but this does not obstruct the public footpath which runs along the top of an enormous sea-wall. During the early

1980s, this embankment was greatly enlarged using thousands of tons of domestic refuse. Most councils are desparately short of landfill sites, and the construction of large coastal defences offers an ideal solution to the problem. This method of disposal solves two problems at once, since the large embankments also help to protect the nearby land from flooding.

About two hundred yards west of the bridge, the sea-wall begins to zigzag wildly in and out of the marshes. It has already been described how, until the mid-1900s, Two-Tree Island was only accessible by two tidal fords across Leigh Creek, one at each end of the island. For a short time, however, there was a third access point. Old maps show that a small path across these saltings led to a footbridge across Leigh Creek. This route does not appear to have lasted very long, and although today there is no sign of either the footbridge or the path, it is still possible to pinpoint the precise location where the footbridge crossed the creek. At this point, the remains of a large wooden hulk stand in the middle of Leigh Creek, forming an artificial island near the centre of the water channel. It is even possible that the hulk was used as a bridging point, since this would have allowed the footbridges to be much shorter.

Hadleigh

The meandering footpath continues westwards towards the Haughness ford. Inside the sea-wall here, the reclaimed marshland has been carefully drained for growing crops. On older Ordnance Survey maps, one of the original creeks was marked as Mill Fleet, a name which suggests that there was once a tidal mill nearby.

This area is known as Hadleigh Marsh, after the town of Hadleigh just over a mile inland. The town was first recorded around the year 1000 as Haethlege, a name derived from the Old English words "haeth", meaning heather, and "leah", which referred to a clearing in a forest. Although the buildings of Hadleigh are out of sight from the sea-wall, the town's most famous landmark is in full view at the top of the hill.

Hadleigh Castle

Hadleigh Castle was built in 1230 by Hubert de Burgh, who had obtained the manor of Hadleigh from Henry III just three years earlier. Roads were obviously poor in those days and most building materials were therefore brought in by boat. The county of Essex consists only of clay and alluvium, and has no native stone. The castle was therefore constructed mostly out of ragstone imported from Kent, generally known as "Kentish rag", being the nearest available stone. Many old buildings around the Essex coastline are constructed out of ragstone, and until recently it was often used as a protective facing on sea-walls.

The castle was given back to Henry III in 1239, and it soon fell into disuse. Under Edward III, a lot of rebuilding took place between 1360 and 1370. This was probably part of a new defence strategy for the River Thames, because Cooling Castle in north Kent was built around the same time. Lord Riche bought the land in 1552, and after removing all the useful parts from the castle, he allowed the buildings to fall into disuse once more. The ruins that you see today have therefore been uninhabited for more than four hundred years.

The castle walls formed a rough octagon, with four circular towers at strategic points. Today, only the two eastern towers remain, and a landslide in 1969 caused further damage. Because of the instability of the ground, the whole site is gradually slipping away down the slope, and more landslides are inevitable.

The ruins of Hadleigh Castle were immortalised in a famous painting by John Constable. After visiting the site in June 1814, he wrote:

"At Hadleigh there is a ruin of a castle from which its situation is a really fine place – it commands a view of the Kent hills, the Nore and the North Foreland and looking many miles out to sea."

Today the castle ruins are managed by English Heritage and are open to the public (admission free). From the centre of Hadleigh, they can be reached from Castle Lane, and although the small car-park rapidly fills up at weekends, the panoramic view of the River Thames makes a visit well worth while.

Back at the shoreline again, the sea-wall continues westwards beside the creek, finally leaving the last vestiges of Two-Tree Island behind. The surroundings are extremely quiet and rural, and yet this stretch of coastline has a lot of hidden history. In 1865, Reverend William Booth and his wife Caroline began church mission work in the east end of London. They were appalled by the conditions in which some people lived, and therefore in 1878 they set up the Salvation Army, a religious organisation particularly aimed at the "submerged" classes.

William Booth was the first general of the Salvation Army, and with a growing band of supporters, he decided in 1890 to puchase a large plot of land near Hadleigh. He bought most of the open ground between Leigh-on-Sea and Benfleet, including the buildings of Park Farm and Sayers Farm. Near the ruins of Hadleigh Castle, William Booth opened the Home Farm Colony for "criminals, the pauper, the reckless and helpless". The aim of the enterprise was to train people in various practical skills, usually before sending them out to occupy British colonies overseas. Cecil Rhodes, for example, is known to have taken 90 men from Hadleigh to work on his poultry farm in South Africa.

The Home Farm Colony was completely self-supporting and employed about 200 men by the turn of the century. As well as a farm and a market garden, the colony also had engineering shops, a library, a hospital and a research laboratory. Just below Hadleigh Castle, they built a pottery with its own lime-kiln, and it is still possible to find shards of pottery scattered about the site.

There were also several brickworks around the colony – one up near Sayers Farm and two more at the foot of the hill. Because Essex has no rock of its own, local builders were faced with a choice. If they were to avoid spending large sums of money bringing in stone such as Kentish ragstone from outside the county, they had to buy their materials from one of the local brickworks. Using local clay, the Salvation Army brickworks managed to satisfy much of the local demand. The bricks were taken by tram to an enormous jetty on the shoreline, where they were loaded onto barges. A small bridge carried the tramway over the main Southend-on-Sea railway-line. The colony fell into steep decline after the First World War. Today, only a small commercial farm remains, although the land is still owned by the Salvation Army.

Near a sharp bend in the sea-wall, several lines of stout wooden posts are embedded vertically in the mud. These tall posts, many standing over six feet high, are all that remain of the large jetty, once known as General Booth's Jetty. The tramlines were pulled up before 1940, although parts of the red-brick tramway bridge can still be seen on either side of the main railway-line. One map, drawn up around 1900, shows that a second tramway from the jetty crossed the main railway-line further to the east. Passing right round the hill, this branch-line climbed up a small valley behind Hadleigh Castle to reach the main buildings of the Home Farm Colony. This tramway was also pulled up, and its route is now hard to trace.

From General Booth's Jetty, the coastal footpath continues westwards along the shoreline, soon leaving the ancient district of Rochford Hundred and entering Barstable Hundred. The enormous sea-wall here prevents the sea from flooding the wide area of reclaimed land, which is variously known as Benfleet Marsh or Casey Marsh. This land forms part of the Hadleigh Castle Country Park, and is used for grazing horses and cattle. Immediately below the sea-wall, the wide borrow-dykes are filled with brackish water. Together with the ditches that cross the marshes, they provide a wide variety of habitats for wildlife.

Further inland, the tranquillity is occasionally interrupted by a train running along the railway-line. In 1911, the Salvation Army refused to allow a railway station to be built on their land, and although some residents of Hadleigh still rue that decision, it has protected these marshes from development.

Beyond the railway track, the ground rises rapidly to a series of steep undulating slopes known as the Benfleet Downs. The downs support a delightful mixture of woodland, scrub and open grassland, and are criss-crossed by a confusing network of footpaths. These slopes once formed the original banks of the River Thames, and although the sea-defences have forced the waters to retreat a short distance, the sea occasionally re-asserts its power. The waves broke through the original sea-wall, and a few yards of new embankment had to be built further inland to protect the rest of the farmland. This new sea-wall forms a tiny inlet about a mile from General Booth's Jetty, and the Ordnance Survey's "Explorer" map still shows the public right of way following the route of the older, abandoned sea-wall.

It is clear that civilisation is not far ahead now. Just before a fence across the sea-wall, the footpath climbs down off the sea-wall and heads towards a gate. This marks the boundary of the Hadleigh Castle Country Park. Until a few years ago, this area was used as a landfill site, but the skills of the engineers have transformed this site into a

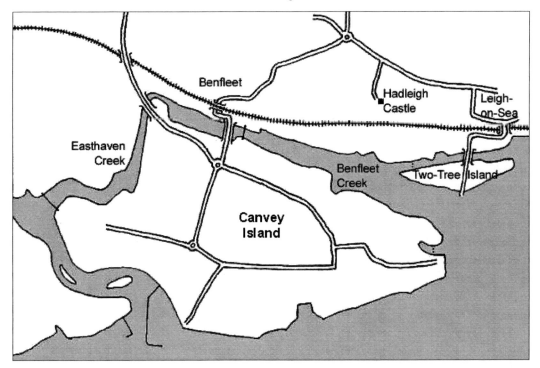

green oasis. The railway-line runs very close to the coast here as it approaches the small town of Benfleet. Most people who have walked this far along the sea-wall from Leigh-on-Sea will now want to push on quickly to the railway station in order to catch a train back to their starting point.

At Benfleet, a large flood barrier has been built across the creek. This concrete and red-brick structure is designed to protect the land beyond from high tides. Following devastating floods in 1953, the Government set up a committee to investigate the various methods of flood protection around the low-lying coasts of east England. As a result, Parliament passed the Thames Barrier and Flood Protection Act of 1972, calling for the construction of a massive barrier across the River Thames near Woolwich. This will be discussed in more detail later in this book.

In addition, the 1972 Act allowed for various other improvements to the sea-defences, such as a small dam near Mucking and floodgates at the entrance to Tilbury Dock. It also proposed that flood barriers should be constructed across several of the smaller tributaries of the River Thames. In the London area, these included structures across Barking Creek and Dartford Creek, whilst Essex was given flood barriers at Benfleet, Fobbing Horse and East Haven Creek. These measures also reduced the cost of maintaining the sea-walls further upstream.

The Benfleet barrier has three opening spans, each 39 feet wide. The central gate is nearly 20 feet tall, though the side gates are slightly shorter. When an unusually high tide is expected, the barrier can be quickly closed, but under normal circumstances the gates are lifted, leaving a height clearance of more than 6 feet above the water-level.

Canvey Island

From the Benfleet barrier, the public footpath continues westwards past a short slipway and meets up with the busy B1014 road from Benfleet. At this point, a low bridge carries the road over Benfleet Creek and onto Canvey Island. Until recently, this road regularly became congested during the rush hour, and so a second road onto the island was built a few years ago. One hundred years ago, however, the inhabitants of Canvey Island found it much more difficult to travel to and fro, since the only route across the creek onto the island was a ford which could only be used for a few hours around low tide.

The Canvey ford was situated just to the west of the point where the modern bridge crosses the creek. Even at the lowest point of the tide, the ford was usually under a few inches of water, but pedestrians could still cross the creek dryshod by following a line of stepping stones alongside the ford. As the tide turned, the stones and the ford were soon covered by the rising water, and a series of small rowing dinghies ferried people backwards and forwards across the creek.

Needless to say, this state of affairs led to considerable delays and caused inconvenience to the increasing number of inhabitants of Canvey Island. In May 1930, construction began on the first bridge across Benfleet Creek. The Colvin Bridge was opened at a formal ceremony by the chairman of Essex County Council, on 21st May 1931, followed by a large parade and celebrations across Canvey Island. At a cost of £20,000, the construction included a level-crossing over the railway and a new road onto the island.

At that time, many boats still plied up and down Benfleet Creek, and the new bridge had a large opening section. Using electrical power, the roadway could slide back on rollers, leaving a channel 60 feet wide for boats to pass, although it was often incorrectly referred to as a swing bridge.

Signal from the old Colvin Bridge

The Colvin Bridge was a great improvement for the islanders, and the easy access provided an immense boost for local industry. The tidal ford and stepping stones were rapidly forgotten. Four of the stones were removed and placed in the grounds of the local council offices, but the rest of the stones were left in place. They are now covered with mud, and even at low tide this route is now completely impassable.

Although the bridge radically improved the access to Canvey Island, it soon became clear that it was too low. During spring tides, the road often flooded and the island would once again become cut off from the mainland. The Colvin Bridge was last opened for water traffic in 1968, and work began on the construction of a replacement bridge alongside. This opened in 1973, along with a new road underneath the railway-line on the mainland, thereby removing the bottle-neck at the level-crossing. By this stage, the only boats sailing up Benfleet Creek were small pleasure craft, and so no attempt was made to provide an opening mechanism for the new bridge. The old Colvin Bridge was soon demolished, though some of the signalling lights can still be seen nearby at the Dutch Village Museum.

History of Canvey

The discovery of Roman houses at Thorney Beck and Leigh Beck indicates that Canvey Island has been occupied for at least two thousand years, though these early buildings were only simple constructions made of mud and wattle with tiled roofs. During Roman times, the island was known as Convennos Insula, the word "insula" being Latin for island. It is not clear what "Convennos" means, though some sources suggest that the name is simply derived from "Canna's Island".

By 1255, it had become known as Canaveye, eventually leading to the present "Canvey Island", although technically this name is a tautology. That is to say, the word "Island" is unnecessary because the suffix "ey" already indicates that the place is an island. Many Essex islands have been named in this way, a few examples including Horsey, Northey, and Rushley. The spelling has also been corrupted over the centuries in such place-names as Mersea, Wallasea and Osea.

Being so close to sea-level, the marshes around Canvey Island were always extremely damp, and were only suitable for grazing animals. From their milk, farmers often manufactured their own cheese, as described by John Norden in 1594:

"Nere the Thames mowth, below Beamflete, are certaine ilandes, called Canuey Ilandes, low merishe [marshy] grounds; and for that the passage ouer the creeks is unfit for cattle, it is onlie conuerted to the feeding of ews, which men milke, and thereof make cheese (suche as it is), and of the curdes of the whey they make butter once in the year, which serueth the clothier."

In John Norden's day, deep creeks divided the marshes into several separate islands, which were collectively known as the Canvey Islands. Some of these islets were permanently inhabited, and it is likely that these farmers protected their land with embankments to prevent the fields from being flooded at high tide. One document from 1438, for example, describes the construction of a mile of sea-wall. However, it was not until the 17th century that a concerted effort was made to reclaim all of the Canvey marshes.

In 1622, Sir Henry Appleton raised the funds for a Dutchman named Joas Croppenburg to construct a single sea-wall around the whole of Canvey Island. By this time, Dutch engineers had gained considerable experience in building sea-defences, and it was arranged that the Dutch would perform the necessary work in exchange for one third of the reclaimed land. This was known as The Third Acre Agreement. The enormous undertaking was carried out under the leadership of the famous engineer Cornelius Vermuyden. Although these days he is renowned for his successful enterprise on Canvey Island, his failure at several earlier drainage projects, including the Fens, is often forgotten.

As a brief aside, East Anglian farmers had managed for years to foil all attempts to drain their Fenlands, perhaps fearing the changes that this would bring about in their lifestyle. One of the most vociferous campaigners against drainage was Oliver Cromwell, who had been brought up in the town of Ely. However, when Cromwell came to power, he switched his allegiance and instigated a scheme to drain the Fens, against the wishes of the locals. Ironically, he died in 1658 of malaria, probably contracted during a visit to low-lying marshes in Ireland.

Back on the Essex coast again, many Dutchmen took advantage of the Third Acre agreement to settle on Canvey Island, though the onset of war between Holland and England in 1665 caused most of the Dutch population to flee back to their home country. A substantial number remained behind however, to tend sheep for their meat, wool and milk, and in time the Dutch community grew so large that they petitioned the king for permission to hold church services in their own language. Today, the Dutch connection remains in many of the road-names.

Over the years, new sea-walls were built around the fringes of Canvey Island, increasing its size and adding new areas of grazing pasture. Extra sea-defences were constructed at the eastern end of the island between 1622 and 1770, and a further bout of land reclamation took place from 1850 to 1860 under the direction of a man named Mr. Hilton. Even though the old sea-walls were no longer required to hold back the sea, they were usually still kept as flood protection, in case one of the main sea-defences should fail. These counterwalls also proved useful as roads, since they provided dry and direct routes around the poorly-drained marshland.

Fresh water proved troublesome for the local farmers, since all supplies of drinking water had to be painstakingly carried across from the mainland. During the 19th century, however, Mr. Hilton dug wells over 250 feet deep in order to provide fresh water to the local inhabitants. This enabled many more people to settle on Canvey Island, but proved a headache for the authorities because the marshes had originally been divided up amongst many of the mainland parishes. With a rapidly growing population, this situation eventually became unworkable, and in 1881 Canvey Island was finally made into its own separate parish.

A much more serious problem facing the islanders, however, has always been the unpredictability of the tides and the constant threat of floods. From the earliest records, these low-lying coasts have been at risk from the sea. In November 1099, it was recorded that the *"sea flood rose to such a height and did so much harm as no man remembered that it ever did before."* These shores were struck on the 12th November 1236 by *"the most violent wind and damaging of sea and river"*, and floods in 1251 and 1294 forced the government to pass a law making it the duty of landowners to maintain their sea-walls. This law stood for nearly 700 years, until the Land Drainage Act of 1930 passed the burden to the local water authorities.

A storm on the 18th January 1881 washed away over three miles of sea-defences along the southern side of Canvey Island. A large chunk of land at the eastern tip of the island was completely devastated by these floods, and had to be abandoned. When the Third Acre agreement had been drawn up in the 17th century, the Dutch owners of the Third Acres had accepted all responsibility for the sea-defences of Canvey Island, including the rest of the island, known as the Freelands. Following the 1881 floods, however, these landowners were unable to meet the cost of the necessary repairs, and the government therefore introduced the Canvey Island (Sea Defences) Act of 1883. This largely replaced the original Third Acre Agreement, although it was not until 1933 that the agreement was completely superseded.

On Monday 29th November 1897, a freak tide caused immense damage down the eastern coast of England, inundating a total of 30,000 acres of farmland, but Canvey escaped relatively lightly with only minor flooding at the north of the island. A further storm struck in 1928, but once again Canvey escaped by the skin of its teeth. On that occasion, the tide stopped just six inches from the top of the island's sea-defences, but the greatest flood of all was yet to strike.

The Great Flood of 1953

On 31st January 1953, the local MP visited Canvey Island to open the Memorial Hall in memory of those who died in the Second World War, but outside a violent storm was growing. It is a common phenomenon that the low pressure underneath an atmospheric depression causes the sea-level to rise by up to a foot. Such a small rise may not appear to be particularly significant, but a hump of water perhaps a thousand miles across, moving at 40 or 50 miles per hour, contains an enormous amount of energy. As the depression approaches the shallow continental shelf around the British Isles, the hump is greatly magnified to a height of ten feet or more.

Once in a while, the timing of the storm coincides with a high spring tide, and a strong north wind brings the powerful mound of water down through the North Sea. If this happens, an exceedingly dangerous surge tide can be created, because the English Channel creates a bottle-neck around Dover, and the rotation of the Earth throws the surge tide westwards towards Britain. On the night of 31st January 1953, the highest surge tide ever recorded in the British Isles pounded the eastern coastline of England. On one of the coldest nights of the year, with the countryside in complete darkness and most people fast asleep, ice-cold sea-water poured over the sea-walls or simply broke through, wreaking havoc in low-lying areas of reclaimed land. Many people were awoken by the sound of the water and fled in pitch darkness upwards into the attic, sometimes having to break through the roof-tiles to escape the ever-rising tide. Canvey Island had a large proportion of bungalows, and therefore many people perished from exhaustion or exposure after clinging to their freezing roof all night through the raging storm.

Holland was hit particularly hard and it is estimated that 3000 people drowned, but England also faced very serious problems. The islands around Foulness and Wallasea were completely inundated, with five people drowned. The evacuation of the survivors was extremely difficult because all roads were underwater. Six more fatalities were reported from Great Wakering where a new housing estate had been flooded, and two people drowned in Southend-on-Sea. All down the eastern coast of England, factories and oil refineries were ruined, and it was years before the farmland would produce any significant crops again because salt had leached into the soil.

The area around Canvey suffered badly because the island had no high ground to which the inhabitants could flee. A total of 58 people drowned on the island that night, and not a single building escaped the floods. With no electricity, heating, sanitation or food, over 25,000 people had to be evacuated by boat to higher ground. In Operation King Canute, the army was immediately drafted in to help repair the sea-defences, many of which had simply been swept away in the night. In order to avoid further flooding, it was important that the sea-defences were re-built before the next spring tide, which was due on the night of the 16th February. By the 13th February, it became clear that the stock of 20 million sandbags would not be sufficient. An emergency operation, code-named Operation Sandbag, was initiated to speed up the supply of sandbags. With an immense effort over the next couple of days, the majority of the sea-defences were repaired, albeit in a very temporary state, and the spring tide passed without further incident.

The task of clearing up the damage took years to complete, and the government decided to set up a committee to investigate how to protect the coastline against future surge tides. As already discussed, this led to the construction of the Thames Barrier and several smaller flood barriers around Essex and Kent. The sea-walls surrounding Canvey Island are now stronger and higher than ever and numerous systems have been implemented to warn the island population about impending floods, complete with detailed evacuation procedures.

Nevertheless, surge tides continue to cause some concern to the authorities, and over recent years Canvey Island has experienced several narrow escapes. On Christmas Eve 1988, the Thames Barrier was used for the first time in an emergency, but the closing of the gates sent a reflected wave back down the River Thames. The Ministry of Agriculture sent a Scale Three flood warning from its centre from Bracknell, which should have invoked most of the anti-flood procedures around Canvey, but there was a breakdown in communications somewhere along the way. As a result, the police and the local emergency authorities received a warning of a Scale One tide, which is a much lower level of danger. Fortunately, on this occasion the flood-water eventually stopped rising just inches from the top of the sea-defences, and Canvey Island remained secure. There was little wind that day, but the situation could have turned into a full-scale catastrophe if a strong northerly wind had been blowing.

Detailed description of Canvey

Canvey Island has a public right of way all around its outer edge, a distance of about thirteen miles. Although this is too far for most people to walk in one go, it can be neatly subdivided into three convenient shorter strolls. The north-eastern edge of the island follows the banks of Benfleet Creek, with views of saltings and deep marshy inlets. The south-eastern sea-wall looks out across the River Thames, which is nearly two miles wide at this point, but this section of the island is too busy and built-up to provide much enjoyment.

The third walk, around the western end of Canvey, is in complete contrast to the rest of the island. This walk is relatively quiet and rural, and the few vestiges of industry that remain here do not generally intrude upon the tranquillity of the scenery. Indeed they even serve to add more interest to one of the finest and most varied walks in this part of Essex. The following text describes each of these three sections in turn, beginning at the bridge over Benfleet Creek and working clockwise around the island.

Crossing the bridge onto Canvey Island, the road passes through an area of low-lying marshland. Before the construction of the Benfleet flood barrier, this stretch of the road was often flooded at high tide, creating considerable delays for the islanders. Where the road cuts through the sea-wall, you can see slots either side of the carriageway where wooden planks were lowered into place to prevent the flood-waters from spreading into the interior of the island.

Leave the road where it cuts through the sea-wall and follow this embankment eastwards. A large boat-yard has been built nearby on reclaimed land. From here, a public footpath heads eastwards along the top of the main sea-wall, following the southern bank of Benfleet Creek.

Along the top of the embankment, a concrete crest-wall provides a few vital extra feet of flood protection. A good footpath runs alongside, and although this is a quiet stretch of coastline, you are never far from suburban sprawl. This part of the island was given the unoriginal name of New Lands when it was reclaimed from the sea towards the middle of the 1800s.

The view outside the sea-wall is much more interesting, with a wide-reaching panorama of the downs of the Hadleigh Castle Country Park. To the east, the ruins of the castle itself stand proudly at the top of a hill overlooking the Thames estuary. Much of this land is owned by the Salvation Army, whose Home Farm Colony was described earlier. Closer to hand, a line of rectangular pits can be seen along the foot of the sea-wall. Hundreds of years ago, shallow pools were often dug in the salt-marshes in order to cultivate oysters. Until the beginning of the 20th century, a lot of the isolated marshland communities were employed in this thriving industry, and the remains of oyster-beds can frequently be found up and down the tidal creeks of Essex.

The oyster industry has now virtually disappeared, and Benfleet Creek is used instead by the yachting fraternity. Hundreds of boats are moored out in the deep water channel. A muddy footpath leads across the marshes to a small jetty at the edge of the saltings. This footpath was marked on maps dating back to 1867, suggesting that it was originally built to give local wildfowlers better access to the salt-marshes.

About a mile and a half from the bridge, the main sea-wall turns sharply to the south and enters a small inlet. At this point, a deep creek used to penetrate about 700 yards inland. It was known as Tewkes Creek, a "tewk" being another name for a redshank. When Canvey's sea-defences were repaired after the devastating floods of 1953, a dam was constructed across the mouth of this creek. This shortened the line of the sea-wall. The dam was finished in 1955, but you can still see the old route of Tewkes Creek winding its way inland between the original sea-walls. One map dating from 1876 shows what appears to be the remains of an earlier barrage across Tewkes Creek. It seems likely that Mr. Hilton tried to dam this creek whilst reclaiming his New Lands nearby, but the sea broke through and he soon abandoned the attempt.

Beyond Tewkes Creek, the sea-wall resumes an eastward direction. This section of the island is another part of the estate reclaimed from the sea by Mr. Hilton between 1850 and 1860. Like the area known as New Lands further to the west, two large embankments were built across the middle of this land. These counterwalls were designed to limit the damage caused by any breach in the main sea-defences. The original Dutch sea-wall, now some distance inland, was not abandoned however. Since it was raised above the level of the marshy surroundings, it became used as a main thoroughfare across the island, and the eastern half of Canvey High Street still follows this route today.

By 1876, a small farm called Sunken Marsh had been set up on this newly-reclaimed land. In the early 1900s, the farm-buildings were demolished to make way for a large housing estate, but the name of the original farm was retained. In the disastrous floods of 1953, all the buildings around Sunken Marsh were inundated, though the old counterwalls proved to be extremely useful. Since they were higher than the flooded surroundings, they provided a dry route across the island, enabling the emergency services to move in quickly to repair the main sea-walls.

Walking eastwards past the remains of more oyster-beds, you soon draw level with a large slipway on Two-Tree Island. When the Essex flood-defences were being reviewed, it was suggested that a barrier could be built across Hadleigh Ray at this point. The proposed barrier was similar to the Thames Barrier near Woolwich, but on a larger scale with eighteen pilings sunk into the river-bed. When a surge tide was expected, gates could quickly be lowered into position, protecting the Benfleet Marshes and the northern edge of Canvey Island from flooding. Under normal conditions, four of these gates could be fully opened to provide navigation channels, each up to 60 feet wide. By adding a carriageway that slid back on rollers, the flood barrier could also provide a useful road link for the inhabitants of Canvey Island to the busy town of Southend-on-Sea. Needless to say, this ambitious scheme was soon dropped in favour of the cheaper flood barrier at Benfleet.

Just inland here, an enormous grass-covered mound towers over the sea-wall. This was once the site of Hoppet Cottage, but the council decided to use this land as a domestic refuse tip. When dumping finished, the ground was subsequently covered with a layer of topsoil and seeded with grass.

Outside the island, a wide area of saltings extends up to the foot of the sea-wall. If you keep a careful look-out, you may spot one of the old footpaths which used to lead across these saltings. Heading directly out from the shore, a low embankment was built across the marshes, probably to enable local wildfowlers to get closer to their prey. Unfortunately, this path can no longer be walked because the tide has eroded a deep channel through the saltings, washing away the first few yards of the embankment.

About two hundred yards further on, a second marshland path leaves the main sea-wall. Instead of using an earth embankment to cross the saltings, two lines of vertical stakes support a series of rickety wooden platforms. This precarious pathway leads to a flimsy bridge over a channel of deep mud before heading out across the saltings. Although it eventually reaches the banks of Smallgains Creek, a blue notice-board carries a prominent warning that the bridge is now dangerously unstable, and walkers should no longer attempt to follow this path.

It is likely that this route was originally used by yachtsmen to reach boats moored out in the deep water, and a few vessels still use these jetties. The local Ordnance Survey maps provide another insight into the history of these marshes. The detailed "Explorer" maps show that this reach is also known as Oyster Creek, and aerial photographs taken at low tide reveal a series of hollows in the muddy bed of the creek. There are around fifty of these pits, each about five yards long. Many of them are rectangular in shape, and it is quite likely that they were dug out of the creek bed in order to cultivate oysters.

Continuing along the main sea-wall, you soon reach the shores of Smallgains Creek, a wide stretch of water which forces you to make a short detour to the west. Originally, this would have entailed a walk of over a mile westwards to the head of the creek, and then another mile back along its southern bank to reach the corresponding position on the opposite bank. Following the great floods however, a large dam was built across the creek in 1955, although a public right of way still exists along its original sea-walls. This dam now provides a convenient short-cut and also offers a good view of the reclaimed land inside, where a large pond is usually thronging with birds.

At low tide, there used to be an even quicker route across Smallgains Creek. Just a couple of hundred yards from the mouth of the creek, a tidal ford once led across the river-bed to a concrete slipway on the opposite bank. At one time, even cars were known to use this ford, but today it is covered with soft mud and is no longer usable.

The ford and slipway are owned by Halcon Marine, part of the Halcon Group. Their bar is housed in the distinctive "Mississippi Steam Boat" which is moored alongside the slipway. The boat-yard also has jetty moorings for up to 300 vessels, including 10 berths set aside for visitors.

A large floodgate stands at the top of Halcon Marine's slipway. This is one of several floodgates to be found around the edge of Canvey Island. For most of the year, they are left open to provide access to the shoreline, but when a surge tide is predicted, the gates are all closed to stop the flood-water from pouring into the island.

Heading eastward along the sea-wall from the slipway, it is only two hundred yards to the eastern end of Canvey Island. Here the road climbs over the top of the sea-defences and leads towards a second slipway into Smallgains Creek. The Island Yacht Club owns a long line of jetties along the water's edge, but the creek dries out within a couple of hours of high tide. This region has been a popular sailing centre for many years, and local maps show that sailors have given names to most of the marshland features. For example, the creek leads out into the deep-water channel of Hadleigh Ray at a junction known as Sluts Hole, and at low tide the receding waters reveal a large expanse of mudflats nearby known as the Bergander Sands, a bergander (or bargander) being another name for the shelduck.

Canvey Point

During the 17th and 18th centuries, a large area of marshland off the eastern tip of Canvey Island was reclaimed from the sea, thereby extending the island eastwards by nearly a mile. The newly reclaimed land was divided into four sections by a series of earth embankments, and the ground was probably used for grazing animals. This narrow promontary was always vulnerable to flooding however, and old maps show that some of it was flooded by 1860. In 1881, a surge tide swept away the sea-defences along its southern flank, and the land was finally abandoned to the tides.

In contrast, the sea-wall along the northern edge of the reclaimed land escaped relatively unscathed, but a few sections are now starting to erode away, and a prominent notice-board warns you that it is often covered by the tide. This embankment obviously no longer serves as a sea-wall, but it does provide a very enjoyable stroll out across the saltings, although a few stretches are very muddy. *Before leaving the main sea-defences of Canvey Island and heading out along this embankment, it is essential to consult a tide-timetable. As with all tidal footpaths, it is not sufficient merely to look and see that the tide is out, since the water-levels can rise dangerously fast around the Essex coastline, and it is easy to underestimate your distance from the shore.*

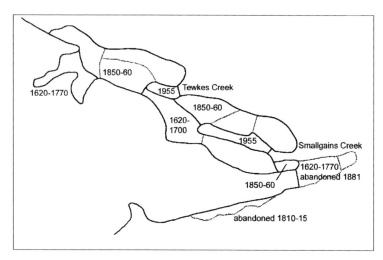

Having ascertained that the tide is not about to come in, the old embankment provides much more peaceful surroundings than the walk along the top of Canvey's main sea-defences. In places, you can see the remains of the old sea-walls where rows of wooden stakes stick up out of the mud. These marshes all belong to a nature reserve owned by the Essex Wildlife Trust, and are often teeming with wildfowl, particularly during the winter months. Maps show that several features of this peninsula have been given individual names, such as Leighbeck Point and Cockleshell Beach, but the area as a whole is usually referred to as Canvey Point.

This promontary of abandoned marshland has also given its name to the local council. During the re-organisations of 1974, the district council on Canvey Island was merged with the mainland council, and a public competition was held to select a name for the new authority. Out of all the entries, the name which was eventually chosen was "Castle Point", a name derived from two of the region's most distinctive features – Hadleigh Castle and Canvey Point.

Just over half a mile from the shore, the embankment eventually peters out in an area known as Clock Bank. Walkers must turn round here and head back to dry land, but the mud and sand-banks continue eastward for another three miles. These sand-banks were once referred to as the Popling Sands, although they are now generally known as the Chapman Sands. It was recently suggested that an enormous barrage could be built across the Chapman Sands from Canvey Point to Southend-on-Sea. Despite the disastrous consequences that this would inevitably bring upon the local ecology, this proposal was seriously considered during the investigation into a possible Maplin Airport, though the cost ultimately proved too high.

Returning back to the main sea-defences around Canvey Island, the coastal route heads southwards past the wreck of a wartime ammunitions ship. Following the top of the massive sea-wall, the footpath soon turns sharply to the right and begins a long stretch along the southern edge of the island. This is one of the highest embankments around the Essex coast, and although it serves an essential purpose in keeping out the tides, its towering height gives the local housing estate a very claustrophobic atmosphere.

This area is known as Leigh Beck, after a small tributary of the River Thames which runs close to the sea-wall at this point. When it is exposed at low tide, you can see that it runs parallel to the shore and penetrates a long way into the Chapman Sands. In 1850, a small lighthouse was erected here to warn sailors of the sand-banks just under the surface. Known as the Chapman Lighthouse, it consisted of a powerful light supported by a simple hexagonal structure and held above the waves on top of six narrow metal pillars. Some sources say that it was finally removed around 1910, although others indicate that it was not demolished until 1940.

Around the beginning of the last century, an entrepreneur named Frederick Hester attempted to transform the island into a popular seaside resort. As well as considerable construction on the mainland, he built a short pleasure pier out from the shore in 1901. The pier projected 220 yards into the waters of Leigh Beck, but it had to be removed at the outbreak of the First World War.

About ten minutes' walk from the corner of the island, the enormous embankment veers slightly to the right. The original sea-wall, built by the Dutch engineers during the 17th century, used to continue straight on at this point, but by the beginning of the 19th century it had become badly eroded. Between 1810 and 1815, it was decided that it was no longer possible to maintain the original embankment, and so new sea-defences were built a little further inland. The old abandoned sea-wall was rapidly washed away by the waves, although at low tide you can still see its original route, indicated by a line of rubble on the mud.

Along most of this stretch of coastline, a tall concrete wall divides the crest of the sea-wall into two separate footpaths. Since the land inside is mostly occupied by suburban housing estates, most people choose to walk on the seaward side of the wall. Although this can hardly be described as a salubrious promenade, it does provide refreshing views of the River Thames, which is over two miles wide at this point.

On a clear day, it is possible to make out several features on the opposite bank. Most of the prominent landmarks are inevitably man-made, such as the tall chimneys of the power stations at Kingsnorth and the Isle of Grain, and it is easy to spot the large caravan park on the hillside near Allhallows-on-Sea, but there is also plenty of interesting countryside in this part of Kent. Along its northern edge, a new public right of way has recently been opened around the coastline from High Halstow to Cliffe, providing a marvellous walk through the remote Cliffe Marshes. A few miles to the south, the estuary of the River Medway is littered with abandoned islands, most of which once harboured their own small community. Today, these islands are all deserted and their people entirely forgotten, but, for the yachtsman with a keen sense of exploration, the hidden corners of this estuary are an endless source of fascination.

Coming back to Canvey Island, the footpath continues westwards from Leigh Beck for just over a mile before turning right and entering a small inlet. Known as Thorney Bay, this was once the mouth of a creek which used to penetrate deep into the island until the Dutch engineers built a sea-wall around Canvey during the 17th century. Its waters can still be seen snaking their way inland, forming a shallow ditch called Thorneycreek Fleet.

The narrow bay, containing a small beach of sand and shingle, provides a brief but welcome respite from the oppressive concrete footpath. It also signals a change in the character of the surrounding land, because the shops and housing estates die out at this point, only to be replaced with the remains of heavy industry, largely the remnants of an enormous oil and gas terminal. The first oil storage tanks were built on Canvey around 1933, despite opposition from the new District Council. Once a bridge had been built onto the island, more industry sprang up, including large tanks to store liquefied natural gas from Algeria. These industrial areas were inevitably one of the first targets of German bombers during the Second World War.

After the war, the large oil companies had big ideas for Canvey Island. Around 1965, an Italian company, with an American associate, bought up most of the western half of the island with plans for new oil refineries. As it turned out, only the Italian company ever started construction work, and after spending £64 million, their project was also abandoned. In recent years, the methane storage has been scaled down, and Texaco announced in 1985 that they would be closing their oil storage plant. Whilst some islanders breathed a sigh of relief that their neighbourhood was not after all destined to become a giant oil refinery, the factories would have brought money and jobs to the area, and their departure also leaves behind large areas of derelict land.

From Thorney bay, the coastal path rejoins the banks of the River Thames at a slight promontary known as Deadman's Point, before resuming its westward course past the remains of the oil and gas works. Several long jetties project out into the deep water channel. During the Second World War, this region played a vital role in the protection of London. In order to prevent enemy submarines and small ships from passing up the River Thames unnoticed, a long wooden boom was placed right across the river to the western side of St. Mary's Bay in north Kent.

The wartime boom was nearly two miles long, and had a movable middle section to allow Allied shipping to pass through unhindered. On the edge of Canvey Island, a series of spotlights and batteries were built to detect and destroy any enemy ships, whilst at the Kent end a small generator provided power for three Defence Electric Light stations. These powerful spotlights were situated in the middle of the river, and were accessible from Kent by means of a narrow-gauge railway which ran for 1400 yards along the top of the boom. The entire structure was removed after the war.

About half a mile west of Thorney Bay, the sea-wall veers to the right slightly. This is the southernmost part of Canvey Island, a point once known as Scar's Elbow. At low tide, you can see a line of rocks and stones placed on the river-bed just offshore. This causes encroaching waves to break early, and helps to reduce their erosive power.

After a mile or so, the footpath arrives at a corner known as Holehaven Point. Here, the sea-wall leaves the River Thames behind. It turns sharply to the right, and heads northwards along the banks of a wide inlet called Holehaven Creek. An enormous jetty crosses the mouth of this creek, leading out almost a mile to a platform enabling large oil tankers to berth safely without having to risk the shallow sand-banks.

Standing just inland at this point, a white weather-boarded building is almost dwarfed by the tall sea-defences. This is a pub called the Lobster Smack. Parts of the building, previously called the Sluice House and The World's End, are said to date from 1510. Drawings from around 1900 show that, although it has been enlarged considerably, the Lobster Smack's olde-worlde appearance has remained unchanged over the years. It was even mentioned in Charles Dickens's "Great Expectations". The settings for his novel were remarkably true to life, and include an accurate description of the prison hulks which were moored in the River Thames just across from the Lobster Smack during the 19th century. Most of the story was centred around the northern shores of Kent, although many of the descriptive passages could have applied equally well to the remote marshlands of south Essex.

Near the Lobster Smack, an enormous three-storey hotel was built in 1900. Known as the Kynoch Hotel, it served the oil refineries at Kynochtown, just across Holehaven Creek, and was connected to the factories by a small rowing-boat ferry which operated across the wide creek. After the war, the building was converted into oil company offices and later demolished in 1960.

For people walking around the Essex coastline, the road leading up to the Lobster Smack is significant because it provides the last public access to the sea-wall until you reach the bridge at Benfleet, nearly five miles further on. This stretch of sea-wall offers some of the best scenery to be found around the area, because this western half of the island has so far managed to escape the sprawl of new housing estates which have already over-run the rest of Canvey Island.

This may all change in the future, however. A few years ago, Peter de Savary applied for planning permission to build a new town near the western end of the island. Covering 1350 acres, the plans included 4000 new houses, as well as a shopping centre and a business park, at a total cost of £300 million. The plan was eventually abandoned after opposition from local inhabitants, who maintained that the existing road links onto Canvey Island were already full to capacity and that any more large-scale developments would only exacerbate the existing traffic problem. However, it is inevitable that applications to develop this part of the island will re-appear at frequent intervals.

From the Lobster Smack, the route finally moves away from the main channel of the River Thames, following a good footpath along the top of the sea-wall in a north-westerly direction. The route soon passes underneath the head of the jetty which crosses the mouth of Holehaven Creek. The path continues along the shores of the creek past the ruins of the oil refinery.

About six hundred yards further on, you encounter a small plot of land, semi-circular in shape, standing at the foot of the embankment on the seaward side. This was once the quay for a nearby coastguard station named "The Emulous". Old photographs of the area show that a large two-storey building stood just inside the sea-defences here around 1900.

The sea-wall veers to the left here, passing the rusting remains of more oil containers, once the site of a small farm called Little Brickhouse. At this point, Holehaven Creek is still about half a mile wide, but at low tide you can see that it splits into two deep channels. There is a small island of saltings between the channels, which is known as Lower Horse. (A "horse" is an old local word for an island or a mudbank in the middle of a river.)

As the name suggests, Lower Horse is the first of two such islands in the middle of Holehaven Creek. Its companion, Upper Horse, comes into view as you follow the sea-wall around the corner to the right, although it is not named on the local "Landranger" map produced by the Ordnance Survey. Unlike its southern neighbour, it appears that the inhospitable saltings of Upper Horse were used for grazing animals at one time.

If you look carefully, you may spot the remains of a low earth embankment running across the islet. From the air, you can clearly see that the embankments form a rectangle about 100 yards long by 80 yards wide, and a detailed map of the area, drawn up in 1876, seems to show a small building or hut inside these walls. In addition, two short embankments led from the main rectangle in a north-westerly direction down to the water's edge, presumably providing a dry route to a boat landing-stage. However, it appears unusual today that an enterprising farmer should go to such great lengths in return for such a small area of poor quality grazing land. Some sources have even suggested that these embankments are the remains of a Roman encampment!

The surroundings are quiet and peaceful, but the scenery is spoiled by the view of tall chimneys and oil tanks on the far side of Holehaven Creek. These belong to the three refineries at Coryton, which will be described later on. Closer to hand, you can see the remains of past industry on Canvey just inside the sea-wall. According to old maps of the area, this was once the site of West Wick Farm, one of the oldest farms on the island, but the area is now just a series of mounds and deep pits, probably the result of gravel extraction. At weekends, motorcyclists frequently use this area for scrambling, although there are several notices at the road-end near Northwick warning people that technically there is no right of public access.

Because of the poor communications to Canvey Island, most of the gravel was carried out by boat, and you can see the remains of the quay just along the coast. It was served by a short tramway which used to head inland for about a quarter of a mile, although the tracks have now been pulled up. Nevertheless, the wooden substructure of the jetty still remains at the foot of the embankment, but the platform on top has disappeared, and the blackened surfaces of the timber beams suggest that the jetty was burned down.

Continuing northwards along the shoreline, the footpath soon turns to the right where a narrow tributary flows into Holehaven Creek. This small offshoot, known as East Haven Creek, penetrates several miles inland before joining up with Benfleet Creek, thereby separating Canvey from the mainland.

Flood barrier across East Haven Creek

A large barrier has been built across the mouth of East Haven Creek. Its design enables it to be used as an escape route from the island in times of serious flood, but its primary purpose is as a flood barrier, similar to the one at Benfleet. The East Haven barrier has a large central gate 40 feet wide by 30 feet high, and has two smaller side gates. Under normal conditions, the gates are held open, 11 feet above high water to allow small boats to sail up East Haven Creek, but when an exceptionally high tide is expected, the gates are lowered into position to hold back the flood. A third flood barrier can be seen at Fobbing Horse, two-thirds of a mile to the west, but this will be described in more detail later.

Leaving Holehaven Creek behind, the footpath follows the crest of the sea-wall along the south bank of East Haven Creek. The Ordnance Survey maps show a second right of way running parallel just a few yards inland, although it is not obvious on the ground. This second path follows the route of the original Dutch sea-wall around the island, but another strip of land has since been reclaimed by the construction of a new embankment, and it is this new sea-wall which forms the coastal route today.

This part of the island, originally known as Southwick Marsh, was once served by a nearby farmstead called Tree Farm, but these buildings have now all gone. Although the road-end at Northwick is only a few hundred yards away as the crow flies, there is no public access between the road and the sea-wall. This seems a shame because the southern shores of East Haven Creek contain some of the most beautiful countryside around Canvey. In order to enjoy these pleasant surroundings, walkers are forced to tramp around the coastline for five miles, and it is therefore not surprising that people rarely visit this corner of the island.

On the other hand, the lack of public access means that this area remains delightfully quiet, with tranquil meadows stretching up to the foot of the sea-wall. The situation is quite different on the opposite bank of East Haven Creek. Looking across the water, you can see that the land on the far side has been raised many feet above the level of the surrounding marshes, and lorries can occasionally be heard thundering about in the distance. Once the site of a remote farm called East Haven House, the area has unfortunately been turned into an enormous dump for industrial refuse.

Nevertheless, the south bank of the creek retains an unspoilt rural atmosphere, the scenery changing with the daily rhythm of the tides. As the water-level drops, the creek dimishes to leave just a shallow channel flowing between deep banks of mud. This type of landscape is also more vivid during the cold winter months, when the air comes alive with flocks of migrating wildfowl and a bitter wind surges across the bleak marshes.

The sea-wall soon turns sharply to the right. At this corner, a large drain passes through the embankment, emptying excess water from the inland ditches into East Haven Creek. The footpath heads around the outside of a small inlet, now covered with saltings but once the mouth of a long creek. On an Ordnance Survey map, you can still trace the meandering route of the creek for over a mile inland.

A wide ditch runs parallel to the shoreline just inside the sea-wall. Although this is now principally used to drain the fields during the wet winter season, its original purpose was to provide earth in order to build up the sea-defences, and hence it is known as a "borrow-dyke". Three hundred yards further on, a turf bridge across the borrow-dyke indicates the site of Pantile Farm. This was another of the old farmsteads on Canvey which have since been demolished, although piles of bricks and rubble can still be found hidden amongst the undergrowth.

The sea-wall continues almost due north, heading towards a long bridge which carries the new A130 road onto Canvey Island. Known as Canvey Way, this busy road seems particularly intrusive amongst these quiet meadows, but few people would deny that the island desperately needed a better road link to the mainland. Shortly after passing underneath the road bridge, the sea-wall reaches the northernmost point on Canvey and then veers slowly to the right. This is the tip of a short promontary called Newlands, a name which reveals that this piece of land was reclaimed from the sea only relatively recently.

When the Dutch built the original sea-wall around Canvey Island in the 17th century, they divided the newly reclaimed land into two regions. Under their contract, the Dutch engineers were entitled to one third of the land, the "Third Acre Lands", whilst English farmers occupied the rest of the island, an area known as "The Freelands". Any marshland which has subsequently been added to the island, like this promontary at Newlands, is usually referred to as one of the "outlands". It is still easy to find the remains of the original sea-wall, now forming just a low earth embankment along the edge of a field.

A large pill-box appears on the opposite bank, a brick construction built during the Second World War. The Benfleet flood barrier comes into view ahead, indicating that you are now approaching the older road-bridge across Benfleet Creek and the end of the walk around Canvey Island. The sea-wall turns right at a sharp corner, but if you look ahead in a straight line you may be able to spot the remains of a low earth embankment crossing the saltings. Although this embankment has now been breached in several places by the tide, maps drawn up in 1876 and 1898 show that this was originally a continuous wall across the marshes, presumably used by local wildfowlers.

The footpath soon turns back to the left and heads due east towards the bridge, with open meadows on one side and the wide channel of Benfleet Creek on the other. Unfortunately, the sea-wall runs very close to Canvey Way and the constant noise of the traffic can be quite distracting. Along this shoreline, the remains of oyster-beds can be seen just outside the sea-wall, forming a line of rectangular pits in the saltings. Cultivating oysters was once an important industry around the Essex salt-marshes – detailed information is given earlier in this book, in the description of Mersea Island.

Another wildfowlers' footpath can be found about three hundred yards from the corner, where the sea-wall veers slightly to the left. At this point, you may just be able to spot the remains of an old embankment heading directly out from the shore across the mudflats. Old maps from 1843 and 1876 show that this originally formed a raised pathway across the marshes, but the swirling waters of Benfleet Creek have slowly eroded it away and the tide has now managed to break through in several places.

As you approach the bridge over Benfleet Creek, another curious feature can be seen a few yards before the buildings of Waterside Farm. From the main sea-wall, two earth embankments head out across the saltings, running parallel just over ten feet apart. A narrow footpath follows the crest of these embankments almost to the water's edge, where a large hut is used as the headquarters of the local boat club, although it is not immediately clear why the boat club requires two embankments. In fact, these embankments pre-date the boat club by hundreds of years because this was the original road onto Canvey Island. Until 1931, the only dry route onto the island was via the tidal ford, mentioned earlier. With a line of stepping stones alongside for pedestrians, this led across the muddy saltings towards the island, with a low earth embankment on either side to keep the track dry. The ford and stepping stones were abandoned soon after the construction of the first bridge in 1931, and are now said to be under several inches of mud, but it appears that the embankments have been maintained for use by local boatmen.

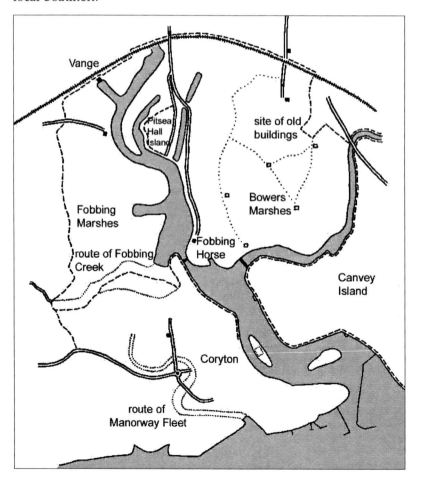

Holehaven Creek

The sea-wall quickly leads back to the main road, hence completing the circumnavigation of Canvey Island. At this point, the coastal route returns to the mainland and heads west past the town of Benfleet, but before leaving the island, it is worth visiting the Dutch Village Museum on Canvey Road. The museum is housed in a tiny thatched Dutch cottage that dates back to 1618, before the construction of the island's main sea-defences. It is open from the Spring Bank Holiday (Whitsun) to the end of September, on Wednesdays and Sundays 2.30 to 5.00. It is also open most Bank Holidays, and admission is free. (It may be advisable to check these opening times.)

Benfleet

Back on the mainland at Benfleet, a good footpath follows the north bank of Benfleet Creek. As you head westwards, the sea-wall steadily gets taller, protecting the low-lying road alongside from flooding. Like most of the small towns around south Essex, a large proportion of the Benfleet inhabitants work up in the city of London and commute to work every day by train, and hence the large railway car-park takes up an enormous area of land. When this railway-line was being constructed in 1855, it is said that a large amount of burnt wood was found just under the surface. Some sources also report the discovery of the remains of Viking long-boats.

Historians believe that a large fort was built by the Viking chief Haelstan just a hundred yards north-east of the site of the present railway station. It was attacked in the Battle of Benfleet, in 892 AD (some sources say 896). Edward, son of the Saxon king Alfred, came down from London and surprised the Viking settlement, storming the fort and setting fire to their houses and ships. It has been suggested that this was the source of the burnt wood discovered nearly one thousand years later. It also appears that history has a tendency to repeat itself, for the original railway station burned down in 1903. The station was rebuilt further to the west, and was eventually re-opened in 1911.

Continuing westwards from the railway station along the shoreline, the road veers off to the north underneath the railway-line. As mentioned earlier, this road was built in 1973, when the original Colvin Bridge across Benfleet Creek was replaced. Before that time, a small creek used to flow underneath the railway-line here, and it is still possible to trace its route for a few hundred yards inland by leaving the coastline for a moment and following a small footpath underneath the railway bridge. Emerging near the centre of the old village of Benfleet, you can clearly see the dry bed of the creek winding its way between the old sea-walls. Old picture postcards of the village show that a quay here was accessible by small boats around high tide. Until the late 19th century, the village was called Beamfleet. "Fleet" was a local word for a small creek, and hence the name refers to a "beam" or plank bridge which originally crossed this narrow side-creek, although some people have confused it with the main Benfleet Creek.

Returning underneath the railway to the shoreline, the footpath continues westwards along the banks of Benfleet Creek past a row of derelict moorings. About half a mile from the road, near a sewage works, a large brick pill-box from the Second World War stands on the edge of the creek, overlooking the tidal marshes. This area of rough ground is often used by local motorcyclists for scrambling practice.

The footpath soon approaches the new road-bridge which carries Canvey Way over the narrowing creek. Beyond the bridge, the ground level is much higher than the usual surroundings, perhaps as a result of domestic waste-tipping. At this point, the right of way leaves the coastline and heads inland across a vast expanse of meadows known as the Bowers Marshes. Although the sea-wall continues southwards along the banks of

East Haven Creek, maps indicate that there is technically no public right of way along its top. This seems a pity, since this district contains some of the most beautiful countryside in the area, and there are no houses or farms nearby.

The worn state of the grass suggests that people do frequently walk along this stretch of private sea-wall, but in any event the route is soon barred by a tall barbed-wire fence. A warning notice on the fence reveals that the long diversion inland is caused by the presence of a large dumping ground for industrial waste just around the coast. The site handles all grades of toxic waste, and this is certainly not an area to visit when the wind is blowing in your direction!

From the bridge over East Haven Creek, the coastal route follows the public right of way inland across Bowers Marshes. The footpath is unmarked on the ground and wanders backwards and forwards around the fields without any apparent purpose. Under these difficult conditions, the Ordnance Survey's "Landranger" map is not really sufficient to find the correct route through the maze of ditches, fields and fences. In these circumstances, their "Explorer" map (in an orange cover) proves invaluable because it contains many useful details, although it can be a little out of date. For example, the "Explorer" map marks a farm building beside the footpath. (It was originally called Newbarn, and was later renamed to Rookery Barn, but neither of these names are marked on the map.) In practice, this farm was demolished some years ago, and only a pile of bricks and rubble hidden in the undergrowth gives a clue to its original location.

At the site of Rookery Barn, the track splits into three. The leftmost fork soon dies out, but it originally led southwards nearly two-thirds of a mile to a small farmstead called South Staines, the buildings of which disappeared long ago. The middle track continues in a south-westerly direction. This used to lead to a farm called North Staines. Once again, this farm was demolished many years ago, and its remains are only visible in the form of a series of unnatural mounds in the otherwise flat landscape.

At one time, a narrow creek threaded its way right across Bowers Marshes from East Haven Creek to North Staines. By 1768, a dam had been built across the creek near Rookery Barn, and it was eventually cut off completely by a second dam built near its mouth towards the end of the 19th century. Although it no longer flows into the sea, the bed of this creek still holds brackish water, and it is now overgrown with bulrushes.

From the site of Rookery Barn, the public right of way takes the rightmost of the three forks, heading northwards towards a footbridge over the railway-line. This scenery is quite different to the typical marshland scenery encountered around the Essex coastline, but these wide open meadows, undisturbed by housing developers and intensive farming, have their own sense of subtle beauty, and to anyone who spends a few carefree hours wandering around the Bowers Marshes, it is clear that this landscape is a haven for wildlife. The site is important for its birdlife, particularly species such as reed and sedge warblers, and is popular with wintering wildfowl such as teal, the smallest duck living in Europe. Nevertheless, the Bowers Marshes are still threatened by developers who want to build a large golf course here, with accompanying club buildings, although the RSPB has pledged to fight these plans.

The public right of way heads northwards towards a small bungalow which was built recently on the site of an old farm called The Rookery. A small bridge carries the footpath over the top of the main railway-line, finally leaving the Bowers Marshes behind. On the far side of the bridge, a small lane leads off towards the buildings of

Jotmans Hall, but the coastal route turns left and follows the railway-line westwards along the edge of a series of open fields.

Passing a tall electricity pylon, the path soon emerges onto a quiet country lane. St. Margaret's Church stands beside the road, a low squat building with a short wooden tower. There is usually a little space here for several cars to park. It seems odd to find a church in the middle of the deserted countryside, but presumably it was once connected with Bowers Hall, the large farm a few hundred yards up the road. At the top of the hill, the lane crosses over the top of the busy A13 road and leads to Bowers Gifford, a village on the outskirts of Basildon.

In the other direction, the lane passes through a bridge underneath the railway-line and heads out across the marshes towards a set of farm buildings called Great Mussels. The name of this farm, and its original neighbour Little Mussels, is probably related to the nearby marshland, which was recorded as Moushold Marsh in 1569. Although the surface of the road quickly deteriorates into a muddy ooze unsuitable for cars, this is the quickest means of access to the Bowers Marshes. Unfortunately, there is no public right of way beyond the railway bridge. At one time, a second track forked off to the west and headed right through the interior of the marshes, leading from one small farm to another. Known as Manor Way, this wide track led past the buildings of Old Barn and eventually reached East Haven House, a remote farmstead over two miles away on the banks of East Haven Creek. All these buildings were demolished many years ago, but it is still possible to trace the meandering route of Manor Way across Bowers Marshes.

From the remote outpost of St. Margaret's Church, there are no public footpaths across Bowers Marshes, and so the coastal route has to stay on the north side of the railway. A good footpath follows westwards along the foot of the railway embankment with gates leading from one field to the next. It is advisable to wear good boots along this stretch because poor drainage and the presence of cattle can make the ground quite muddy, particularly after heavy rainfall.

Pitsea

After a mile, the path enters the town of Pitsea along a residential side-street. Following this side-street to the west, you soon reach a main road through Pitsea. Just to the left, a bridge carries the main road across the railway-line, which splits into two at this point. The southern branch is the original line to Fenchurch Street station in London. Built in 1854, it follows a very circuitous route past Tilbury Docks. When the line was extended in 1888 to reach the growing seaside resort of Southend-on-Sea, the northern line was opened, providing a more direct route from London. In order to serve the new line, Pitsea railway station had to be moved to its present position, nestling in the junction between the two branches, although you can still see the sidings of the original railway station a few hundred yards to the west.

Before continuing around the coastline from the railway station at Pitsea, it is worth taking a short detour southwards down the main road. At first the scenery is not particularly salubrious. A scrap-metal yard stands on one side of the road, a domestic waste site on other, and a private track forks off to the left towards the enormous industrial waste tip on the Bowers Marshes. As if to cap it all, the main road continues southwards past a sewage works. However, this road is known as Marsh Road, a name which suggests that there is better scenery just around the corner, and indeed within half a mile you reach Pitseahall Island and the Wat Tyler Country Park.

Pitseahall Island

The layout of the land around Pitseahall Island can appear rather confusing at first sight. The town of Pitsea stands near the head of Holehaven Creek, which follows a long and meandering route through remote countryside, shunning all centres of population, before eventually flowing into the main channel of the River Thames some five miles away. The creek also has lots of smaller tributaries, including Timberman's Creek and Pitseahall Fleet. These two offshoots flow either side of a raised patch of ground known as Pitseahall Island. This is no longer a true island in the modern sense of the word, but our ancestors tended to use the word "island" to describe any plot of land which was surrounded by marshy or boggy ground. (The "Isle of Ely" is a well-known example.) Indeed, when Pitsea itself was recorded in the Domesday Book in 1086, it was known as Piceseia, which means "island of Pic".

A dam was built across the mouth of Pitseahall Fleet many centuries ago, probably for flood protection. Hidden behind the hedges on the left of Marsh Road, you can see that the channel is still full of water. Pitseahall Fleet now contains the largest reedbed in south Essex, consisting mostly of common reed (*Phragmites australis*), although the brackish nature of the water has led to the growth of some sea club-rush (*Scirpus maritimus*). The area also supports a large amount of birdlife and has been designed a Site of Special Scientific Interest (SSSI), despite the construction of a line of electricity pylons nearby.

Around 1900, Pitseahall Island was bought by the British Explosives Syndicate. For several decades, the site was used as an ammunitions store, and you can still find the remains of protective earth embankments amongst the undergrowth. In 1984, Basildon Council turned the 120-acre site into a country park, complete with an information centre, craft workshops and a museum of rural life.

This type of leisure development is becoming increasingly popular with both local inhabitants and out-of-town visitors, and it deserves full support. However, the idea of an environmental "country park" is a very dangerous one if it concentrates people's attention on the ecology of just one small area. Pitseahall Island is surrounded by unimproved marshland which is all under constant threat, and although the designation of SSSI allows wardens to vigorously exclude individual walkers on the excuse that they will disturb the wildlife, this countryside remains unprotected from the much greater danger of corporate development. This may be in the form of council authorities who consider unimproved marshland to be "waste" ground suitable only for dumping rubbish, or in the form of private businesses who are allowed to purchase and develop enormous plots of land at reduced rates. Country parks are a welcome addition to the leisure industry, but it seems that their increasing popularity is being used as an excuse to neglect the rest of our valuable countryside.

The country park at Pitseahall Island has plenty of amenities for visiting families, including the National Motor-boat Museum, with free admission. There is also a small cafe, and a miniature steam railway runs alongside the road during the summer months. This area is now known as the Wat Tyler Country Park, after the leader of the Peasants' Revolt. Although it is believed that Wat Tyler himself came from Kent, the villages of south Essex played an important role in the uprising.

By 1380, the lower classes were becoming extremely unhappy with the disproportionate wealth and power of the upper classes, and matters were not improved by the introduction of a third poll tax, unrelated to people's income. Riots occurred when three men from Fobbing, Coryton and Stanford-le-Hope attacked lawyers in a Brentwood court, and anarchy quickly ensued. Thomas Baker of nearby Fobbing became the first rebel to be hanged for his part in the riots, but the people remained undeterred. Crowds from Essex and Kent marched on London, led by Wat Tyler and attacking all members of the aristocracy in their path.

In an effort to quell the riots, the young King Richard II confronted the mob and gave in to their demands. He agreed to abolish all bishoprics and lordships, to confiscate all land owned by the church, and to pardon all the rebels who had been arrested for the riot. However, during the mayhem, the Mayor of London knocked Wat Tyler off his horse, and whilst the rebel leader lay on the ground, an unknown person fatally stabbed him. Despite this disturbance, the young king managed to persuade the crowd to disperse, but Parliament refused to carry out any of his concessions. The unpopular social system continued unabated, and the leaders of the rebellion were eventually hanged for their crimes.

The road through the Wat Tyler Country Park soon ends at a small car-park beside a wide creek. This is the main channel of Holehaven Creek, although along this upper stretch it changes its name to Vange Creek. A wooden jetty projects out from the shoreline and a short slipway gives access to over a hundred moorings out in the deep water, the uppermost moorings in Holehaven Creek. This is known as Pitseahall Wharf, and is part of the Wat Tyler Marina owned by Basildon Council.

From the wharf, a footpath heads eastwards along the top of a sea-wall. Beyond the ruins of a wartime pill-box, the sea-wall enters a small inlet. At this point, Pitseahall Fleet originally flowed out into the main channel of Holehaven Creek – this "sea-wall" is actually a large dam constructed many centuries ago. At the far end of the dam, a tall wire fence stretches across the footpath. This is the boundary fence for a large industrial waste site, and since it blocks any further progress, this marks the end of the footpath in this direction.

Retreating back to the end of the road at Pitseahall Wharf, a wide footpath heads around the coastline in the opposite direction. It follows a marked trail around the edge of the Wat Tyler Country Park, and wooden bird hides have been built at appropriate intervals overlooking the tidal waters of Holehaven Creek. After a few hundred yards, beyond a wartime pill-box, the path veers gently to the right and follows the narrow channel of Timberman's Creek upstream. Along the banks of this tributary, a small area of saltings has built up over the years. The plants which thrive in this intertidal zone can tolerate the salty conditions at high tide, but they must also be able to withstand the heat of the sun when the mudflats are exposed during the day.

On the far side of Timberman's Creek, the bank rises up steeply to a raised platform about twenty feet higher than the usual surroundings. This land was once used as a rubbish-tip, but the site has now been grassed over. Because of the flatness of the surrounding marshland, this green hillock can be seen for miles in every direction. After walking for nearly two-thirds of a mile, you finally reach the head of Timberman's Creek, and a tall fence forces you to head inland through the woods. A confusing network of footpaths through the trees leads you eventually back to the main road near the entrance to the country park, thereby completing the circumnavigation of Pitseahall Island.

Once you have completed the pleasant diversion around Pitseahall Island, you need to return back up the road to Pitsea railway station in order to rejoin the route around the coastline. The head of Holehaven Creek lies just a few yards to the west of the road, near the buildings of Marsh Farm. There was once a small wharf at the head of the creek here, but the area is now cordoned off with tall fences capped with barbed-wire.

The next stretch of coastline is quite difficult to walk because a new dual carriageway was built to bypass the towns of Pitsea and Vange. The construction of this new A13 route, complete with an enormous roundabout, has obliterated many of the old public rights of way. It appears that many people choose to avoid walking alongside the busy roads by cutting through the derelict ground just to the north of the railway-line, although it must be pointed out that this is private land.

Three hundred yards from the road, a public right of way crosses over the Tilbury railway-line. *Since there are no gates or signals here, extreme caution should be taken when crossing the track, and this is obviously not a place to allow children to wander around unsupervised.* Once you have safely crossed over to the south side of the railway-line, an indistinct footpath leads through an area of rough grassland.

To the left, you can see the low line of a sea-wall running parallel to the path about two hundred yards away. It seems a shame that the right of way stays inland here, because the crest of this sea-wall would provide a marvellous footpath, offering a beautiful view of Holehaven Creek. The creek has narrowed considerably by this point, and along this reach it is usually referred to as Pitsea Creek. When the tide drops, Pitsea Creek dries out almost completely, leaving just a narrow trickle of water in the middle of the muddy channel. The region is rich in birdlife, including waders that probe underneath the exposed surface of the mud for worms and insect larvae.

Inside the sea-wall, the ground is a curious mixture of rough grassland and undrained marsh, intersected by a series of deep ditches and brackish ponds. Meanwhile the footpath crosses a few low ridges and mounds. These are sometimes used for scrambling practice by motorcyclists, but most of the time this corner of the countryside remains quiet and undisturbed. This was once the site of Kiln Farm, but these buildings were demolished many years ago. Older maps indicate that there was once a small wharf beside the creek here. One map dating from 1876 shows a simple farmtrack leading to a large hut in the tidal marshes outside the sea-wall, although its precise purpose is not clear.

Vange

The footpath eventually reaches a group of buildings clustered around the head of a small creek, another tributary of Holehaven Creek. It is known that this site was occupied during Roman times, for a coin discovered here was found to date from the reign of Emperor Gratian (375-378 AD). Until relatively recently, the land supported a small farm called Merricks Farm. Because road communications were so poor, a lot of trade was traditionally carried out by boat and each marshland community tended to maintain its own small wharf. Merricks Farm was no exception, and indeed the wharf here was amongst the largest on Holehaven Creek. This wharf was generally known as Vange Wharf, since it served the nearby town of Vange, which has now been engulfed by the rapid expansion of Basildon nearby.

In 1949, Basildon was designated a New Town, although the name is certainly not new. It was recorded in the Domesday Book of 1086 as Berlesdune. Since "dun" was an Old English word for a hill, the name is thought to mean "Beorhtel's Hill". Linguistic experts believe that the local Essex accent gradually transformed the initial vowel "e" into an "a", and hence the area became known by 1510 as Bartelisden, although it is not until 1594 that the name becomes recognisable as Basteldon.

The area around Vange Wharf is now used by a small private company called W. C. Ware. A public right of way follows the boundary fence around the buildings to a small level-crossing. Here, an access road links the site to the busy A13 dual carriageway and there is just enough space to park a car, although the gates of the level-crossing make the approach quite awkward.

Vange Wharf marks a significant turning point, because here the footpath begins to head southwards, following the western bank of Holehaven Creek back towards the open waters of the River Thames. Indeed, Holehaven Creek is the last major creek encountered in the walk around the coast of Essex. Unfortunately, the public right of way leaves the creek behind for the next few miles and detours inland, and the footpath is often indistinct on the ground. Walkers who are brave enough to attempt this route must be proficient at orienteering and must expect to tackle several hurdles and obstacles on the way.

From Vange Wharf, the route heads westwards past a farm known as Gouldings and then crosses a series of small fields. After veering southwards through an overgrown and water-logged meadow, the public right of way reaches a concrete farmtrack. This is an important but confusing junction. To the right, this leads up the hill to the buildings of Marsh Farm, which was once a brick and tile works, whilst to the left it heads directly towards the sea-wall. In this easterly direction, the concrete track passes a small isolated building called Marsh House, now boarded up and derelict, and continues towards a small wharf on the banks of Holehaven Creek. This area was a hive of industry in the 1920s, but the remains of the wooden jetty are now hard to find. The wharf, originally called Old Dock, was served by a short tramway, which was probably connected to the brick and tile works at the top of the hill.

From the junction, a second concrete track leads straight ahead (southwards) across the flat expanse of the Vange Marshes. This used to lead to a remote building, originally called White House, but later known as Vange Wick. The building was pulled down, but the Ordnance Survey "Explorer" map shows a right of way in this direction. This right of way leads ultimately to a small tributary of Holehaven Creek called Parting Gut, before looping back to the foot of Marsh Lane. However, this footpath has long since disappeared, and the marshes are intersected by a maze of deep ditches which will quickly ensnare the unsuspecting visitor.

Instead, the walker is condemned to a weary trudge across rough pastures and open farmland. From the confusing junction, you should instead take a second public right of way which forks off to the right, following the foot of a gentle escarpment. The footpath is generally indistinct, and a few ditches and fences only serve to make the route more difficult. It is a great shame that there is no right of way along the top of the sea-wall, because this would provide an easy path. Despite a few ins and outs, the sea-wall route is shorter and far more interesting than the tortuous route inland.

Because of the valuable wildlife, a few sections of this coastal marshland have been designated as Sites of Special Scientific Interest (SSSI), and local authorities often cite this as a reason to exclude the public. However, this is a lame excuse because a new coastal footpath from Marsh House to Fobbing would not actually pass through any of the SSSIs in the area. On the contrary, it would provide a very useful amenity to the public, allowing walkers to enjoy this beautiful countryside.

After about a mile, the right of way reaches the foot of Marsh Lane, a grassy track which leads down the slope from the main road. Because of the difficult nature of the footpath, one could be forgiven for abandoning the walk at this point and retreating up the hill, continuing along the busy road towards the village of Fobbing, now just half a mile away.

Fobbing

At the end of all the obstacles, the public right of way eventually reaches Fobbing. It enters the village along the foot of Wharf Road, a small side-street which leads down the hill from the main road. The lane is narrow and parking space is always limited, and local residents would probably prefer visitors to leave their cars near the church at the top of the hill.

During the 19th century, Fobbing was a centre for the local brick and tile industry, with clay pits both to the south and east of the village. Until seventy years ago, the tidal waters of Fobbing Creek used to flow right up to the houses at the foot of the hill, and tall sailing barges often unloaded their cargo at the wharf here. By the beginning of the 20th century however, improved communications allowed most businesses to switch to overland transport. The shipping industry went into serious decline, and water traffic virtually disappeared from Fobbing Creek between the wars. In order to save the expense of maintaining the sea-walls on either side of Fobbing Creek, a dam was built across the mouth of the creek around 1940. The creek gradually dried out, and today the village is over a mile from the open river.

From the village of Fobbing, a public footpath heads eastwards across open pastures towards Holehaven Creek. Due to the activities of the oil companies just around the coast, this route is unfortunately now a dead-end, although this is only shown on the most up-to-date maps. Even though you will have to retrace your steps back to Fobbing, this path is still strongly recommended because it provides the last public access to the shores of Holehaven Creek and the surrounding countryside is delightfully unspoilt.

The footpath starts from the houses at the foot of Wharf Road, leading along the crest of a raised earth wall. This embankment was built across the channel of Fobbing Creek, forming a dam, presumably to protect the farmland beyond from being flooded during exceptionally high tides. After about a hundred yards, watch out for a smaller embankment which bears off to the left. At this point, you should turn left and follow the lower embankment eastwards across a wide area of rough grassland known as the Fobbing Marshes. This embankment originally formed the south bank of Fobbing Creek, and in some places the channel still carries a small trickle of water.

In 1989, the Essex Wildlife Trust bought 187 acres of land around Fobbing Marshes, helped by a generous anonymous donation. The Essex Wildlife Trust was keen to acquire the Fobbing Marshes because the unimproved marshland supports many threatened species of birds and animals. The marshes, which have also been designated a Site of Special Scientific Interest (SSSI), provide one of the last habitats for barn owls in Essex, and are home to the emerald damselfly or dragonfly (*Lestes dryas*), a very rare species which was believed to be extinct until it was rediscovered in 1983. There are also plans to raise the water-table in order to increase the diversity of wildlife.

After half a mile or so, the footpath gradually becomes indistinct on the ground and difficult to follow. The area is quite confusing, and it is easy to get lost. Some of this confusion can be resolved by a 1768 map of the region. This clearly shows that Fobbing Creek was split into two channels, separated by a small island of marshy ground. At a later stage, a new sea-wall was built across this marshy island, cutting off the south channel with a small dam at each end. It doesn't matter too much whether you follow the original sea-wall to the south, or the newer embankment to the north, because they are both rights of way.

The footpaths continue in an easterly direction through some of the most unspoilt countryside in this corner of Essex, but Fobbing Marshes were not always as isolated as they are today. The marshes have had a succession of farms, with names such as Slated House, Great Ellford Farm and New House. In 1789, Great Ellford Farm was put up for auction. Rather than mentioning the remoteness of the farm, the auctioneers stressed the convenience of its location: *"These marshes are very conveniently situate for shipping and landing Goods to and from Fobbing Creek."*

Just over a mile from the village of Fobbing, the footpath eventually reaches the large dam at the mouth of Fobbing Creek and the landscape suddenly changes from wide grassy meadows to tidal mudflats and saltings. Outside the dam, the channel of Fobbing Creek meanders wildly, and so you must walk another few hundred yards eastwards along the sea-wall before you reach the shores of Holehaven Creek proper.

Half a mile upstream, on the far bank, you can see the blue cranes of Martins Wharf, built on the site of a small farm called Little Mussels. However, attention is instead drawn to the enormous concrete structure which towers over Holehaven Creek just a few yards downstream. This is the Fobbing Horse flood barrier, built around 1980 to protect the low-lying farmland upstream from surge tides. During the description of Canvey Island earlier, it was discussed how the concepts of flood protection were revised after the devastating floods of 1953. After years of careful planning, it was eventually decided that a series of tidal flood barriers should be built across the main creeks of south Essex and north Kent, in conjunction with the Thames Barrier.

In order to protect the land around Holehaven Creek, the original plan was to build a sliding barrier further downstream, near the island of Upper Horse, but this idea was soon changed to the current design at Fobbing Horse. The structure is quite impressive, with a single opening nearly 120 feet wide and a height clearance of around 30 feet at high tide. When an exceptionally high tide is anticipated, an enormous floodgate is swung down into position to block the channel completely.

Flood barrier across Holehaven Creek at Fobbing Horse

Fobbing Horse was once the name of two small marshy islands which stood in the middle of Holehaven Creek at this point. During the 19th century, two tidal causeways linked the islands to the mainland so that sheep could graze on the saltings there. By 1950, a sea-wall had been built around the two pieces of marshland to form a single island. Around 1970, a dam was built across one of the channels of Holehaven Creek at each end of the island, thereby joining Fobbing Horse to the mainland. The remaining channel of Holehaven Creek was relatively narrow, and so this was a natural choice for the site of the new barrier.

The footpath continues beyond the barrier along the top of the sea-wall for a few yards, but it soon reaches a tall wire fence which blocks any further progress. At one time, the public right of way continued around the coastline for another six miles to the town of Stanford-le-Hope, but the footpath was closed in 1987. The nearby oil companies of Shell, Mobil and BP had attempted to close this right of way for many years, claiming that it posed a threat to their security. Each time, the local borough council refused their request, pointing out that the footpath offered good views of Holehaven Creek and the River Thames, and it therefore provided a useful amenity for the local people.

Following another refusal in 1976, the oil companies agreed to help the council to improve the sea-defences around the coast, by building a new concrete crest-wall on the seaward side of the footpath. In most places, it was more than six feet high, and walkers could no longer see the riverside. Without the pleasant view, the footpath was now of little value, and so the oil companies were able to return to the council with a stronger argument for closing the footpath.

At the subsequent public inquiry, one Mobil witness even suggested that the footpath posed such a serious threat to their security that the company might have to consider moving the entire refinery to another site. However, even the inspector of the inquiry believed that *"the risk of a serious incident initiated by a member of the public is probably low,"* and that, in any event, the closure of the footpath would not deter a determined terrorist or vandal. The oil companies had continued to invest heavily in new machinery over the previous few years, despite the presence of the right of way, and yet very little money had been spent on improving the security of the site. It was even suggested that the oil companies' operating licences should be removed if they considered that the site was not safe.

Nevertheless, the closure of the footpath was confirmed in 1987 by the Secretary of State, and 7½ miles of public right of way were extinguished on the 7th September. It seems that the decision was largely based upon an offer made by the oil companies to create a new footpath further inland, although the inspector accepted that this was hardly a replacement for a coastal route with wide views overlooking Holehaven Creek and the River Thames. He claimed that the route of the proposed new footpath *"was almost universally disparaged by the objectors' witnesses... I fully accept the objectors' arguments that the new footpaths would have very real shortcomings; their combined lengths would be very much shorter and they would not be along the riverside."*

In this way, one of the best circular walks in this corner of Essex was closed, and so you now have to retrace your steps across Fobbing Marshes back to the village of Fobbing. From here, most people will choose to follow the footpath westwards towards the town of Corringham, but there is another route which runs closer to the coastline. This starts from the houses at the foot of Wharf Road, following the dam at the head of Fobbing Creek. Instead of turning off into Fobbing Marshes, this time you should continue southwards along the top of the main embankment.

Although the embankment gradually dies away, the route of the footpath is obvious. Beyond the site of an old farm called Marshroad, it emerges onto a wide and busy road, the A1014. Known locally as Manorway Road, it links the Coryton oil refineries to the nearby town of Stanford-le-Hope. Large lorries speed up and down this road at all hours of the day, and it can become quite congested during the rush hour. In order to cope with the volume of traffic, Manorway Road was rebuilt just south of its original position, and much of the route was converted into a dual carriageway.

History of Coryton

Although the oil refineries around Coryton can hardly be described as beautiful walking territory, the development of the industry is an interesting and integral part of the history of the coastal salt-marshes, and a description of the region is therefore included for background interest. Heading eastwards along Manorway Road towards the centre of Coryton, a wide stream can be seen to the side of the road. Known as Manorway Fleet, this was once a tidal creek flowing into the River Thames, but the channel was dammed near its mouth many centuries ago.

Manorway Road eventually ends at a small roundabout with side-lanes leading off in all directions. The second road from the roundabout continues in an easterly direction across the channel of Manorway Fleet, which is sometimes known as Salt Fleet along this reach. The area's industrial history began in 1895 when the land was purchased by Kynoch and Co. Ltd from Birmingham. They started an explosives factory here, with large earth embankments around each building for protection against accidents. The Kynoch brothers chose two lions as their emblem, and these figures, which once stood on either side of the entrance gate, can still be seen on the lawns of the nearby Mobil refinery.

In 1897, an extremely high tide flooded much of the low-lying land along the east coast of England, and the Kynoch explosives factory was badly damaged. Nevertheless, the site was rebuilt with massive investment, and in 1899 a small village was constructed for the workers. Known as Kynochtown, it had forty houses, as well as a shop and a school for the employees' children.

The factory employed around 600 people from nearby towns and villages, but transport was a problem. The 2½-mile Corringham Light Railway was therefore built in 1901 to carry goods and workers from Corringham. It crossed Manorway Road just west of Ironlatch farm and led to a small jetty beside Holehaven Creek.

In 1923, Corringham Marshes were purchased by the Cory brothers, who renamed the village Coryton, a name now used to describe the whole area. A large oil refinery was built on the site, but this was sold in 1950 to the Vacuum Oil Company, who immediately began major reconstruction. The new company re-instated the railway link from Coryton to the main railway-line at Thames Haven, but they felt it was no longer necessary to maintain the rest of the track up the hill to Corringham. This line was closed in 1952, and the rails and sleepers were soon removed.

All remains of the level-crossing on Manorway Road were removed when the carriageway was rebuilt recently, but it is still possible to follow the line of the light railway up the hill. It appears that many local people still frequently walk this route, although it should be noted that technically the land is private. At the top of the hill, the station building has been converted into a private residence, and the final few hundred yards of the railway-line have been fenced off as a private garden, but a public footpath conveniently leads back to Fobbing village.

Following the major reconstruction work carried out by the new owners, the oil refinery finally came back on stream in the afternoon of the 31st January 1953. The timing was extremely unfortunate because that evening the Essex coastline experienced the highest tide ever recorded. During a night of devastating storms, many miles of sea-defences were swept away, allowing sea-water to flood the vulnerable low-lying marshes. Fortunately no lives were lost in the Coryton area, but the damage to the refinery was immense. Nevertheless, the Vacuum Oil Company managed to repair the plant, and the refinery was soon back on line.

In 1956, the company became part of Mobil Oil, and their refinery is still operating today. It occupies a peninsula nearly a mile long, stretching from the Manorway Road roundabout to the tip of Shellhaven Point. This is the point where Holehaven Creek flows into the main River Thames, and hence it was originally known as Holehaven Point. The village of Coryton was closed in 1969 and the tenants all moved out. Along the road known as Fleet Street, all the buildings were demolished by 1974, and the new Fluid Catalytic Cracker was completed by 1981.

In general, the safety record of these oil refineries has been good, and accidents are surprisingly rare considering the dangerous nature of the work. However, problems have inevitably cropped up. In October 1990, for example, Mobil accidentally pumped 25 tons of heavy fuel oil into the River Thames, causing untold damage to local wildlife. The worst disaster occurred in 1970 when a 10,000-ton passenger ship, the Monte Ulia, crashed into the refinery's jetty and poured hundreds of tons of oil into the river. The oil promptly caught fire and began to spread across Holehaven Creek towards an oil tanker which was discharging on Canvey Island opposite. Fortunately, favourable winds prevented a major disaster.

Back at the Manorway Road roundabout, the third road heads southwards over a small level-crossing. This was once the site of a remote farmstead called Oil Mill Farm, an appropriate name considering the later development of the area. The farm was auctioned off in 1789 but it is known to date back to at least 1638. It also gave its name to the nearby Oilmill Fleet, a narrow creek which originally joined up with Manorway Fleet nearby. Many centuries ago, a dam was built just below the confluence of these two creeks, and the present road still follows the line of this ancient dam. If you drive a short distance down this road, you can still see Manorway Fleet to the left, now overgrown with reeds. Most of Oilmill Fleet has now been drained, but a few small sections are still marked on the Ordnance Survey map to the south of Manorway Road.

Below the dam, the water originally flowed southwards towards the River Thames. This last stretch was once known as Shellhaven Creek. At one time, the creek was crossed by a tidal ford near its mouth. As part of the local flood protection scheme, a large dam was constructed across the mouth of Shellhaven Creek soon after 1958. Since then, this final section of the creek has gradually dried out, although it still carries a narrow trickle of water.

The channel of Shellhaven Creek conveniently separates the Mobil refinery at Coryton from the nearby area of Thames Haven to the west. Thames Haven once supported a small fishing community, and the railway from Tilbury was extended to a small jetty here to serve the fishermen. (Speculators had planned to create an enormous deep-water dock here, but these ideas never came to fruition.)

The community fell into decline and all passenger traffic ceased by 1880. By then however, the jetty had a new role in transferring oil from large ocean-going vessels onto smaller barges for local transport. In 1876, the Petroleum Storage Company built a series of warehouses on the site, using the new railway to carry oil up to the London markets. Although the pier was finally abandoned in 1920, the Shell oil company had begun their own operations beside Shellhaven Creek in 1916, although few people realise that the similarity in the names is entirely coincidental.

Shell constructed a large refinery on the site, and in recent years BP has also moved into the Coryton area. Before building new plant, all these companies have had to spend large sums of money draining the land. Manorway Fleet and Oilmill Fleet have already been mentioned, but the region was also crossed by a third tidal creek, known as Rugwood Creek. This was blocked off near its mouth before 1768, and is now marked on the Ordnance Survey's "Explorer" map as Shelly Bay.

The land to the west of Thames Haven was originally occupied by Curriemarsh Farm, but this was demolished around 1880 to make way for a second explosives factory. This was known as the Miners Safety Explosives Factory, although it was renamed the Curry Marsh Factory between the wars. This factory was closed during the 1960s. After the oil refineries around Coryton, visitors must return back up the Manorway Road towards Corringham.

Corringham

The town of Corringham was first recorded in the Domesday Book as Currincham, an Anglo-Saxon name which simply means "Curra's homestead". From here, our coastal route now aims westwards towards the neighbouring town of Stanford-le-Hope. For car drivers, this is a simple matter of continuing up Manorway Road and turning left at the first large roundabout. However, walkers have the opportunity to enjoy a much more enjoyable back-route, and since this runs closer to the shoreline, it can be described as the true coastal route. Just after the B1420 side-road from Fobbing joins the main Manorway Road from the right, a small footpath heads off to the left towards the farm buildings of Old Hall. Instead of entering the farmyard, the public right of way follows a small track to the right. Shortly before reaching the Manorway Road again, a footpath disappears off to the left across a couple of open fields.

This footpath soon emerges onto a narrow country lane, where a building called Spring House once stood. This quiet lane passes through some marvellously undisturbed countryside, and as you follow the lane to the left, you get the impression that this corner of the county has been completely forgotten by the sprawl of suburban housing estates nearby. After two hundred yards, a couple of tracks lead off to the left towards the twin farms of Old Garlands and Great Garlands. At one time, a farmtrack continued beyond Old Garlands for over a mile, crossing the remote marshes on its way to Curriemarsh farm. This farmtrack was the original Manor Way, but the name has now been stolen by the busy dual carriageway to the north.

Stanford-le-Hope

The narrow country lane eventually emerges onto Rainbow Lane, a back-road of Stanford-le-Hope. The town's name originally referred to a "stone ford", probably across the nearby Mucking Creek. The suffix "le-Hope" is a convolution of "hop", an Old English word describing a valley. Although it has been largely swallowed up by the rapid growth of Corringham, the town still manages to retain its own identity, and it also offers the only public access to the coastline for several miles in either direction.

From a sports ground on the outskirts of Stanford-le-Hope, Rainbow Lane leads past the farm buildings of Broadhope and comes to an abrupt end near an electricity sub-station, just a few yards from the banks of the River Thames. The railway-line to Thames Haven runs right along the shoreline here, with a simple pedestrian level-crossing providing access to the coast. Mobil and Shell stopped using the railway many years ago, but BP still occasionally run freight trains along this line. *There are no warning signals, so you should take great care with children around this area.*

The level-crossing leads to a small bay known as Stanford-le-Hope Marshes. Along the foot of the sea-wall, a narrow strip of rough grassland has built up, but this quickly

Flood defences near Stanford-le-Hope

gives way to an area of tidal marshland called Earl's Hope Saltings. These saltings are usually only flooded by the highest spring tides, and are criss-crossed by a network of tiny muddy channels which fill up at each high tide, cutting them off from the mainland.

The Ordnance Survey maps show that the public right of way used to head eastwards across these saltings along the top of an earth embankment. This was the original sea-wall around the coastline, but it appears that the sea-defences were washed away some time after 1860, perhaps during the storms of 1897. The footpath now runs parallel to the shoreline just inside a new concrete sea-wall.

The remains of an outfall pipe can be seen 300 yards east of the level-crossing. This once flowed out into a deep water channel called Carter Creek. Beyond the outfall, the public right of way continues eastwards around the coastline for a short distance, but because of the closure of the Coryton footpath in 1987, this route is a dead-end and is now used mainly by fishermen.

To the west however, an enjoyable footpath follows the grassy top of a large sea-wall around the coastline towards the village of Mucking. At low tide, the receding waters reveal a wide area of mudflats known as Mucking Flats. During the First World War, damaged ships were moored here for repairs. The landscape gives the impression that you are never very far from civilisation. There are wide views across the River Thames of the Cliffe Marshes in north Kent. Looking inland, the monotonous panorama of arable fields is broken only by the ditch which runs along the foot of the sea-wall. This is called a "borrow-dyke" because it provided much of the material for the original sea-defences. It is now used to drain the fields.

After half a mile, the sea-wall begins to veer to the right and head inland along the north bank of Mucking Creek. The land to the south of the creek has been used as a refuse tip for many years, and the level of the ground there is now considerably higher. The tip is one of the largest in the country, serving a large part of the London area. A lot of refuse is brought in by barge and offloaded at a large jetty down the coast.

A good footpath follows the meandering creek inland for a short distance, but the public right of way soon leaves the water's edge behind and heads northwards along a rough track called Wharf Road. Until recently, it was possible to drive almost to the edge of Mucking Creek, but it is now accessible only on foot.

If the tide is out, it is worth following Mucking Creek inland for a few yards further in order to look for the wooden remains of Stanford-le-Hope wharf. This was once the base for a coastguard ship called The Vigilant. The creek now meanders gently to the south, but its course was changed by the expansion of the nearby refuse tip. The remains of a second small wharf, known as Mucking Wharf, were buried as a result.

Only the most recent Ordnance Survey maps show the dam which was built across Mucking Creek in the 1980s. This dam is part of the flood protection scheme for the

Essex coast, and has two openings each 5 feet square to allow a normal flow of water. The land beyond the dam appears to be used for scrambling practice by motorcyclists, but it is privately owned and you should therefore return to the rough track. This heads northwards between two large ponds, used by fishermen. These are the flooded remains of two gravel pits which were worked during the early 1900s. A simple tramway once ran along the track, carrying extracted gravel to barges at Stanford-le-Hope wharf.

The track continues northwards towards the centre of Stanford-le-Hope, passing underneath the Thames Haven railway-line, but our coastal route turns off just before this bridge. From this point, a good footpath leads to the left, crossing Mucking Creek with a small footbridge which is not marked on the Ordnance Survey maps. Despite the construction of a dam across Mucking Creek further downstream, this waterlogged mire was never properly drained. In recent years, this land was turned into a nature reserve called Stanford Warren. Fortunately, an earth embankment has been built across the marsh, allowing people to walk along the footpath dryshod.

Mucking

The footpath leads directly into the centre of Mucking, a tiny village which now contains just a few farmhouses and a church, although it did have its own public house around 1900. Like the Anglo-Saxon place-names of Fobbing and Corringham, the name Mucking means simply "Mucca's people". Today, the village is largely associated with disfiguring industries, such as the refuse tip and gravel works, but this quarrying has uncovered a large number of antiquities dating back to the Bronze Age. In one gravel pit, an Iron Age fort dating from around 500 BC was discovered, and the Ordnance Survey's "Explorer" map indicates that Roman pottery and burial remains have also been found close to the village.

Because of the refuse dumping operations, the coastal route once again has to take a detour inland for a few miles. A small country lane leads westwards out of the village. This is known as Mucking Wharf Road, after a small wharf which once stood near the mouth of Mucking Creek. The coastal route follows the lane over a level-crossing and then along Walton's Hall Road, a busy road which heads southwards through open countryside.

Despite a series of sharp bends, drivers often race along Walton's Hall Road at ridiculous speeds, and pedestrians should take great care. On a couple of the bends, you can escape the road and walk across a field to cut off the corner, but these are only short detours and the footpaths can be quite wet underfoot. After just a quarter of a mile, another level-crossing leads back across the railway-line to a large building known as the Golden Cottages, but unfortunately this is a private track.

The road continues in a south-westerly direction past the farm buildings of Walton's Hall. An interesting farm museum was opened here recently, and is well worth a visit. On the hillside behind the farm, aerial photographs have revealed an amazing collection of crop-marks. A series of lines and circles indicate that this was once one of the largest ancient settlements in this corner of Britain. Archaeologists carried out a careful investigation of the site, uncovering both Bronze and Iron Age settlements, as well as a Romano-British field system and a series of small Anglo-Saxon huts dating from around 400 AD. Their findings have been published in a small booklet which can be purchased at local museums.

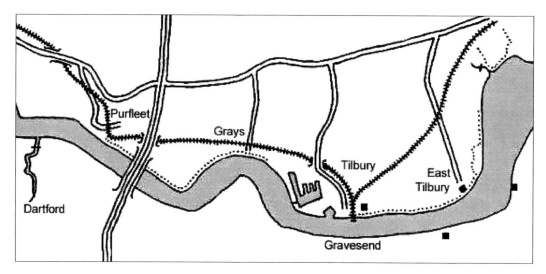

East Tilbury

Beyond Walton's Hall, a country lane leads to the village of Linford, where the coastal route turns left. The main road passes a pub in the hamlet of Muckingford and eventually reaches the outskirts of East Tilbury, a small village which should not be confused with the much larger town of Tilbury nearby, which has grown up relatively recently around the massive docks. There is also another tiny village nearby called West Tilbury, where Queen Elizabeth I is said to have reviewed her troops in August 1588 shortly before the onslaught of the Spanish Armada.

The centre of East Tilbury lies just a few hundred yards further along the main road. The village has expanded rapidly in recent years with the construction of hundreds of new houses, but the site has been occupied for at least a thousand years and it even appeared in the Domesday Book in 1086. Many inhabitants work at the large Bata shoe works, but the gravel extraction industry has also employed many local people over the centuries..

Until very recently, a quiet footpath forked off to the left across the fields to rejoin the banks of the River Thames. The footpath is currently closed and walkers are forced to continue along the main road through East Tilbury. After nearly two miles, the road ends at Coalhouse Fort, right on the water's edge. The fort has a large car-park, just beyond the church of St. Catherine. Visitors generally pay very little attention to the church itself, which is a shame because it was the scene of one of the lesser known battles in English history. In 1667, an invasion fleet sailed across from Holland and moored at the mouth of the River Thames. They easily overran the fortifications at East Tilbury and, on the orders of Admiral de Ruyter, destroyed the church. The raiders next turned their attention to the north Kent shores, attacking the fort at Sheerness on the Isle of Sheppey. It took the Dutch army just three days to capture the fort. Buoyed up by their success, the fleet headed northwards up the coast to Landguard Fort, near Felixtowe. Here, on 7th July 1667, the Dutch forces were finally defeated.

Coalhouse Fort

The village of Tilbury was recorded in the Domesday Book of 1086 as Tilibria. The suffix "bria" corresponds to the modern "bury" or "burgh", and refers to a castle or fort. The name therefore means "Tila's fort", although nothing is known of these early fortifications. A rampart with towers was built here around 1410, although it was not until 1539 that a large blockhouse was also constructed. This was part of a general defence scheme for the River Thames, with another stronghold at Tilbury to the west and two more blockhouses in Kent, at Gravesend and Shornemead.

With the Spanish Armada preparing to invade in 1558, the East Tilbury blockhouse was hurriedly improved, although Tilbury acted as the main centre of defence, with an 800-yard-long boom across the River Thames to block all enemy ships. When the threat subsided, these defences were not maintained, and they were said to be virtually useless when the Dutch raided these shores in 1667. As a result, plans to improve the Thames naval defences were accelerated, and a large fort was built at Tilbury between 1670 and 1684 on the site of the older blockhouse.

The Napoleonic wars led to the reconstruction of Coalhouse Fort between 1796 and 1799, along with new forts in Kent at Gravesend, Shornemead and Cliffe. These were all enlarged around 1850, and in 1861 it was decided that Coalhouse Fort and Shornemead Fort should be entirely rebuilt.

Coalhouse Fort was withdrawn from active service in 1920. The guns were removed and the buildings were turned into store-rooms. When the Second World War broke out, a series of anti-aircraft guns were rapidly installed, and many of these wartime relics can still be seen around the fort today. The British coastal artillery was disbanded in 1957, and the buildings were finally abandoned, although it was not until 1962 that the Ministry of Defence handed over control to the local council.

The interior of Coalhouse Fort is only open to the public on occasional Sundays and Bank Holidays, but the site can be quite busy at weekends because this area is used for general recreation. A small playground has also been provided for young children. Since 1983, local volunteers have worked hard to restore the buildings, and the fort also houses the Thames Aviation Museum, a small collection of wartime memorabilia.

The buildings facing the car-park are relatively recent additions to the fort, so you must walk around to the riverside in order to see the original fortifications. Overlooking the shores of north Kent, the strong semi-circular walls of the fort are surrounded by a wide moat, although a stone dam had to be built to prevent the water from flowing away into the low-lying fields to the west. In any event, the moat may soon disappear, because wave action is rapidly eroding the earth embankments along the banks of the River Thames.

From the fort, it is possible to walk back along the riverside towards Mucking and Stanford-le-Hope. After two miles, the footpath is blocked by the enormous landfill site at Mucking, so you will have to retrace your steps back here to the fort again, but this is a beautiful stretch of wild and remote coastline, with good views of the north Kent marshes opposite, a flat landscape known as Redham Mead ("mead" being an archaic version of the word "meadow").

This a marvellous walk, particularly during the winter when the mudflats are thronging with wildfowl. It is highly recommended as a short stroll, and therefore described here in detail. If you are using the Ordnance Survey's 1:25,000 "Explorer" series, you will need map number 163 (Gravesend & Rochester).

For the first half-mile or so, the sea-wall used to skirt around the edge of a wide inlet with far-reaching views over an enormous area of saltings. However, a large tract of land was reclaimed a few years ago from the river by constructing a new embankment outside the original sea-defences. In order to consolidate this marshy ground, the new land was divided into seven sections by means of small earth embankments. One by one, each section was filled with mud and silt which was pumped through a floating pipeline from a platform anchored out in the deep water. As dredgers plied up and down the river to maintain the depth of the navigation channel, they moored up against this platform and offloaded their dredgings into the pipeline, thereby slowly raising the level of the newly reclaimed land. The ground is now overgrown with bulrushes and even a few small trees, but be warned – there are still some a few shallow pools and boggy marshes hidden amongst this ground, and it is dangerous to stray from the footpath. A similar land reclamation scheme has been carried out in north Kent on the island of Hoo Marsh.

At the end of this reclaimed land, the sea-wall returns to the river's edge. Along this stretch, the "Explorer" map marks a row of four groynes projecting out from the banks of the river, presumably to prevent erosion of the sea-wall. Older maps show five "hards" running out across the mudflats in roughly the same location, but all these features have now disappeared.

In order to minimise the risk of flooding, a tall concrete wall has been built alongside the footpath. The National Rivers Authority added nine duck-ramps to this wall. Shelduck make their nests and lay their eggs amongst the rough ground further inland. When the young chicks are born, they need to reach the safety of the river in order to scavenge for food. The new sea-defences act as a considerable barrier to the weak chicks, and the engineers have therefore designed a gentle slope leading up either side of the sea-wall to enable the birds to reach the water more easily. You will notice that each slope is carefully labelled "duck-ramp", though it is questionnable whether the shelduck chicks have learned to read at such a young age!

The sea-wall soon veers slightly to the left. In this shallow bay, clumps of rough vegetation have managed to colonise the mudflats to form a small area of saltings. In one place, a tiny raised island has begun to form, complete with several bushes and low trees. During the 19th century, local fishermen dug a series of rectangular holes in these saltings in order to cultivate oysters. The oyster trade was once a thriving industry around the salt-marshes of Essex, and a few remains of these oyster-beds can still be seen today near the foot of the sea-wall.

If the tide is out, look out for a narrow channel of water winding its way across the deep mudflats from a pipe outfall. This is now only used for drainage, but old maps indicate that it was once the head of a large creek which penetrated inland for roughly a mile. It was known as Gobions Creek, after the nearby farm buildings, but the channel was blocked off when the original sea-wall was constructed.

Before long, the concrete surface gives way to a rough footpath. During the summer months, this can get quite overgrown, and many people choose to turn around here and return to the fort. In any event, the right of way comes to an end shortly afterwards. Looking ahead, you can see an enormous jetty where containers of London refuse are offloaded from barges by large cranes. This is clearly not the first heavy industry to despoil the landscape, as demonstrated by the remains of a couple of wooden jetties nearby. With all this industry, it seems appropriate that this reach of the River Thames is known as The Lower Hope, and the promontary on the far bank is called Lower Hope Point.

❋ ❋ ❋

Chapter seven – the Thames estuary

Tower near East Tilbury

Westwards from Coalhouse Fort

Returning to the buildings of Coalhouse Fort, the coastal route now heads westwards, following the shores of the River Thames towards the town of Tilbury, three miles away. Over the last hundred years, various industries have robbed this stretch of coastline of its natural beauty, but they have at least left several features of interest. The footpath passes a series of ruins from the Second World War and leads towards a small tower beside the shoreline. This curious hexagonal structure was built in 1941 as a wartime radar tower, although some sources have also suggested that it was used by the coastguard.

The tower stands near a small promontary known as Coalhouse Point. The name is derived from a nearby coal wharf, of which a few large concrete blocks remain. Coal was offloaded onto trucks which ran along a light tramway towards the village of East Tilbury. The track was pulled up many years ago, but you can still follow the tramway embankment back towards the car-park, and a few wooden sleepers can be seen embedded in the ground.

Four hundred yards further on, the footpath climbs up onto a raised area of land known as the East Tilbury Marshes. At this point, the Ordnance Survey maps show that the footpath veers inland a few hundred yards. This is just an anachronism. The public right of way follows the route of the original coastline, but new land was reclaimed about thirty years ago, and most people these days keep to the riverside. This occurs twice more over the next mile.

Historians believe that a Roman road once led to the shoreline three-quarters of a mile west of Coalhouse Fort. Around 1900, it was reported that, following a night of violent storms, workers discovered a stone-laid track leading down into the water at this point. It seemed almost certain that they had inadvertently stumbled upon the remains of the Roman road. Unfortunately, the site was lost when the tide covered the stones with a fresh layer of mud, and archaeologists have never managed to relocate the site. The Roman road probably led originally to a small jetty or wharf, although some writers have made the strange suggestion that there was a tidal ford across the River Thames during Roman times.

The riverside footpath soon arrives at a wartime pill-box which is embedded into the surface of a small wharf. The wharf has fallen into disuse, and the skeletal remains of a wooden jetty are slowly rotting away. The footpath then crosses a region of rough grassland sometimes known as the West Tilbury Marshes.

The open ground eventually comes to an end at a tall fence surrounding the enormous buildings of Tilbury power station. Fortunately, a narrow strip of land along the river-bank has been left clear for a public footpath, but the view across the River Thames is obstructed by the presence of a large jetty with eight tall cranes.

When the public footpath reaches the end of Tilbury power station, the sea-wall makes a brief detour around the edge of a small inlet. This was originally the head of a narrow creek which meandered inland for about a quarter of a mile. Known as Bill Meroy Creek, it was dammed near its outflow into the River Thames, although the old channel can still be seen inside the sea-wall.

Tilbury Fort

The footpath is now approaching the town of Tilbury, and a line of tall cranes stretches along most of the western horizon. Before you reach this busy industrial centre, however, the coastal footpath passes the buildings of Tilbury Fort. The fort is a popular tourist venue and is signposted for many miles around. It should not be confused with Coalhouse Fort, a much smaller building three miles downriver near the village of East Tilbury. Coalhouse Fort was described a little earlier, along with a brief history of the other naval defences around the mouth of the River Thames.

Like most of the forts along the north Kent shores, Tilbury Fort was used during the Napoleonic wars to prevent enemy ships from sailing up the River Thames and attacking vulnerable sites around London. A blockhouse has stood on this site since the reign of Henry VIII, although the present building dates from the end of the 17th century. A few modifications were made around 1868, but the military authorities only left in 1950.

The barracks and associated buildings are protected by a high wall in the shape of a pentagon, and extensions were added at four of the five corners so that the flanks could be protected by crossfire. In order to make an enemy attack even more difficult, Tilbury Fort was surrounded by two separate moats, and these were both overlooked by gun-positions inside the parapet. The fort was never used in battle, but around ten large cannons still stand on the parade-ground as a testimony to its potential strength.

Tilbury Fort is now owned by English Heritage, and the site is open to the public for a small admission fee. There are two entrances into the fort – one beside the river and another facing inland. The riverside entrance is through a prominent archway in the curtain wall. This is known as the Water Gate because, at high tide, the waters of the River Thames originally flowed right up to the gate. This enabled naval ships to offload easily, but in recent years an enormous sea-wall has been built along the coastline here as part of the flood prevention scheme.

Most visitors to Tilbury Fort use the landward entrance, called Landport Gate. From the car park, a small track crosses the moat complex using a series of wooden drawbridges. From April to September, the fort is open daily between 10 am and 6 pm, but during the winter months the buildings close earlier, at 3.30 pm, and are only open on certain days of the week. If you are considering a visit, it is therefore worth making a telephone call to check the current opening times before you set out.

Tilbury

From Tilbury Fort, a footpath leads westwards along the coastline past a pub called The World's End. This was built in 1694, and acted for many years as the local ferry house. It is now only a short walk along the riverside to the outskirts of Tilbury itself.

Although the nearby villages of East Tilbury and West Tilbury have been in existence for many centuries, the town of Tilbury only grew up relatively recently during the railway era. In 1854, a railway-line was opened from Fenchurch Street station in London to a small pier here, at the southernmost point in Essex. As its name suggests, Tilbury Ferry Pier was the landing-stage for a ferry across the River Thames to the town of Gravesend on the opposite bank.

Gravesend was already a sizeable town by this stage, and this stretch of the river became known as Gravesend Reach. During the last hundred years, almost all the ferries in Essex have closed, but the Tilbury ferry has remained running to this day, although it stopped carrying cars in 1962.

Tilbury Docks

Tilbury Ferry Pier was also the boarding point for ocean-going liners, carrying both passengers and cargo, but the real impetus for the growth of Tilbury came with the construction of Tilbury Docks. A purpose-built dock on this site was first proposed in 1882 by the East & West India Dock Company, and it took four years to construct. The 75-acre site had three enormous docks leading off a central basin. The company made use of the existing rail link to London, but they decided to build a new station for cruise passengers, with a large hotel alongside. The central basin was linked to the tidal River Thames by a large lock, 700 feet long by 80 feet wide, with an average depth of roughly 44 feet.

The project was huge, with an initial cost of £2.8 million (the equivalent of well over £100 million today), but the new Tilbury Docks failed to make a profit. In 1888, with an increasing burden of debt, the docks fell into receivership. However, fierce competition with the docks in central London led to a price-cutting war, and Tilbury eventually managed to attract enough trade to balance the books by 1893.

Compared to some others docks further upriver, Tilbury had the advantage of space, thereby enabling a fast turn-around, and could handle extremely large ships at any state of the tide. Trade began to boom, and by 1900 the docks were handling over a million tons of cargo each year, mostly tobacco, tea and meat.

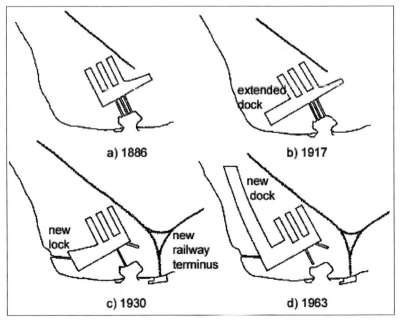

Stages in the development of Tilbury Docks

In 1909, the site came under the control of the Port of London Authority, who decided to construct a large western extension to the docks. Opened in 1917, this new basin was 1600 feet long. Between the wars, a new lock was built to the west in order to handle even larger ships, although the old lock remained in use until 1967.

In addition to the cargo trade, around 300,000 passengers passed through the docks every year. In order to cope with this increasing traffic, a new passenger terminal was opened in 1930 by the prime minister Ramsay MacDonald, and the original railway station was converted to freight use (and is still in operation today). Trade was obviously quiet during the Second World War, although the Tilbury Docks were occasionally used to practise troop landings. Following the war, the concept of a standard container size led to the container revolution of the 1960s, and Tilbury was quick to take advantage of the greatly increased efficiency of this new system through the construction of an enormous new western dock in 1963.

With the closure of other docks upriver in the 1980s, Tilbury now handles almost all the bulk trade for London. Forestry products form a large portion of the cargo, but the docks also handle over 2 million tons of grain every year. The Northfleet Hope Terminal also boasts the largest refrigerated container store in the world, capable of handling 1500 units at a time. Its 24-acre site was built on reclaimed land to the north-west between 1976 and 1978, although it has not yet been marked on Ordnance Survey maps.

Although the Tilbury Docks provide a valuable source of employment for thousands of people, they also inevitably act as an obstacle to people walking around the coastline of Essex. At the Tilbury Ferry Pier, the coastal route has to make a long detour inland.

Grays

From Tilbury, it is only a couple of miles along the road to the suburbs of Grays. This town was originally known as Thurrock, and was recorded in the Domesday Book in 1086 as "Turroc". This name is believed to derive from "thurroc", an Old English word used to describe the bilges of a ship, referring in this case to the marshy ground on which the town stood. From the end of the 12th century, the local manor was held by the family "de Grai", who are said to originate from a village in Normandy called Graye. By 1248, the town had become known as "Turrokgreys", and until just a few years ago it was still officially called "Grays Thurrock". Today, the town takes the shorter name of Grays, although both the urban district and the borough council maintain the older name of Thurrock.

The town also marks the boundary between two of the ancient divisions of Essex. As you pass through the town, you leave the area known as Barstable Hundred and instead enter Chafford Hundred (often spelt with just a single 'f'). This is the last of the ten "hundreds" to be encountered around the coastline of Essex. Under the original county boundaries, you would also pass through Becontree Hundred a few miles further upstream, but this area has now been completely absorbed into the Greater London area.

Grays is now surrounded by several large chalk quarries, remnants of the lime & cement trade, but this industry is far from new. On the north-eastern edge of town, archaeologists have found a series of "dene-holes" in Hangman's Wood. These originally consisted of a shaft leading vertically down into the ground towards a large chamber, often up to 20 feet square and 12 feet high. These were almost certainly used to extract chalk for use as local fertiliser.

For the remainder of the coastal route, you will need the Ordnance Survey Explorer map 162 (Greenwich & Gravesend). The main railway-line passes right through the centre of Grays, with an inconvenient level-crossing dividing the town in two. From the railway station in the centre of the town, a footpath follows the north bank of the River Thames in a south-easterly direction, heading back towards the Tilbury Docks for half a mile or so until a large jetty blocks any further progress. This short footpath is technically open to the public, but all signs of natural beauty have been obliterated by a combination of concrete and graffiti. This stretch of the river is called Northfleet Reach, after the small town of Northfleet in Kent, although the view across the river consists mostly of rough grassland near the tip of a long peninsula called Broad Ness.

Another footpath leaves the town of Grays, this time in the opposite direction, heading westwards along the riverside through a dilapidated area of abandoned buildings and ruined jetties. Officially, there are no further points of access until you reach the town of Purfleet, over four miles further on, although it appears that local people do use some of the private tracks from time to time.

The right of way closely follows the banks of the river, a stretch known variously as Fiddler's Reach or St. Clement's Reach, for just over a mile before reaching an enormous power station. At this point, an overhead power cable crosses the River Thames, supported by a massive pylon on either bank of the river and forming a single span nearly a mile wide.

Within half a mile, the River Thames begins a sharp bend to the right around a short peninsula known as Stone Ness. Unlike the surrounding land, Stone Ness has managed to avoid industrial development, perhaps because of the marshy nature of the ground. The fields also lie very close to sea-level, and only the presence of a large sea-wall prevents them from being inundated by high tides. According to one old map, these sea-defences were breached in 1805, leading to severe floods.

The footpath along the top of the sea-wall overlooks these marshes, offering a wide view across one of the last pieces of open countryside on this coastal route. However, most walkers will already be looking ahead at the enormous Queen Elizabeth II Bridge, which crosses the River Thames about a mile beyond the promontary of Stone Ness. This bridge, the furthest downstream, is by far the most impressive structure around the Essex coastline, completely dominating the skyline for many miles around.

The Queen Elizabeth II Bridge stands beside the Dartford Tunnel, which was opened in November 1963. The tunnel between Essex and Kent proved very popular because it avoided the traffic further upstream in central London, and the two lanes were soon filled to capacity. A second tunnel was built alongside the first, but the area soon became congested again. The opening of the M25 led to regular queues on both sides of the river, with tailbacks sometimes stretching back ten miles during the rush hour. Incidentally, it should be noted that the road at the Dartford Crossing has been designated as the A282, and does not have the status of a motorway. This enables learner drivers and other restricted vehicles to use the tunnel, but it also means that the M25 is not technically a complete orbital motorway.

In an effort to remove the bottle-neck, a private company called Dartford River Crossing Limited began the construction of a new bridge over the river in 1988. The work was completed within just three years and with towers over 400 feet high, the Queen Elizabeth II Bridge was at the time the longest cable-stay bridge in Europe (and the second longest in the world). The concrete and steel structure cost around £86 million and was finally opened by the Queen on the 30th October 1991. From the sea-wall, the most striking feature of this bridge is its incredible height – even the roadway stands hundreds of feet above you.

As you walk underneath the bridge, the footpath passes a curious circular building topped by a tall cone-shaped structure. This is one of the ventilators for the Dartford tunnel. For the next mile or so, a public right of way sticks closely to the coastline along a straight stretch of river known as Long Reach. A series of factories line the river-banks, along with a collection of associated jetties and piers. Although there is no natural beauty to be found in these surroundings, the varying industries can provide an interesting landscape. The right of way passes directly through a working environment where hundreds of people make their living, and the footpath occasionally has to weave in and out of temporary obstacles. Nevertheless, this stretch remains a fascinating footpath, with a hive of activity going on all around you.

Purfleet

About a mile beyond the Queen Elizabeth II Bridge, the right of way eventually leaves the coastline and begins to head inland. The footpath joins a narrow track which leads alongside the main railway-line towards the centre of Purfleet. This town was recorded in a document in 1285 as Purteflyete, a name which means "Purta's Creek". This probably refers to the Mar Dyke, a wide stream which flows into the River Thames half a mile further on.

The narrow track soon emerges onto the main A1090 road almost directly opposite Purfleet railway station. This railway-line is ideal for coastal walkers because it provides a direct link between the towns of Purfleet and Grays. From the station, the coastal route continues westwards for just over a mile before reaching the county boundary, but most of this route is along busy roads with very few items of interest to the walker, and so, for most people, Purfleet marks the end of the walk around the coastline of Essex. The last section of the coastal route beyond Purfleet is only described in this book for completeness.

From Purfleet railway station, the coastal route heads westwards along the A1090, which changes its name here from London Road to High Street. Just after a large hotel, a public footpath leads off to the left to a causeway beside the River Thames, where a small ferry used to operate. Across the water, you get a good view of the flood barrier at the mouth of Dartford Creek.

Rainham Marshes

At this point, the coastal route leaves the River Thames behind for the last time, because the next stretch of coastline is out of bounds to the public. For many years, the Ministry of Defence used the Rainham Marshes as a rifle-range. Because of the presence of the MOD, the marshes escaped all industrial and housing developments, and several square miles of unspoilt countryside have therefore been retained. This is now some of the closest open land to the heart of London, and has been designated a Site of Special Scientific Interest (SSSI).

In the 1990s, there were plans to sell a large portion of the marshes to the Music Corporation of America (MCA) for the construction of a large film studio. Not surprisingly, the decision to build on this last fragment of open land caused some controversy. The corporation agreed to set aside 400 acres as a nature reserve and to build a riverside ecology park, but environmentalists pointed out that the marshes were effectively a nature reserve already. Many people were outraged that the sale was conducted by private treaty, because this method stops other interested organisations from making a bid for the land.

The status of SSSI is supposed to afford a certain degree of environmental protection, but Havering Council still gave permission for the development to go ahead. Furthermore, the Secretary of State for the Environment also refused to hold a public inquiry to discuss the issue. This decision only served to confirm the widely-held belief that designations such as SSSI and AONB (Area of Outstanding Natural Beauty) carry no environmental protection whatsoever. Our last vestiges of open countryside are still under threat from unwelcome and inappropriate development, despite the rhetoric from the major political parties assuring us of their "green" credentials. A commitment to improve the environment is worthless unless it is accompanied by urgent and positive action, and it is clear that many politicians are failing in their duty to protect our countryside.

Fortunately, public pressure saved the Rainham Marshes, and in July 2000 the land was finally sold instead to the RSPB (Royal Society for the Protection of Birds), at a cost of £1.1 million. However, it is estimated that it will take another 15 years to clear the site of unexploded shells. Furthermore, the western edge of the marshes is still threatened with "development".

Returning to the busy A1090 route through Purfleet, the road turns sharply to the north. Heading inland, it passes a large housing estate that stands between the main road and Mar Dyke. Near the mouth of Mar Dyke, sluices control the flow of water into the River Thames, although an extra floodgate was added after the 1953 floods. The floodgate is lowered vertically into position when a very high tide is forecast.

A small bridge carries the main road across the Mar Dyke about half a mile inland and joins a busy trunk route into London. The boundary between Essex and Greater London lies about half a mile to the left, just before the road splits into a dual carriageway.

At the Essex border, the landscape is a far cry from the remote coastal salt-marshes which form the backbone of this book, but it is worth remembering that the county of Essex originally stretched much further to the west, only crossing into the old county of Middlesex at the River Lee, just before the Isle of Dogs. Under these old county boundaries, this book would have included several extra tributaries of the River Thames, including Rainham Creek, Beam River and Barking Creek. The Hornchurch Marshes would have been described in detail, as well as the industrial centre at Dagenham and the housing developments around the Royal docks. During the re-organisation of the county boundaries, Essex lost a strip of coastline to London. Some parts of the northern bank of the River Thames even belonged to Kent, a curious anomaly that has now been cleared up.

Thames flood barrier

In particular, the old boundaries would have placed the new Thames flood barrier within the county of Essex. Although the Woolwich Reach is now firmly within the Greater London area, it is probably worth mentioning the flood barrier at this point, since it is inextricably linked to the problems of sea-defences and flood protection which have troubled Essex over the centuries.

As long ago as 1663, the famous diarist Samuel Pepys recorded that *"there was last night the greatest tide that ever was remembered in England to have been in this river."* Even in 1907, engineers suggested building a barrage across the River Thames from Tilbury to Gravesend, effectively turning the upper reaches of the river into an enormous dock. Needless to say, the plan soon faltered and all ideas of flood protection were forgotten.

The description of Canvey Island earlier in this book mentions how this part of the coastline was devastated in 1953 by the highest surge tide ever recorded in this country. Within a single night, over 160,000 acres of farmland were flooded, as well as 24,000 houses, 200 miles of railway-line and 2 major electricity generating stations. Over 100,000 tonnes of gypsum were subsequently required to bring the salt-infested farmland back into a useful state. Although the loss of human life was miraculously small, about 11,000 cattle drowned that night, along with 9,000 pigs.

The business of flood protection returned to the limelight with a jolt. The city of London had escaped relatively lightly, but it was clear that the potential for a major disaster was very real. An engineers' report examined the effect of raising all the sea-walls alongside the River Thames, but concluded that this approach would be too expensive and unreliable, and that a large flood barrier near Purfleet was the only sensible alternative.

In March 1960, a blue paper suggested three possible types of barrier. A lifting barrier, like the current bascule bridge over Havengore Creek near Southend-on-Sea, was believed to be too expensive on this large scale. A barrier opening like a swing bridge was also considered, but the cheapest scheme was found to be a rectractable barrier. This was priced at £15 million, but it was then too late to proceed with the plan at Purfleet because new jetties had been built on the site.

Proposals for a barrier nearby at Crayford Ness were estimated at between £25 and £40 million, and there were even serious suggestions of an enormous barrage across the mouth of the Thames estuary from Clacton-on-Sea to Herne Bay in Kent. This massive project would have helped the supply of fresh water to the region, and could also be linked to the plan for a third London airport on the Maplin Sands. Once again, the costs proved prohibitive, and the concept of a London flood barrier reached stalemate.

In 1965, the impasse was broken by another dangerously high tide. Co-ordinated by the new Greater London Council, Professor Bondi was commissioned to write a report on the available options. It was even suggested that the Cliffe marshes in north Kent could be deliberately flooded whenever a very high tide was expected. By spreading the surge tide over a wider area, it was believed that the level of flood-water could be significantly reduced. Under careful examination, however, this technique was found to make matters even worse.

By 1969, after considering numerous other designs, the engineers had finally settled on the idea of a barrier in the Woolwich Reach of the river. The construction began in earnest in 1975, taking seven years to complete at a cost of £1 billion. The barrier stretches for a third of a mile across the river, and is powered by hydraulics. There are three independent electricity supplies, with another three back-up generators on site.

As well as the main Thames flood barrier, many of the smaller creeks downstream were provided with their own flood barriers, and a retractable barrier was built across the mouth of Tilbury Dock. Since their construction, ever-rising tide levels have meant that these flood barriers have been deployed many more times than originally envisaged.

Recommended bibliography

Southend past 1865-1940 – John Smith
The story of Southend pier – E. Shepherd
Old Leigh – H. Bride
Hadleigh Past – Ian Yearsley
A history of Canvey Island – Fred McCave
Invaders of Canvey – Olivia Whitcomb
Canvey Island in old picture postcards – European Library
The great tide – Hilda Grieve
The east coast floods – Dorothy Summers
North Sea surge – Michael Pollard

Essex and the sea – Essex Records Office
A history of Benfleet – Harold Priestley
Coryton – Winifred Scott
The Corringham light railway – I. Gotheridge
The Mucking crop-mark sites – M. James
Resist the invader – P. Gifford
Defending London's river – Victor Smith
Coast defences of England & Wales – Ian V. Hogg
Tilbury Fort – A. D. Saunders
Thurrock in old picture postcards – European Library
The Thames Barrier – Stuart Gilbert & Ray Horner
A portrait of the London river – Basil Cracknell
Estuary – A. Astbury
Maunsell Sea Forts – Frank Turner

Chapter eight – wildlife of the Essex coastline

The wildlife of the Essex coastline is potentially an enormous subject for study, and this book can obviously only mention a few of the most common birds and plants. Furthermore, it only covers the flora and fauna that are clearly visible on a typical walk.

Around the Essex coastline, the natural environment is harsh. This is especially true of the tidal saltings, which have to withstand a wide range of temperatures and salinity – the mudflats are daily inundated with salt-water and then exposed to the air, sun and wind. As a result, only a few hardy plants can grow here. This in turn limits the insects that feed on these plants, and so on further up the food chain.

As a result, only a few animals live near the coastline. Foxes and voles are probably the most common mammals to be found here, but keen naturalists may find more variety in the moths, crickets and other insects. Further out to sea, seals are also occasionally spotted basking on the sand-banks. In the summer months, you can sometimes take a boat from Wallasea Island to visit the seal colony off Foulness Point.

Industrial pollution sometimes limits the wildlife around the coast, but Essex has suffered less than many other counties. However, there is still concern about the effects of intensive farming practices. For example, the massive grain subsidies of the 1980s led to the drainage and "improvement" of many large fields around Essex. The wide use of chemicals also contributed to a sterile monoculture, but fortunately this attitude is gradually being replaced with more environmentally friendly forms of farming. During the 1990s, the concept of "set-aside" land and a softer approach to sea-defence helped to ease the pressure on the coastal wildlife. Many areas of marshland are now left deliberately undrained in order to support a greater diversity of plants and animals.

At the same time, it is still clear that most forms of official protection are virtually useless. Sites of Special Scientific Interest (SSSI), for example, are intended to prevent vulnerable countryside from being swallowed up by inappopriate development, but these official designations are immediately swept aside when money becomes involved. Our wildlife seems to be more effectively protected by private bodies, such as the Essex Wildlife Trust or the Royal Society for the Protection of Birds (RSPB).

Organisations like the Essex Wildlife Trust help to maintain nature reserves all around the county. These special reserves only protect a tiny proportion of our coastline, but they do form a useful introduction to anyone who wants to find out more about their local wildlife. The following list suggests a few places around the Essex coastline where you might like to start

Wat Tyler Country Park

Operated by Basildon Council, this small park includes saltings and freshwater wetlands. The scrubland of Pitseahall Island also supports birds such as fieldfare and redwing.

Northey Island

This small island near Maldon is more difficult to find. You need to arrange each visit with the National Trust in advance, but the wardens have created a wide variety of habitats for birds. Several important experiments in land reclamation have taken place on Northey Island.

Fingringhoe Wick

Sited just south of Colchester, Fingringhoe Wick is the headquarters of the Essex Wildlife Trust. This is one of the most interesting nature reserves around the Essex coastline, and an ideal place for budding naturalists to start from. The trust produces a wide variety of leaflets, and there are several marked trails. These take you around saltings, disused gravel workings and scrub.

Old Hall Marshes

These undisturbed marshes are operated as a bird reserve by the RSPB. Hen harriers and short-eared owls are relatively common here, and you can also see large numbers of brent geese during the winter months.

These nature reserves are only a first step; some of the best wildlife can be found along the remote sea-walls, many miles from the nearest village. In particular, the Maplin Sands deserve a special mention, along with the islands that form the Essex Archipelago. This region is not a special nature reserve, but the Ministry of Defence has excluded the public for many years. As a result, many rare birds have been allowed to thrive undisturbed, including the colourful mandarin duck (*Aix galericulata*) and the elusive garganey (*Anas querquedula*).

The government has come up with many ideas over the years to protect landscapes and wildlife. At the larger end of the scale, National Parks were introduced in the early 1950s. Despite their name, National Parks are not centrally owned, but merely have an extra tier of management, taking over some of the planning duties from the local councils in order to maintain a healthy balance between nature and local business. The government can also designate "Areas of Outstanding Natural Beauty" to help local authorities to discourage unsuitable development. There are currently around 40 of these areas, which tend to be smaller than National Parks. On the more local level, the range of schemes becomes even wider:

- National Nature Reserves – designated (and sometimes owned) by the government to protect special areas of flora or fauna.
- Sites of Special Scientific Interest – relatively small areas of land, particularly concerned with special examples of wildlife or geology. There are now over 6000 SSSIs, covering a twelfth of the country. However, these have virtually no protection. Between 1991 and 1995, for example, only two landowners were ever prosecuted for damaging SSSIs.
- Green belts – first proposed for London in 1944, and extended to the rest of Britain in 1955. However, it could be argued that these are intended more as a method of preserving the quality of towns, rather than the countryside.
- Ramsars – wetlands of national importance (they are named after the town of Ramsar, in Iran, where the international agreement was drawn up). The United Kingdom currently has 126 Ramsar sites, including virtually all the Essex coastline.

- Special Areas of Conservation – these are offshore marine areas, designated under European Union laws. There are 12 candidate sites within the UK, but none are planned for the seas around Essex.

As well as various countryside stewardship schemes, small country parks are operated by various councils and other private organisations, such as the RSPB (Royal Society for the Protection of Birds). Within Essex, perhaps the most important non-governmental organisation is the Essex Wildlife Trust (previously known as the Essex Naturalists Trust). Despite their very limited resources, the trust manages to run 93 nature reserves around the county, as well as 6 visitor centres.

It is also worth mentioning the role of central government in managing the countryside and preserving its wildlife. Over the years, this role has been carried out by a number of departments and organisations, and these are re-organised so frequently that this book is almost certain to be out of date even before it is published. For example, the Nature Conservancy Council used to have a direct responsibility for managing National Nature Reserves, as well as scheduling the SSSIs. This was replaced recently by three separate departments:

- English Nature (not to be confused with English Heritage, who protect *historical* sites)
- Countryside Council for Wales
- Scottish Natural Heritage

The Joint Nature Conservation Committee was also created as a forum to oversee the three. (Northern Ireland has its own separate Environment and Heritage Service.)

This confusion of departments may explain why the government seems incapable of translating positive ideas into actual practice on the ground. Furthermore, as if this maze wasn't complicated enough already, there is yet another governmental body to advise ministers on rural policy matters. This used to be the Countryside Commission until it merged with the Rural Development Commission to form the Countryside Agency. And then there is the Environment Agency, a separate organisation whose task is to protect the overall *quality* of the environment and its resources. For example, they monitor water quality and pollution, and are responsible for maintaining inland flood-defences (though not coastal defences, for some inexplicable reason). This agency replaces the old National Rivers Authority, HM Inspectorate of Pollution, and several other small agencies.

Perhaps it is easy to understand why the most successful countryside preservation is carried out not by government, with its labyrinth of committees, but by individual landowners who respect and take pride in their natural surroundings, and enjoy the beautiful marshlands of Essex.

Recommended Bibliography

A new guide to the birds of Essex – Simon Cox
The ecology of a salt marsh – L. Pomeroy
Essex – a guide to the countryside – County Guide Publications
Flora of Essex – Stanley Jermyn
The natural history of Britain's coasts – Eric Soothill and Michael Thomas

Index